O'Brien, Lawrence
No final victories

DATE DUE

#47-0108 Peel Off Pressure Sensitive

NO
FINAL
VICTORIES

Lawrence F. O'Brien
NO FINAL VICTORIES

A Life in Politics—
from John F. Kennedy to Watergate

DOUBLEDAY & COMPANY, INC.
GARDEN CITY, NEW YORK
1974

Time Magazine cover reprinted by permission from *Time*, The Weekly News-magazine; copyright © 1961 by Time Inc.
Portion from Jimmy Breslin's column first appeared in the New York *Post*, copyright © 1968 by Jimmy Breslin. Used by permission.

Library of Congress Cataloging in Publication Data

O'Brien, Lawrence F
  No final victories.

  Autobiographical.
  1. O'Brien, Lawrence F. 2. United States—Politics and government—1945– I. Title.
E840.8.024A36   329'.0092'4 [B]
ISBN 0-385-02484-3
Library of Congress Catalog Card Number 73-22535

In memory of my parents,

LAWRENCE F. O'BRIEN, SR.,
and
MYRA SWEENEY O'BRIEN

who came to this country with no money and
little education but by their hard work made
a good life for themselves and their children

AUTHOR'S NOTE

This book reflects one man's life in politics and what I have liked least about writing it is the number of times the word "I" appears. Throughout my political life the advice, assistance, and encouragement of literally thousands of people have sustained me. Some of them appear in this book, most do not, but all of them have my thanks and enduring gratitude. There are, all across America, men and women who bear the still-honorable title of "politician," with whom I have been associated in campaign after campaign and in government. We have been together in good years and bad, through triumph and heartbreak, and I can never thank them all, no more than I could ever forget them.

I have also shared my ups and downs with many fine members of the American press and I wish it were possible to thank each of them personally for their friendship, their fairness—and even their occasional criticism.

A few individuals were close to the preparation of this book and deserve my special thanks: Phyllis Maddock Nason, who not only lived through many of these experiences but at great personal inconvenience made sure my memories found their way onto paper; Patrick Anderson, for his advice and assistance in its writing; Janice Akerhielm, for her research and her contributions to its content.

Finally, my thanks to my family, who contributed so much: my wife Elva's constructive criticism and needed encouragement, my son Larry's significant editing, and my daughter-in-law Helen's contribution of its title were most welcome as I struggled with the book's final draft.

Lawrence F. O'Brien
February 1974

CONTENTS

NO
FINAL
VICTORIES

INTRODUCTION

I spent the month of April 1973 on a long-delayed vacation trip to Ireland, working on this book and also trying to relax. It was during that month that the Watergate case broke wide open, and when I returned to Washington in early May it was a different city. One day soon after my return I went for lunch at Duke Zeibert's restaurant, one of the traditional gathering places for politicians in Washington. The unfolding Watergate scandal was virtually the only topic of discussion at Duke Zeibert's that day. A steady stream of people came by my table with the newest Watergate rumor or Watergate joke, and I detected a good deal of gloating among my friends and acquaintances.

I could not share in the gloating. True, it was my phone that the Watergate burglars tapped and my personal files that they photographed, but I had long since come to regard the whole sordid affair as a national tragedy. Not the least of the tragedy was the cynicism the Watergate scandals had engendered in millions of Americans. During the 1972 presidential campaign, when I was the national campaign chairman, we had tried to raise the Watergate break-in as a serious and legitimate political issue. Our efforts failed, because the hard evidence was still hidden from view, and most of the press and the public still regarded Watergate as a joke, a "caper." Time and again, I sensed that the public reaction was, "So what? That's just politics as usual."

Well, it's *not* politics as usual! I've been a politician for most of my life and I've never dreamed of bugging an opponent's telephone or breaking into his office. If a generation of Americans becomes convinced that burglary and wiretapping are "politics as usual," then there's not much hope for our political system.

I'm proud to be known as a politician. I've known hundreds of honorable, dedicated men and women, of both parties, who have entered upon the uncertainties and frustrations of political life because they consider it a high calling, one that would permit them to contribute to a better America and a better world. It pains me more than I can say to see these people and our entire political system discredited by the criminal acts of a misguided band of zealots. One of the reasons I've written this book is to show what the world of politics is really like, not an underworld of cloak-and-dagger activity, but a vast public arena in which men and ideas do battle and in which great deeds can sometimes be achieved.

I do not claim that politics is always a genteel, kid-gloves pursuit. Perhaps the toughest political fight I've ever been in was the 1960 Kennedy-Humphrey primary race in West Virginia. It was no holds barred, but Kennedy and Humphrey could still end that encounter as friends, as political pros with mutual respect; and it was that victory in West Virginia that enabled Kennedy to emerge as the outstanding President and world leader that he became. A great statesman must first be a great politician, as Jack Kennedy was and as I remember him. Indeed, Kennedy often quipped: "Mothers all want their sons to grow up to be President, but they don't want them to become politicians in the process!"

It has been my privilege to know most of the Democratic leaders of my time. As a boy, I shook hands with Al Smith and Franklin D. Roosevelt when they campaigned in my home town of Springfield, Massachusetts, during the 1928 and 1932 campaigns. I joined forces with Jack Kennedy in 1951, and a decade later I accompanied him to the White House. I served both President Kennedy and his successor, Lyndon B. Johnson, as director of congressional relations; I served in President Johnson's Cabinet as Postmaster General; I have twice been Democratic National Chairman; and have played a major role in the past four Democratic presidential campaigns.

In this book I have tried to portray accurately the men and events I have known. The Presidents and would-be Presidents I have worked with were not paragons; they were men, human beings, with the mingled capacity for nobility and folly that all men share. I remember Jack Kennedy as a great and inspiring political leader, but I also remember him as the carefree young congressman who almost blew his 1952 race for the Senate with an impulsive prank. I remember Bob Kennedy as a passionate champion of human rights in the 1960s, but my most enduring memory of him may be the time I watched him participate in a bloody fist fight. I remember Lyndon Johnson as the President who passed the greatest legislative program in American history, but I also remember him as a fellow who could never understand why I wouldn't join him for his famous in-the-raw dips in the White House pool.

I have many warm memories of my political career, of good friends and good times, but politics is more than that. It is a deadly serious business. I admit that when I started in politics as a young man I viewed it largely as an exciting game. Winning elections was my business, and I didn't worry much about what my candidates did after they were in office. But that, in time, was to change. When I became the White House director of congressional relations I found myself deeply involved in momentous legislative proposals—the civil rights bills, federal aid to education, Medicare, the minimum-wage bill, to name a few. I was called upon daily to make decisions that would affect the lives of millions of Americans. At that point, politics was no longer a game. It was a heavy responsibility and a rare opportunity, and nothing I have ever done has given me more pride than my role in helping enact the historic New Frontier and Great Society legislative programs.

Over the years, my political role changed. As a young man, I was an organizer, a specialist in registration drives and telephone campaigns and get-out-the-vote techniques. But during the 1960s, because of my association with Presidents Kennedy and Johnson, I was in a position to serve as a party strategist and spokesman. When I was called back to be chairman of the Democratic Party for a second time in 1970, I assumed a role of leadership in a deeply divided party. I spoke out on the issues and I made well known my criticisms of the Nixon administration. I worked for party unity, and although our efforts were not successful in 1972, I believe the Democratic Party can once again be united, can once more win the trust of the American people, and can once more assume leadership in this troubled nation.

My dedication to the Democratic Party is no secret. Our party is far from perfect; it has made mistakes and it has paid for those mistakes; but I continue to believe that ours is the party that will best serve the interests of the vast majority of the American people. Still, despite my beliefs, I do not intend for this to be entirely a partisan book. It is not partisan to want fair elections, to want honest, public campaign financing, or to want equal access for both parties to the powerful medium of television. I have spoken out on those issues not for partisan gain, but because I believe reform is imperative if our two-party system is to survive.

As I write these words, our nation faces a crisis of confidence as serious as any crisis since the Civil War. Can politicians be trusted? Can our democratic institutions endure? I believe our system can endure, but only if the American people regain their trust in our political system and those who work within it. And the essential first step in regaining that faith is for all politicians to quit the double-talk, quit the secrecy, quit the pie-in-the-sky promises and level with the American people. In this book, I've tried to level. I've called upon my memories and my experiences and my memoranda to try to show the political world as I have known it, to try to show how politics can contribute to the progress of America. If this book, reflecting one man's life in politics, can contribute to better public understanding of what politics is, and what politics can be, then it will have served its purpose.

I

A POLITICAL APPRENTICESHIP

MY EARLIEST MEMORIES are political. In 1924, when I was seven, my father attended the Democratic National Convention, and I can remember him returning home with a souvenir hat shaped like a teapot—a jibe at the Republican Teapot Dome scandals. I remember my father taking me up to shake hands with Al Smith during the 1928 presidential campaign and with Franklin D. Roosevelt four years later. I remember evenings when I would walk with my father through working-class neighborhoods in our home town of Springfield, Massachusetts, as he was getting names on nominating petitions or urging people to register and vote. On one such evening, as we walked along together, my father told me something I never forgot, "The votes are there, Lawrence, if we can only get them out."

His name was also Lawrence Francis O'Brien. He was born in County Cork, Ireland, and came to this country at the turn of the century. He first settled in upstate New York where he worked as a machine operator in a factory; later he crossed over into Massachusetts and found a job tooling rifles at the armory in Springfield. There he met and married my mother, Myra Sweeney, a handsome, intelligent woman with a marvelous personality. She, too, was from County Cork, one of ten children who had emigrated from Ireland to America.

By 1914 my father had saved enough money to lease the Roland Hotel, a small building in downtown Springfield, which he and my mother operated as a rooming house and restaurant. My mother, who was a wonderful cook, ran the kitchen, assisted by student waiters from nearby Springfield College. I was born in the Roland on July 7, 1917, and my sister Mary was born there four years later. Soon after Mary's birth, my father bought another rooming house, on Mattoon Street, where our family lived for two decades.

My father was a good businessman, and throughout the 1920s he increased his real estate holdings. Then, at the decade's end, the Depression struck. My father had bought several fine homes for rental properties, but as the Depression worsened he couldn't meet the mortgage payments, nor could he find tenants. Slowly, painfully, my father lost everything. Either he sold his properties at a loss or the banks would foreclose. Yet he would never file for bankruptcy. He was a proud, stubborn Irishman, and he believed a debt was a debt.

In December 1932, as the holidays neared, we had no Christmas tree. We couldn't afford one. Still, I was sure my father would get one somehow. On Christmas Eve our doorbell rang and I dashed to open the door, sure that our tree was being delivered. But it was more bad news—a telegram demanding that my father pay some debt. That was the low point of the Depression for me.

With his property gone, my father had to find another way to make a living. One of his buildings in downtown Springfield, one the bank had taken back, had a small cafe in it, and we leased the cafe and ran it as a family enterprise. The specialty of the house was a large bowl of my mother's beef stew and dumplings for twenty-five cents. We also got a liquor license, and at age eighteen I became a bartender. It was a struggle for my parents. My father was then past sixty. But we made a go of it, so much so, that in the late 1930s my father began buying real estate again. In the 1940s, during the wartime boom, our cafe was quite successful and some of my father's real estate holdings proved to have been good investments.

As far back as I can remember, my father was active in Democratic politics. As a young immigrant, he had seen the signs outside factories that said "No Irish Need Apply," and he and other Irishmen soon realized that the men who owned those factories were the same white, Anglo-Saxon, Protestant Republicans who controlled local and state politics—the WASPs, as we scornfully called them. My father believed that they were holding his people down, and he saw the Democratic Party as a means through which the Irish and other immigrant groups could fight back.

He helped organize the Democratic City Committee in Springfield, and in time he served as one of the two western Massachusetts members of the state committee. He was a partisan and proud of it, at a time when Democratic partisanship was not wise for a businessman in Springfield. He was the kind of man who would give fifty dollars to the party when he should have applied it to one of his mortgages. This was not always easy for my mother to understand, for she was not a political person. I remember once when U. S. Senator David I. Walsh, one of the first successful politicians of Irish heritage in Massachusetts, came to our house to talk politics with my father. The senator picked up the phone and began making long-distance calls to political leaders around the country. My mother watched from the kitchen, horrified by the expense, but my father didn't care—this was politics. Finally the coal truck came to make a delivery and the clatter of the coal forced Walsh to stop his calls. My mother almost wept with relief. She never complained, but I think she worried a lot about my father's devotion to politics.

My father was a rather short, stocky, red-haired man who worked hard, didn't drink, and was strict with his children. His formal education had been limited, but he read widely and took correspondence courses in real estate, business, and law. Books were our only luxury during the Depression. He was immensely proud of his library, where his fine sets of Shakespeare and the classics and the great historians covered all four walls from ceiling to floor. He kept a large dictionary there and whenever he had to look up a word he put a check mark beside it. He was always angry with himself if he had to look up a word a second time.

As a Democratic leader, he had to persuade people to run

for office at a time when Democratic candidates were not too likely to win in Springfield. Often, he had to do all the work for the candidate he wanted—fill out the filing papers, get signatures on the nominating petitions and so on. I wanted to help him all I could, so many days, after school, I'd find myself going around our neighborhood asking for signatures on a half-dozen nominating petitions. On Election Day, I'd ring door-bells, pass out literature, and help with the car pools we used to get our people to the polls. That kind of work, as a teen-ager during the Depression, was my political apprenticeship.

My first political hero was James Michael Curley. He and David I. Walsh were the first Irish politicians to have major success in Massachusetts; Walsh as U.S. senator, Curley as mayor of Boston, congressman, and governor. But Walsh was not really thought of as an "Irish politician," and it was Jim Curley who became the hero of the Irish. The Yankees detested him and many of the Catholic Church leaders attacked him and considered him a rogue, but to the average Irish-American Curley was the symbol of the breakthrough the Irish were be-ginning to make. We rejoiced in the way he could thumb his nose at the Yankee establishment.

Our town, Springfield, was a hundred miles west of Boston and, to most Democratic politicians in Boston, it might have been a thousand. The rule for the Democrats in those days was that if you could carry Boston by a hundred thousand votes you could carry the state, so they concentrated on Boston. But some Democrats would explore the rest of the state and they would usually wind up talking politics with my father in the O'Brien kitchen. Curley was a visitor there in my youth. When I was about sixteen, and Curley was running for governor, I toured our area with him. At the start of his political rallies, I would make a short speech about young people taking part in politics. Next, Rabbit Maranville of the Boston Braves, a Springfield native, would talk baseball. Finally at the right dramatic moment Curley would march down the aisle—waving and shaking hands as he passed through the audience—and climb onto the stage to make his speech. I still think he was the best orator I have ever heard.

He spoke in the old-school, passionate, evangelical style. He would exhort the audience to start at the bottom of the ballot and work up, putting their mark by every name with the Democratic "D" beside it. "Elect every Democrat," he would cry, "that's our salvation!"

Curley and my father were two of the very few Irish Democrats in the state who favored Franklin Roosevelt over Al Smith for the Democratic nomination in 1932. My father ran as a pro-Roosevelt delegate on a ticket headed by Curley and which included FDR's son James. For my father, or any Irishman, to oppose our fellow Catholic, Al Smith, was almost like leaving the Church. My father's brother, my Uncle David, didn't speak to him for a year. But my father, stubborn and independent as ever, thought Roosevelt could win and Smith couldn't. The pro-Roosevelt slate lost by about ten to one, but Roosevelt, of course, was nominated at the Democratic Convention. We had a little store adjoining our restaurant that my father donated for the Roosevelt headquarters, the only one in western Massachusetts. Roosevelt visited Springfield during the campaign and my father took immense pride in greeting him and in making sure that I shook the great FDR's hand. After Roosevelt took office and began his historic battle against the Depression, we felt vindicated in our support of him. He proved himself a great leader who was fighting heroically to solve the economic problems that had hit the O'Brien family and millions of other families so hard.

My early years were not entirely devoted to politics, of course. As a boy growing up on Mattoon Street, I loved to play basketball. I wasn't good enough to make my high school team, but I spent many hours shooting baskets at the YMCA court that was only a block from my home. As I grew older, I developed a love of the theater that continues to this day. I went to see all the plays and vaudeville shows I could. Sometimes the traveling actors and musicians would eat in our cafe and even stay at our rooming house and I was always thrilled at meeting them.

Mattoon Street was only two blocks from Springfield's Main Street. Our block consisted mostly of fine old homes that now, like ours, had become rooming houses. Our neighbors were a full spectrum of American immigrants—Irish, Polish, Scandinavian, Italian—people who, like my parents, had worked their way up to the point of owning property. They were united by the common bonds of immigration, of ambition, and of sharing the ups and downs of the rooming-house business.

I graduated from Cathedral High and would have loved to attend Notre Dame, but my family lacked the money, and I enrolled instead as a night student at Northeastern University's Law School in Springfield. I continued to work as a bartender at our cafe and in 1939, in my only venture into office-seeking, I was elected president of the local bartenders' union. In due course, I received my law degree, but my real passion in life was politics, not law. I was anxious to pursue a career in politics—just how, I wasn't sure—but before I could, World War II began.

I applied for a commission in the Navy but was turned down because of poor eyesight. Finally the Army drafted me for limited service. I was ultimately assigned to Camp Edwards, a classification center in Massachusetts, where my job was to interview and assign draftees and men who had gone absent without leave. My experience in life had been largely limited to Springfield until then, and while talking to those AWOLs, many of them blacks or poor whites from the South and many of them illiterate, I began to sense the vastness of this country and the dimensions of its social ills.

Camp Edwards was only about a hundred miles from Springfield, so I was able to get home many weekends, and I began to date Elva Brassard, a pretty blonde who was a friend of my sister. On May 30, 1944, when it appeared that I was about to be sent overseas, Elva and I were married. Elva's parents were both of French-Canadian extraction, and she sometimes joked about ours being a "mixed marriage," but in fact she and my family were extremely close. Elva continued to live with her parents and continued her job as a clerk with a local company, and I came home to Springfield as many weekends as possible. Finally, on November 1, 1945, I was discharged from the Army.

Our son, Lawrence F. O'Brien III, was born only two months after my discharge, on December 31.

When I returned to Springfield, our cafe and the adjoining garage and parking lot were doing well but my father's health was failing. I took over the management of our family interests, and my first task was to see a local banker to settle a debt on a piece of property my father had lost during the Depression. It was his last debt. The banker gladly accepted the money, then asked why I was paying a debt that was legally unenforceable, as the statute of limitations had run.

"It's my father's wish," I explained. "My father wants the record to show he has paid off all his debts."

In the next few years, until his death in 1950, my father was often hospitalized, and it took something over $20,000 to care for him. We were able to pay those staggering medical bills, but we knew many people who could not. I often thought of my father's long, expensive illness during the fight for Medicare nearly twenty years later.

I was soon back into politics. Our cafe was a natural political gathering place—the Springfield Central Labor Union Building was just across the street, and we were only a block from Court Square and the various city and county offices. Politicians and would-be politicians gathered daily at the O'Brien Cafe to exchange gossip and spin out their tales. I'd known most of them for years, and soon after my return from the service I was seeking their support for a bright, personable, young lawyer named Foster Furcolo.

Before the war, in one of my law school classes, I had met a pretty Irish girl named Katherine Foran Furcolo, and soon I'd become friendly with her husband, Foster, who was the son of a prominent Springfield doctor. No Italian-American had ever been elected to a major office in the Springfield area, but Foster and I believed he was the man to break that tradition. In 1942, just before I left for the service, I helped Furcolo campaign in the Democratic primary for district attorney. He didn't win—he hadn't expected to—but the race helped to make

his name known and to set the stage for a postwar political
career.

I managed three congressional campaigns for Furcolo—
1946, 1948, and 1950. In each campaign I was applying at the
congressional district level the organizational techniques that
I'd previously used at the ward and city level and that I
would later use at the state and national level. I began with
the assumption that far more could be done in the basic nuts
and bolts of campaigning—in registering voters, in getting them
out on Election Day, in personal contact with the voters—than
was traditionally done in our area. Furcolo was an appealing
candidate who attracted volunteer workers, and I was fascinated by the various ways we could make use of this free
manpower and womanpower. We wanted to organize these
volunteers for letter-writing campaigns, telephone campaigns,
door-to-door canvassing, and a myriad of other activities. Political organization is not complicated, but it is hard work, and
not many people care to perform it ten or twelve hours a day.
I was intrigued by the challenge of organizing a campaign in a
congressional district that included some forty cities and towns,
and as 1946 began I threw myself into the Furcolo campaign.

One of the hoary old rules of politics in those days was
"Don't peak too soon," or "Don't bother the voter before Labor
Day." I knew that wouldn't work for Furcolo. He faced, first,
a tough Democratic primary, then, if he won the primary, an
uphill race against a popular and able Republican incumbent,
Charles Clason. The January snow was still on the ground
when I began driving around our district to find local supporters who could head up Furcolo-for-Congress committees in
their communities. Once I had found our local workers, I prepared several pages of instructions outlining basic campaign
procedures. Those mimeographed pages of political advice
were the forerunner of what became known as the O'Brien
Manual, which was eventually used in the presidential campaigns of 1960, 1964, and 1968 and in political campaigns in a
dozen foreign countries.

Furcolo entered and won a crowded Democratic primary
that included several World War II veterans who hoped to

start careers in politics. In the general election he lost to Clason by 3,500 votes, but we considered that a strong showing in what was generally a Republican year. We started to plan for the 1948 election immediately. Our first tactic was to demand a recount, not because we expected it to change the result, but to get some free publicity and to spread the idea that it had been a close election.

In 1948, Furcolo was again the Democratic nominee. During the campaign, we avoided any identification with Harry Truman's seemingly doomed presidential campaign, and when Truman spoke outside the Springfield City Hall, Furcolo arrived late, stayed on the far end of the platform, and left early. That was our mistake, for Truman carried the district and the state. I often thought of that episode twenty years later when I was managing Hubert Humphrey's trouble-ridden 1968 presidential campaign and again in George McGovern's 1972 campaign, when local candidates were hiding from Humphrey and then McGovern all over America. Despite the snubbing of President Truman, Furcolo beat Clason handily and he asked me to come to Washington as his administrative assistant. I accepted with enthusiasm. To work in Washington, in the political big leagues, seemed an immensely exciting prospect.

Elva and I and Larry, who was four, drove down to Washington in January, and we were soon settled in a furnished house in Bethesda, Maryland, not far from the East-West Highway.

My enthusiasm for my job soon began to dwindle. Running a congressman's campaign was more exciting than running his office. I put out press releases and helped constituents with their problems and did all the routine things that congressional aides do. I found that, while a member of Congress is a very important man in his district, a first-term member of Congress is not very important in Washington, and his administrative assistant is just another guy named Joe. The hours were long and many nights I had to have dinner with constituents. Often I would call Elva at the last minute and ask her to join me for dinner, but she would have baby-sitter problems and usually could not. Socially, we saw a good deal of Foster and Kay, and we enjoyed Washington's restaurants and theaters, but we were homesick for Springfield.

Furcolo did not share my discontent, for he was busily and successfully making a name for himself. He became a protégé of John McCormack, who was then the majority leader and who ruled Massachusetts patronage with an iron hand, and with McCormack's backing won appointment to the powerful Appropriations Committee. Furcolo was aggressive and had a knack for publicity, and he was soon regarded as a man with a political future.

But I knew my future was not with him. I could see making a career as a congressman, but not as a congressman's assistant. I felt that I owed it to Furcolo to finish out his first term with him and to manage his 1950 re-election campaign, but after that election was won, I told him at lunch one day I wanted to return to Springfield. He did not take the news well. He was hurt and angry. We were close friends and he seemed to regard my departure as a rejection, even a betrayal.

"Larry," he told me bitterly, "I'm going to spend my life in politics, and I'll never allow myself to have a close personal relationship with anyone again!" I could never understand why he took it so personally.

I left Washington soon after that, and my resignation was a big story in the Springfield papers. Furcolo hinted to reporters that he wasn't sorry to see me go; that, in fact, he had reason to be glad. He left it vague, so people could draw their own conclusions. I found when I returned to Springfield that many people in politics felt they had to choose between Furcolo and me. Many chose Furcolo, for he was the local political power. A few times I saw old associates cross the street rather than speak to me. It was a good lesson to learn, if I hadn't already, that in a showdown many people go where the power is.

My feelings were hurt, but I tried not to show it. I had promised myself I was finished with politics for good. I was going to devote myself to the O'Brien Cafe and to our real estate holdings. But I had been back in Springfield only a few weeks when a chance encounter started me toward my political association with Jack Kennedy.

II

JOINING JACK KENNEDY

EARLY IN 1951, not long after my return to Springfield, a fellow I knew in the Elks Club came into our cafe and asked if I knew Congressman Kennedy.

"I know him," I said, "but not intimately."

My friend explained that the Elks hoped Kennedy might address a large outdoor gathering they would be having in the spring and wondered if I might extend the invitation. I said I would be glad to and I wrote Kennedy and explained why this would be a good speaking engagement for him—it was non-partisan, there would be a big crowd, and so on. I knew Kennedy well enough to suspect he would jump at the chance to address a large audience in western Massachusetts, where he was not so well known.

I had first met Jack Kennedy back in 1947, when he was serving his first term in Congress. I had been talking with my good friend Eddie Boland, who was then the registrar of deeds in Springfield, when Eddie reminded me that young Congressman Kennedy was speaking that afternoon to a labor convention at the Springfield Auditorium, just across Court Square from Eddie's office.

"Have you heard about this guy?" Eddie asked me.

"Yeah, I've read about him," I said.

"He's a real comer," Eddie said. "He could be President someday. Let's go take a look at him."

I agreed and we left Eddie's office and walked to the auditorium. I was curious. I didn't know much about the young congressman, but I knew about the Kennedy family, for it was the most prominent Irish-Catholic family in Massachusetts. The Kennedys were known not only for their wealth and for their generous contributions to charities and to the Church, but also because Joseph P. Kennedy had been Roosevelt's ambassador to England. We all had read about Joe, Jr.'s death during the war and Jack Kennedy's heroism when his PT boat was sunk, and we knew there were other brothers and sisters whose pictures appeared in the society pages from time to time. The Kennedys were a Massachusetts legend even then, and if Jack Kennedy was speaking in Springfield, I thought I'd better have a look at him.

His speech struck me as routine. The important fact was not what Kennedy said but simply that already, as a young first-term congressman, his name brought him speaking invitations all over the state. After the speech, Eddie Boland and I went up and Eddie introduced me. Kennedy had to hurry off to a radio station, but he asked Eddie and me to meet him for a drink after his interview. We met at the Kimball Hotel—our drinks were Cokes, I recall—and talked for an hour or so before he drove back to Boston. Nothing memorable was said, but he was pleasant and likable. Certainly he made a favorable impression on us, which was what he intended. Even then he knew it was worth an hour of his time to cultivate a couple of local politicians who might someday be useful to him.

When I arrived on Capitol Hill in 1949, I looked Kennedy up and we had lunch at Mike Palm's Restaurant a couple of times. At first I was trying to advance Furcolo's interests, trying to persuade Kennedy to co-sponsor this or that bill of Furcolo's. But Kennedy wanted as little as possible to do with Furcolo. He had rejected our request that he campaign for Furcolo in 1948 and he wasn't interested in sponsoring Kennedy-Furcolo bills. I assumed that he regarded the ambitious Furcolo as a potential rival for state-wide office.

I had no luck helping Furcolo with Kennedy, but we remained friendly. We were almost exactly the same age—he was born about six weeks before I was born in 1917—and we shared an interest in politics. He was very young and casual in those days. I recall his wearing sneakers and khaki pants one day when we lunched on Capitol Hill, and he was considered rather offbeat by congressional standards. For his part, Kennedy was bored by the House and was often conspicuous by his non-participation in its affairs. You sensed, without his telling you, that he would not be making a career of the House, yet you did not have to be a genius to see that he had a real future in politics.

I liked Kennedy and enjoyed his company, but when I left Capitol Hill and returned to Springfield I had no reason to think I'd ever be seeing him again. Then, a few weeks after I wrote him about the Elks Club speaking invitation, I got a call from Frank Morrissey, who was an aide to the congressman and later a judge in Massachusetts. Morrissey said Kennedy would be in the Springfield area soon and would like to talk with me. I said that would be fine, and on a Sunday in March we had dinner at Kelly's Lobster House in nearby Holyoke. Kennedy was not long in getting to the point.

"Larry, I'm not going to stay in the House," he told me. "I'm not challenged there. It's up or out for me. I'm definitely going to run for state-wide office next year. I don't know many people in western Massachusetts and I'd like your help."

"What are you running for?" I asked.

"I don't know yet," he admitted. "I want to run against Lodge, but if Dever makes that race I'll run for governor."

His reply and his uncertainty reflected his status in the state's politics at that point. Henry Cabot Lodge, the respected Republican senator, was up for re-election in 1952 and was widely viewed as unbeatable. Paul Dever, the aging "boy wonder" of Massachusetts politics, was the state's Democratic governor. If Dever wanted to run against Lodge, the Democratic nomination was his for the asking. Only if Dever decided to play it safe, and run for re-election as governor, could Kennedy make the race against Lodge.

I admired Kennedy's audacity, for here was a fellow in his mid-thirties who was eagerly seeking a race against one of the most popular senators in Massachusetts history. But I discouraged any thought that I might be involved in his campaign. The memories were still fresh from my Washington experience and my break with my friend Furcolo.

"I need your help, Larry," Kennedy kept saying. "You did some terrific organizational work for Foster and I don't have anybody who can do that."

"Thanks but no thanks," I told him emphatically. "I'm out of politics. For good."

Kennedy was a hard man to say no to. He thanked me for telling him about the Elks Club speech and asked if I'd let him know about other good speaking engagements in my area. I said I would. Then, as a follow-up to our talk, Frank Morrissey sent me some Kennedy literature and asked if I'd pass it on to people who might be interested. I kept the material in my cafe, where some of the town's Democrats would have a chance to look at it. Later in the spring Kennedy called me.

"Larry, I want to talk to you," he said in that distinctive Boston accent of his. "Do you ever come to Boston?"

"Not often," I said. "I might be in to see the Red Sox this spring. I'll call you if I am."

As it turned out, I went to Boston for a Memorial Day double-header between the Red Sox and the Yankees. I called Kennedy in advance and we agreed to meet for dinner at the Ritz-Carlton Hotel after the game. We had a long and pleasant talk, which essentially covered the same ground as our talk in March—Kennedy was still planning to run for either senator or governor the next year and he still wanted my help. For my part, I said again that I was definitely out of politics.

"Larry, I want to meet the party workers in western Massachusetts," he said. "You can at least help me there, can't you?"

It seemed like a modest request, so I said yes, I could probably help in that regard.

"How should we do it?" he pressed. He knew that the kind of gathering he would hold in his highly political district in Boston might not be appropriate for the lower-keyed politics of Springfield.

"I'd suggest an informal reception early in the evening," I said. "Just coffee and sandwiches, no drinks. You meet everyone personally, shake their hand, and make brief, informal remarks."

"Terrific," Kennedy replied. He was leaning forward over the table, eagerly taking in everything I said. This was politics —this was progress. "Where will we have it?"

"I'd suggest Blake's Restaurant," I told him. "They've got an upstairs room that will hold several hundred people."

"What about the invitations?"

"I can take care of them," I said. "I've got lists of all the people you ought to meet."

Kennedy was beaming when we left the Ritz-Carlton. Then a few weeks later, after I'd sent out the invitations to the reception, which was in June, I received an unexpected call from Kennedy.

"Larry," he said, "your friend Furcolo just called me and said he was really bulled off about my coming into his district without clearing it with him. It doesn't bother me, but I thought you ought to know."

"It doesn't bother me," I assured him.

I understood Furcolo's anger, of course. It's traditional that if one congressman is visiting another congressman's district, he "clears" the visit, or at least gives advance notice. That way, the host congressman won't be embarrassed by having some constituent or reporter break the news of the visit to him. He can always say, "Why, yes, of course, I told my distinguished colleague he was welcome to visit our district."

Kennedy could play by the rules when he chose to, but he didn't choose to with Furcolo and he wasn't about to clear anything with him.

But that wasn't the end of it. The day before the reception, Kennedy called again, this time from New York. I took the call in the phone booth in the cafe.

"Larry," he began. "Foster called again."

"Yeah?"

"He says I should cancel our reception."

"For any particular reason?" I asked. This whole thing was getting absurd.

"Yeah," Kennedy replied. "He said he hated to tell me this,

but I should cancel because O'Brien was in trouble and might have some legal problems."

I couldn't believe what I was hearing. I had no legal problems, none whatsoever. I could only assume that Furcolo was so anxious to keep Kennedy from association with me that he had fabricated the story as a desperate ploy to scare Kennedy into canceling the trip. I was stunned, then increasingly angry. I had thought I was out of politics, but here I was in the middle of the worst kind of political back-stabbing.

I bit my lip and cursed silently, until finally Kennedy said, "Well, what do you think of that?"

"I haven't any comment on it," I said.

"What's your advice?"

"My advice, if you're worried about it, is to forget the meeting tomorrow. It doesn't matter to me, one way or the other."

Kennedy paused a minute, then said: "Where am I supposed to meet you and what time?"

"At noon outside Howard Johnson's Restaurant," I told him.

"I'll see you there," he said and hung up.

In the dozen years ahead, when I was impatient or angry with Kennedy, I would sometimes think back to that time when he had to make a quick judgment between Furcolo and me. Furcolo was a member of Congress; I was a cafe owner whom Kennedy knew precious little about. The easy thing, the safe thing would have been to plead illness and cancel the reception. Why risk involvement with some local pol who might be in some sort of trouble? But Kennedy chose to trust me rather than Furcolo, and I would have to say that I don't know another man in politics who would have made the same decision.

I met Kennedy at noon the next day. He had driven from Boston with Morrissey and with Bob Morey, his regular driver in those days. We went to lunch, then went to my mother's apartment to talk until it was time to go to the reception. My father had died the previous year and he, to my knowledge, had never met Kennedy, but Kennedy and my mother became friendly. She was a woman of great poise and self-assurance and Kennedy was intrigued by her.

"Mrs. O'Brien," he said with a twinkle in his eye, "why don't you have more of a brogue?"

She laughed and explained that in the part of Ireland she and her husband had come from, many people didn't have pronounced brogues. She went on to say, "But in fact I have a sister who has acquired a brogue since she came here." They moved into a conversation about local politics, for if my mother was not an activist she nonetheless had acquired a good deal of political know-how. She certainly knew aspects of Springfield politics that Kennedy didn't know, and he was fascinated to hear her views.

Kennedy's curiosity was one of his most striking qualities. He had led a life, somewhat sheltered from the workaday world that most of us know, and so he moved through life with an insatiable curiosity about many things that most of us take for granted. Once he came to my cafe and tried his hand at drawing beer from the taps. I had probably drawn my first glass of beer at age fifteen and several thousand more after that, but it was an entirely new experience to Kennedy. Next he wanted to know where the beer came from.

"For Pete's sake, Jack," I protested. "It comes from barrels down in the cellar."

"Let's take a look," he insisted, and nothing would do but that we go down for a guided tour of the walk-in cooler where we kept our barrels of beer. This led, finally, to a detailed discussion of the profit margin on each glass of beer sold.

Finally, that June afternoon, we left my mother's apartment and proceeded to the reception at Blake's Restaurant. We arrived early, when the big hall was empty except for the refreshments and the red, white, and blue bunting we had put up for decoration. Slowly, the party workers began to file in and I stood with Kennedy near the door to make the introductions. Each guest, before he or she reached Kennedy, was asked by a hostess to sign a guest book—it seemed like a "social" touch, but in truth I wanted all the names for follow-up mailings.

Kennedy was warm and gracious to the people who filed past him. He had the ability to focus exclusively on each person for a few seconds, establishing real human contact, making the person feel that he would remember and treasure those few seconds of conversation.

In political situations, such as a receiving line, a politician often has about ten seconds to give an impression that may last a lifetime. In Kennedy's case, because of his youth and his wealth, many people would be ready to dislike him if he appeared standoffish. Although he was reserved, Kennedy had a genuine interest in people. I could literally see this reflected in the faces of the people who filed through that receiving line to meet him—nervous or hesitant as they approached him, loosening up as he took their hand, and finally beaming with pleasure as they walked away from their first encounter with one of the famous Kennedys.

His remarks were low-key. He was pleased to be in Springfield, pleased to meet all of them, and he hoped to come back again, perhaps someday—this said lightly—as a candidate for office.

As we left the reception, Kennedy knew it had gone well. "God, what a great meeting," he kept saying. Then, as we drove away, his mood changed.

"Let me ask you something, Larry. What would you have done if I had called off this reception because of what Furcolo said?"

"That's very simple," I told him. "I'd have gone to the meeting and told them exactly what happened."

"Do you mean you would have told them I canceled because Furcolo said you might be in legal difficulties?"

"That's absolutely right. And the papers would have picked it up—it would have made an interesting story."

"You'd really have done that?"

"Why not? What would you suggest I do with several hundred of my friends gathered there at my invitation?"

Kennedy shook his head in bewilderment. "Politics," he muttered. "What a business."

The next day I mailed him the guest book and he wrote

everyone a note of thanks. He loved that guest-book idea, and it became a fixture of his later campaigns.

One result of the reception at Blake's Restaurant was Kennedy's determination to have me on his campaign team. And, in retrospect, it's clear that my resolve to stay out of politics was weakening. Part of it was my long-time love of politics, but more of it was my growing affection and respect for Jack Kennedy. He represented something new in Massachusetts politics.

When I was growing up, Jim Curley had been my hero— a two-fisted, flamboyant Irishman who had fought his way up from the slums. But Curley had fallen on bad times. He had been a congressman, governor, and in 1945 he was elected mayor of Boston for the fourth time. But in 1947 he was convicted of using the mails to defraud and sent to prison. John Kennedy, who had been elected to fill Curley's old House seat, was the only Democratic congressman from Massachusetts who refused to sign a petition asking President Truman to pardon Curley. Nonetheless, his prison sentence was commuted a few months later and he was granted a full pardon by Truman in 1950. At the time, because of my old affection for Curley, I had resented Kennedy's refusal to sign the petition, and yet I had understood the political reasons for his decision. He sensed even then that the Curley era was ending and a new era, a Kennedy era, was beginning, and it was not in his interests to be identified with the Curley tradition.

Kennedy represented a new generation, a new kind of Irish politician, one who was rich and respectable and could do battle with the Lodges and the other Yankee politicians on their own terms. I would always feel an affection for Curley, but the practical politician in me saw that Kennedy was the man who could lead my generation.

However, despite my growing interest in Kennedy, a misunderstanding soon threatened our relationship. To follow up on the reception in June, we scheduled an organizational meeting for a Sunday afternoon in September in the ballroom of the Kimball Hotel in Springfield. I invited roughly the same group that had attended the reception, but this was no social, get-acquainted session. This was a sit-down meeting, a business meeting. Kennedy was coming to state unequivocably that he would be running for governor or senator the next year—he still didn't know which—and to ask for commitments of support.

The meeting was set for 2 P.M. and Kennedy had said he'd meet me there. At about one, I went to the hotel to check on the arrangements. I ran into an associate who had some news for me.

"Say, Larry, what do you think about this secret meeting Kennedy's having?"

I must have shown my surprise—I knew Kennedy was going to a communion breakfast in a nearby town that morning, but I knew nothing about any secret meeting.

"Sure," my informant said, "I hear Jim Reed arranged it and there's a number of your friends there, too."

Jim Reed was a Springfield man whom Kennedy had known in the Navy and who happened to be President of the local Young Republicans. Most of the others at the meeting were Democrats, some of whom were invited to my meeting that afternoon.

I was furious. I thought I at least deserved the courtesy of being informed if Kennedy scheduled a political meeting, particularly one that included Republicans. It looked to me as if he was going behind my back, trying to play both sides of the street, and that wasn't the way I thought the game was played.

Kennedy arrived at my meeting promptly at two and I opened the meeting. I thanked everyone for coming; I said that Kennedy would be a strong candidate; and that the people in that room could build a first-rate organization for him. I went on to declare that I was not going to direct that organization. Then I introduced Kennedy, who was ill at ease and made a very short talk. When he finished, I suggested that he shake hands with everyone as they left, since he hadn't when they arrived. I went to a room upstairs in the hotel and talked with some friends. About a half hour later, Kennedy came in.

"My God, what happened down there?" he asked.

"What do you mean?"

"You asked everyone else to support me but you 'resigned,'" he said. "I thought you were going to put this together for me. What's wrong?"

"If you don't know what's wrong," I told him, "there's no point in discussing it. I'll be damned if I'll work for a candidate who holds secret meetings behind my back."

"Oh, *that*," he said.

"Yes, that," I repeated.

"That was just a meeting with some old friends," he said. "But I should have thought to tell you and I assure you it won't happen again."

His manner disarmed me. I calmed down, our talk returned to politics, and before the evening was over I had agreed to start driving to Boston two days a week to help organize his campaign. Our misunderstanding had brought us closer together. It had cleared the air. He understood me better, and I appreciated his conciliatory manner. Had he said, "Oh, to hell with you, O'Brien," which he certainly could have, my future would have turned out quite differently. But, once again, his instincts were good, and I, despite all my disclaimers, was committed to an active role in another political campaign.

Throughout the winter of 1951–52 I was in Boston two or three days a week. Kennedy had a man named Mark Dalton, a dedicated supporter, running his headquarters in Boston. He also had two young field men who had traveled around the state interviewing local political leaders and filing reports on them. I read the report they had written on me and discovered that they hadn't been very impressed with me. That was amusing, but the general situation wasn't. Kennedy had to have a state-wide organization. He was traveling around the state making a good impression on people, but there had to be organizational follow-up. Most of my efforts in those early months went into contacting political leaders throughout the state who might form the nucleus of a Kennedy organization.

We still didn't know what Kennedy was going to run for. We were waiting for Governor Paul Dever to decide whether he would seek re-election or challenge Senator Lodge; Kennedy would enter whichever race was left over.

It appeared that Kennedy would be better off running for governor, if Dever left the office, than running against the popular incumbent Lodge. But that was not what Kennedy wanted. He kept an apartment in Boston, across from the State House, and one day, while looking out the window at the State House, he said to me, "Larry, I don't look forward to sitting over there in the governor's office and dealing out sewer contracts." He viewed the governorship as a mundane administrative post and the Senate as the place where the action was.

One Sunday afternoon that spring, Kennedy called me, as excited as I'd ever heard him. "I've just talked to Dever," he exclaimed. "He's running for governor again. Here we go, Larry —we've got the race we want!"

I wasn't so sure. He faced an uphill battle against Lodge, perhaps an impossible battle. But I tried to sound as excited as he was. Whatever happened, I was aboard, all the way.

A little later, Kennedy's father called a meeting in a Boston hotel to discuss campaign strategy. About a dozen people were present, including the candidate, his campaign manager, Mark Dalton, his two field organizers, and his brother Bob who was about twenty-five then and who I had never met before.

The elder Kennedy dominated the meeting. Jack Kennedy didn't say much; I think he took his father with a large grain of salt. Mr. Kennedy's monologue jumped around from the strategy we should follow to the kind of campaign lapel buttons we should have. Little was accomplished. Eventually the elder Kennedy began making such rough criticisms of Mark Dalton's performance that Dalton rushed from the room distraught— he was out as campaign manager.

When that meeting broke up, Mr. Kennedy said he wanted to talk to me privately. He later came to my office in our campaign headquarters on Kilby Street. There we sat down and Mr. Kennedy abruptly said, "Larry, I want to go over in detail my concept of this campaign and how it should be organized."

This was my first visit alone with Mr. Kennedy, whom almost everyone called "the Ambassador." I had been warned that he liked to run over people, so I felt I had about five seconds to set the tone of our relationship.

"Mr. Kennedy," I broke in. "Maybe it would be better if I gave you *my* concept of how the campaign should be organized and then you can tell me *your* reaction."

I started talking and he listened intently. The essence of what I said was that we must build a Kennedy organization separate and independent from the regular Democratic organization, because the regulars would be concentrating on reelecting Governor Dever and wouldn't worry much about Kennedy's race against the "unbeatable" Lodge.

When I finished, Mr. Kennedy nodded and said, "That's about the way I see it. Feel free to call me anytime."

He started to leave, then sat back down and chatted for a while. He was quite cordial and in parting he gave me some advice I've always remembered. "Whenever you're dealing with someone important to you," he said, "picture him sitting there in a suit of long red underwear. That's the way I've operated in business."

I thanked him for his advice and, in the years ahead, whenever I've had to deal with the important and the self-important, I've often followed it.

Later that day, perhaps after talking with his father, Jack Kennedy called me and said he was naming his brother Bob to be his campaign manager and he wanted me to be his director of organization. I accepted. I was still involved only part time, but it was obvious that I was moving toward a full-time commitment to the Kennedy cause.

I try to be a perfectionist in political organization and I've spent a lifetime being frustrated by the imperfections and inefficiencies of the campaigns I've directed. The Kennedy campaign of 1952 was the most nearly perfect political campaign I've ever seen. It was a model campaign because it had to be. Jack Kennedy was the only man in Massachusetts who had the remotest chance of beating Henry Cabot Lodge that year, and even Kennedy couldn't have won without an exceptional political effort.

At the outset I doubted that Kennedy could do it. But I didn't care. Win or lose, I was proud to be associated with him. I viewed the Kennedy-Lodge race as a historic confrontation between the flower of the Yankee establishment and the best that we newer Americans could put forward as our champion.

In the pre-Kennedy era of Massachusetts politics, despite the occasional successes of a Jim Curley or a David I. Walsh, the immigrant groups had traditionally accepted the political leadership of the Yankee Republicans: the Cabot Lodges and the Leverett Saltonstalls and the Christian Herters. In years past, I must have heard Irishwomen say a hundred times, "What a fine gentleman Senator Saltonstall is—he has Irish maids in his home and he treats them very well."

Too many of the immigrant groups, even when they were nominally Democratic, tended to turn Republican when they made a little money and moved out to the suburbs. Republicans were respectable. Republicans didn't get thrown in jail like Jim Curley. But Jack Kennedy was different. If the Yankee politicians had their snob appeal, so did the Kennedys. Those suburban sons and daughters of immigrants might not say "I'm a Democrat," but I hoped they could be brought to say "I'm for Jack Kennedy."

We weren't going to win on snob appeal alone, however. We could win, I believed, only if our extremely attractive candidate was supported by an organizational effort unprecedented in Massachusetts politics. The Democratic Party regulars weren't going to do anything for Jack Kennedy. They regarded him as a rich kid who had entered a hopeless race. They would be concentrating on Governor Dever's tough re-election race against Christian Herter. Kennedy interested the Democratic regulars only insofar as he might be persuaded to contribute some of his money to the Democratic ticket.

For our part, we saw little to be gained by close identification with Paul Dever. Dever had once been the "boy wonder" of Massachusetts politics, but no longer. That summer, in a televised speech he made to the Democratic National Convention, he had come across as a portly, perspiring old pol —his inept performance was the talk of the state. Dever's star was fading and Kennedy's, we hoped, was rising. Thus, we would let the regulars do or die for Dever; our only hope was to build our own independent Kennedy organization, city by city, town by town, and, if possible, to build it without offending the party regulars. That was our job and the challenge fascinated me.

I had learned early, from my father, how important the nuts and bolts of politics can be. The organizational end of politics always appealed to me more than the office-seeking end. I observed that many people like the rallies and the torchlight parades, but few want to work year in, year out, at tasks like voter registration. Perhaps that's why I concentrated on organizing, because I saw so much to be done and so few people doing it.

I don't mean to overstate the importance of good organization. Obviously the candidate and his ability and personality are extremely important, and in recent years the effective use of television has become increasingly vital. But I believe that effective organization can affect perhaps 3 to 5 per cent of the total vote, enough to win or lose a close election. I believe it made the difference in the Kennedy-Lodge race in 1952.

There was little difference between the two candidates on the issues. Lodge's record was so resolutely middle-of-the-road that there was some debate within our camps as to whether Kennedy should criticize him for being too conservative or too liberal. Actually, Kennedy hardly criticized Lodge's record at all, since his own voting record in the House was so similar. The "issue" became which of them could funnel more federal largesse back home from Washington. Thus, Kennedy's posters proclaimed "He Can Do More for Massachusetts" and Lodge's countered "He Has Done the Most for Massachusetts."

Lodge was so confident of victory that he spent a great deal of time traveling about the country as Eisenhower's national campaign chairman. He didn't realize until too late that Kennedy was steadily closing the gap between them.

The key to the Kennedy organization in 1952 was the network of three hundred local campaign directors we recruited, the Kennedy secretaries, as we called them. The title was significant. We could have called them Kennedy chairmen, but that might have offended the local party chairmen, who in theory were still chairmen of everything—our campaign included—so we settled on the more modest title of secretary. I had the primary responsibility for selecting these men, and I was looking for fresh faces, people who had been active in community life but not necessarily in politics.

Once we had our secretaries, we had to be sure they carried out the program of political activity we envisioned. To that end, I wrote a more detailed version of the O'Brien Manual —containing instructions on telephone campaigns, voter registration, press relations, and so on—and I also frequently organized meetings around the state with groups of the secretaries to discuss implementation.

Bob Kennedy regularly accompanied me to those meetings, but one could not say that he took to politics like a duck to water. Irish politicians in Massachusetts in those days often greeted people they met with a hearty "How's the family?" —if you knew nothing at all about a fellow, you could at least assume he had a family and would report on it. I never heard Bob Kennedy ask anyone "How's the family?" The entire hand-shaking, small-talking side of politics was repugnant to him; he often said to me, "Larry, I don't know how you stand it."

When we met with the secretaries, I sometimes introduced Bob, who was of course the campaign manager, as "the candidate's brother," which was usually good for a chuckle. Bob was all business. He would explain what he wanted done, and no one could deny that he was setting an example with the fifteen- and twenty-hour days he was working on Jack's behalf. Bob was sensitive about his age and his lack of political experience and he worked terribly hard to compensate for it. On balance his zeal and the unique trust his brother placed in him more than made up for his inexperience.

Early in the campaign, Jack Kennedy told me that Ken

O'Donnell, a close friend of Bob's from Harvard, was leaving his job with a paper company to join the campaign full time. I knew a little about Ken, who had been Harvard's football captain back when Bob was scrambling to make the team. I knew more about Ken's father, Cleo O'Donnell, who was the widely admired coach of the Holy Cross College football team.

Ken was a wiry, sharp-featured, tight-lipped young man who wasted no words. He proved to be a natural politician, to love the game, and to thrive on it. He was no back-slapper, but other men liked him and respected his bluntness.

I saw relatively little of the candidate during the campaign. I had my assignment and I was largely left to do it as I thought best. It became a joke between Jack and me that he was always going out the door as I came in or vice versa. Yet I saw enough to have an ever-increasing respect for him. He could not be called a natural politician; he was too reserved, too private a person by nature. To stand at a factory gate and shake hands with the workers was never easy for him, nor was he ever fully at ease with the old-style political leaders of Massachusetts. But he knew what he wanted and he would force himself to do whatever was necessary to achieve it. Throughout the 1952 campaign he became more at ease with strangers, a better public speaker and a more confident campaigner. I think people too often regard politicians with awe and too rarely realize that they are men with all the frailties of other men. Among politicians, as among teachers, barbers, or bartenders, some are mediocre and some are exceptional. Some take pride in their work and some are content with a sloppy performance, if it gets the job done. Kennedy had talent and he worked hard to perfect it; above all, he was a proud man who took intense pride in every aspect of his work.

Our biggest worry throughout the campaign was his health. It was well known that he had injured his back during the war, and the last thing we wanted was any suggestion that he still had a health problem of any kind. The truth was, however, that his back was bothering him. And on one of his visits to Springfield, he stopped in a local fire station, went up to the third floor shaking hands, then impulsively slid down the fire pole to the first floor. He landed with a jolt and doubled up with pain. We hurried him to his hotel and called a doctor, who confirmed that Kennedy had aggravated his old back injury and would have to use crutches.

We were desperate to keep Kennedy's health from becoming an issue so early in the campaign. We canceled his schedule for the next day and said he had to return to Washington because of urgent congressional business. I doubted that the story of Kennedy sliding down the fire pole and injuring his back would stay secret long, however, so I called an editor of the Springfield paper and leveled with him and asked him to help us out. He did, and the paper went along with our story about Kennedy's return to Washington.

Throughout the campaign Kennedy had recurrences of both malaria and his back problem. He sometimes appeared in public on crutches, but only when it was imperative. I saw him several times stand for hours in a receiving line when I knew he was in severe pain. Occasionally he made the usual complaints of a candidate about being overscheduled, but I never heard him complain about his health. I think that Jack's wartime experience, coming so close to death in his PT-boat mishap, had toughened him tremendously—not only physically but in his outlook toward life, so that he could withstand whatever came along, including all the name-calling and back-stabbing of Massachusetts politics. He was a courageous man in every regard.

Early in my political life I decided that womanpower was the great neglected resource of American politics. Women had time and energy and political concern, and the candidate who could arouse their enthusiasm would be all but unbeatable. Certainly, in 1952, womanpower was basic to the Kennedy campaign, both in the contribution made by the candidate's mother and sisters and in the mobilization of thousands of women volunteers across the state.

We started with the fact that our candidate was young, rich, handsome, and unmarried, a combination that women of all ages seemed to find irresistible—the young ones wanted to marry him and the older ones wanted to mother him. We also discovered that the candidate's mother, Rose Kennedy, the dynamic matriarch of the Kennedy clan, was just as big an attraction as her son and that his sisters, Pat, Eunice, and Jean, along with Bob Kennedy's wife, Ethel, could draw large and enthusiastic crowds. We, therefore, began a series of receptions or teas under the direction of Polly Fitzgerald, a Kennedy cousin (we called them receptions, but the papers called them teas) featuring Jack and his mother and his sisters.

These were political functions, as far as I was concerned, but we tried to make them appear to be social functions. Our local Kennedy secretary would send out printed invitations to local Democratic women and, if there was any doubt about a good turnout, we would put an ad in the paper on the day before the reception. We held thirty or forty receptions that summer and fall, with the smallest attracting a few hundred women and the largest several thousand.

At every reception each guest was asked to sign one of the guest books that had become a fixture of the campaign. The guest books were passed on to the local Kennedy secretary for the appropriate follow-up and often today's reception guest became tomorrow's volunteer.

The general format was for the women to assemble in whatever hall we used and to hear a brief talk from Jack, if he was present, then a longer talk from his mother, who was a star attraction. She would speak as a mother, to other mothers, recalling the joys and tribulations of raising a large family. She would speak of Jack as a boy and of the scrapes he had gotten into and, in passing, she would mention that she thought he would make a fine senator. A reporter wrote of one large reception, "An air of pleasant, chattering amiability prevailed in spite of a few splattered dresses and two faintings. When the handshaking in the ballroom was finally completed around 10:30, the Kennedys, looking wilted but determined, came in for tea themselves."

My wife, Elva, once organized a reception in Springfield for Mrs. Kennedy. There was some complaint in the final days before the reception that not everyone was invited, so Elva went on television to reassure the ladies of Springfield that they were all welcome to come to meet Rose Kennedy. The ladies of Springfield took her at her word. They poured into the Sheraton Hotel by the thousands. The ballroom became so packed that Elva feared those coming in might crush those already inside. She therefore positioned the receiving line so that after each lady had greeted Mrs. Kennedy she could be guided down the fire escape to the street.

I had met Mrs. Kennedy several times at Hyannis Port, but she tended to keep to herself. That summer she had a little cabana down at the beach and you would see her disappear there in the morning, carrying a book and wearing a floppy straw hat, and she might not reappear until evening. At dinner she would be quite gracious, but the dinner-table conversation was usually dominated by her husband. Elva and I thought of her as a pleasant but rather reserved woman and, thus, we were delighted when, during cocktails and dinner at her home just after the election, she entertained us with hilarious, and devastating, imitations of Henry Cabot Lodge and other politicians she had met over the years.

Once during the campaign I asked Elva to pick up Mrs. Kennedy at the Roger Smith Hotel in Holyoke, where she had attended a reception, and drive her to Bradley Field in Connecticut, where she would meet Jack and me and they would catch a plane home. Elva asked our friend Anita Shea to come along to talk with Mrs. Kennedy while Elva concentrated on the driving. After Elva and Anita got to the hotel and called up to Mrs. Kennedy's suite, there was a long wait. Elva was becoming worried that they might miss the plane. She didn't realize that it was a private plane and wasn't going anywhere without Mrs. Kennedy. Finally Mrs. Kennedy's maid came down with a bellhop carrying a half-dozen bags. He put the bags in the trunk of our Buick and stood waiting until Elva handed over a five-dollar tip. When Mrs. Kennedy came down, Elva made no mention of the five dollars, but Mrs. Kennedy presented her with an orchid that she guessed had been given her at that day's reception. Mrs. Kennedy, Elva, Anita, and the maid got into the car, and Anita was just about to strike up a conversation when Mrs. Kennedy said, quite graciously, "Would you forgive me? I'm very tired and don't feel like talking." So they made the hour's drive to the airport in total silence.

Jack and I met the ladies at the airport and as we were hurrying across the lobby Jack dropped a large brown paper bag he was carrying and out spilled his week's supply of dirty laundry. We all helped gather it up, to the amusement of the passers-by. Jack was also carrying a suitcase which he had apparently packed in haste, for it had socks and shirttails hanging out of it.

"Jack, that suitcase is a disgrace," his mother said. "Put it down and let me fix it for you." Jack sighed and put down his suitcase, and our party stopped in the middle of the terminal while his mother tidied up his suitcase to her satisfaction.

Eventually, it all began to come together. The teas and the tireless campaigning of the Kennedy family generated enthusiasm and thousands of volunteers. Our organization was in place and was able to use those volunteers in our telephone campaigns, our mailings, distributing our tabloid, registering voters, and getting them out on Election Day. Our secretaries were making weekly reports to me and they were growing more sophisticated from week to week. It was with great satisfaction that I watched the smoothly operating campaign organization that we had created from scratch, the sort of satisfaction that a political organizer experiences only rarely.

For a long time neither Lodge nor the Democratic regulars realized what we were doing. They knew we had opened some offices and were making some telephone calls, but no one knew the scope of our operation. When Lodge finally realized he was in trouble, he hurried back from the Eisenhower campaign and, among other things, agreed to a series of debates with Kennedy. But Lodge, like many others, underestimated Kennedy. Jack won the first debate hands down and, thereafter, Lodge was unavailable for a rematch.

The Democratic regulars, preoccupied with the Dever campaign, had largely ignored us, but eventually they began to sense that something was happening, that their man was in trouble while our man was looking stronger each day. At that point, in the final weeks of the campaign, things began to get sticky. Dever's people started demanding joint Dever-Kennedy headquarters, joint appearances, joint advertisements, a combined effort all the way. We had in fact co-operated with Dever in Boston, where the party organization was strong, but we knew that association with Governor Dever beyond that would hurt us. Yet we didn't want an angry, public break with the regular organization, so we had to handle the situation with extreme care. Kennedy maintained that his schedule was set and wouldn't allow for more than a few appearances with Dever. The regulars would send us pictures of Dever to hang in our local headquarters, but our people would be awfully slow in unpacking those pictures.

We succeeded in fuzzing over the situation. We kept our distance from Dever, but we avoided an open break with the regulars. We wished Dever well, but he was falling behind while we were pulling ahead; and we didn't intend to blow a year of work in the last two weeks of the campaign.

On Election Night, the polls had hardly closed when the word went out that Eisenhower was carrying the state by a landslide.

"My God, it's over so quick," I told Kennedy.

Kennedy shook his head. "I can't think of anything we could have done that we haven't," he said.

One Boston paper projected Lodge's victory in its first edition, but as the night wore on we began to get encouraging reports from around the state. We were running strong in the towns and villages that Lodge had to carry to win, but where our Kennedy secretary operation had taken root. By dawn we knew we had won. Eisenhower had swept the state, Herter had beaten Dever by a slim margin, but Kennedy had beaten Lodge by 70,000 votes.

Soon after victory was assured, Kennedy took a long-distance call. I heard him saying, "Well, thank you, Senator, thank you very much." When he put down the phone he looked at me with a puzzled expression.

"That was Lyndon Johnson in Texas," he told me. "He said he just wanted to congratulate me. The guy must never sleep." What neither of us realized was that another election that night had opened up the post of Senate majority leader and Johnson wasn't wasting any time in courting Kennedy's support.

We were exhausted but bursting with pride. Jack Kennedy sat cross-legged on a table in our Boston headquarters surrounded by laughing, weeping, cheering volunteers. We all wondered when Lodge would concede. His headquarters was down the street from ours, and just after dawn Jack looked out the window and said, "Look, there's Cabot coming out."

Lodge climbed into a car that was headed our way and we assumed he was coming in to congratulate Kennedy. Jack jumped off the table and posted himself near the door.

"Everyone be polite to him," Jack ordered. "Give him a hand when he comes in." We were all poised for a show of good will, even though partisan feelings had been running high in both camps in the final days.

Lodge's limousine approached, then whizzed on past our door without slowing down.

"Son of a bitch," Kennedy muttered. "Can you believe it?"

III

LOOKING AHEAD

"LARRY, I want you to go to Washington with me," Kennedy had said in those early morning hours when he knew he was the new senator from Massachusetts.

"I appreciate it, Jack," I told him. "But I haven't any interest in going back to Washington."

The next Saturday he was in Springfield for the wedding of his friend Bob Cramer, and we met at the Kimball Hotel to discuss my post-election work—grading the performance of each Kennedy secretary, compiling lists of all our volunteers, double-checking our financial records. And it was agreed that Jean McGonigle, who had been my campaign secretary, would join the senator's Washington staff to maintain these records.

We were particularly concerned that all our financial records be in perfect order, because a Republican administration was about to take over in Washington and we thought it possible that they might undertake an investigation of the man who upset Henry Cabot Lodge, if only to try to embarrass us and to raise the issue that Kennedy money had won the election.

That afternoon at the Kimball, Kennedy again said he wanted me on his Senate staff and I again declined. "I'd rather stay in Springfield," I told him. "I can keep some of your fences mended here, and if you want me for special assignments I'll be available at the drop of a hat."

He realized that I was not turning down his offer because of any lack of respect or affection for him. But I had served two years as a congressional aide and I had learned I was not cut out for staff work. Foster Furcolo and I had been good friends, closer friends than Kennedy and I were, and my working for Furcolo had ended unpleasantly. I didn't want that to happen between Kennedy and me, and I suspected that it might if I went on his payroll. If you work for a politician, he tells you what to do, but if you maintain your independence, you can now and then tell him what to do.

No year had ever been more thrilling for me than 1952. I had seen my candidate defeat the pride of the Yankee establishment. But now the game was over—other men could go to Washington and worry about legislation and the problems of government. My life was in Springfield and I had plenty of business to attend to there.

Our cafe was doing well and I had become active in the Western Massachusetts Cafe Owners Association, which represented about 150 cafe owners in our area. My father had helped organize the association before the war. Once, when he was representing the association and I was president of the bartenders' union, he and I had sat across the table to negotiate a contract. The association negotiated industry-wide with the unions representing the waiters, cooks, and bartenders, and it also spoke for the cafe owners in dealings with local and state agencies on such matters as liquor licenses, zoning laws, and so on.

In 1951 the Cafe Owners Association had agreed to establish a health fund for the employees. We decided that, rather than pay an insurance company to run the health fund, we would have our own self-administered fund, and I was selected to be the administrator. We opened offices at the corner of State and Main streets in Springfield, just a block from O'Brien's Cafe, and I was able to divide my time between the two responsibilities. In December of 1952, I hired a petite young brunette from Springfield to assist me in my health fund office. Her name was Phyllis Maddock and she would soon become a close friend of Elva's and mine. Phyllis, who later married and became Phyllis Nason, has continued to be a close and valued associate of mine up to this very day.

As it turned out, I was not to be in the cafe business much longer. Our cafe and the adjoining garage and parking lot occupied about a third of a city block that was only one street over from Springfield's Court Square. For several years the owner of the three Springfield newspapers, Sherman Bowles, had wanted to buy our property as well as the rest of the block. Bowles, who was a cousin of Ambassador Chester Bowles, was something of an eccentric—he sometimes drove a newspaper truck, he never wore an overcoat in winter, and he chose to live in a hotel near his newspaper rather than in his family's estate.

Bowles already owned the block in front of us. He hoped to own our block also and to join the two blocks by an overhead walkway. When he died he left the newspaper to its employees, apparently with the admonition that they pursue his plan of buying our block. One day the trustees of the newspaper came to my office and said they wanted to buy our property. I told them, as I had in the past, that the cafe was a family business and my mother and sister and I had no wish to part with it.

"Just give us a price, Larry," one of them urged.

Somewhat annoyed, I threw out what seemed to me a ridiculous figure, one well above what I felt to be the property's market value. The trustees only nodded and said they'd be back in touch with me. A few days later they came back and said they would pay my price.

I was surprised. I talked to my mother and my sister, Mary, and we concluded that the offer was too good to refuse. We sold the property and invested the money and the income which, while by no means making us rich, made it possible for my mother to live in comfort until her death in 1958 and has continued to provide a degree of financial independence for Mary and me.

Mary, I should add, had married Frank Placzek, a lawyer I had known when I was in law school. Frank eventually became a probate judge in Hampden County in Massachusetts and Frank and Mary and Elva and I have remained close over the years.

The mid-1950s were a good time for Elva and me. I had the leisure to dabble in politics and still have time for my family.

Early in the fifties we had bought a comfortable home on Roosevelt Avenue in the Forest Park section of Springfield. Roosevelt Avenue always had a special meaning for me, for when the Depression struck in 1929 my father had owned a beautiful home on that street. We used to drive out and look at it on Sundays, but we couldn't rent it and we couldn't afford to live there ourselves and eventually the bank foreclosed and took it back. Our new home on Roosevelt Avenue was within walking distance of our church and of Larry's public school, and we lived there until we went back to Washington in 1961.

Two of our favorite pastimes in the 1950s were basketball and the theater. I had always been a frustrated basketball player and I would drive to Boston in snow or sleet to see the Celtics play. That was the era when Bob Cousy and Bill Russell were leading the Celtics to the championship year after year.

My love of the theater, which had begun when I was a boy, continued as an adult, but my mobility increased, so that I would see virtually every play that passed through our part of Massachusetts. I can't stand a bad movie, but I will sit through almost any play, no matter how inept. If the script is poor, I'm content to study the actors. I've always been fascinated by the similarity between actors and politicians. Certainly there are a lot of frustrated actors in politics, as well as some very good actors. In both professions you must concern yourself with timing and inflection and the subtleties of human relationships. If you care about the comedy and the tragedy of human life, you have to love the theater, and the dramas that are played out on the political stage as well.

The new senator and I kept in close touch. Not long after the election he invited the O'Briens and the O'Donnells for a weekend at the Cape. That was the visit during which Mrs. Kennedy surprised us with her imitation of Henry Cabot Lodge. That was also the visit when, in the midst of some cheerful cocktail conversation, Joe Kennedy said abruptly to his son Bob:

"Well, what are you going to do now?"

"What do you mean?" Bob asked.

"You've got to get to work," his father said. "You haven't been elected to anything."

Bob must have taken his father seriously, because in a few months he joined Senator Joe McCarthy's Subcommittee as a counsel and later became chief counsel of the "rackets committee" headed by Senator John McClellan that led to his conflict with, among others, Teamster President Jimmy Hoffa.

During the campaign, Kennedy had sometimes borrowed coins from me to place long distance calls to a girl named Jackie who seemed to divide her time between Washington and New York. I believe it was in the spring of 1953 that I first met the beautiful Jacqueline Bouvier one weekend at Hyannis Port. During those weekends, since I didn't play touch football and she seldom did, we would sometimes sit together on the porch and watch the others play. She was always relaxed and pleasant, but we didn't have a great deal to talk about. She was young and rather shy but very much her own woman and not absorbed by the Kennedy family.

Elva and I were guests at Hyannis Port one weekend in the early summer that year when Jackie was visiting the senator. One afternoon we were all sitting around in casual attire, bathing suits or Bermuda shorts, when two young Europeans in business suits appeared. We soon learned that they were from Van Cleef and Arpels, the exclusive New York jewelry store. They were delivering Jackie's engagement ring. The senator slipped the ring on his fiancée's finger and we all gathered around to admire it—an emerald and diamond ring, the loveliest I had ever seen. Jackie insisted that the other women try it on and the senator beamed. Kennedy, in fact, was so pleased that he invited the two men to stay for a swim with us.

Kennedy and I wanted to keep the Kennedy secretary organization intact, at least informally, for use in future campaigns and we used his wedding, in September 1953, as an occasion to call together all the secretaries. I arranged a stag dinner, which was held on the roof of the Parker House in Boston on a hot night in early September. About five hundred men attended and one woman, the senator's sister Pat Kennedy.

It was fascinating to look out over that group and see almost none of the familiar faces of Massachusetts politics. This was a new political force that we had developed, and in my remarks as toastmaster I stressed the importance of keeping our group together.

The wedding itself, and the reception following it at Hammersmith Farm, Jackie's mother's estate in Newport, Rhode Island, was a curious mingling of Jack's political friends and Jackie's society friends. Some of Jackie's friends must have thought us a pretty rowdy bunch, and, for our part, we doubted that many of them voted the straight Democratic ticket. Ken O'Donnell in those days drove an old car with a door, on the passenger's side, that wouldn't open unless he kicked it and then jerked it up off the hinges. He drove up to the portico of Hammersmith Farm amid a long line of limousines, stopped in front of the mansion, and got out, walked around, and casually kicked his car door open to let his wife, Helen, out. After the wedding reception, his car wouldn't start, and we pushed him for miles before we finally gave up.

I was one of the few wedding guests, at least from our crowd, who'd made a hotel reservation in Newport so we wouldn't have to drive a great distance after a long, liquid reception. It turned out that a dozen people converged on our hotel room that night. Elva finally gave up and went to sleep in the middle of a roaring party. She recalls that when she got up the next morning she found one of our guests asleep in the bathtub.

In 1954 Bob Murphy was the Democratic candidate against Governor Herter, and Foster Furcolo was the Democratic candidate against Senator Saltonstall. Our network of Kennedy secretaries was working actively for Murphy, but some were doing little for Furcolo. The fact was that Kennedy probably preferred the Republican Saltonstall with him in the Senate rather than the Democrat Furcolo. Kennedy had a good, nonpartisan relationship with Saltonstall, and he felt that Furcolo would be a rival and a potential source of trouble. Thus,

Kennedy endorsed Murphy and virtually ignored Furcolo, and many in our organization followed his example.

Yet Kennedy could ill afford an open break with Furcolo lest he alienate Furcolo's Italian-American supporters. Furcolo knew this and insisted that Kennedy appear on television with him and give him a firm endorsement. Kennedy had to agree but he insisted that Bob Murphy also be included on the program.

The television show was set for October 9, the night before Kennedy was to enter a New York hospital for an operation on his back. He and I had lunch that day at the Ritz-Carlton Hotel in Boston, and his mind was obviously much more on the back operation than on the television appearance.

"This is it, Larry," he told me. "This is the one that cures you or kills you."

It was not our most cheerful talk but when it was over, he hauled himself up on his crutches, grinned at me, and said, "I'll be seeing you," and hobbled out to his car.

I drove back to Springfield and watched the Kennedy-Furcolo-Murphy appearance at my home. I saw that Kennedy was quite cool to Furcolo, but it was not until later that I understood why.

An advance script had been agreed to by the three participants. When Kennedy arrived at the studio, on crutches and in considerable pain, Furcolo demanded that Kennedy not only endorse him but strongly attack Saltonstall. If Kennedy didn't, Furcolo warned, the Italian-American voters would feel that Kennedy had double-crossed him.

Kennedy was furious. "I didn't know whether to take a swing at the guy or clout him with my crutch," he told me later. Instead, he hobbled out of the studio and only returned, seconds before air time, at the urging of Bob Murphy.

That was the situation as the state's leading Democrats went on the air in a show of party unity. Kennedy, in his remarks, praised Bob Murphy, said he supported the entire Democratic ticket, and barely mentioned Furcolo's name.

The incident might have ended there, except that a reporter overheard part of the angry Kennedy-Furcolo exchange and the papers were soon filled with reports of a break between them. Kennedy was by then in the hospital and said he stood on the record—Furcolo had asked him to go on television with him and he had done so.

Furcolo lost to Saltonstall by 29,000 votes and some Furcolo supporters blamed Kennedy for his defeat. It was also said that Kennedy's lukewarm support was due to me, which was certainly not the case. Kennedy, for his part, was flabbergasted that Furcolo would make such demands on him just before the show began. I wasn't surprised—I had known Furcolo long enough to know he was a gambler. If he could scare Kennedy into a stronger endorsement, it was worth a try. Kennedy now felt he had been right in his early judgment of Furcolo. The two were destined to be rivals, never allies.

Elva and I visited the Kennedys in their Georgetown home not long after they were married. Jackie had encouraged Jack to take up oil painting and during our visit she insisted that I give it a try. I did and proved conclusively that my talent is not for painting. One evening the Kennedys took Elva and me to a cocktail party given by one of their neighbors. As we went up the front steps, we could see, through the window, the guests already gathered in the living room. "I'm always frightened whenever I enter a roomful of strangers," Jackie whispered to Elva. Elva was constantly amazed that Jackie, who was so beautiful and vibrant, seemed genuinely surprised that people were interested in her.

One afternoon that weekend, the three Kennedy brothers and I and several of their friends walked to a nearby park for a game of touch football. Jack was still on crutches and I was never a touch-football player, so we watched while Bob and Ted and their friends played.

At the other end of the park some young fellows, who we assumed to be Georgetown University graduate students, were hitting fly balls, and their baseball kept landing in the middle of our game of touch football. Ted yelled to them to stop but the ball kept coming, until it was apparent that it was deliberate. Finally Ted and one big fellow exchanged angry words and I could see a fight was coming. Ted was ready and willing, but Bob broke in and announced that he'd do the fighting. It was like a scene in ancient Rome, with both sides putting forth their gladiator.

Ted was the biggest of the brothers and would have had no trouble with the fellow, but Bob gave away about thirty pounds. It was an uneven match, which was no doubt what Bob wanted, but no one tried to stop it. The two of them fought their way all around that park, with the rest of us in a circle around them, shouting encouragement. It became a bloody brawl, with each man determined to score a knockout. But neither could and finally the fight stopped when they simply couldn't raise their arms any longer.

Throughout the battle, I kept suggesting to the senator that perhaps he and I should return to his house and await the outcome there. I thought it was foolish for Bob to get into a public brawl, and I was afraid that the police might come or the newspapers might learn that Bob Kennedy had been in a fight while Senator Kennedy cheered him on. It wasn't exactly the image we wanted for our senator. But Jack was not about to leave. I thought to myself, "My God, this is the story of my life."

The incident epitomized for me the competitive drive of the Kennedy family, and particularly of Bob Kennedy. He was the smallest of the brothers, so naturally he had to take on a bigger man to prove his toughness. If Bob had been beaten, Ted would have stepped in, and if Ted had been beaten I suppose the senator would have gone after the fellow with his crutches. And if their father had been present, he would have heartily approved. That was how he'd raised his boys.

That night, back at Jack's house for dinner, Ethel Kennedy commented on the condition of her husband's face.

"Goodness, Bobby, you're all bruised up. That must have been a rough game of touch."

"Yeah," Bob mumbled, and went on with his eating.

After our visit to Washington, Elva sent Jackie a pink and silver shawl she had knitted herself. In return, Elva received a long, lovely note from Jackie in which she said how she loved the shawl, that she had been wearing it in bed when she read at night, but that it was so pretty she'd worn it to a party and Ethel Kennedy had liked it so much she nearly snatched it off her shoulders. In this and other instances, Jackie impressed Elva and me with her extreme graciousness.

Kennedy was a U.S. senator now, a rising national figure, yet his roots were still in the rough-and-tumble world of Massachusetts politics, often to his dismay. In 1956 Ken O'Donnell and I led Kennedy into a wild battle for control of the state Democratic committee. Before it was over, the struggle had turned into a test of strength between Kennedy and John McCormack, who was then still House majority leader, but that was not what Ken and I had intended. The episode began because we were annoyed that the state committee, with its potential for leadership, was inactive. I felt that Kennedy had a responsibility to work for a strong Democratic Party in Massachusetts, and the state committee was the logical starting point. Also we contended that the struggle was necessary to insure control of the delegation to the Democratic National Convention.

The state committee had eighty members who were elected every four years. There wasn't much interest in their elections, and I thought it would be relatively easy to elect a few dozen Kennedy people around the state. Once we had a majority we could elect our own chairman and control the organization.

Kennedy never was enthusiastic about the plan. His instinct was to avoid internal party fights. Ken and I kept pushing him until he gave reluctant approval, but he also told us to keep him out of direct involvement. That wasn't realistic, since we were obviously his agents, but we proceeded on that basis.

Our takeover plan became a Kennedy-McCormack fight when a McCormack loyalist, Onion Bill Burke, a big, balding tavern owner and onion farmer, was seeking re-election as chairman of the state committee. Thus we headed for a showdown: either a Kennedy man or a McCormack man would head the state committee. For a while I hoped to solve the problem by arranging for Onion Bill Burke to be defeated when he ran for re-election to the committee in his home district. I persuaded a popular druggist, a Kennedy supporter, to run against him. But Burke said that he didn't have to be a member of the state committee to be elected its chairman.

By this time, the newspapers were playing up the state committee contest as a Kennedy-McCormack fight. Kennedy was furious. "What the hell are you guys doing to me?" he kept asking, and we kept assuring him it would all work out fine.

In truth, we didn't even have a candidate for state chairman. Then Ken came up with Pat Lynch, the mayor of Somerville, a feisty little man who was famous for his colorful speech. He would say of a verbose politician: "He can talk a dog off a meat wagon" and of a political enemy: "If you dropped him out a window, he'd go up." He would call an Irish-American who didn't impress him a "two-boater," which meant that he or his parents hadn't had enough money to sail directly from Ireland to Boston, but had to stop off in Nova Scotia.

Lynch was willing to be our candidate for chairman, so we took him to see Kennedy, who was concerned that our man was a professional politician, not a fresh new face. But Ken and I convinced him that Lynch was the best candidate we had.

The new state committee was elected in April and was to meet and elect its new chairman in mid-May. In the final days, both we and the McCormack people were using all our powers of persuasion on the uncommitted members to vote for our man. Onion Bill Burke charged that Kennedy was trying to buy the state committee, which so angered Kennedy that he agreed to personally contact several undecided committee members.

Burke reported to McCormack that he had the votes to beat Pat Lynch, which led McCormack to announce that this was indeed a test of strength between him and Kennedy. Our head count showed us with the votes to win, but Kennedy had no assurance that our head count was better than McCormack's, and he was shaken to his boot tops. He saw himself losing a highly publicized fight he'd never wanted to get involved in. By then he was wishing he'd never heard of O'Brien and

O'Donnell, and we suspected we might not be seeing too much more of Senator Kennedy if we blew this one.

Finally the election was held, at a meeting in the Bradford Hotel in Boston. We argued that Onion Bill Burke shouldn't be allowed to attend the meeting, even if he was running for state chairman, since he was not a member of the committee. To back up our ruling, we had two tough Boston cops guarding the door, one of whom had reputedly killed a man in a barroom brawl. Burke arrived with some tough guys of his own and, after some pushing and name calling, he and his men went to a room upstairs in the hotel. Kennedy was also upstairs, fretting. Eventually he left the hotel room to wander on Boston Common while awaiting the outcome.

Just as the meeting was about to begin, Onion Bill Burke and his men charged out of the elevator and broke past our guards. One of their leaders was "Knocko" McCormack, the majority leader's two-fisted three-hundred-pound younger brother. As shouting and shoving spread across the meeting room, I called the Boston police commissioner. He arrived minutes later.

"I'm O'Brien," I told him. "You've got to get those troublemakers out of here."

"One more word out of you, O'Brien," the commissioner replied, "and I'll lock you up!"

I hadn't known the commissioner was a McCormack man.

The whole thing was a scene out of *The Last Hurrah*. The two candidates for state chairman, Burke and Lynch, almost settled matters by a fist fight. There was shouting and confusion, and as the roll call began, one member who had gotten drunk attempted to vote twice. But we won—Pat Lynch was elected by a two to one margin. Onion Bill Burke angrily announced his intention to run against Senator Kennedy in 1958. Kennedy, who was mightily relieved, told the press that the election marked a "new era" in Massachusetts politics—but he knew better than that.

In retrospect, I was wrong to lead Kennedy into the state committee battle. We won control of the committee, but the contention that this was necessary to insure our role at the National Convention was not valid and we did not revitalize

the Democratic Party in Massachusetts. One reason was that
the party was too diverse for any quick or easy unification. Another was that, after 1956, Kennedy's attention was increasingly directed away from Massachusetts toward the national
scene.

Once during the 1952 campaign I'd spent a few days at the
Kennedy home at Hyannis Port while I searched for Kennedy
secretaries in that area. Joe Kennedy invited me to join him for
breakfast one morning, and as we lingered over coffee he
looked me in the eye and made a statement I never forgot:

"Larry, Jack is a man of destiny. He is going to defeat Lodge
and serve with distinction in the Senate and eventually he is
going to be President of the United States."

I suppose it was a historic moment and I should have been
awed. Instead, I was rather annoyed. I thought to myself:
"Fine, but why am I knocking myself out helping to build a
political organization for Kennedy if destiny is going to take
care of everything?"

I thought of Mr. Kennedy's prophecy four years later as I
sat at home watching on television while Jack Kennedy was almost nominated for Vice President at the 1956 Democratic
National Convention. It was all so unexpected and all so perfect—perhaps, I thought, shaking my head in wonder, Joe Kennedy had been right and Jack was indeed destiny's child.

A week before, the senator had visited Springfield to receive
an honorary degree. A cloudburst had grounded his plane, and
he came to my home and we talked about the upcoming National Convention while he waited for the weather to clear.

He told me he had spoken to Adlai Stevenson, who was
the likely presidential nominee, and received the impression
that Stevenson would choose Senator Estes Kefauver as his
running mate.

Ted Sorensen, who had joined Kennedy's Senate staff in
1953, believed that Kennedy needed the vice presidency as the
first step toward the presidency. Ted was a rather quiet, book-
ish young man, totally devoted to Kennedy. I knew how highly
Kennedy valued Ted, but I had not gotten to know Ted well.

Ted had been planting stories in the newspapers and magazines for months about how Kennedy's religion would actually be a plus, not a minus, if he were Stevenson's running mate. My impression was that Kennedy regarded all this as good publicity, but he didn't think Stevenson would choose him and he wasn't at all sure he wanted the honor. Certainly, as we talked that afternoon in my home, he gave no indication that he was about to seek the vice presidency. To the contrary, we discussed whether I should go to Chicago for the Convention and agreed there was nothing for me to do there.

Kennedy was as stunned as everyone when Stevenson left the selection of his vice-presidential candidate to the Convention. Suddenly, Kennedy and Kefauver were locked in a close, dramatic race for the nomination. Kefauver won, and Kennedy made a graceful call for party unity. We could not have written a better scenario ourselves. If Kennedy had won the nomination, his Catholicism might have been blamed for Stevenson's defeat. But his dramatic loss to Kefauver gave him priceless national exposure on television. In one evening, he became a contender for the presidential nomination in 1960.

The episode jolted all our thinking. If Kennedy had previously thought of running for President in 1960, he had not informed me of it. But given his growing national reputation and the defeat of the Stevenson-Kefauver ticket, we all knew we were in a new ball game.

As 1957 began, Kennedy accepted more and more speaking engagements all over America, particularly in the West, to gain exposure and to establish political contacts for a national race. Meanwhile, in Massachusetts, my concern was his 1958 race for re-election to the Senate. That he would be returned to office was a foregone conclusion. Our need was to produce a massive, record-breaking victory that would gain national attention and thus help move him toward the 1960 presidential nomination.

One obstacle we faced was the ill will of John McCormack and his followers as a result of the state committee fight. To try to smooth this over, we arranged for the state committee to hold a Kennedy-McCormack unity dinner, attended by some six thousand Democrats—the biggest dinner ever held in Massachusetts. The dinner didn't solve all our problems, but it gave the political columnists something positive to write about, instead of constant stories of a Kennedy-McCormack feud.

Another problem was apathy. Why should our people make a major effort in a campaign that was obviously going to be won? To combat that kind of thinking, we kicked off the 1958 campaign with a luncheon in Boston on April 19. About four hundred of our secretaries and the regular party's Boston ward chairmen attended. In my remarks, I stated candidly that we wanted a maximum effort because we saw 1958 as a steppingstone to 1960. All three Kennedy brothers made rousing speeches, and the senator announced that his brother Ted would be his campaign manager that year. The meeting was a success. Our people left the luncheon fired up, ready to do or die for Senator Kennedy. We only hoped we could keep them that way for the next seven months.

Ted Kennedy at that point was twenty-six years old and a law student at the University of Virginia. I didn't know him well. He had been in the Army during the 1952 campaign and he had not had much political experience. The senator viewed Ted's role as campaign manager as a kind of on-the-job training.

"Teddy's starting from scratch," Jack told me. "Push him. Make him work."

I soon found that no one had to push Ted. He was, like Bob in 1952, an eager and tireless worker. Whenever he was in Springfield he would stay in our home and he became Elva's favorite house guest. He loved Elva's cooking, particularly her salads, and he would lavish praise upon her while devouring everything in sight.

Ted's days began before dawn when he was staying with us. Eddie King, my old friend and a staunch Kennedy worker, would come for him bright and early, and if Ted had overslept Eddie would throw pebbles at his window until he arose. When he was touring Springfield with Eddie, Ted would often station himself beside a stoplight and ask motorists if he could put a Kennedy sticker on their bumper while they waited for the light to change. I recall his doing that for hours one day in a pouring rain, wearing my son Larry's Boy Scout poncho.

Elva tells of the time when Ted came home after a long day's campaigning to have dinner with her and Phyllis Maddock.

"Ted, you must be exhausted," Elva said when he came down for dinner.

"I've got loads of energy," Ted told her. "Didn't you know I climbed the Matterhorn on my last trip to Europe?"

"Weren't you frightened?" Elva asked.

"There's nothing to it," Ted said. "You just put one foot in front of the other and up you go—it's just like climbing those stairs."

To dramatize his point, he began climbing up the outside of our stairs, holding the banister, until his head grazed the ceiling.

"If you get stuck," he called down to Elva and Phyllis, "you just pull yourself up by the ropes."

To show what he meant, he gave a pull on the banister, which suddenly broke with a loud crack, and Ted dropped down to the floor, uninjured but terribly embarrassed.

Ted's mind was not exclusively on politics that summer. He was courting Joan Bennett, his future wife, and no matter how late he arrived back at our house he would always hurry to our upstairs telephone for a lengthy long-distance call to her in New York. They were married just a few weeks after the election.

Foster Furcolo was then the governor of Massachusetts and was running for re-election. Both he and Kennedy were unopposed in the Democratic primary that summer, but Furcolo received more votes than Kennedy did. It was assumed, although there was no actual evidence, that Furcolo, because of the continuing Kennedy-Furcolo feud, had passed the word to his Italian-American followers to vote for Furcolo but not for Kennedy and, thus, to embarrass Kennedy.

Kennedy reacted strongly. "Damn it, Larry, I didn't go into politics to run behind Foster Furcolo," he told me as the results came in. "We've got to do better in the general election."

I agreed, but Kennedy himself caused us a serious problem in our effort to turn out a maximum vote against the Republican Party's token candidate, Vincent Celeste. He spent the late summer on an extended vacation in Europe, and it was difficult for us to keep our workers excited about a candidate who was sunning himself on the Riviera.

Ken O'Donnell and I went to New York to talk to the senator and his father on the day he arrived back from Europe. I had prepared a detailed schedule which called for Kennedy to devote twenty-three days to intensive campaigning, nineteen of them outside Boston, to guarantee the record vote we wanted. Ken and I went first to Mr. Kennedy's Park Avenue apartment before the senator's ship arrived, and it was soon evident that the elder Kennedy did not care for my plan.

"It's crazy," he declared. "You're going to kill him. You don't have to run him all over the state, just put him on television."

I responded, as tactfully as I could, that Vincent Celeste's main campaign issue was Kennedy's wealth and that a massive television campaign would only support his argument. Thus, I said, we had to minimize television and maximize personal contact with the voters.

By then it was time for the senator's ship to arrive. We were getting nowhere with Mr. Kennedy, so Ken and I excused ourselves and hurried to the dock so we could get a word with the senator before his father did. We met Jack and Jackie as they stepped off the gangplank and I began outlining my plan.

"It looks all right to me," Kennedy said.

"Your father doesn't like it," I warned.

Kennedy shrugged. He hadn't realized he'd stepped off the boat into the middle of a fight between me and his father. "We'll see what happens," he said.

While he went through customs, Ken and I dashed back to the elder Kennedy's apartment, not mentioning that we'd talked with his son. When Kennedy arrived a few minutes later, he kept the secret. I outlined my campaign plan and he listened intently as if it was all new to him.

His father didn't like my plan any better the second time.

"Jack, they're trying to kill you," he declared. He turned to me. "O'Brien, you'll wind up with a dead candidate on your hands and you'll be responsible. This schedule is ridiculous and I'm completely opposed to it."

"It is pretty rugged, Larry," the senator injected. "Can't you give me some time off? Dad's got a valid point about my health."

I saw what Jack was doing. He was trying to be diplomatic, trying to keep his father happy without angering me. "Suppose I try the first day or two and see how it goes?" he suggested. "Let's give it a fair try, Dad."

His father reluctantly agreed.

The first day was a long, full one. It started at Lynn in the early morning, included brief stops at Marblehead, Salem, Beverly, Gloucester, Danvers, Peabody, and Swampscott, and ended back at Lynn with a big rally, complete with searchlights and a band. A tour like that demands split-second timing—you have to keep your candidate on schedule or the crowds at each stop will get tired of waiting and drift away. We went to great lengths to make this first day letter-perfect, and it was good that we did, for I soon learned that Mr. Kennedy and Frank Morrissey followed the tour all day. I assumed that Mr. Kennedy was just looking for something to criticize. Fortunately, everything went beautifully.

At the end of the day, the senator, O'Donnell, and I returned to Boston and went to his father's apartment near the Common.

"Don't argue with him," Jack instructed us.

But the elder Kennedy continued with his remarks about having a dead senator on our hands until I began to respond with some sarcasms of my own. Jack quickly pulled me aside.

"Don't," he ordered. "Just ride with it. Your point is valid, but just don't make it."

So I kept quiet and nothing more was said about canceling the tour.

Jackie Kennedy was a major new attraction of the 1958

campaign. She appeared with Jack and also made separate appearances of her own. She spoke both French and Italian and would delight Italian-American and French-American audiences by addressing them in their native tongues.

Elva once helped arrange a reception for Jackie at a parish hall in Chicopee. When they arrived only a handful of people were present. The monsignor, terribly embarrassed, took Jackie next door to his home, where they chatted in French and she admired his antiques. Jackie didn't mind if there was no crowd—she was delighted to visit with the monsignor— but Eddie King, who was traveling with her, was furious. He rushed to a nearby Catholic girls' college and soon reappeared with several dozen school girls in tow. I appeared on the scene and blamed Elva for the fiasco, but Elva insisted she was innocent—the monsignor had neglected to announce that Mrs. Kennedy was coming.

I always felt that Jackie was amused and somewhat intrigued by politics, by the people and by the sheer spectacle of it. She joined us on the traditional election-eve tour of the Boston wards, which in those days culminated at a big delicatessen in Blue Hills. She shared a bag of chocolates with me and, since she did not think she should be seen smoking, I would hold a cigarette for her and she would take furtive puffs from time to time.

In the end, our efforts were repaid. Kennedy beat Celeste by 874,608 votes—a new record for Massachusetts and the biggest win any senator scored that year. The national media gave good coverage to Kennedy's spectacular win. We had taken another step toward 1960.

Kennedy could have been nominated in 1960 without his big 1958 win, but it was not a chance we could afford to take. Because Kennedy was young, because he was Catholic, because he was rich, he could never afford to be an average candidate. He had to prove something in every election he was in.

After the election, I did the things I always did following a campaign—closed our headquarters, wrote thank-you notes, compiled the records we would need for the next election. Yet I had a distinct feeling it would be a long time before I was again engaged in a campaign in Massachusetts. We were moving on to another arena.

IV

1960: THE PRIMARIES AND THE CONVENTION

THE FIRST STRATEGY meeting for the 1960 campaign was held at Joseph Kennedy's Palm Beach home on the first two days of April 1959. Those present were Mr. Kennedy, who was to play a significant behind-the-scenes role in his son's quest for the presidency, Senator Kennedy, Bob Kennedy, Steve Smith, who had married Jean Kennedy, pollster Lou Harris, Ted Sorensen and Bob Wallace from the Senate staff, Ken, and I. Most of our talks were held at poolside, so the Kennedys could take a quick dip whenever they felt like it. I didn't swim, but I managed to get a terrible sunburn.

We discussed our strengths and weaknesses, our political allies and potential allies, who would control which states' delegations, which primaries Kennedy might enter, and what kind of organization we needed. Our main conclusion was that America is one hell of a big country and no set of rules applied to all its states. There was some discussion of whether we should seek a big-name campaign manager, but finally we realized that we didn't know any such person and that, in fact, *we* were the Kennedy organization. On a national scale we would use the same people and the same basic techniques we had successfully applied in Massachusetts. As the meeting closed, I could sense an undercurrent of excitement. We were pledged to an all-out effort to capture the presidency.

Steve Smith had already opened a campaign office in Washington, a few blocks from the Capitol. Steve was a handsome, wiry, hard-driving young man from an old New York family.

After he married Jean Kennedy he had begun managing the Kennedy family business interests, which suggests in what high regard he was held by his in-laws. As our Palm Beach meeting ended, it was agreed that I would begin working three days a week in the Washington campaign office.

My main job, in those early months, was to go on the road, to travel around America to build a campaign organization, as seven years earlier I had traveled through Massachusetts in search of Kennedy secretaries. I would pay special attention to the potential primary states, since we knew that Kennedy would have to score well in the Democratic primaries to have any chance for the nomination.

A week later, on April 10, I visited my first primary state, Indiana, a state I'd never set foot in before. I wanted, eventually, to make a judgment on whether or not Kennedy should enter the Indiana primary, almost a year away, and I wanted to base my judgment on firsthand, face-to-face political intelligence. So there was nothing to do except to go there and talk to the local politicians. I had a few leads, but essentially I was going in cold. I spent five days in the state, driving from city to city, talking to mayors, sheriffs, state legislators, union officials. I introduced myself as a representative of Senator Kennedy, a potential candidate for President in 1960.

I soon realized that I was a long way from Massachusetts, that most often Jack Kennedy was just a name, an image on a television screen. People were polite, sometimes interested, but there was no great groundswell for Kennedy. I found some support, a sheriff here, a mayor there, but perhaps more important, I found concern about Kennedy's religion, particularly as I moved southward in the state. If you had lived your life, as I had, in Massachusetts, you take the Catholic religion for granted. But as I traveled through southern Indiana and politician after politician shook his head and reminded me that this had once been a heartland of the Ku Klux Klan, I began to realize what a continuing problem Kennedy's religion was going to be.

My trip to Indiana was intended, to some extent, to keep Senator Stuart Symington uncertain about Kennedy's intentions. Symington was a possible candidate for the nomination and we felt that Indiana would be a natural primary for him to enter since, besides being Protestant, he was from nearby Missouri and was well known. By sending me to Indiana, Kennedy was warning his friend Symington that he might not get Indiana for free, that he might face a tough fight there. As elsewhere, we tried to keep our potential opponents off balance.

From April 25 to May 8 I was in California, another state I had never visited before. I started in Los Angeles, where I talked to two young lawyers who wanted to form a Kennedy for President Club. I feared that their activity might be premature and might cause us problems with the state's Democratic leaders. I had to slow them down without discouraging them, for we would need them later. Meanwhile, I wanted to sound out the established political figures.

I paid a courtesy call on Governor Pat Brown in Sacramento. Brown was considered a dark-horse possibility for the presidential nomination or, more likely, the vice-presidential nomination. He was in a difficult position. Stevenson had a great deal of support in California, and I assumed the Stevenson people were hinting that Brown might be Stevenson's running mate if he would deliver his state to their man. Brown certainly knew that, as a Catholic, he wasn't going to be on the ticket with Kennedy. I hinted broadly to Brown that Kennedy might enter the California primary. I assumed Brown wanted to win the primary and to go to the Convention as his state's favorite son, so my hints were to keep him unsure about Kennedy's intentions. We had a pleasant talk, but we both were playing our own little games.

I also met with Jesse Unruh, the astute Democratic leader in the State Assembly. He and Bill Munnell, another Democratic Assembly leader, arranged for Senator Kennedy to address the state legislature on a subsequent trip to California. I regarded both Unruh and Munnell as the kind of first-rate professionals we needed on our side, and both of them announced their support for Kennedy. Later, when the going got tough, Munnell switched to Lyndon Johnson, but Jesse Unruh stuck with us when it counted.

"Jesse," I used to tell him, "Senator Kennedy has every politician's name written in one of three books and your name is written in Book One, in gold letters."

I was on the road for at least half of the remainder of 1959. In addition to Indiana and California, I was in Nebraska, Montana, Wyoming, Colorado, New Hampshire, Oregon, Maryland, Wisconsin—which included every primary state we ultimately entered except West Virginia, which turned out to be a crucial one.

As I look back on my travels, the thing that amazes me is that we had the field almost entirely to ourselves. No one representing Johnson or Humphrey or Symington had preceded me to the statehouses and union halls. Somehow, because of the complexity of national politics and the uncertainty of his opponents, Kennedy was able to work unopposed toward the nomination for months, at least so far as grass-roots American politics was concerned. He was running free.

As I moved from state to state making friends, nailing down support, I kept waiting for the opposition to show up, but it never did. Kennedy's opponents had placed their hopes elsewhere. Johnson and Symington were counting on political leaders they thought could deliver their states; Humphrey and Stevenson were apparently counting on their popularity in past years. Meanwhile, Kennedy had his man out in the field building an organization.

It always amazed me how other politicians underestimated Kennedy. Johnson and Symington weren't taking him any more seriously in 1959 than Henry Cabot Lodge had in 1952. His opponents never discovered just how tough, gutty, and ring-wise he was, until it was too late. We were lucky in 1959, because if his opponents for the nomination had started earlier and worked harder, they could well have blocked Kennedy's nomination. Instead, they sat tight, the Washington columnists kept writing about what a political genius Lyndon Johnson was, and we kept locking up delegates.

Kennedy announced his candidacy on January 2, 1960, and Bob Kennedy joined us as campaign manager. One of my most lasting memories of Bob's first days in the campaign is the substantial portion of his time he devoted to making contacts throughout the country seeking job opportunities for his former associates on the McClellan committee. Bob could be tough, and he was not the most gregarious man in politics, but he was unfailingly loyal to those who had been loyal to him—or to his brother.

Soon the first primaries were upon us. We had spent hundreds of hours trying to decide which of the sixteen primaries Kennedy should enter; we had to consider geography, timing, finances, the religious issue, probable opponents, and many other factors. We eventually settled on seven primaries—New Hampshire, Wisconsin, Indiana, West Virginia, Nebraska, Maryland and Oregon. Of these, the two in which Humphrey challenged Kennedy, Wisconsin and West Virginia, were to prove crucial. But others were also important to our plans, including the first primary, New Hampshire, on March 8. Kennedy's strength there, as a New Englander from neighboring Massachusetts, was such that no serious candidate chose to oppose him. Our goal, therefore, was to roll up a record margin of victory, primarily for publicity.

The state was ideal for our type of organization. It was small enough so it could be saturated with phone calls and door-to-door canvassing and the candidate could make a significant personal impact. Kennedy could give only four days to New Hampshire, but we scheduled him tightly, from 10 A.M. until 8 P.M., up and down streets, into factories and stores, pushing him harder than we ever had in Massachusetts. I was amazed that Nelson Rockefeller didn't make a similar effort in New Hampshire. He was well known and could have received a huge vote, perhaps bigger than ours, and perhaps begun a successful drive for the Republican nomination. If he had been nominated, he might well have defeated Kennedy for the presidency. Kennedy fully shared my view, and we never understood Rockefeller's inaction.

One day Bernard Boutin, our campaign chairman in New Hampshire, called me with some unexpected news:

"Guess what? We've got an opponent!"

"A what?"

"An opponent. Somebody running against Kennedy."

I couldn't believe it. Could Humphrey or Symington or Stevenson have taken leave of his senses?

"Bernie, which one is it?"

"Paul Fisher."

"*Who?*"

"Paul Fisher. He's from California. He makes ballpoint pens."

"What the hell is going on?" I asked. "Is this guy for real?"

It is not unheard of for men to exercise their right to enter political campaigns and then to withdraw for a price. We determined that this was not Paul Fisher's motive for entering the New Hampshire primary. To this day I'm not sure what his motive was. He could have been acting in the interests of one of our serious opponents, but my best guess is that he was simply a publicity-seeker.

To that end he was successful, for the reactionary newspaper the Manchester *Union Leader* was happy to portray him as the underdog businessman doing battle against the millionaire playboy Kennedy. The Fisher candidacy presented a touchy situation for us. If he received any significant vote, Kennedy might be laughed out of the presidential race.

So our policy was to ignore the penmaker, but it was not always easy. One day when Kennedy arrived at the University of New Hampshire for a question-and-answer session with students, Fisher was backstage, insisting he was going to share the platform with the senator.

The press was delighted at the prospect of a David and Goliath political story—"Penmaker Upstages Senator"—and that was exactly what we were determined to avoid.

"Larry, get rid of that character," Kennedy told me. But getting rid of Fisher was not simple. I politely suggested that

he have a separate Q & A session of his own and I got the
university officials to join in the request, but Fisher declared
he was going to share the stage with Kennedy. One of our people offered to throw Fisher out of the auditorium bodily, but
I vetoed the idea. It was a nightmare, with Kennedy fuming,
the students waiting, the officials pleading, and Fisher standing fast. Finally Kennedy began to address the students and
Fisher took a chair behind him on the stage.

When Kennedy finished speaking, Fisher stood up, prepared
to move to the microphone. Before he started forward, however, one of our cohorts pulled the curtain, trapping Fisher
behind it. As Fisher struggled to get past the curtain—we could
hear his muffled cries of indignation—we made a hasty exit.

On election eve in New Hampshire, we had a little fun. We
learned that Governor Wesley Powell, who was Richard Nixon's New Hampshire campaign manager, was en route to a
Manchester television station to repeat charges he had been
making that Kennedy was "soft" on communism. Bernie Boutin, Pierre Salinger, and I hurried to the studio and paid sev-
enty-five dollars for fifteen minutes of time immediately following Powell's talk. When he left the microphone, the governor
was stunned to see Boutin step up. While Powell was speaking,
Salinger had begun writing a speech for Boutin and fed him
additional pages while he was on the air. It was a rough
rebuttal to Powell, including a denunciation of his tactics.
Powell stood outside the studio, infuriated. At the finish he
turned to me and said, "I'll see you in Wisconsin," an obvious
reference to the upcoming primary. I said to the governor, "I'll
be happy to buy your plane ticket." The incident proved to be
a last-minute diversion.

The next day, Kennedy defeated Paul Fisher the penmaker
by a nine-to-one margin, which was better for us than an unopposed victory would have been. The luck of the Irish seemed
to be holding. Just after New Hampshire, two other Kennedy
men and I bet Pat Morin of the Associated Press one hundred
dollars that Kennedy would be nominated on the first ballot
in Los Angeles. Our growing optimism was based in part on
a major breakthrough in Ohio, which occurred as early as

January 5, 1960. Kennedy had agreed to stay out of the Ohio primary, and in exchange, Ohio's favorite son, Governor Mike DiSalle, had assured Kennedy of seventy-four convention votes on the first ballot at Los Angeles. That early development, coupled with the New Hampshire victory in March, bolstered our confidence. But it was that very optimism that led us to bungle the next primary, Wisconsin.

We had debated at length whether Kennedy should enter the Wisconsin primary. We knew Humphrey, from neighboring Minnesota, was very popular there, and, beyond that, the question was whether we were spreading ourselves too thin. However, the polls looked good and we had some solid people committed to us, including Ivan Nestingen, the mayor of Madison; Pat Lucey, who later became governor; and Jerry Bruno, a fiery little dynamo whom we discovered in Kenosha and who became the best advance man in the business.

If we could beat Humphrey in his own backyard, as I thought we could, we would take a big step toward the nomination. However, we foolishly let our optimism show, and Humphrey started playing the underdog role that should have been Kennedy's.

Kennedy did *his* part in Wisconsin, campaigning hard for twenty days, but the rest of us didn't do our part. We got cocky and talked about the big victory we were going to win. Some of our people predicted that Kennedy would win eight or nine of the state's ten congressional districts. The result was that when Kennedy won 56.5 per cent of the vote and six of the ten congressional districts, he was in the incredible position of being regarded as the loser and Humphrey the winner. The newspapers, taking their lead from our optimism, had written that anything less than a landslide would be a defeat for Kennedy. There was a terrible sense of gloom in our headquarters on Election Night as the results came in. Kennedy was pacing and shaking his head and biting his fingers—all the nervous habits he possessed. We watched Humphrey on television talking about the moral victory he had won. I felt sick. I looked at Kennedy and thought: "Here is a man who stood in zero weather outside factory gates shaking hands until his own hand bled, a candidate who's won a strong victory against a tough opponent—and somehow he hasn't won anything."

Humphrey immediately announced that he would carry his campaign on to West Virginia and, unexpectedly, it became the make-or-break primary for us. It was being said that the Catholic vote had won for Kennedy in Wisconsin, and if Humphrey could beat him in Protestant West Virginia, Kennedy would be finished.

We saw Humphrey as a spoiler. We didn't think he could be nominated, but if he could win in West Virginia he could ruin Kennedy's chances and open the nomination to Johnson or Symington. We had a suspicion that Humphrey was acting on behalf of Johnson or some other contender. Despite the poor-boy role Humphrey had played, his Wisconsin campaign had been well financed. But Humphrey had played his role to the hilt and we assumed he would repeat it in West Virginia.

Bob Kennedy, Ken O'Donnell, and I flew to West Virginia the morning after the Wisconsin primary. We were delayed at the airport because the Kennedy family plane, the *Caroline*, had a flat tire, and Bob was furious. We were all aware that we had only a month to take our West Virginia campaign off the back burner, where it had been for a year, and carry out a make-or-break effort.

Fortunately, we were not starting from scratch. The story of the Kennedy effort in West Virginia really began at the Democratic National Convention in 1956, where Kennedy met Bob McDonough, a lean, taciturn politician and printing-shop operator from Parkersburg. McDonough supported Kennedy's bid for the vice presidency and decided he'd like to see more of the senator. Thus, two years later, McDonough invited Senator Kennedy to address a luncheon on behalf of a candidate he was supporting in Parkersburg. Somewhat to his surprise, Kennedy came and brought his wife—a combination which sold out a five-dollar-a-plate luncheon, a record price for a political affair in that area.

Kennedy invited McDonough to visit him in Washington, and when he did, they had a long talk about West Virginia politics. Even then, McDonough was urging Kennedy to enter his state's primary in 1960. Kennedy was interested enough to send Ted Sorensen down to talk to other political figures in the state. This led to the creation of West Virginians for Kennedy, but we continued to have serious doubts about Kennedy's entering the primary. The religious issue was a consideration as was the fact that most of the state's politicians did not seem much interested in the presidential primary, one way or another. Bob McDonough kept working on Kennedy's behalf, but the state remained low on our list of possible primaries. I never bothered to go there during 1959.

Our thinking began to change late in 1959 when a Lou Harris poll showed Kennedy beating Humphrey handily in West Virginia. We began to hope that Humphrey would enter the primary, thinking he could win it without opposition; then we could quickly jump in behind him. That was exactly what happened, just before the filing deadline. Then, to our dismay, Lou Harris came up with another poll that showed Humphrey leading. Lou explained, rather lamely I thought, that at the time of the first poll most West Virginians didn't know Kennedy was a Catholic, but by the time of the second poll they were starting to find out. Whatever the reason, we were in trouble.

I visited the state for five days in February of 1960 and came away perplexed. The religious issue bothered me, as well as the strong support for Humphrey among union leaders. In my talks with Bob McDonough and other Kennedy backers, I stressed the need for carrying out the classic Kennedy campaign procedures—the receptions, the tabloid, the telephone campaign, and so on.

"We can do all that," McDonough told me. "But that won't be enough."

He was right, and the longer I was in West Virginia, the more I realized that we would have to do more there than just our traditional volunteer effort. West Virginia is a poor state where the patronage jobs available to county and state officeholders are highly prized. This leads to a tough, skillful brand of politics. We could hold our receptions and distribute our tabloids, but we would also have to forge personal alliances with dozens of local politicians who influenced thousands of votes. The Humphrey people were, of course, trying to forge alliances with the same people, so the West Virginia primary became one of the most challenging head-to-head political contests I have ever been involved in.

The great art of West Virginia politics is the process called slating. In each county, in the days before an election, the various political factions determine which candidates they will support. Finally a slate is formed and a hand card is passed to the faithful outside the polls: A for Governor, B for County Clerk, C for Sheriff, and following that: D for President and so on. Our job was, first, to determine which faction was the strongest in each county and then to persuade that faction, and perhaps competing factions, to put Kennedy on their slate.

At first, the politicians I talked to were not particularly interested in Kennedy or any other presidential contenders. Sheriffs and county clerks controlled patronage, but presidential candidates meant little or nothing to them. As Kennedy increasingly campaigned in the state and showed signs of growing popularity, however, the local leaders began to think he might add strength to their slates. Moreover, we were willing to pay our way, both in manpower from our volunteer organization and for legitmate Election Day expenses. At no time did I think we were being "taken" for our money. We paid our fair share, which was always less than that of candidates for sheriff and the other more "important" offices.

I negotiated our payments for campaign expenses. Neither Jack nor Bob Kennedy knew what agreements I made—that was my responsibility. I had to have cash at hand and I usually left it with my secretary, Phyllis Maddock, for safekeeping. On one occasion, in the lobby of Charleston's Kanawha Hotel, I completed agreements with the leaders of slates in two extremely important counties, representing the largest single expenditure of the campaign. I called Phyllis on the house phone and whispered, "Bring me five." Phyllis kept the money in her suitcase under her bed, and in a moment she appeared in the lobby and slipped me five hundred dollars, not the five thousand I'd agreed to.

"Not five *hundred*, Phyllis," I told her. "Five *thousand*." Phyllis was stunned, as this just about depleted our exchequer.

I have no apologies about the money we spent in West Virginia. Our total outlay state-wide was about $100,000 including radio and television, less than a candidate for Congress in any *one* congressional district would expect to spend. But there were charges that Kennedy bought the West Virginia primary. In one speech, Humphrey said, "I can't afford to run around this state with a little black bag and a checkbook . . . I can't buy an election."

After the primary, many of the nation's top investigative reporters spent weeks in West Virginia searching for evidence that we had bought votes or engaged in other financial improprieties. They found nothing, as we knew would be the case. Because of his family's wealth, accusations of vote-buying had haunted Kennedy's political career from the first and led him to be meticulous in his financing, for he realized that charge would always follow his political victories.

The irony of Humphrey's charge was that about a week before the election a nationally known politician, a man I assumed was working in Lyndon Johnson's behalf, appeared in Charleston carrying, literally, a black bag filled with money to invest in the Humphrey campaign. He approached a local political leader, a man who had pledged his support to Kennedy, and said he had $17,000 to spend on behalf of Humphrey.

The local man stalled the visitor and came immediately to report the matter to me.

"I appreciate this," I said. "But let me ask you something. Why are you telling me this?"

"We have an understanding," the local politician said. "Our organization is for Kennedy. I thought you'd want to know, because I suspect this fellow is going all over the state."

"How long do you think he'll wait for your answer?" I asked.

"Perhaps forty-eight hours."

"Then let him cool his heels," I suggested. "That'll give me time to alert our people around the state."

"Fine."

"My only other suggestion," I added, "would be that you take his money and donate it to your favorite charity."

He laughed and departed, and I never knew if he made a charitable donation or not.

There is a postscript to the story of the mysterious bagman. Some years later I told the story to one of Lyndon Johnson's closest associates.

"That son of a bitch," he exclaimed. "We gave him $20,000— he skimmed $3,000 off the top!"

The truth is that no one can buy an election in West Virginia. That was the first thing Bob McDonough told me when I arrived there. Perhaps I was cynical at first, but I found out he was right. The politicians there were proud men, men whose word was their bond, and the only way we Kennedy men, as outsiders, could win their support was to earn their personal regard, to win their respect as professionals. That was what we set out to do and it was not a quick or easy process.

I went one day to the rather dilapidated courthouse in Charleston to see the Kanawha county clerk, a very important man in local politics. I explained to his secretary that I was there on behalf of Senator Kennedy and she invited me to have a seat on a wooden bench. I sat and sat and sat, doing a slow burn, because I was convinced the clerk was in—other people were going in and out of his office. Finally the secretary said he was running behind schedule and couldn't see me that day— perhaps I'd come back another time.

I returned the next day with John Bailey, the Connecticut political leader who is known for his sagacity as well as his eyeglasses perched on his forehead and his cigars. John and I sat on the wooden bench for a while, then the county clerk finally called us into his office. He seemed to know who we were—I assumed he'd checked us out—and he was pleasant, but indifferent to our political needs. John and I left after a brief chat.

I went back a third time, however, and made my pitch.

"Senator Kennedy is going to be the next President," I told

him. "It's early in the game and the people who help us now will be remembered later." I paused and said dramatically: "I want you to know that if you help Jack Kennedy now the door of the White House will always be open to you!"

The county clerk chewed on his lip while he thought that one over. "Well, Mr. O'Brien, I'll tell you. I've never been to the White House, and I don't know anyone in Kanawha County who's ever been to the White House, and to tell you the truth I don't think many of us are real interested in going to the White House, but we have a great interest in this *courthouse.*"

I saw that I had blundered, and I withdrew as gracefully as possible, suggesting that we might chat again sometime. And, in fact, we did chat again, and as the weeks passed we became friends. After our third or fourth talk, he introduced me to some of his friends. And so, slowly, in county after county, we began to break through on the personal level that was the route to political success in West Virginia.

As I was carrying out my political negotiations, the candidate was carrying his case to the people of West Virginia. The agonizing problem was the religious issue. Kennedy's candidacy had given some of the state's Protestant clergymen a new cause in life—to save their flocks from this devil who was passing among them. It was a difficult issue to deal with, an underground issue, an emotional issue, and we felt the only answer was for Kennedy to get out and meet the people and win them on a personal basis. He undertook a tremendous schedule. Some days he would rise at 4 A.M. to be at the coal mines when they opened and wouldn't get to bed until one the next morning. We could see him gradually overcoming the resistance to him. One day I watched him walk up to a mine entrance where twenty miners were staring at him and spitting on the ground as he approached. He asked them to hear him out, and they talked for an hour and shook his hand when he left.

Another time, at an outdoor rally, a woman in the audience asked Kennedy: "How does your Catholicism square with your desire to be President? Isn't there a conflict?"

That was the issue in a nutshell, and Kennedy, speaking with a microphone in his hand to the three or four hundred people, said that of course he was Catholic, and proud of it, but he couldn't accept that his religion barred him from the presidency. He noted that he had served in Congress, served in the war, lost a brother in the war, and no one had questioned his religion or his patriotism. The people listened intently, and as I watched I had a feeling that Kennedy was getting to them, that a corner was being turned, that the fair-minded people of West Virginia were starting to reject the bigots. But my hunch was a long way from proven.

There was some ill feeling toward Humphrey in our camp, for it was felt that although he was not encouraging the anti-Catholic feeling, neither was he actively discouraging it. Also, we continued to see Humphrey as simply a spoiler. In turn the Humphrey camp became rightly infuriated with Kennedy as a result of an incident involving Franklin D. Roosevelt, Jr.

President Roosevelt was still regarded as a savior in West Virginia. I was in many homes where the only pictures on the walls were of FDR and John L. Lewis, the former leader of the mine workers. We therefore considered it a great breakthrough when Franklin D. Roosevelt, Jr., agreed to campaign for Kennedy in West Virginia. As it turned out, Frank Roosevelt caused the most controversial incident of the campaign when he criticized Humphrey for not serving in the military during the Second World War. We were stressing Kennedy's record as a war hero, of course, and we hoped the voters would contrast it with Humphrey's lack of a war record. But the Roosevelt incident went beyond that.

We had received, from an anonymous Minnesota source, supposed copies of correspondence between Humphrey and his draft board. We decided to do nothing with this for the time being, but we agreed that if Humphrey hit us with some extremely low blow, we might use the material to retaliate. We determined that if retaliation was decided upon, it would come from Frank Roosevelt, not directly from us, and we turned the material over to Frank.

We had assigned Frank an assistant, Fred Forbes, who had worked for us in New Hampshire. His job was to be with Roosevelt constantly to be sure his speaking schedule was met. One day Roosevelt and Forbes and a reporter were driving along and the reporter kept bringing up critical things Humphrey had been saying about Roosevelt. Finally, when Forbes left the car for a minute to make a phone call, Roosevelt angrily pulled the Humphrey material from his pocket and handed it to the reporter. "Here," he said. "If that's what Humphrey's saying about me, just look and see what kind of a fellow he is."

The story was promptly published and the Humphrey camp exploded. Retractions were demanded, and Roosevelt apologized and offered to leave the campaign immediately.

Kennedy was to introduce Roosevelt at a rally in Charleston that evening, and some liberal reporters warned me that if Kennedy didn't disown Roosevelt that night, they would "get" Kennedy. But Kennedy felt to disown Roosevelt would be a grandstand play and an injustice, since Roosevelt had publicly regretted and apologized for the incident. So Kennedy defied the critics and spoke warmly of Roosevelt, and Frank continued to be an effective campaigner. Looking back on it, the incident is one of my few regrets in campaigns. We should have destroyed that rubbish, not turned it over to Frank Roosevelt. We had to accept the responsibility for the incident, even though it happened inadvertently.

Another of our most active and effective campaigners was Ted Kennedy. He had visited West Virginia and he had crisscrossed the state for weeks speaking on his brother's behalf. Ted had served his political apprenticeship, and now he was demonstrating his considerable political skill. Later in the campaign, he would serve as our campaign chairman for the thirteen western states.

The West Virginia campaign was nothing if not hectic. Once Bob McDonough and I were flying high above the mountains in a single-engine plane when its engine conked out. We watched the stricken pilot wrestle with every button in reach as he veered for an emergency landing along a river bank. Suddenly the engine restarted, but the pilot continued to play with the controls. I'll never forget McDonough yelling to him, "God damn it! Will you stop trying to be a mechanic up here!" We returned safely to the airport, but that was the end of single-engine planes for me.

On the Sunday nine days before the election, McDonough, Phyllis Maddock, and I hedge-hopped across the state—in a twin-engine plane this time—making perhaps ten stops to meet directly with local political leaders. Once I confirmed that our slating arrangement was firm, I would hand over our agreed-upon share of the expenses and we would take off for the next stop. We shuttled from tiny airport to tiny airport, sometimes landing in open fields. Late that night we made a landing in a field with only the headlights of three automobiles to guide us —the end of a harrowing day, but a successful one.

Both Phyllis Maddock and Eddie King, my old friend from Springfield, played key roles in my work in West Virginia. Another invaluable campaign worker was Matt Reese, a gregarious West Virginian who weighed some three hundred pounds. Every morning Matt would arrive at our office in the Kanawha Hotel laden with cartons of Coca-Cola and huge bags of potato chips, which he would consume while spending hours on the telephone keeping order in our campaign.

One local volunteer was a young man who we later discovered had a history of mental illness. He took a dislike to some of the female members of our staff and entered their bedrooms while they were at work and ripped their clothing to shreds. In Phyllis' case he restricted himself to putting cracker crumbs in her bed. Phyllis wasn't too happy about that, but her real concern was whether he had discovered the suitcase *under* her bed, the one she kept the money in. Fortunately he had not.

The Sunday before the election was a rainy, dreary day. Kennedy, Dave Powers, and I went to Mass. The only Catholic church we could find was some distance outside Charleston and we drove over in the rain, a pretty sad group. Kennedy was losing his voice, we weren't sure if he could make his final campaign appearances because of flying conditions, and the latest polls showed him behind. We all prayed pretty hard that morning.

On the ride back to the hotel, I thought of a speech Abraham Ribicoff had made a few years before when he was running for governor of Connecticut. Abe had also faced religious prejudice, and he had made a very dramatic talk on television about his parents being immigrants and recalling how as a little Jewish boy selling newspapers in front of the State Capitol in Hartford he dreamed that some day he might become governor —the American Dream.

I recalled Ribicoff's performance to Kennedy and asked, "Well, are you ready to cry a little?"

"I'm desperate but not that desperate," he said grimly.

Back in the hotel room, we discussed how we would respond to a defeat. We agreed that if we lost by no more than 53–47 we would try to claim a moral victory, as Humphrey had done in Wisconsin. There was no suggestion that Kennedy would quit if he lost in West Virginia.

That afternoon we drove to a television studio where Kennedy was to make his last major campaign appearance. I, and others from the staff, sat on a wooden bench to watch. We were a gloomy bunch. Originally, Kennedy was to have had a question-and-answer session with Franklin D. Roosevelt, Jr., as moderator, but toward the close of the program, he changed the format. He spoke to the people of West Virginia in a direct, low-key, conversational manner, particularly about his religion. There was nothing emotional or tear-jerking or apologetic in what he said. As in an earlier rally in the campaign, he noted that his religion had not kept him from serving in the war or his brother from dying in the war. No one can say what affect his talk had on the viewers, but our gloom disappeared and all of us in our group felt a great surge of pride as he finished. It was one of the great moments I've had in politics. And that pretty well wrapped up the campaign for us. Our candidate had acquitted himself with honor and courage.

The first returns to come in that night were from strong Humphrey precincts—the kind that broke 104–12—for Humphrey had done some slating too. Bob Kennedy turned to me and exclaimed, "What's happening? You told me that everything possible had been done."

I shared Bob's concern but told him not to worry and soon the Kennedy trend began. It became one of the easiest election nights I'd ever spent. Kennedy won by a 61–39 margin and carried forty-eight of the state's fifty-five counties.

When Humphrey conceded, Bob Kennedy went to his headquarters and escorted him back to ours. Humphrey was gallant and gracious. Jack Kennedy, who was in Washington, flew down on the *Caroline* to thank our workers and, upon his arrival, we were able to give him additional good news. Nebraska's primary had also been held that day and Kennedy had received the largest Democratic vote since Roosevelt in 1940—89.1 per cent. I stayed overnight to wind up some affairs, then Phyllis and Eddie King and I caught a commerical flight back to Washington on Wednesday morning.

My thoughts should have been on the primaries ahead, but they were still very much on West Virginia. I thought how gloomy things had looked a month before. I thought of the fantastic job done by Bob McDonough and more than nine thousand volunteers. I thought most of all of Jack Kennedy and how he had come to know and love the people of West Virginia. He had been to schools where the children took their free lunch home to share with their parents. He had met the miners with ravaged lungs and proud hearts. He had gone to these people and they had accepted him and turned their backs on the bigots. He would never forget them and they would never forget him.

I sank in my seat, completely exhausted, then noticed Hubert and Muriel Humphrey sitting nearby. I had not known Humphrey before this primary, but one evening at the Charleston Press Club he had come to my table and kiddingly said, "O'Brien, I'm hearing a lot about you. You're causing me problems." And we went on to have a pleasant talk. I had liked him immediately—he was a warm and sensitive man.

When the plane was aloft, I went over to speak to the Humphreys. Hubert and I agreed that it had been a hard fight, but fairly fought. As we talked, some Kennedy workers sitting in the back of the plane, perhaps unaware that Humphrey was aboard, began singing a parody of the "Hubert, Hubert Humphrey" song that had been set to the tune of "Davey, Davey Crocket." I sent Phyllis back to tell them to stop. I felt nothing but respect for Hubert Humphrey at that point. We were professionals and he had engaged in one of the great encounters of his career. There were no hard feelings, and it would not be long until Humphrey and I became close friends.

I have detailed the West Virginia primary because I think it tells something about American politics, something that isn't found in the civics books. Making slates, sitting on wooden benches in county courthouses, seeking the votes of hard-bitten miners at a slag mine—that is the stuff of politics. Kennedy became a statesman, but he was a politician first, a tough and resourceful one, the best of his time.

After West Virginia, and before flying out to Oregon, Kennedy spent a day of intensive campaigning in Maryland. I had spent time in Maryland previously and we had put together a first-rate Kennedy organization there. We had an opponent in Maryland, Senator Wayne Morse, who we believed was getting substantial financial support from the Teamsters union as a result of Jimmy Hoffa's feud with Bob Kennedy. Morse campaigned in Maryland far more extensively than Kennedy, but Kennedy won the May 17 primary by 70.3 per cent to 17.2 per cent.

Indiana's primary election was held on May 3, a week before West Virginia's. We had only two minor opponents there—Lar Daly, the perennial candidate in an Uncle Sam suit, and another man of no political significance. Yet on Election Night as our co-ordinator, Eddie King, called the result to me, I began to feel concern. Kennedy was taking about *eighty* per cent of the vote, which is certainly a landslide, but the fact that two nonentities were getting *twenty* per cent of the vote was a danger signal. In effect, one voter in five had cast a protest vote against Kennedy, and we had to assume this was mainly be-

cause of the religious issue. I couldn't help wondering what
kind of vote Stu Symington might have gotten in the Indiana
primary if two fringe candidates had received twenty per cent.

The Pennsylvania primary on April 26 was a unique situation.
We did everything we could *not* to get votes there. Governor
David Lawrence was running as a favorite son, and he was
sensitive about his prerogatives. In California, we had pushed
Pat Brown, warning him that if he ran in his state's primary as
a favorite son and didn't support Kennedy, Kennedy would
run against him in that primary. You didn't treat Dave Lawrence that way. The difference was that Brown, although the
governor, had no real organizational base and thus had little
control. Lawrence, along with Congressman Bill Green, the
Democratic leader in Philadelphia, did have a political organization, one that exercised considerable control. We had to
respect their power, just as we respected Mayor Daley's in
Chicago. If Lawrence wished to run in his state's primary, we
accepted that; and we would negotiate with him later for his
support at the Convention. We wanted to do nothing to offend
Lawrence or Green and, in particular, we wanted no pro-Kennedy write-in movement that could be interpreted as an effort
by us to put pressure on Lawrence and Green. All of Kennedy's
political operatives were given strict orders not to set foot in
Pennsylvania.

Nevertheless, a write-in movement for Kennedy developed,
and on Election Night he received an amazing 183,073 votes
or 71.3 per cent of the total vote. I called and woke him up to
give him the first returns and we were both surprised and
thrilled. Some skeptics persisted in thinking we had helped
organize the write-in vote, but that wasn't the case. The risk of
offending Dave Lawrence and Bill Green was too high. When
Green later learned that one of his Philadelphia precinct cap-
tains had supported the write-in effort, he immediately had the
man fired from his city job. Later, during the campaign, Ken
O'Donnell and I persuaded Green to reinstate him.

The write-in vote in Pennsylvania was ideal so far as Kennedy and I were concerned. The record was clear that we had
not sought it, yet Lawrence and Green had to be impressed

by the pro-Kennedy groundswell. Eventually, they would produce 64 of Pennsylvania's 81 delegate votes for Kennedy at
the Convention.

Oregon was the final contested primary—May 20—and two
days after his West Virginia victory, Kennedy flew out on the
Caroline for a week of campaigning. He had lost his voice and
he communicated with us, on the long and bumpy flight, via
notes and sign language. One additional problem arose when
he remembered there were only two bunks on the plane and he
indicated, again by sign language, that the two women aboard
—Congresswoman Edith Green, his Oregon campaign chairman, and Phyllis Maddock—should have them. But Phyllis persuaded him that he and Mrs. Green should have the bunks and
she could manage in her seat.

Upon our arrival in Oregon, we discovered that our Oregon
people had been using the traditional Kennedy campaign
techniques far less than we had expected. Someone explained
to me that our methods were just too "high-pressure" for Oregon's low-key brand of politics.

"Too high-pressure?" I said. "If I had enough time, I could
elect a Chinaman as governor of this state."

My quip found its way into a newsmagazine, and I had the
problem of explaining to Congresswoman Edith Green that
no criticism of her leadership, or indeed of the Chinese, was
intended.

Kennedy swept Oregon with 51 per cent of the vote. The
state's own Senator Wayne Morse, was second with 32 per cent.
Farther back, Humphrey received 5.7 per cent, Symington 4.4
per cent, and Johnson just under 4 per cent.

After the Oregon primary, I came up with what I thought
was a brilliant idea. Why didn't Kennedy, on his way back
east, stop off in Illinois and pay a courtesy call on Adlai Stevenson? Surely Stevenson, impressed by Kennedy's string of primary victories, would take the occasion to advise him that he
would not contest Kennedy for the nomination. Ken O'Donnell
and I sold Kennedy on this plan, although against his better
judgment. He went to see Stevenson, who was cool and aloof,
seemed confused by the visit, and gave no indication he was

prepared to announce his retirement from politics. Kennedy was furious that he'd put himself in such an awkward position, and I'm sure it took a while for him to regain confidence in our political judgment.

We went to the Democratic Convention in Los Angeles confident we had the delegates for a first-ballot nomination. Our basic strategy, determined some eighteen months before, had succeeded: Kennedy entered and won the primaries and thereby convinced party leaders like Dick Daley and Dave Lawrence that he was a viable candidate, a winner. Yet caucuses were still to be held and we could take no risk of slippage amid the confusion and pressure of the National Convention. We therefore set up an elaborate intelligence system so that we would know what was happening in each state delegation at all times. One of our trusted people was assigned to each delegation as a permanent liaison. He was to eat with the delegates, live with them, and know exactly where each delegate stood at all times.

This was a delicate assignment. Our people were sure to be regarded by some delegates as spies, but we were willing to run that risk in order to have up-to-the-minute intelligence. For the assignment we called on people who had proven themselves during the primaries, including Byron R. (Whizzer) White, who worked with the Colorado delegation; John Bailey with Connecticut; Joe Tydings, Delaware and Florida; Ted Kennedy, Hawaii, New Mexico, and Wyoming; Edith Green, Oregon; and Eddie Boland, Ohio.

In the weeks prior to the Convention, we compiled a file card on each of the 4,509 delegates and alternates, giving each one's occupation, special interests, political background, and so on. Throughout the Convention, our liaison people submitted daily written reports to me on developments in their delegations. Beyond that, we had a twenty-four-hour telephone operation headed by Dave Hackett, Bob Kennedy's old friend from Milton Academy days, so our liaison men could call any time one of our delegates appeared to be wavering. Bob Kennedy or I could then be summoned to talk to the uncertain delegate. It was a massive operation. No doubt there was a degree of overkill in it, but it achieved its purpose, and no matter what the newspapers said, no matter what rumors swept the Convention, we *knew* at all times just how many delegates we had. Our communications system in Los Angeles in 1960 was to be the forerunner of the increasingly complex systems, involving telephones and walkie-talkies and other devices, that candidates in both parties would use at future National Conventions.

We were thankful for our intelligence-gathering system when waves of pro-Stevenson enthusiasm swept the convention hall and, seemingly, all of Los Angeles. There was no denying Stevenson's popularity in Los Angeles. We found that we had no such support there. One day Phyllis Maddock managed to obtain several hundred extra tickets to the convention hall's galleries, but we simply didn't have the people to fill the seats. When Stevenson made his first appearance in the hall, his followers set off a wild demonstration, a truly heartfelt show of their affection for one of our party's leaders.

As the pro-Stevenson cheers filled the hall, I was being interviewed by Mike Wallace of CBS in a television booth high above the convention floor. Mike began by saying something like, "Isn't this exciting? Isn't this remarkable? It's the first real excitement in this Convention. How do you feel, Larry, as a Kennedy man, about this great outpouring of support for Stevenson?"

I replied rather heatedly, "It's a fine demonstration but I don't think it's changing any delegate votes. It only shows Stevenson might be elected mayor of Los Angeles."

The fact was that any chance of Stevenson's being nominated had evaporated the previous Sunday when Illinois, his home state, gave 59½ of its 69 delegate votes to Kennedy. That action reflected Mayor Daley's dispassionate judgment that Kennedy, not Stevenson, was the party's best candidate in 1960.

Early in the convention week, Kennedy and I were driving across Los Angeles from a meeting with one state delegation in one hotel to a meeting with another delegation in another hotel. It gave us a little time to talk and his thoughts returned to a challenge that Lyndon Johnson had issued to him the pre-

vious day. Johnson, still seeking to contrast "young Jack's" supposed immaturity with his own presumed wisdom, had urged
Kennedy to debate him in a joint appearance before the Texas
delegation. We had at first regarded the invitation as a Johnson
ploy that we had best ignore. We were ahead, so why take any
chances? But as we drove through the seemingly endless gilt
and glitter of Los Angeles, Kennedy reconsidered.

"I'm going to do it, Larry," he told me. "I'm sure as hell not
afraid of Lyndon. It could be fun."

I wasn't enthusiastic, but I accepted his decision without
further comment. He accepted the challenge and in the ensuing "debate" he deftly and humorously turned aside all of
Johnson's heavy-handed criticisms. He set the tone when he
told the delegates and the audience on television,

"I come here today full of admiration for Senator Johnson,
full of affection for him, strongly in support of him—for majority
leader of the United States Senate."

It was, to my mind, a classic instance of Kennedy's natural
political style. Most politicians would have played it safe,
would have avoided a confrontation where they had far more
to lose than to gain. But Kennedy relished the challenge, the
sheer joy of political combat, and once again his instincts had
been good, for when he finished his remarks Johnson was de-
flated and even the Texas delegates were cheering Kennedy's
performance.

When the roll call finally began on Wednesday night, Kennedy was watching from the privacy of his hideaway, but I
was standing in an aisle on the convention floor, waiting
tensely for the final tally. There was nothing left for me to do
except to compare the actual count with our projections and to
be available in case any crisis erupted. I stood near the California delegation, which was in disarray, as it had been for
weeks because of Governor Brown's inability to make up his
mind between Kennedy and Stevenson. He eventually lost control of his delegation, and California cast 33½ of its 81 votes
for Kennedy, probably all we deserved because of Stevenson's
genuine strength in the state. As the roll call proceeded, I
found that our estimates were on target. We had projected that

Wyoming would cast the final votes to give us the nomination. Ted Kennedy, who had been working with Wyoming and the other western states, had posted himself in the midst of the Wyoming delegation. When they did in fact put us over the top, he grabbed the Wyoming standard and waved it wildly.

Chaos erupted. We had seen the nomination coming, but there was no way to prepare for it emotionally. Somehow, Ted Kennedy and I fought our way through the crowd and threw our arms around each other. We both had tears in our eyes, and when we tried to shout congratulations to each other, we couldn't make ourselves heard above the din. It didn't matter. We both knew what we were trying to say. The great political victory that the experts said was impossible had happened. A journalist called it "the changing of the guard" and the expression was apt. This was a "new generation" victory, a victory for the men who had fought in World War II and returned home determined to have a voice in their nation's future. Our candidate, at forty-three, could be the youngest man ever elected President. I was the same age, Bob Kennedy and Ken O'Donnell were in their mid-thirties, and Ted Kennedy was still in his twenties. No matter. We had learned the political game and we had played it well. Our leader was now the Democratic nominee for President of the United States and we had little doubt of victory in November.

The tears and the cheers and the congratulations went on in the hall until, finally, Kennedy left his hideout and made a brief appearance before the Convention. I think I cheered louder than anyone when he entered the hall. I had been in politics a long time and I had never been so moved than at that moment.

V

KENNEDY VERSUS NIXON

THE CELEBRATING WAS SOON over. Early the next morning I was called to Kennedy's suite, where already a heated discussion was taking place about his decision to offer the vice-presidential nomination to Lyndon Johnson. Bob Kennedy led the opposition to Johnson. He reflected the bitterness that we all had felt at the allegations about Kennedy's health that the Johnson people had made during the Convention, particularly John Connally of Texas. But it was apparent we had to put that behind us. Our major problem was obviously going to be the South, and Johnson might be the running mate who could do us the most good there.

Throughout the morning, Kennedy's suite and the hallway outside were jammed with political leaders hoping to get a word with Kennedy about the vice presidency or some other matter. I recall Kennedy once going off by himself, standing at his bedroom window looking out at the city, saying to no one in particular, "You'd think you'd have a little time to enjoy your nomination. Our problems are just beginning."

Among those who were ushered in that morning were Senators Jackson and Symington, both of whom had been under consideration for the vice presidency. Once the Johnson decision was made, they had to be informed. In Jackson's case, Kennedy arranged a consolation prize—Jackson would be chairman of the Democratic National Committee for the campaign period. The only complication was that Kennedy had promised the chairmanship to John Bailey, the Connecticut leader, in exchange for his early and active support. It was, to my knowledge, the only commitment for a specific job that Kennedy made to anyone. Bailey graciously agreed to postpone his appointment until January, so Jackson could have the position throughout the fall.

Lyndon Johnson and I met for the first time that day. When he entered Kennedy's suite, he was a symphony in brown— brown suit, brown shirt, brown tie, brown shoes. He and I were introduced and he took my hand and pulled me close, until we were standing nose-to-nose, and that, in terms of noses, was a summit conference.

"Larry," he began, "you don't know me, so let me tell you a little about myself."

That set him off on a five-minute monologue, which I punctuated with an occasional nod or grunt. The thrust of what he said was that he wanted to be part of our team, that he would work tirelessly for the ticket, that he had nothing but admiration for the job we had done—that he was a pro and respected us as fellow pros. It was my first exposure to the famous Johnson "treatment"—I would see more of it in years to come—and I found it intriguing. You had to be impressed with his energy and the sheer impact of his personality.

Even as Johnson and I spoke, however, opposition to his nomination was spreading, particularly among some elements of organized labor. Walter Reuther, the United Auto Workers president, had deep doubts about Johnson's commitment to both civil rights and to the labor movement. Our trouble spot, as we looked ahead to a roll call vote on Johnson's nomination, was Michigan, where both Reuther and Governor G. Mennen Williams were in opposition. We devised a plan to avoid a roll call after Johnson's name was placed in nomination. Congressman John McCormack, the leader of the Massachusetts delegation, would ask Governor LeRoy Collins of Florida, the convention chairman, for recognition to suspend the rules and take the nomination by voice vote. In case there was any foulup, Governor Abe Ribicoff, the leader of the Connecticut delegation, would be prepared to seek recognition for the same purpose. I stationed myself next to Ribicoff just in case. But the plan went off perfectly—Collins recognized McCormack who made the motion, Collins then informed the Convention that a two-thirds vote was required to suspend the rules and he put the motion to a vote. To a chorus of ayes and a scattering of no's, Collins declared Lyndon B. Johnson nominated by acclamation.

On the next evening, Kennedy in his acceptance speech called for a "New Frontier" in America. From all reports it was an inspiring moment, but I was not present to savor it. I was to be director of organization for the campaign and that night I was busy preparing for the Democratic National Committee meeting the next morning, where Kennedy would make this announcement.

At the DNC meeting and in informal meetings after it, Bob Kennedy and I introduced party leaders to the basics of a Kennedy campaign. Once again we passed out the O'Brien Manual and explained our registration drives, telephone campaigns, and tabloid distribution system. Throughout the rest of the day, Bob and I met with party leaders who deserved our special attention. These sessions became rather chaotic, for it was well past the hotel's checkout time and, as we talked, we found ourselves being moved from room to room so cleaning women could change the beds and telephone workers could dismantle our communications network. The hotel officials made it clear that we had overstayed our welcome and as we shuttled about amid the debris of our hectic and victorious week, I was suddenly reminded of the inescapable fact that life does go on, that these rooms would soon be occupied by salesmen and tourists and honeymooners, that politics is not all of life.

The *Victory Special,* a chartered plane, carried us from Los Angeles back to Boston on Sunday afternoon. It was a joyous occasion. Kennedy wandered up and down the aisles chatting with us, and the champagne flowed freely. After a few hours, however, exhaustion caught up with us, and one by one people began dropping off to sleep. From Boston, Ken O'Donnell and I and our wives flew to Hyannis Port, where we had cottages at the Poponesset Inn. The idea was that we would spend a few days combining campaign planning and relaxation. The days ahead turned out to be more work than play, however, for the immensity of the job we faced immediately began to sink in. For more than a year our thoughts and energies had been focused on the nomination; now we had to organize a *national* campaign.

My instinct told me that we must apply on a national scale the same techniques that we had used successfully in Massachusetts and the primary states. First, I wanted to hold a series of meetings, just as in 1951–52 we had held regional meetings with our Kennedy secretaries. We began, on Tuesday, August 2, a cross-country tour. Our traveling party included Campaign Manager Bob Kennedy, Byron (Whizzer) White, head of the Citizens for Kennedy, Margaret Price of Michigan, who had become vice chairman of the DNC, several of our campaign specialists, and myself.

Our first regional meeting was at two that afternoon in the ballroom of the Sheraton Hotel in Philadelphia. I outlined our basic campaign activity and stressed that we wanted every state to carry out this traditional program. I then introduced Bob Kennedy who spoke and took questions from the floor and was followed by other members of our traveling team. We then called upon Bill Green, the Philadelphia Democratic chairman and congressman, who gave a fascinating talk on how *his* organization carried out voter registration.

"Bill, I want you to go with us," Bob Kennedy told Green at the end of the meeting.

"You mean to the airport?" Green asked.

"No, to Boston. I want the people up there to hear what you say about registering voters."

"I can't just up and go to Boston," Green protested. "I haven't even got a clean shirt."

"We'll buy you a shirt, Bill," Bob told him, and the next thing Green knew he was on a plane headed for Boston.

We met that night at Boston's Parker House with party leaders from the New England states. The next morning we flew to Chicago for a meeting with Democrats from Illinois, Wisconsin, Indiana, Michigan, Ohio, and Minnesota.

Upon our arrival in Chicago, where we were to have a luncheon meeting, Bob Kennedy and I discovered we had a problem. In our haste to set up the meetings, someone on our staff had simply called Mayor Daley's office to notify him of the Chicago session and our hope that he would be its host. That was a mistake. You don't notify Mayor Daley about political meetings in Chicago. You seek his approval of political meetings. We got the word, loud and clear, that Mayor Daley was likely to have other business to attend to that noontime. Bob and I hurried to see him at his office in the Morrison Hotel—his Democratic Party office—and found Daley rather aloof and obviously indignant. We hastened to apologize for our failure of communication. We also understood that Daley was dubious about his hosting a regional political meeting, which had never been done before in Chicago, and we explained why we felt the meeting was of extreme importance to us. The mayor listened intently to our apologies and explanations, was satisfied by them, and a few hours later graciously hosted our regional meeting.

We raced on across the country—Denver on Thursday, San Francisco on Friday morning and Los Angeles on Friday evening, Kansas City and St. Louis on Saturday, and finally back to New York for a meeting with a thousand Empire State politicians in the ballroom of the Biltmore Hotel on Sunday night. The New Yorkers were not as impressed by our traveling show as some of the regional groups had been and a number of the local pols had more than a few words to say. The whole thing turned into something of a pep rally, rather than a business session, a typical New York political meeting, I thought. But that didn't disturb us. The speechmaking, the show of unity, the getting acquainted was as important as our lectures on campaign techniques. We finished that hectic week with the knowledge that we had touched base with thousands of state and local Democratic leaders and labor leaders, we had demonstrated that we planned an aggressive campaign, we had listened to their thoughts and problems, and we had exposed them to the mechanics of a Kennedy campaign. It was a week well spent.

The South remained a problem. Our meeting in St. Louis with border-state Democrats had not been successful. Liberal leaders had attended but very few leaders from the state party organizations. We therefore decided against having a meeting with Deep South Democrats until we had given more thought to the matter. Outside the South, we could assume that Democratic leaders wanted to work for the ticket. We couldn't make that assumption in the South, because of the problems created by Kennedy's religion and his position on civil rights.

We asked Senator George Smathers of Florida, an old friend of Jack Kennedy's, to be our co-ordinator for the southern states. George agreed and set up several meetings with southern leaders. The first was in Tennessee and its highlight was an impassioned speech by Senator Albert Gore on the religious issue.

"This is the greatest challenge the South has faced in a hundred years," Gore declared. "The Kennedy candidacy is putting our people to a truly historic test to show the nation we are not people with religious prejudice. I intend to spend every waking moment working for the Kennedy-Johnson ticket, not simply because it is a great Democratic ticket, but because I love the South and I want to help our people meet this great challenge."

Gore finished to a standing ovation and we immediately asked him to join our tour and repeat his remarks at other meetings of Southerners, which he did.

Our next stop was Atlanta, where Smathers had arranged a luncheon for Deep South party leaders. The night before the luncheon I met in a hotel room with five southern governors, several senators and other party leaders. All of them told me that the key figure in Georgia, perhaps in the entire South, was Senator Herman Talmadge. Nothing, they said, could have a more favorable impact than for Talmadge to endorse the Kennedy-Johnson ticket.

At that time we did not even know if Talmadge was going
to attend our luncheon. He had been invited, of course, but
he had been noncommittal. The next morning, Smathers rushed
up to me with the news that Talmadge had called and he was
coming to the luncheon. We were both overjoyed—this might
be our big breakthrough in the South. At the luncheon, we
watched intently when Talmadge was introduced and stood
up to say a few words.

Talmadge said he was glad to be present with all these fine
Democrats. He said it was certainly an outstanding group.
However, he never quite got around to mentioning the Kennedy-Johnson ticket. When he sat down, amid great applause,
George Smathers looked stricken, and probably I did too. But
we had to settle for just having Talmadge present, even if
he wasn't ready to publicly support the ticket yet.

When I got to know Talmadge in Washington, I reminded
him of this episode. He, in turn, reminded me that he had
indeed worked for the ticket. He added, "Don't forget, Larry,
that my state gave Jack Kennedy a better vote than yours did."

That was true. Kennedy received 62.6 per cent of the vote in
Georgia and only 60.2 per cent in Massachusetts.

The last stop in our southern swing was a luncheon in
Shreveport, Louisiana. The discussions did not go well. The
low point of the visit came when a party leader from Mississippi delivered an anti-black tirade while black waiters were
serving our food. I departed from the meeting and from
Shreveport as quickly as I could.

It became apparent in terms of the South that we were most
fortunate to have Lyndon Johnson on the ticket. He campaigned intensively throughout the South and the border states
and aroused increasing support for the ticket. Johnson deserved great credit for his campaign effort and Kennedy's decision at Los Angeles to select him as his running mate proved
to be an excellent one.

Nevertheless, we were pleased to do as well as we did in
the South, winning Arkansas, Georgia, Louisiana, the Caro-
linas, and Texas. Few southern leaders would work openly for
us and clergymen continued to attack Kennedy from pulpits

every Sunday. We owed much to men like Governor Terry Sanford of North Carolina, Carl Sanders of Georgia (who later
became governor), and Louisiana AFL-CIO President Victor
Bussie, who challenged the prevailing prejudices of their re-
gion under the most difficult circumstances.

Back in Washington, our group took over the offices of the
National Committee and we began to consider the basic problem of co-ordinating a campaign in the fifty states. We couldn't
control what the state organizations did, but we wanted to
know what was going on and we wanted some influence over
local decisions. Obtaining accurate political intelligence was a
major task—who were the state political powers, what were the
local issues, who were the strong candidates, what were our
prospects? We might talk to four or five people and get four or
five answers. We tried to deal with the state party chairman
whenever possible, but often we found that he had priorities
and problems different from our own.

I kept returning to the idea of assigning our own representative to each state, much as we'd assigned our liaison men to
each delegation at the Convention in Los Angeles. To do so
would be a gamble, for if our man, an outsider, offended the
locals, we would have to remove him fast. Moreover, as some
of my colleagues protested, our man might not have detailed
knowledge of the state's politics. But my experience in my
travels in 1959 and 1960 proved to me that if one knew politics
one could go into any state and size up the situation pretty fast.
The scenery and the accents differ, but politics is about the
same everywhere. I thought this new approach—and it was,
to my knowledge, unprecedented—was our best bet and Bob
Kennedy agreed with me.

We assigned our Kennedy co-ordinators, as we called them,
to forty-two states, excluding only those southern states where
they would probably have been resented as outsiders. Some
of our co-ordinators were the same men and women who had
been our liaison people at the Convention. We found the co-
ordinators were well received. The local people knew they had
no vested interests, that on the day after the election they
would pack their bags and leave. For our part, we backed our

co-ordinators. They had a direct line to the national campaign, they made on-the-spot decisions, they had a say on where the candidate appeared and whom he met when he campaigned in their state. As a result they had clout with the state political leaders.

The experiment with the state co-ordinators was, in my view, a success. Our political intelligence was good and many potential problems were spotted early and resolved. My belief in this system was reinforced four years later when President Johnson rejected this approach in favor of co-ordinators from within each state. We then spent long hours searching for someone who was acceptable to all factions in his state, and often he proved to be acceptable only because he was innocuous and wasn't a threat to anyone. In the 1964 landslide it didn't matter if we had this kind of state co-ordinator, but it might have been fatal in 1960.

I was with Kennedy during his four televised debates with Richard Nixon. When the networks proposed the debates, Kennedy accepted without hesitation. He had no doubt that he could hold his own against Nixon. The first debate, in Chicago on September 26, proved to be the crucial one. I thought the drama before the two men went on the air almost equaled that of the debates themselves. Each candidate visited the studio about an hour before air time to check the cameras, the lighting and so on. We could see that Nixon was nervous. He tried to be hearty, but it didn't come off. Kennedy for his part was cool and businesslike. Both candidates were assigned holding rooms. Mr. Kennedy, Bob, Ken, Ted Sorensen, and I joined our candidate, who was easily the calmest man in the room. He drank some tea, but a plate of sandwiches went untouched. There was a little small talk, but mostly we watched the clock. The network official had said they would notify us when it was time to return to the studio.

I became nervous. Finally ten minutes or so before the debate was to begin, I left the room and went back to the studio. To my surprise, Nixon was already there pacing up and down along the far wall. He was alone, except for some technicians who were too busy to pay any attention to him. I stayed out of sight and watched him. He went onto the platform a time or two. He mopped his brow with his handkerchief. Even from across the studio I could see how awful his make-up was—he was in unbelievable shape.

The countdown commenced over the loudspeaker: "Five minutes to air time." Nixon began watching the studio door. "Four minutes," the loudspeaker said, "Three." Nixon was still watching the door, as tense a man as I had ever seen. By then, I was sure that no one had summoned Kennedy, and I was about to dash after him, when the door swung open. Kennedy walked in and took his place, barely glancing at Nixon. Moments later, they were on the air.

Kennedy had played the clock perfectly. He had thrown his opponent off stride. Nixon was ill at ease throughout and it was widely believed that he had "lost" the debate. It was a turning point—perhaps *the* turning point in the campaign. I should not have been surprised. Kennedy took Nixon the way he had taken Lodge in 1952, Humphrey in the West Virginia primary, and Johnson in their "debate" at the Convention two months earlier. Again, his opponent had underestimated him.

There was rising optimism in our camp during the final weeks of the campaign. Ken O'Donnell and others who were traveling with Kennedy would call me in Washington with excited reports of the huge crowds that greeted Kennedy in city after city. Some of our people said it was all over—the only question was the size of the victory. I never shared this optimism, partly because of my pessimistic nature, partly because I wasn't there to see the cheering crowds, and partly because of an incident I remembered as a youngster in my home town during the 1928 presidential campaign. Al Smith, the Democratic candidate that year, was greeted in Springfield by a wildly cheering crowd of 50,000, the largest crowd in the city's history. A little later his opponent, Herbert Hoover, came to town and was met by perhaps half that number. But on Election Day, Hoover easily carried the city.

Kennedy was glamorous and controversial and people wanted to see him. He had the "jumpers and screamers," as the press called the young girls who greeted Kennedy with an excitement usually reserved for movie stars. But, once again, the actual voting proved that cheering crowds are not an accurate gauge of the votes to be cast.

I was also skeptical about the effect of Kennedy's comments on his religion before a group of Protestant ministers—the Greater Houston Ministerial Association—on September 12. He made an excellent presentation, one that would have impressed any fair-minded person, but I suspected the majority of the people who were upset about the religious issue were not fair-minded and were not going to be swayed by even the most rational statement by the candidate. No doubt Kennedy's remarks, and our use of films of the remarks, had some impact, but I never thought, as some did, that it would turn the issue around, and I think the election returns supported my view.

I resisted optimism, but it became difficult in the final days of the campaign, particularly when I joined Kennedy's final swing through the East. There was the fantastic ticker-tape parade in New York City. There was the 30,000 people in Waterbury, Connecticut, who greeted him at three in the morning when he was running way behind schedule. There was the pandemonium in Boston the night before the election. It took hours for Kennedy to be driven from the airport to his hotel to the Boston Garden, for his car had to inch through a sea of humanity—the car was so scratched and dented that it was scrapped the next day. Finally, when Kennedy reached the Garden, there was an explosion of total, deafening shouting, stomping, unrestrained enthusiasm—I've never experienced anything like it, before or since.

The next morning, Election Day, we flew up to Hyannis Port to await the returns. At the Logan Airport in Boston, for some reason, we had to get our chartered plane off the ground in a hurry, but once we were aloft we had a pleasant and leisurely flight. Campaign staffer Chuck Roche was singing over the intercom, the stewardesses were serving champagne and chicken Kiev, and the pilot took us on an aerial tour of the Cape. The flight lasted less than an hour, and it was only when we landed that we learned that, during our hasty departure from Boston, one of the baggage handlers had accidentally been locked in the baggage compartment and had enjoyed our flight far less than the rest of us.

We had set up, at Bob Kennedy's house at Hyannis Port, a nationwide telephone system that was intended to give us the earliest possible election returns, earlier than those the news media would have. We had selected a number of "weathervane" precincts across the country and arranged for our local people to call us directly with the results. Dick Donahue, Ralph Dungan, and Joe Napolitan, three of our most effective political operatives, directed the ten volunteers who were manning the telephones. I was told our phone bill for that one day and night was about $10,000.

Election days are maddening. There is nothing left to do. The tension builds, the minutes pass slowly, and all you can do is wait and sweat. The Kennedys tossed a football around and walked on the beach, and I busied myself with long-distance calls here and there, but we were all just killing time, waiting to see if we were heroes or bums.

Kennedy came over to inspect our telephone setup during the afternoon. He was wearing khakis and a tan sweater, and his voice was hoarse.

"Let's see how well that works," he told Dick Donahue. "Get me John Bailey."

Donahue quickly had Bailey on the line. "John," he said, "somebody here wants to speak to you." He then handed the phone to Kennedy.

"John, how's it going?" Kennedy asked.

Bailey, confused by all this, asked who it was.

"Jack," Kennedy said.

"Jack who?" Bailey asked.

"Your candidate," Kennedy replied, and I thought I heard the distinct sound of John Bailey swallowing his cigar.

The group of us spent most of Election Night watching the returns together—Jack and Jackie, Bob and Ethel, Ted and Joan, Steve Smith and Jean, Sarge Shriver and Eunice, Peter Lawford and Pat, Sorensen, O'Donnell, Salinger, Lou Harris, and others. There was tension, but we felt reasonably confident. Drinks and a buffet supper were served. Jackie, who was pregnant at the time, spent part of the evening studying a stack of pictures taken of her and Jack during the campaign. Caroline was there for a while, wearing overalls and with a scratch on her face, chasing her Scottie, Charlie, all over the house.

It turned out, of course, to be a long night. Kennedy sipped a beer and watched calmly as the returns see-sawed back and forth. Lyndon Johnson called and Kennedy broke the tension momentarily by quipping: "Well, I see you lost Ohio and I won Texas."

Nixon appeared on television around 3 A.M. but refused to concede.

"Why don't you give up?" someone said angrily to the image on the TV screen.

"Why should he?" Kennedy remarked. "I wouldn't, in his place."

There was also an interview with Nixon's running mate, Henry Cabot Lodge, who was known as a man who liked to get a good night's sleep—it was said he even took daily naps while out campaigning.

"Cabot looks like he's having a hard time staying awake," Kennedy said of his 1952 opponent.

Kennedy left us around four, saying he was going to bed. I always wondered if he really did, and whether he slept if he did. I couldn't. I went back to my hotel and watched the returns on television while the sun came up. By then we were sure we had won. I was sure after I had called an election official in Illinois who told me that the Democratic margin in Chicago was big enough to offset any possible late returns from the downstate Republican strongholds.

There were later charges, which Richard Nixon encouraged, that Mayor Daley had "stolen" the election for Kennedy in the Democratic precincts of Chicago. Here again, as in the vote-buying charges in West Virginia, the best reporters in America searched for hard evidence for weeks and found none. The fact was that Republican poll-watchers had the Chicago polling places covered like a blanket. Our fear was that Republicans would do some vote-stealing of their own in their strong-holds in downstate Illinois, where we lacked the manpower for extensive poll-watching. I don't know whether they did or not, but I certainly wouldn't make the charge without evidence. As for Nixon's complaint that the election was stolen from him in Chicago but that he was too good a fellow to complain, that's perfectly absurd. If he had evidence of vote fraud, he had a duty to come forth with it, and I have no doubt that he would have. The 1960 election is history now, but those people who encourage the myth of its being stolen should either put up or shut up.

In late morning, with victory assured, I showered and shaved and joined the others at the National Guard Armory in Hyannis where the President-elect appeared with his family to claim victory. As he approached the stage through the crowded hall, he stopped for a moment, greeted Elva and me warmly, and expressed his thanks for my efforts over the years. I was deeply touched.

At mid-morning the next day, Bob, Ted Kennedy, Ted Sorensen, Ken, Pierre Salinger, Steve Smith, Sargent Shriver, and I waited expectantly at Bob's house for the President-elect to arrive. When the door opened and he entered, relaxed and smiling, we sprang to our feet. He was different now; he was to be President of the United States and I suddenly realized that I would never call him Jack again.

I took a few days off, relaxing first at Hyannis Port and then back in Springfield, but on the Monday morning after the election I was at my desk at the DNC office in Washington. My first assignment given me by the President-elect was to start thinking about which of our campaign supporters should be offered positions in the new Administration. In the weeks ahead, there was a good deal of jockeying about as various Kennedy advisers tried to influence the top-level appointments. Ken O'Donnell and I were in the middle of the action, because we wanted to see the people rewarded who had given us their all.

In mid-November our talks moved down to Palm Beach,

where we met as usual at poolside so the Kennedys could take
a plunge now and then, and as usual I suffered in a long-
sleeved shirt to avoid sunburn. We were inside occasionally,
however, for I recall that it was in the President-elect's bedroom that Sarge Shriver first introduced the name of Robert
McNamara, then the new president of the Ford Motor Company, as a possible Secretary of Defense.

"McNamara?" someone said. "Is he Catholic?"

No one knew, and Shriver promised to find out because if he
had been, even a McNamara would have had a hard time
winning an appointment in an administration that already included a Catholic President and potentially a Catholic Attorney General.

One man was all set to be Secretary of Agriculture until he
met with Kennedy. He proved to be so verbose that Kennedy
wanted nothing more to do with him—the man literally talked
himself out of a job. I was pleased because this made possible
the appointment of liberal Governor Orville Freeman of Minnesota.

One typical bit of by-play over patronage pitted Ken and
me against Bob and Ted Kennedy on the appointment of the
new Director of the Internal Revenue Service. Bob and Ted
wanted the post to go to Mortimer Kaplan, who had taught
them tax law at the University of Virginia Law School. Ken
and I had a candidate, John O'Connell, the Attorney General
of the state of Washington, a man who'd been an early and effective Kennedy supporter. I pleaded our case to the President-
elect one day in his suite at the Carlyle Hotel in New York,
and he told me to go ahead and pursue the possibility. I did,
but our candidate decided that to be the nation's chief tax
collector would not further his political career, so Bob and
Ted's man got the job.

Postmaster General was the last cabinet post to be filled.
Pierre Salinger and others from California were pushing State
Senator Hugo Fisher of San Diego. I had met Fisher during my
California travels and had worked hard to get his support for
Kennedy. He had backed Kennedy but not as early or actively
as others, and I was not persuaded he was our top prospect in

California. Sarge Shriver told me about Fisher's candidacy one midnight in the lobby of the Mayflower Hotel where I was staying during the pre-Inaugural period. I immediately went up to my room and called O'Donnell. I then called Jesse Unruh in California and asked him for recommendations.

Jesse suggested Ed Day, an insurance executive who'd headed a group of businessmen for Kennedy. Day had been a strong Kennedy backer, a fact that was all the more impressive because he had once been Adlai Stevenson's law partner. Early the next morning, I talked to Kennedy and told him that all things being equal, the appointment should go to someone we had worked with early rather than someone who came aboard later. He said he had about made his decision but he'd think it over and get back to me. Later that morning he called me to get Ed Day's phone number.

In California that same day, Governor Pat Brown advised a luncheon group which included Ed Day that a Californian had been selected the previous evening to serve in Kennedy's Cabinet as Postmaster General and the announcement would be made momentarily. That afternoon—after returning to his office from the luncheon—Ed Day received a call from the President-elect asking him to come to Washington immediately. Day met with Kennedy, was offered the Postmaster Generalship and accepted. He was stunned, of course, because he recalled Pat Brown's announcement of the previous day that someone else had the job.

As the story of Day's appointment suggests, Kennedy took office with no commitments to anyone and he had a free hand in selecting his Cabinet. As a result, some of the men he chose were strangers to him and to politics as well. He and I agreed that I should meet with his Cabinet designees to discuss with them their role with the White House. I held a series of dinner meetings with some of them at my Mayflower suite at which I emphasized that there would be but *one* Administration legislative program—the President's; that we were all to be part of *one* team and would maintain close contact; that major appointments would be cleared by the White House; and that we should not forget we had another election coming up in 1964.

These sessions went well, and I particularly recall one with Bob McNamara, who was to be Secretary of Defense. I was immediately impressed with his razor-sharp, unblinking, no-nonsense manner. Dick Donahue, who is as astute a lawyer as he is a politician, was also present, and he and I were both astonished when McNamara told us the extent of the financial loss he was taking voluntarily to join the government.

"You don't have to go that far," Donahue said, speaking as a lawyer who was familiar with the conflict of interest laws.

"I think I do," McNamara told us.

Throughout November and December, as we placed other men in jobs, I had no idea what assignment, if any, I might be offered. I assumed Kennedy would let me know in due time, so I never raised the question. One day in mid-December, Bob Kennedy dropped by my office in the DNC and abruptly brought up the subject.

"Larry, the spot for you is Deputy Postmaster General," Bob said. "That's the number two spot in the Post Office and John Bailey won't stay on as national chairman forever."

I was taken aback by the suggestion, literally stunned and I reacted brusquely.

"I haven't any interest whatsoever in that spot," I said, "and furthermore you needn't be concerned about me. I have no problem in just going back to Springfield."

Bob was annoyed at my reaction and indicated that perhaps my return to Springfield might not be a bad idea, and we left the matter there. He gave no indication whether the Post Office spot was his idea or the President-elect's. In retrospect, I suppose Bob felt there was a certain logic to it. The Post Office Department had traditionally been a political arm of the party in power. But Bob should have realized that, after working closely with Jack Kennedy for eight years, I wouldn't be content being second-in-command to Ed Day, the California businessman whose appointment I'd myself encouraged. So I began to think I would be back home in Springfield as soon as I had wrapped up loose ends in our campaign.

The matter was resolved over Christmas when I was named special assistant to the President for congressional relations and personnel. The President-elect told me, "Larry, I've decided congressional relations is the right role for you and the personnel slot seems to go with it." I had no real concept of the role but I was pleased that I would have an opportunity to participate, particularly in the White House.

In later conversations with Professor Richard Neustadt, who had served on Harry Truman's staff and who was advising Kennedy on White House organization, I learned he had recommended to Kennedy that he give a high priority to congressional relations, and Kennedy concurred. I think it pleased Kennedy to add "and personnel" to the job title to show that one person could handle posts that required two men in the Eisenhower administration.

Thus, as January began, I was still involved in patronage and Inaugural planning, but I also was trying to look ahead to my new assignment on Capitol Hill. I wanted to meet with Bryce Harlow, who had handled congressional relations for Eisenhower, but I just could not find the time, so I sent Phyllis Maddock to the White House where she had a good meeting with Harlow and his staff. I met with Harlow later and was highly impressed by him and the advice he gave me. We became friends and have maintained our friendship since.

On January 13 I began interviewing candidates for my congressional relations staff. I had decided to consider people with prior Capitol Hill experience and those without it as well. Those who had worked on the Hill would have built-in friends, enemies, prejudices, and so on; on the other hand, they would obviously have useful experience. For the most part, however, I felt that sound political judgment was more important than prior Hill experience.

To concentrate on the Senate I chose Mike Manatos, who was then administrative assistant to Senator Joseph C. O'Mahoney of Wyoming, had been on the Hill for many years, and was well regarded. By contrast, I chose Henry Hall Wilson, a tall young North Carolinian—a man with no previous Hill experience—who had served in his state legislature and worked closely with Governor Sanford on the Kennedy campaign, to work in the House, particularly with the southern delegations. Dick Donahue, a long-time political associate from Massachusetts, agreed to join the staff to assist Wilson with the big-city congressmen of the north and east. Claude Desautels, administrative assistant to Congressman Wayne Aspinall of Colorado, agreed to serve as my administrative assistant. Phyllis Maddock continued as my personal secretary and trusted assistant.

Later, three other men would join our congressional relations staff: Chuck Roche, who had been a Harvard classmate of Bob Kennedy's and a Boston newspaperman before joining our 1960 campaign staff; Chuck Daley, who once had been a summer intern in Senator Kennedy's office and later was a vice president of the University of California; Dave Bunn, a Coloradan who worked on congressional relations at the Post Office before I brought him to the White House. Thus, I had a staff as Inaugural Day neared.

For weeks before that great day I was bombarded by old friends and would-be friends who wanted tickets to the Inaugural ceremony and various other Inaugural functions. At the last minute I realized I needed a top hat—I'd never owned a hat of any sort—and finding one for my size 7¾ head proved something of a problem until Alex Rose, the president of the hatters' union, saved the day. Then there was a snowstorm. But finally, amid pageantry and a dazzling winter sun, John F. Kennedy took the oath of office and became the thirty-fifth President of the United States.

President Kennedy had issued orders that afternoon before the Inaugural Ball that all members of the White House staff were to report for work at eight o'clock the next morning. With only a few hours sleep, a "Gung-ho" staff gathered in the "Fish Room" across the hall from the President's Oval Office.

The President gave a brief, "let's get going" pep talk, and we all hustled around the West Wing to claim office space. None of us on the staff had felt authorized to make office assignments, so the supposedly tight-knit, disciplined Kennedy team began scurrying in every direction to claim "squatter's rights." It was every man for himself.

I needed several offices for my staff, so I headed for the second floor, just above the President's office, where Bryce Harlow previously had his office. I commandeered that office and the adjoining offices on each side of it. Down the corridor I also found a paneled corner office with an adjacent conference room. Mike Feldman, who was to be a deputy to Ted Sorensen, had placed his briefcase on the desk; however, I suggested to Mike that perhaps I should have that office and he readily agreed. Meanwhile, some of my colleagues who had sought space on the first floor, to be nearer the President, gradually lost out because of the limited space available, an occurrence that others of us found amusing.

As I settled into my new working quarters with their bare walls, empty file cabinets, and mysterious phone systems, I realized, and I think all of us did, just how abrupt the transition between administrations is. None of us knew how to send a memo from one office to the next, and for a time we were totally dependent on the telephone operators and messengers and civil service people who stay on while Presidents and their immediate staffs come and go. As I contemplated this bewildering situation, the other special assistants to the President were being sworn in downstairs. I missed the ceremony and later was sworn in alone by Bill Hopkins, the long-time permanent chief clerk of the White House.

VI

CAPITOL HILL

As THE Kennedy presidency passes into history, Kennedy seems to be best remembered for his personal magnetism, for the new spirit he brought to America, and for his successes and failures in foreign policy. A myth has arisen that he was uninterested in Congress, or that he "failed" with Congress. The facts, I believe, are otherwise. Kennedy's legislative record in 1961–63 was the best of any President since Roosevelt's first term. We did not get everything we wanted. We won some legislative battles and we lost others—you don't "win" or "lose" with Congress the way you win or lose an election. Even when we failed, we were building toward the future. We could not pass Medicare in 1961–63, but we raised the issue, we forced our opponents to go on record against it, and we paved the way for its eventual passage in 1965. I would take nothing from Lyndon Johnson's brilliant and tireless performance with Congress, but I believe that, had Kennedy lived, his record in his second term would have been comparable to the record Johnson established.

The reality Kennedy faced as he looked toward Capitol Hill was that he had, at best, a slender Democratic majority there. Our party had lost twenty-one congressional seats in the 1960 election. Kennedy had no sweeping mandate from the voters, and he had few, if any, representatives or senators who owed their election to his political coattails. The balance of power in the House of Representatives was held by southern Democrats who might or might not support a young Catholic President with a commitment to civil rights.

The difficulty of the situation was brought home to us abruptly on Tuesday, January 24, just four days after his Inauguration, when Kennedy held the first of his weekly breakfast meetings with Democratic leaders of the House and the Senate. That morning, Sam Rayburn, the venerable Speaker of the House, dropped a bomb in the new President's lap.

"Mr. President," Rayburn said, "I don't believe we have the votes to expand the Rules Committee."

Kennedy was stunned, as was I. It had been agreed, at a meeting in Palm Beach in December, that Rayburn would take the necessary action to stop "Judge" Howard Smith of Virginia and other conservatives on the Rules Committee from bottling up liberal legislation in the committee, as they had been doing for years. Rayburn had decided to back a plan to add three new members to the Rules Committee and thereby give it a more liberal majority. We had assumed Rayburn was on top of the matter and we had held no further discussions with him. So we were astounded to hear Rayburn report that the expansion plan would probably lose by a handful of votes.

The loss would be devastating. If the Rules Committee was not expanded, little if any of the Kennedy legislative program was likely to be passed. Beyond that, the defeat would be a stunning blow to his prestige, both nationally and internationally, at the very start of his Administration.

Following the legislative breakfast, Kennedy and I talked at length. We were particularly concerned that Rayburn did not have a head count—he didn't know exactly how many votes were for or against us or who was leaning which way. Head counts were basic to the Kennedy style of operation, but Rayburn's was a lower-keyed style. Our problem, however, was that if Rayburn's methods lost the Rules fight, it was Kennedy who would suffer a humiliating defeat.

Kennedy called Rayburn back to the White House that afternoon and asked him to postpone the vote from January 25, the next day, until January 31. Rayburn was reluctant. My impression was that he thought the battle was lost and wanted to get it over with. But at length he agreed. That gave us a

week to carry out a Kennedy-style campaign to win the necessary votes in the House.

"We can't lose this one, Larry," the President told me. "The
ball game is over if we do. Let's give it everything we've got."

My first job was to take a head count. I was still a virtual
stranger to the House of Representatives and my efforts were
immeasurably helped by such allies as Congressmen Richard
Bolling of Missouri, Frank (Topper) Thompson, Jr., of New
Jersey, and Carl Elliott and Robert Jones of Alabama. Our
count indicated we were likely to lose the Rules Committee
vote by seven votes.

We went over and over the list of congressmen, seeking to
determine which ones might be won over and by whom. We
called in Andy Biemiller of the AFL-CIO to bring what pressure he could to bear. From the Cabinet, Bob Kennedy and
Stew Udall—who had been a member of the House before becoming Kennedy's Secretary of the Interior—were in the thick
of the fight.

Support for the new President was our main argument, not
patronage or arm-twisting.

"Let's win this one for Jack, Jackie, and little Caroline," I
told one congressman. We told the members they just couldn't
undercut the President on this first, crucial vote.

The southern Democrats were the key. The House then consisted of 174 Republicans, 151 Democrats from northern and
western states, 108 Democrats from southern states, and two
vacancies. That meant that if we could hold all the non-
southern Democrats (which would be extremely difficult) and
if we could pick up twenty Republican votes, we still needed
a third of the Southerners for a majority of 218 votes.

Rayburn and Georgia's Carl Vinson—another highly respected congressman—were working on their fellow Southerners. We also asked some southern governors, including
North Carolina's Terry Sanford and Arkansas' Orville Faubus,
to use their influence with their states' congressional delegations. Southerners were under tremendous pressure to oppose
the expansion of the committee. Southern newspapers were
picturing the Rules Committee as the nation's last bulwark

against socialism and civil rights legislation. One Southerner who supported us was Overton Brooks, who represented a district in northern Louisiana where anti-Catholic and anti-civil rights feelings ran high. He later told me about the retaliation he experienced because of his vote. Newspapers in his district attacked him mercilessly. He and his family received threatening calls. And a cross was burned on his lawn.

North Carolina was of particular concern to us. Kennedy had carried the state, he had placed former Governor Luther Hodges in his Cabinet, and he had appointed several other North Carolinians to high office—but we had only one vote, Herb Bonner's, from the state's eleven-man delegation. This situation led to the one instance in which Kennedy personally sought votes in the Rules fight.

Over Rayburn's objections, the President called Harold Cooley, dean of the North Carolina delegation, and urged him to reconvene the delegation to reconsider its members' positions. Cooley did call the delegation back together, but no one's vote was changed. The main result of the exchange was Cooley's telling everyone in earshot the President had called him. This led to reports that Kennedy was busily calling members and pleading for their votes. In reality, the call to Cooley was the only one he made.

We won the Rules Committee fight by a vote of 217 to 212. Our majority included twenty-two Republicans, virtually the high-water mark of our Republican support, and thirty-four southern Democrats or about a third of the Southerners. The southern support was a bright spot, but the fact remained that despite our massive efforts, and those of Rayburn and Vinson, we won by only five votes. Our honeymoon with Congress was over before it began.

With the Rules fight won, I took a few deep breaths and began examining how I could best function in the area of congressional relations. One thing I soon realized was that I should not continue as the presidential assistant for personnel—my congressional work would be more than enough to keep me occupied.

I had already received several messages from the heads of

federal employee groups who assumed I would be the White
House liaison with the federal bureaucracy. I had put aside
their inquiries, but my supposed role as personnel czar required
my immediate attention when a snowstorm swept over Washington in February. As the snowdrifts piled higher across the
White House lawn outside my window, I received a call from
a man who directed a twelve-man personnel office next door
in the Executive Office Building. We'd never met, but I was
his new boss.

"Mr. O'Brien," he said, "we're all looking forward to meeting
you. We know you've been awfully busy, but this snowstorm
requires a decision by you. What time do you want to shut
down the government offices?"

I asked, "Would you please repeat the question?"

"Well," he said, "as the President's personnel assistant, it's
up to you to determine when we close down federal offices because of hazardous driving conditions."

I quickly told him, "Let me call you back."

I conferred with Phyllis Maddock and we determined that
an Under Secretary of Commerce had jurisdiction over the
Weather Bureau. I called the new Under Secretary who happened to be Clarence Daniel (Dan) Martin, Jr., of California,
an old political associate of ours, and persuaded him that it was
proper for his office to determine when government workers
got off during snowstorms. Within a few more days I had arranged for someone else to handle White House dealings with
the federal bureaucracy.

My interest in the personnel area was not with civil service
jobs, but with the top-level political appointments—the ones
that congressmen wanted to influence and that we might use in
turn to influence how those members voted. I felt, however,
that it was important that I not be seen as Kennedy's patronage
chief, lest the ill will from the people I had to say "no" to would
hurt Kennedy on the Hill. Therefore, John Bailey, the new
national chairman, and I worked out an informal arrangement whereby, in effect, I said "yes" for patronage granted and
he said "no" for patronage denied. In other words, John took
the heat when we had to refuse someone and the White House

took credit, for the President, when we made an appointment that pleased some member of Congress.

Patronage aside, the question was how Kennedy could work effectively with a closely divided Congress and thus keep his promise to "get this country moving again." There had been no truly productive relationship between Congress and a President since Franklin Roosevelt broke with Congress over his "court-packing" plan in 1937. Roosevelt had at times dispatched various of his aides, such as Thomas G. Corcoran—the legendary "Tommy the Cork"—to deal with Congress, but he had had no permanent congressional relations apparatus. Harry Truman had had no such apparatus either and his tactic, when his legislative program was blocked by Congress, was to turn the situation to political advantage by running against the "do-nothing" Republican Congress in the 1948 election; he won the election but was never able to pass his program. Eisenhower had a congressional relations office, but its role was largely to discourage or water down Democratic-sponsored bills.

Kennedy and I both believed that he, and I also, would have to take an active, aggressive role with Congress if he was to have any chance of passing his program. Kennedy's view was based, in part, on his own experience in the House and Senate.

"I was up there for fourteen years," he told me once, "and I don't recall that Truman or Eisenhower or anyone on their staffs ever said one word to me about legislation. One time I was about to cast a vote and some White House fellow up in the gallery seemed to be waving encouragement to me, but that was about all. We've got to do better than that."

Kennedy wanted a well-organized, aggressive congressional relations program, just as he had wanted well-organized, aggressive political campaigns. We were haunted by our slender margin of victory in the Rules fight, and we believed that Kennedy's only hope of legislative success was to establish a liaison relationship with Congress—both the House and the Senate—that was new and, in the context of Capitol Hill, revolutionary. Kennedy wanted my staff and me to work closely with congressional leaders on the formulation and passage of bills. We knew this approach was a gamble. There would be mutterings, perhaps outcries, that we were encroaching on congressional authority or even violating the "separation of powers" doctrine. But we felt we had no choice. Either we fought for our program or we would have no program.

I wanted to apply to our congressional relations program the same attention to detail that I think is basic to all political success. To begin with, as newcomers on the Hill, we needed information about the men and women we'd be dealing with. Thus, in my suite at the Mayflower Hotel one night in early February, our three friends in the House who had helped us on the Rules fight—Topper Thompson, Dick Bolling, and Carl Elliott—went through the entire list of the House membership, recalling invaluable details about each member's friends, interests, and voting record, while Henry Wilson, Dick Donahue, and I scribbled notes furiously. This supplemented information from our campaign files. Later we compiled similar data on the Senate. Thereafter, a record was maintained of every contact we had with members of Congress.

I soon realized that our five-man staff was not large enough to perform the task I envisioned. There were, however, congressional relations staffs operating in some forty federal departments and agencies and I wanted them to supplement our White House effort. I called in the directors of these agency congressional relations offices and reminded them that there must be one administration legislative program, not dozens of competing agency programs. We quickly initiated a system whereby each department and agency submitted to Claude Desautels in my office, by each Monday noon, a report of its congressional activity for the week past and its plans for the week ahead. My staff reviewed these reports on Monday afternoon and prepared a summary for the President to review prior to his legislative leaders' breakfast the following morning.

This organizational effort would have meant little if it had not been backed up by Kennedy's personal support and if I, as his agent, had not been regarded as someone who had his ear and his trust. On both counts, he could not have been more co-operative.

Kennedy was well aware that he lacked the necessary degree

of intimacy with his party's congressional leaders, even though he had served in both the House and Senate. Mike Mansfield, the new majority leader in the Senate, had been majority whip under Lyndon Johnson and had favored him for the nomination the previous year; and the new majority whip was Hubert Humphrey, who had engaged in two bruising primary battles with Kennedy the previous spring.

On the House side, Speaker Rayburn had opposed Kennedy at Los Angeles and had obvious reservations about the new President's ability to lead the nation. Majority leader John McCormack had, of course, known Kennedy for a long time, but their relationship had sometimes been marked by conflict. House whip Carl Albert of Oklahoma barely knew Kennedy.

Kennedy knew that personal relationships could make all the difference with Congress and he therefore launched an unprecedented program of presidential activity. My staff maintained records of his contacts with Congress in 1961: he held thirty-two of the Tuesday morning leadership breakfasts and about ninety private conversations with congressional leaders, the type that lasted an hour or two. Coffee hours brought five hundred members of the House and Senate to the White House, and bill-signing ceremonies brought in the same number. All in all, Kennedy had about 2,500 separate contacts with members of Congress during his first year in office, exclusive of correspondence. Then, he used to thank the Democrats who'd helped on a bill with a personal note—that they could use in their campaigns. But he thanked the occasional Republican who needed thanking by a phone call, which could not be reproduced for campaign purposes.

I was forever pushing the President to have another luncheon or reception. A ritual arose between us. I would give him a partial list of the legislators I wanted him to see. He would look at it, groan, and say, "Okay, where's the rest of it?" Then I would hand over the full list and he would OK it.

The scope of Kennedy's courting of the Congress was missed by the press, perhaps because Kennedy insisted that most of the meetings be kept "off the record," lest he appear to be using the congressional leaders for publicity purposes. These were soft-sell sessions. Kennedy rarely asked a member for his vote on a specific piece of legislation. That was not his style. If there were arms to be twisted, that was our job. His responsibility, as he saw it, was to create an atmosphere in which my office could work effectively, and, in that effort, he was entirely successful.

I, too, had to build personal relationships with the men on the Hill. Kennedy gave me a boost during my early weeks in Washington. When his old colleagues from Congress called him with some legislative ideas, he would invariably ask, "Have you taken this up with Larry O'Brien?" Soon the calls began coming to me, which was what we both wanted.

My old friend Eddie Boland, who had become the congressman from Springfield, arranged a series of receptions for me so I could meet and get to know his colleagues. Congressmen Tip O'Neill and Gene Keogh assisted Eddie in this effort. On the Senate side, Ben Smith, who had replaced Kennedy as the junior senator from Massachusetts, and Felton (Skeeter) Johnston, the Secretary of the Senate, did the same for me on the Senate side.

Those first months in Washington in early 1961 were a busy and exciting time for Elva and me. We had rented a house on Thirty-second Street in Georgetown, and our son Larry, was enrolled in Georgetown Prep. It seemed there was some new congressional reception or White House function almost every night. Elva shared my newfound fascination with Congress and would often observe House and Senate proceedings from the visitors' galleries. She was intrigued by the oratory and disillusioned when I told her that the speeches did not mean much, since most members knew in advance how they would vote. Elva and a number of other wives from Massachusetts with husbands in the Administration started a Thursday luncheon club, which featured visits to art galleries and tourist attractions, as well as lunch at a different Washington restaurant each week. Elva's enthusiasm for Washington was undimmed even when, at one White House dinner, a well-lubricated Republican leader managed to spill his dessert into her lap.

As soon as Elva and I had moved into our Georgetown home,

I began weekly Sunday brunches, inviting congressmen, cabinet members, and other administration officials, and newspapermen, and we served them bloody marys, scrambled eggs, ham, bacon, baked beans, rolls, coffee and O'Brien potatoes. One sidelight of these brunches was how often I, the newcomer to Washington, would find myself introducing important members of the House to important journalists, even when both men had been in Washington for years. On one occasion, Walter Lippmann and his wife were among the guests and Lippmann pulled me aside to ask me to identify some of the congressmen present, including Albert Thomas, George Mahon, and Wilbur Mills, three very, very powerful men. By the same token, a few congressmen asked me to identify Lippmann, Joseph Alsop, and other nationally known writers to them. The situation reflected the extent to which the press concentrated on the Senate, despite the equal power wielded by the House.

I had certainly become aware of the immense power wielded by certain members of Congress and I realized that unless I could win the trust of these men, I would not get very far assisting the President on his legislative program.

No man in Washington in 1961, the President not excluded, had more prestige than the Speaker of the House, Sam Rayburn of Texas. In my first months on the Hill I would often drop by his office to chat. For the most part, I would listen while he talked about Texas, often about the Texas Rangers or about his years in Congress. As his eyesight was failing, the blinds would be closed and we would sit in semi-darkness. He would sometimes punctuate his comments with shots at a big brass spittoon and, despite his poor eyesight, they were well aimed. It was on one of these visits that, to my amusement, Rayburn confided to me that he had little recollection of Kennedy from his three terms in the House.

I understood Rayburn's uncertainty about the new White House Office I headed, for it might have been interpreted as a criticism of his leadership or an attempt to bypass him. Rayburn had been in Congress a long time, and I think he feared that we new fellows didn't understand how the game was played and that we might do him more harm than good, perhaps by giving the Republicans an "encroachment" issue. I did everything I could to relieve his fears.

Sam Rayburn was a rugged old gentleman with a fine appetite, and he relished the quantity and quality of the food at our weekly legislative breakfasts. He would tear into the eggs, bacon, ham, toast, juice, jellies, and other items with a gusto that I envied, for my mind was so completely on business at those breakfasts that I would chain-smoke and perhaps only sip some coffee. Mister Sam was never verbose, but by occasional grunts and short, pithy comments he would make his views known. In time, President Kennedy was able to draw him out and we would all enjoy his vast storytelling ability. He would talk about Presidents he had known, commencing with Wilson and Coolidge, and one by one he would take the measure of the giants of American politics in this century. Or he would tell tales of the Texas Rangers, often verbally illustrating that two Rangers comprised an army. Sometimes he would talk about his farm back in Texas—how he used his front porch as an office, how he always advised young congressmen that they could get publicity in national magazines and appear on television and make a hit with the "fancypants" people in Washington society, but unless they kept close to the folks back home they wouldn't be around for long. He told his stories with a snap of his head and a fire in his eyes that enthralled Kennedy.

The Speaker's health began to fail during 1961. This was a matter of great concern to Kennedy, and he asked if he could help. Rayburn complained of a back condition, so Kennedy suggested that he be examined by Dr. Janet Travell, who had done so much to ease Kennedy's own back problem. Rayburn later told us it had disturbed him greatly to have to "drop his trousers" for a woman, but Dr. Travell's treatment seemed to help, for he said he felt better. Mister Sam's attitude toward ill health was that you should ignore it until it went away.

One morning he arrived for a legislative breakfast a few minutes late. The President told a waiter, "Bring the Speaker some breakfast." Rayburn said no, he'd already eaten; he didn't have room for any more. I think we all realized that he was ill, for he had so enjoyed those hearty breakfasts.

Rayburn worked in his office for a few more weeks. I saw him several times and he appeared to be in great pain. The shades would be drawn and he might be napping or his friend and aide, D. B. Hardeman, might be reading him the mail in the near-darkness. Finally, he said it might be good for him to go home to Texas. He returned to his farm, and there he died.

I was with the President in California when the news came. We flew directly to Bonham, Texas, for the funeral on November 18. It was a simple service in Mister Sam's church, with many of his old friends and neighbors gathered to pay their final respects. Also attending were the Vice President, former Presidents Eisenhower and Truman, and numerous congressional leaders. As I watched the mighty and the humble gathered to mourn Sam Rayburn, this great leader who had sprung from the rugged soil of Texas, I had a feeling that this scene embodied something very close to the heart of America, something that helped to explain the toughness and the continuity of our democratic government.

Rayburn's successor as Speaker was majority leader John McCormack, the man we had challenged in the 1956 fight over control of the Massachusetts Democratic Committee—the Onion Bill Burke fight. As majority leader, McCormack could not have been more kind and co-operative with me and I soon came to regard him with the highest degree of affection. This warm relationship was to continue throughout his years as Speaker. In Massachusetts politics, in earlier years, I had regarded him as a symbol of the Old Guard, and we Kennedy men had seen ourselves as the Young Turks of the state's politics. But in Washington I came to appreciate just what a skillful and valuable politician John McCormack was. He was a man with an almost perfect liberal voting record, yet he was widely admired by the southern conservatives and, upon Rayburn's death, could command their strong support for the speakership.

One of the most conservative of the Southerners, Mendel Rivers of South Carolina, used to say, "I'm not a Democrat, I'm a McCormacrat," and from time to time, on close issues,

McCormack would say to him, "Well, Mendel, it's time for you to prove you're a McCormacrat," and he could sometimes swing Rivers' vote.

McCormack was a courtly man who rarely spoke critically of any of his colleagues. The worst thing I ever knew him to say about another member of Congress was, "His colleagues hold him in minimum high regard."

Despite his gentle manner, however, McCormack could be tough. We saw an instance of his toughness in 1965, when the bill to provide federal aid to education was awaiting action by the House Committee on Education and Labor. We felt an urgent need to get the bill out of committee, but the committee's chairman, Adam Clayton Powell, the flamboyant Harlem congressman, was relaxing at his home on the island of Bimini. Henry Hall Wilson of our staff tried in vain to lure Powell back to Washington and finally took the problem to Speaker McCormack. Within hours McCormack told Henry that he had spoken to Powell and gotten his promise to return and convene his committee the following Wednesday.

Wednesday came and went with no Adam Clayton Powell. Henry again went to the Speaker, who was furious, and promised to settle the matter quickly. A day or two later he told Henry he had Powell's written agreement to convene the committee the next Wednesday.

"Mr. Speaker," Henry said, "what will you do if he fails to show up this time?"

"I'll put him in purgatory," McCormack said firmly.

"What does that mean?" Henry asked.

"It means I'll cut off all his prerogatives."

"Have you ever put anyone in purgatory before?" Henry persisted.

"Once."

"Who?"

"Carl Vinson, the distinguished member from Georgia," McCormack said, to Henry's amazement.

"Why?"

"Because many years ago he pledged to vote for me for majority leader and then went back on his word."

"How long did you keep him in purgatory?"

"Twelve years," the Speaker said.

Adam Clayton Powell must have known that story, because he returned the following Wednesday and the aid-to-education bill proceeded on schedule.

If Carl Vinson had spent twelve years in John McCormack's purgatory, he had certainly recovered by 1961, for he then ranked with Rayburn and McCormack in power and prestige in the House. Dick Bolling had stressed to me, soon after the Inauguration, that Vinson was the key to our hopes of winning southern support for our program. He was right. If we could win Vinson's vote on any given issue, that would swing over several other Georgians and Southerners. His support had been crucial on the Rules Committee struggle, and much of our success in 1961 was due to Vinson's voting with us on many major issues, including the minimum-wage bill, the depressed-areas bill, and the foreign-aid bill.

Vinson was a conservative, but he was also a Democrat— proud to see a Democrat in the White House and anxious to work with him. We tried to make that easy for him. He was chairman of the House Armed Services Committee, so Kennedy often sought his views in advance of major military decisions. Secretary McNamara joined in the wooing of Vinson with considerable success. Nonetheless, early in 1962, Kennedy and Vinson found themselves on a collision course, and it was at that point that a year of careful presidential attention paid off.

The issue was an airplane—the RS-70 manned bomber. Vinson sought approximately a half-billion dollars to build the RS-70. McNamara and his Defense Department experts had grave doubts about the RS-70 and they proposed to spend approximately $171 million on further testing and development of it. This was not enough for Vinson, who had included in the military appropriations bill language to "direct" the Secretary of the Air Force to spend the larger amount on the aircraft. While the language was aimed at the Secretary of the Air Force, it was of course intended to "direct" the President. The bill further declared: "If the language constitutes a test as to whether Congress has the power to so mandate, let the test be made. . . ."

We in the White House viewed such a showdown with alarm. At the least, we would lose Vinson's good will and the President might well be drawn into a constitutional crisis.

McNamara finally reported that he could not budge Vinson, so Kennedy called Vinson to his office for a discussion. This was in March. After a while, the two men stepped outside and went for a walk in the Rose Garden, and in that private talk Kennedy persuaded Vinson to withdraw his demand. I never knew exactly what Kennedy said to Vinson, but I imagine it was a very personal and low-key appeal, stressing the harm that a direct collision between the President and the Congress could do to the country. Vinson told me later, "I feel good about this, Larry, because I really want to help the President." Whatever was said during that walk in the Rose Garden, it epitomizes Kennedy's personal success in dealing with Congress.

Politics is the art of the possible, and it is an intensely personal art. I tried to bear in mind, in my work on Capitol Hill, that members of the House and Senate are human beings and they can be vain, stubborn, irrational, and petty, like all human beings, including Presidents and their assistants. I always felt that we could never discount any member of Congress, no matter how much we might disagree with him. The people of his state or his district had elected him; he spoke for them and he was, therefore, deserving of our respect. I felt a great affinity with all elected officials. I knew, from my own experience in Massachusetts, how hard it is to get elected to office. I never expected any member to commit political suicide in order to help the President, no matter how noble our cause. I expected politicians to be concerned with their own interests; I only hoped to convince them our interests were often the same. I've never been entirely comfortable with purists in politics. The purist thinks it's more laudable to accept defeat than to compromise. Maybe, but in a legislative context you strive for the best compromise you can get. That's the purpose of Congress—

to compromise the vast differences of political opinion that exist in this country.

My job had more to do with persuasion than with patronage. A folklore arose that pictured me and my staff trading dams and post offices for votes. In truth, we didn't have much patronage to dangle before anyone's nose. For example, the allocation of most public-works projects was in the hands of powerful members of Congress.

Certainly, when it was possible and proper, we did try to help our friends on appointments in the Administration. In our first month in office, I notified heads of departments and agencies of the procedures for clearance, by the White House, of top-level appointments outside regular Civil Service. We wanted to insure that the recommendations of our friends in the Congress and throughout the country would receive full consideration.

Weekly meetings took place at the White House involving Ralph Dungan of the President's staff, Richard Maguire, a long-time Kennedy associate from Massachusetts, Ken O'Donnell, and me at which we reviewed the openings and the recommendations to fill them.

When appointments were made, we saw that the President got full credit. All this was routine and appropriate political procedure, any suggestion that it "bought" us votes in Congress is ridiculous.

What we did do, and this was a far more intricate and important procedure, was to try to know and understand each individual member of the House and the Senate to determine how far he could go with us without hurting himself politically, to convince him that his constituents had a stake in a particular piece of legislation and that he could support us without political risk or compromise of principle.

Sometimes we succeeded and sometimes we failed. The foreign-aid fight in 1961 brought me into negotiations with two very difficult gentlemen, Representatives D. B. Saund of California and Otto Passman of Louisiana. I didn't do very well in my dealings with either of them, but the problems they posed were typical of the problems we faced in hundreds of encounters.

Saund had supported foreign aid in years past, but he opposed us in 1961 because the Veterans Administration had decided to close a hospital in his district. Every expert involved stated that the old hospital was inadequate and unsafe, but Saund felt that its closing would embarrass him in the eyes of his constituents.

As a means of retaliation, he introduced an amendment to the foreign-aid bill to delete the President's request for long-term borrowing authority. That was just a ploy, of course. Saund wasn't particularly concerned about long-term loans versus short-term loans, but he was extremely concerned about his VA hospital. It was a form of blackmail, and the final decision on how to deal with it fell to me. I decided that we could not bend to that type of pressure. The result was that Saund's amendment passed by a close vote, thereby doing great harm to the foreign-aid program. It was a bitter pill to swallow, but to have bowed to Saund's demands would have been stretching political compromise past the breaking point.

Phyllis Maddock, however, had one small measure of revenge. Saund had sent us a picture of his grandson taken with the President—a large and quite lovely photograph of the President holding the child above his head—which he wanted autographed by Kennedy. Phyllis proceeded to hide the photograph behind a sofa and announced that it had been mysteriously lost. Saund was hysterical and he had half the White House staff looking for it, but not Phyllis. Eventually, she "found" the picture and we had it autographed.

Otto Passman, chairman of the House Foreign Aid Appropriations Subcommittee, was even more difficult to deal with. We at least knew what Saund wanted, but Passman seemed to have an irrational loathing of the entire concept of foreign aid and he gloried in his annual, well-publicized crusade against it. Kennedy met with Passman several times, but all he received was a sampling of Passman's double-talk—triple-talk, I called it, for Passman was a master of evasion. After Kennedy, McCormack, and I held several sessions with Passman, we thought we had his agreement to a four-billion-dollar foreign-aid bill. Within hours of our agreement, however, Passman was declaring we had misunderstood him, and in the end we had to settle for a lesser amount in the House.

In fairness, I should add that when I dealt with Passman on other issues, particularly when I was Postmaster General, I found him co-operative. He simply had a "thing" about foreign aid.

If Otto Passman had a "thing" about foreign aid, Mike Kirwan had a "thing" about an aquarium. Mike was a tough old Democratic pro from Youngstown, Ohio, who liked to joke about having done pretty well for a fellow who had only gone to grade school. He was popular on the Hill and, as a member of the Appropriations Committee and chairman of its Subcommittee on the Interior, he was powerful, too. Mike's annual St. Patrick's Day party was a social "must" in Washington; I recall that the President and I donned green neckties and attended it together one year.

For reasons that were never clear to me, Mike Kirwan wanted to see the world's greatest aquarium built in Washington, D.C. The Washington *Post* derided the aquarium as a blatant waste of money, but Mike's colleagues in the House dutifully supported their powerful colleague's pet project.

The problem arose when Senator Wayne Morse—a former law professor, a brilliant and acerbic man, an important ally of ours on education legislation—made the mistake of criticizing Mike Kirwan's aquarium. No insult was intended; Morse was simply making a speech back home about the waste in Washington and cited the aquarium as an example. But Kirwan heard about the speech, took offense, and proceeded to eliminate from an appropriations bill some major projects for the state of Oregon.

One of Mike Kirwan's favorite expressions was "You get the point I mean?" He did not publicize what he'd done to the Oregon projects but Wayne Morse soon got the point. Unable to make any headway with Kirwan personally, he appealed to President Kennedy to intervene.

We found ourselves squarely in the middle. Kirwan was a

good, down-the-line Democrat whose support we counted on in many areas. Morse had been our invaluable ally on education legislation. We needed them both and it was in our interest to smooth over the quarrel, if we could. Kennedy, therefore, called in Kirwan, urged him to restore Oregon's projects and suggested that an aquarium might not be the District of Columbia's most urgent social need.

Mike Kirwan stood firm. "My aquarium's gotta go through, Mr. President. And Morse has gotta stop badmouthin' me. You get the point I mean?"

The President got the point, and Kirwan's aquarium bill proceeded through the Congress with no objection from us. Eventually it reached the White House for signature and at that point I called Kirwan.

"Mike," I said, "the President is going to sign your bill and we hope this will solve the problem between you and Senator Morse."

"When is he gonna sign it?" Kirwan asked.

I had to admit I didn't know—the aquarium bill wasn't one of our top priorities.

"I want to know when he's gonna sign it," Mike said. "I want to be there to see him sign it."

It was customary for groups of congressmen and senators to witness the signing of important bills, but since Mike was the only congressman with any interest in his aquarium bill, we arranged a special, one-congressman ceremony for him. Mike looked proudly over Kennedy's shoulder as Kennedy dutifully signed the bill into law. Mike was given the pen that signed the bill, a picture was taken, and Oregon soon got back its projects.

Mike's aquarium, incidentally, was never built because his House colleagues failed to vote the necessary appropriations.

There was never any lack of conflict, drama, excitement, suspense and, indeed, humor, on Capitol Hill. I had little time for the theater in Washington, but my work kept me in the midst of an endlessly fascinating series of human and political dramas. Yet it was more than that, too, and looking back on it now I realize that my feelings about politics began to change during

1961. For a long time I had viewed politics as an exciting game and my part in the game as helping win elections. Once that had been done, I hadn't worried much about what my candidates did when they took office.

Capitol Hill was more complex and exciting—more fun, to be honest about it—than any political campaign, but increasingly I realized that I was doing more than playing an exciting game. My work on Capitol Hill dealt with matters of substance, matters of the utmost national importance—the minimum wage, Medicare, civil rights, education and all the rest of the Democratic legislative agenda. How well I did my job could affect the lives of millions of my fellow Americans.

As a youth in the Depression, I had experienced how hard life can be in America. I had grown up knowing the financial insecurities many people faced throughout their lives. To me, there was nothing abstract about the legislation I fought for. The Republicans could call Medicare "creeping socialism," but it meant that people like my parents could face the hazards of old age with a measure of security. When I worked on the civil rights bills, I recalled that my father's generation had known the prejudice—"No Irish Need Apply."

In short, I took my work seriously. I gave it all I had. We made mistakes and, as I have said, we had our failures, but we had our successes, too, and there is nothing I am more proud of than my contribution to the passage of the Kennedy and Johnson legislative programs.

I learned in my years on Capitol Hill just how difficult it is to achieve social progress in America. Powerful forces are arrayed against any legislative proposal they think will affect their wealth or influence—for every Medicare, one might say, there is an American Medical Association. Sometimes in my mind's eye I saw two great armies facing one another across a vast field of battle. One army—our army—was led by the President and included in its ranks the forces of organized labor, the urban political leaders, the emerging black political spokesmen, and many of the nation's intellectual luminaries.

Ours was a formidable force, and yet facing us was a no less powerful legislative army led by such Republican stalwarts as

Ev Dirksen and Charlie Halleck, backed by the vast resources of the American business community, the major corporations and especially the oil industry, as well as the medical profession and important segments of rural and suburban America.

These two armies fought battle after battle on Capitol Hill, with one now gaining the advantage, then the other. In the long view, in terms of my lifetime, the Democratic force has seemed to move ahead, to win more often than it lost, but it was always slow progress, inch by inch, vote by vote, with much bloodshed and heartbreak along the way.

During the Kennedy years, I was sometimes called upon to make difficult and far-reaching decisions, decisions I had not sought and I could not avoid. One of them came on Kennedy's effort in 1961 to obtain a $1.25 minimum wage.

When the President took office, the minimum wage was still a dollar an hour, $40 a week, in the richest nation in the world. Kennedy felt this was a disgrace and he pledged to do something about it. His proposal was to increase the minimum wage to $1.25 and to extend its coverage to about four million Americans who weren't yet covered.

The House Education and Labor Committee reported out Kennedy's bill, but our head count indicated that we did not have the votes to pass it in its existing form. On March 24 Secretary of Labor Arthur Goldberg and I met in Rayburn's office with Vinson, McCormack, Carl Albert, and Adam Clayton Powell. We went over and over the ground. Vinson felt we could pick up some southern votes if we would retreat to a $1.15 minimum wage. Goldberg and I felt the Administration was committed to the $1.25 figure, yet we recognized that some compromise was necessary to pass the bill.

Rayburn turned to Goldberg and said, "I feel this is a decision the Administration has to make."

"This really is a White House decision," Goldberg responded, nodding to me.

I could have called the President, but I felt that this decision was mine to make, that he would want me to make it because I had all the facts at my disposal.

"We've got to hold with $1.25," I said. "We'll have to cut back on the coverage."

We therefore agreed to drop about a half million of the four million workers to whom we'd hoped to extend minimum-wage coverage. It was a hard concession to make. Those to be dropped included several hundred thousand laundry workers, people who had come to be a symbol of underpaid workers in America. But the cold political fact was that we knew of four or five votes in opposition, because of intense pressure from the laundry lobby, that would be gained by dropping the laundry workers.

I also suggested at this meeting, since we so badly needed southern support, that Carl Albert of Oklahoma, then the Democratic whip, lead debate on the floor for the bill.

"I can't do it, Larry," Albert protested. "I'm not well enough informed on the bill."

The others and I persisted, however, and Albert reluctantly agreed to do so. He went home that night, studied the bill and the committee report on it intensively, and the next day made an absolutely brilliant presentation when the debate was held.

Yet, despite all our efforts, we lost on the House floor that day, by a vote of 186 to 185.

I immediately called the White House to break the news to the President.

"One vote! I can't believe it!" he exclaimed when I told him. In his frustration, I later learned, he plunged his letter opener into the top of his desk.

Yet the minimum-wage battle had a happy ending. The Senate passed the administration bill and the House passed a $1.15 version. In the House-Senate Conference, I once again faced a decision as to what the Administration's position should be. My decision was to agree to a two-step increase, starting with $1.15, then raising it to $1.25 in two years. The House approved the Conference Report, 230-196, giving us substantially what we wanted and involving no real compromise with the $1.25 minimum. Kennedy signed the bill into law on May 5. The AFL-CIO's legislative director, Andy Biemiller, our staunch ally all that spring, was among those present when the bill was signed. Moments later he shook my hand and said, "Larry, we in organized labor have been waiting seven years for this moment—not weeks or months, but seven years!"

Yet the $1.25 minimum wage, which seemed such a breakthrough then, would, with the passage of time and the spread of inflation, come to be inadequate. In the years ahead there would be other battles for a $1.60 minimum, a $2.25 minimum, a $2.50 minimum, and each new struggle would be as difficult as the one before. There are no final victories on Capitol Hill, only steps forward or steps backward, a step at a time.

That same week, the anniversary of his victory in the West Virginia primary, Kennedy had proudly signed the Area Redevelopment Act, a four-year, 451-million-dollar program of grants and loans to aid distressed areas of the country, such as West Virginia, with chronic unemployment. It was a proud moment for Kennedy, for he felt that he had kept his pledge to do something to help the economy of the people of West Virginia who had won his heart during his weeks of campaigning in their state.

Of our defeats, none was more bitter than our inability to pass the bill to provide federal aid to elementary and secondary education. No President had ever been able to overcome the massive political and constitutional problems involved in a program of federal aid to education, but Kennedy had dreamed of making this historic first. He failed because, combined with all the other problems involved, his religion became a divisive issue.

Kennedy, as the first Catholic President and one who had in his campaign promised a strict observance of the church-state separation, believed he could not possibly provide aid in any form—directly or indirectly—to parochial schools in his education bills. His position pleased many Protestants, but it served to unite many Catholic leaders against him and their opposition meant that some Catholic members of Congress would oppose the education bill. We already faced the opposition of most Republicans and many Southerners; to also lose votes among the ninety or so urban Catholic representatives proved, in the end, fatal to the education bill's chances. HEW Secretary Abe Ribicoff urged that the door be left open to some accommodation with the Catholics, but there simply was no give on the part of the President.

There were many ironies to the situation. The first Catholic President was being frustrated on one of his top-priority legislative proposals by leaders of his own Church; they, for their part, had come to feel that the Church's interest in education might be better served by a non-Catholic President and indeed they were right. It was a rather delicate situation.

One evening, for example, as I was having dinner at Paul Young's Restaurant in Washington, Richard Cardinal Cushing, the renowned Catholic prelate, stopped by my table. He was, of course, an old and dear friend of the Kennedy family and had presided at the President's marriage and given a prayer at his Inauguration.

"Tell Jack I'd like to see him, Larry," the Cardinal told me. "I see where Billy Graham has been visiting Jack at the White House. You tell Jack I'd like to visit with him too. Tell him it's okay with me if I come in the back door."

Another irony of the education battle was that the bill was stalled in the very Rules Committee that we had supposedly "packed" in 1961.

This came about when Jim Delaney, a Catholic member from Queens with a heavy Catholic population and a Democrat whose vote we normally could count on, decided that it was unconstitutional to provide aid to public schools and not to Catholic schools. Delaney, by joining with the Republicans and southern conservatives on the Rules Committee, could turn our 8–7 majority around and that is exactly what he did.

Nothing could change Delaney's mind. Had he been bargaining, holding out for some patronage plum, we might have done business, but the only thing he wanted was the one thing Kennedy could not give—federal aid to Catholic schools. Ribicoff and I talked to him many times, to no avail. The President had at least two long, off-the-record talks with him in which he tried desperately to bring Delaney around, but Jim was adamant. He sincerely and deeply believed that he was right and we were wrong, and nothing could persuade him otherwise. Eventually, it was a Protestant President, Lyndon Johnson, who succeeded in bringing about passage of the education bill, largely because he was free to view it as a political problem, not a religious issue.

During the Kennedy administration, the education bill stayed bottled up in the Rules Committee and the Medicare bill met a similar fate in Wilbur Mills's Ways and Means Committee. There were other setbacks, but on balance I thought our 1961 record was a good one, even an outstanding one.

We had sent Congress fifty-three major bills and we had won passage of thirty-three of them. Those thirty-three bills were, by way of contrast, more than had been passed in the final *six* years of the Eisenhower administration.

In his effort to combat the economic recession, Kennedy in his first year had won passage of a new minimum wage with the first expansion of coverage since 1938; a program of aid to dependent children of the unemployed; the area-redevelopment program; and amendments to the Social Security Act, including the first reduction in the retirement age for males from sixty-five to sixty-two.

First-year legislation in foreign affairs included the Peace Corps, $500 million for the Alliance for Progress (a ten-year social and economic plan for the Americas), and the establishment of the U. S. Arms Control and Disarmament Agency. To bolster national security, Kennedy obtained a defense authorization $6 billion above the final Eisenhower budget.

In keeping his promise to "get the country moving," Kennedy succeeded in bringing about passage of the most comprehensive housing program in history; a water-pollution-control bill that doubled the existing program; a community health program that included hospital rehabilitation, community services and nursing homes for the aged; an omnibus farm bill that was the most comprehensive since 1938; an emergency feed grains program.

In the areas of justice and civil rights, bills approved included the first anti-crime bill since 1934, including the long-sought ban on transmitting gambling information; the first federal program to combat juvenile delinquency, providing $30 million for local youth programs; and a two-year extension of the Civil Rights Commission.

We were proud of our record and astounded at the number of reporters who were writing that Kennedy had "failed" with the Congress or was "deadlocked" with the Congress. Thirty-three major bills passed is not failure or deadlock.

Many of our congressional allies were as disturbed as we were by the press commentary. They wondered, as we did, if they had really fought all those battles, taken all those beatings, run all those risks, and finally passed all those bills, only to be told in the newspapers that they had accomplished almost nothing. The President lifted their spirits somewhat with two receptions; one for House Democrats and one for Senate Democrats, held just before Congress adjourned on September 27. My staff had prepared charts showing all the legislation passed during the session and we briefed them on the full story. The President told them, "Here it is, in black and white, on the record. You can go back home and point with pride to the record of this Congress." Some of them, just from reading the papers, hadn't been so sure, but the President's words cheered them, and we had many requests for our fact sheets.

The President, frustrated by the newspaper evaluations, told Ted Sorensen to hold briefings with reporters to show them that our record was better than they had written. Ted arranged to meet with a group of reporters at the home of Carroll Kilpatrick of the Washington *Post*. He asked me to join him and be available for questions. I agreed to attend.

About two dozen reporters attended Ted's briefing. Cocktails were served, but the atmosphere was not one of great warmth. Sorensen went over the legislative record, but the reporters did not seem impressed and they proceeded to state their skepticism. I stayed for a nightcap after Ted left to see if I could get a better idea of the reporters' thinking. Our talks were more pleasant than the earlier session, but the reporters still were by no means convinced that they had underestimated Kennedy's record. To the contrary, they resented what they viewed as an administration snow job. Their stories, as they appeared in the next few days, more often denounced the alleged White House effort to dictate to the press than they praised our legislative achievements.

I don't mean to suggest that every reporter was critical of, or underestimated, Kennedy's success with Congress. For example, Neil MacNeil of *Time*, a close student of Capitol Hill, sent a report to his news magazine in August 1961 that I certainly could not fault. He said in part:

"We must remember in judging the performance that the 87th Congress felt hostility toward Kennedy's program. The loss of those 21 House seats partially explained this. So did the central reading a few months back that the people liked Kennedy but were indifferent about his welfare programs.

"And, despite that hostility, the Congress has passed a large part of his program . . . unmatched since FDR's 1933 session. This has been done. . . . at a time when President Kennedy was suffering continuing failures in foreign policy and in his military adventure in Cuba, a record of failure that could only make it more difficult, not less, to pass a domestic program through a reluctant Congress.

"We think it fair to say that the Kennedy success with his program on Capitol Hill has been the one major bright spot in his Administration's career to date."

As the first session of the Eighty-seventh Congress adjourned and the staff and I looked ahead to the second session in 1962, we agreed that we had made mistakes in our first year and we hoped to correct them. We felt that we had introduced some bills later than we should and with insufficient preparation, and we wanted a tighter, earlier agenda for 1962. We also hoped to achieve better press understanding of our legislative program. Pierre Salinger and his White House press staff were not closely attuned to our work, and neither Sorensen nor I had the time or perhaps the talent to deal with the press in any depth. We often spoke of hiring a skilled press relations man to work exclusively on our legislative program.

We never attained that sort of press operation, but we did carry out a first-rate public relations campaign that helped to pass one of Kennedy's most important 1962 bills, the Trade Expansion Act.

The twenty-year-old Reciprocal Trade Act was scheduled to expire in mid-1962 and the first question we faced was whether to seek a new trade bill or simply a one-year extension of the old bill, thus postponing a fight on a new bill until 1963. The State Department argued for the delay, but I recommended Kennedy push for a bill in 1962, primarily because of encouraging talks I had with Wilbur Mills. Kennedy decided to go. The trade bill became a top priority, and we carried out on its behalf the kind of careful packaging and promotion that I wish we could have given every piece of legislation.

We centered our effort for the trade bill in the White House, to avoid the traditional rivalries between State, Commerce, Agriculture, Labor and other departments concerned with trade issues. We brought in Howard Peterson, a Philadelphia banker, to head a ten-man task force that worked with Congress, the departments, the media, labor, the U. S. Chamber of Commerce and other groups interested in trade policy. The President spoke strongly for the trade bill in his State of the Union message and cabinet members were instructed to support the bill in their speeches. Perhaps most importantly, our efforts with the media were rewarded with almost unanimous support for the bill from major newspapers, magazines and television commentators.

The result was that the trade bill passed both Houses of Congress by resounding margins, and President Kennedy signed the Trade Expansion Act of 1962 into law on October 11, calling it "the most important international piece of legislation since the Marshall Plan." My own feeling, as I watched the bill being signed, was that its success reflected how much we had learned about dealing effectively with Congress. I hoped the smooth sailing of the Trade Expansion Act would be a model for many more bills President Kennedy would introduce in the next six years.

Looking back over what I have written, I realize I have focused on our dealings with the House more than with the Senate. The reason for this is that we had fewer problems in the

Senate. The Democrats had a 65–35 majority there, and even granting the defection of southern senators on some issues, our majority usually held solid. The Senate is by its nature a tidier place—it is much easier to deal with 100 members than with 435. We were aided, in our efforts on the Senate side, by the fact that we never had to go through a period of winning the trust of Majority Leader Mike Mansfield, as we did on the House side with Speaker Rayburn. Mansfield could not have been more helpful; among other things, he made one of his conference rooms available to Mike Manatos and me when we needed working space on the Senate side of Capitol Hill. Hubert Humphrey, the new majority whip, was equally helpful. Most importantly, both Mansfield and Humphrey were fully committed to President Kennedy and his program and he in turn had the utmost confidence in them.

The Senate was the scene in 1962 of an unusual battle that developed over our bill to set up a private corporation to build, launch, and operate communications satellites. We were opposed on this bill by a group of Senate liberals, led by Senators Albert Gore, Estes Kefauver and Wayne Morse, who considered the private corporation a "giveaway" to big business. Our attempts to negotiate with the liberal group failed and they responded with a filibuster on the Senate floor. It was, of course, a rare situation in the Senate to have liberals, not southern conservatives, employing the tactic of unlimited debate to defend a minority position.

In late July, after the filibuster had continued for two weeks and with the liberals showing no signs of weakening, we determined to seek cloture—a two-thirds vote to cut off debate. One Saturday afternoon Senator Robert Kerr, an acknowledged shrewd tactician; Bobby Baker, Secretary for the Majority; Mike Manatos; and I pooled intelligence and concluded that a two-thirds vote for cloture was possible but would be very close. Our problem was that many of the Southerners, who wanted to see the liberals' filibuster halted, were nonetheless reluctant to vote against the principle of unlimited debate, which had served them so well in the past.

Our strategy was to persuade these Southerners to avoid the

dilemma by not voting at all. Our strategy worked. On August 14, for the first time since 1927 and the fifth time in history, the Senate invoked cloture by a vote of 63 to 27, so we had three votes to spare. Of the twenty-two senators from the eleven Confederate states, fifteen followed tradition and voted against cloture, two voted for cloture, and five didn't vote. The five we persuaded not to vote provided our margin of victory.

It was, for us, an odd fight, for *we* were aligned with Ev Dirksen and the southern conservatives against liberal senators who were our customary allies. But we remained convinced that ours was the best possible bill and passing it—as well as winning the cloture fight—were victories for the President.

Medical care for the aged—Medicare, as it came to be called —was a constant concern of ours throughout the Kennedy years. Kennedy had supported Medicare as a senator, and as President he made it one of his top priorities. Wilbur Mills, the powerful chairman of the House Ways and Means Committee was not ready to report the Medicare bill out of his committee, and we could not persuade a majority of the committee to report it out against his wishes. To an extent, Mills's coolness toward Medicare reflected its lack of support in the House as a whole. His attitude was that he was doing us a favor to keep the bill in his committee, because if it came to a vote in the full House we would lose. We didn't accept this. We might have lost on the floor of the House, but we were willing to make a fight of it.

In 1962, as our impasse with Ways and Means continued, Kennedy was urged by some of his advisers to "go to the people" on the Medicare issue via speeches and television statements. I questioned this approach, because I believed that, in dealing with Congress, Kennedy could try to work with Congress or he could declare war on Congress. The latter course was more dramatic but less productive. For the most part, Kennedy chose a strategy of conciliation.

Medicare became an exception, however. He took it to the people, but it did not have the desired effect. The National

Council of Senior Citizens was sponsoring pro-Medicare rallies around the country and had scheduled one in Madison Square Garden on May 20. Kennedy agreed to make a nationally televised address at the rally, as he wanted to leave nothing undone in his support of Medicare.

Unfortunately, his speech failed to arouse grass-roots pressure on Congress, and we only succeeded in annoying Mills, which was my main concern. To get a vote on Medicare in the House, we had to persuade Mills, and you don't persuade Mills with a rally in Madison Square Garden. Kennedy understandably wanted to take his case to the people, but in this particular instance that approach didn't work.

Stymied in Mills's Ways and Means Committee, we still pressed for a vote in the Senate, one that would put Medicare's Senate opponents, at least, on record against it. Senator Clinton P. Anderson, therefore, offered Medicare as an amendment to a House-passed public welfare bill in July. This enabled us to bypass Ways and Means. If we achieved Senate passage, Medicare would then go to a House-Senate conference for final determination. It was a shaky way to do business, one that showed the essential weakness of our position, but it was the best we could do, given our inability to get our bill out of the Ways and Means Committee.

As the Senate vote approached I sent the President our head count, which showed the Senate divided 50–50 on Medicare. I added: "Senator Randolph has a problem."

Senator Jennings Randolph of West Virginia soon became *our* problem. He should have been with us, for he was a Democrat from an economically depressed state with a generally liberal record. But we soon began to fear he was following the lead of Senator Robert Kerr, the leader of the opposition to Medicare. Senator Randolph's problem was that his state had overspent its federal welfare funds by some $11 million and he was fearful that the welfare bill would be delayed by attempting to attach Medicare to it. Senator Kerr proposed to help out West Virginia by adding a provision to the welfare bill that absolved the state from having to make up the squandered $11 million. In return, Randolph was expected to vote with Kerr against Medicare.

On the day before the Senate vote, HEW Secretary Abe Ribicoff and Under Secretary Wilbur Cohen went to see Randolph and assured him that he did not have to count on Kerr to take care of West Virginia on the $11 million, because we would do the same. In the meantime, we had been doing all we could to bring pressure on Randolph from back home. We had called every labor leader and politician we knew, urging them to speak to Randolph on behalf of Medicare. All this time, Randolph was noncommittal, stating he hadn't made up his mind. But when the vote came, he stuck with Kerr and we lost by 52 to 48. If Randolph had voted with us, Carl Hayden had promised to do the same. We would have had a tie, which would have been broken by Vice President Johnson.

When you lose, you're supposed to say you didn't do all you should have done, but I don't know what more we could have done to bring Randolph around. At that point, as far as 1962 was concerned, Medicare changed from a legislative issue to a political issue.

When Congress adjourned on October 13, I felt the year had been a successful one, perhaps even more so than 1961. We had failed to pass Medicare, the education bills, or the proposed Department of Urban Affairs, but we had obtained passage of the trade bill, the first omnibus tax reform bill since 1954, the UN bond issue, the International Wheat Agreement (treaty), the Communications Satellite Act, a $435-million Manpower Development and Training Act to provide job training for the unemployed, $400 million in special accelerated public works funds, a record budget of $5.4 billion to expand space exploration, a drug-labeling act, the air-pollution-control study, the poll-tax constitutional amendment, a 32-million-dollar program of assistance to educational television, the creation of the Institute of Child Health and Human Development, the mass immunization bill and increased disability compensation to two million veterans, among others. In all, Kennedy obtained passage of forty of his fifty-four major proposals for 1962 and yet we continued to read about his "deadlock" with Congress.

Those who wrote of a deadlock often attributed it to Kennedy's inability to gain support from southern congressmen. To the contrary, our success in 1962 was largely due to substantial southern support. Our Republican support in the House had diminished steadily. Twenty-two Republicans had voted with us on the Rules fight in early 1961, but by 1962 we were lucky to pick up four or five Republican votes on most bills and often we got none. Thus, we now needed half the Southerners to pass any given bill and more often than not we got them.

The Southerners were never a monolithic bloc. They were individuals with individual problems. They were liberal on some issues and conservative on others. I found the majority of them to be men of purpose, men who wanted to support the President whenever they could and still survive politically.

Henry Hall Wilson compiled the voting records of ninety-nine Democrats from eleven southern states on four key votes in 1962—the recommittal motions on the farm bill, the trade bill, and the tax bill, and the final vote on the debt-limit increase. Forty-two of the Southerners voted with us on all four issues. Twenty-two voted with us on three of the four. Eleven supported us on two of the four votes. Six supported us once and only thirteen did not support us at all.

We felt these figures showed substantial southern support for Kennedy and reflected his increasing personal popularity with the Southerners. They deserved credit for the support they gave us under what was often difficult political circumstances then. They received little in return other than a thank you and a pat on the back.

VII

POLITICS, CAMELOT, AND DALLAS

WITH ADJOURNMENT of Congress, we could turn our full attention to the congressional elections that were only three weeks away. It was imperative that we break the long-standing tradition that the party in power loses congressional seats in off-year elections. We had a slim majority in Congress, at best, and any Democratic losses, especially in the House, would have killed our chances of enacting Kennedy's programs in 1963 and 1964.

I had, of course, been thinking about the congressional elections since I started my work on Capitol Hill. Whenever we tried to force a vote on bills such as Medicare, for which we felt we had popular support, we were in part trying to put the Republicans on record against those programs and thus give their Democratic opponents issues in the 1962 elections. And my office enforced strict rules to insure that Democrats who supported the President could make the first public announcements of federal grants and programs in their states and districts to their advantage back home.

Early in 1962 I sent Kennedy a memo outlining a program for his personal participation in the 1962 congressional elections. I proposed a series of coffee hours for groups of Democratic senators and representatives at which photographs with the President could be taken for campaign use. I urged him to make a series of radio and television tapes endorsing Democratic candidates. Of the final weeks of the campaign, I wrote:

"One suggestion is a nationwide 15-minute television talk for use late in the campaign.

"Your personal tours ought to be concentrated in a key few Senatorial and Gubernatorial races. Activities in the House campaigns are centered in approximately 50–60 key districts (some 30-odd Democratic and 20-odd Republican seats will be the battlegrounds). You could render most assistance to these battleground contests by having the Democratic incumbents or candidates brought in to meet you when you are in the immediate vicinity."

Kennedy followed most of my suggestions, at least until the Cuban missile crisis erupted in mid-October. This forced him to cut off his active campaigning, but his firm resolution of that crisis was to be a main factor in the elections.

Neither our legislative activity nor the congressional elections took place in a vacuum. Both were profoundly affected by external events, both foreign and domestic, that influenced the President's popularity with the Congress and the public. In addition to the missile crisis, two other events in 1962 proved to be political pluses for the President: his bold actions in April to force the steel companies to rescind a price increase that he viewed as inflationary, and his use of federal marshals to insure the court-ordered enrollment of James Meredith, a twenty-nine-year-old Negro, at the University of Mississippi in late September.

Kennedy's firmness in both these encounters, followed by his leadership in the Cuban missile crisis, impressed the public with his courage and therefore bolstered his—and his party's—political standing.

To be sure, the conflict with the steel companies abruptly ended his honeymoon with big business, but that had been an uneasy alliance at best. It isn't realistic for a liberal Democratic administration to expect to be supported for long by big business, not if it pursues its commitments to the workingman and to social reforms. It was probably just as well that Kennedy's break with business came in a clear-cut confrontation in which he was in the right—and in which he prevailed.

The Meredith episode certainly hurt us in the South, but Kennedy's civil rights program had already hurt us there and his firm support of Meredith, on balance, probably helped us more in the rest of the country than it affected our prospects in the South.

I was with Kennedy on the long night of September 30 when the crisis at the University of Mississippi finally erupted. Earlier that week, Mississippi Governor Ross Barnett had sent state patrolmen to stop Meredith's enrollment at the university. Finally, cited for contempt by a federal appeals court, Barnett agreed to admit Meredith and promised the President and Attorney General Bob Kennedy that the state police would keep order. Barnett asked that Meredith enter the Oxford, Mississippi, campus on that Sunday, when most students would be away. Bob Kennedy agreed to this, but sent a force of U.S. marshals to the campus as insurance.

Ken and I were called to the White House about 6 P.M. and went immediately to the Cabinet Room. The President joined us shortly, and later, Bob Kennedy arrived with Burke Marshall, the assistant Attorney General for civil rights. Already we were getting grim reports from Mississippi. Nicholas Katzenbach, the Deputy Attorney General who was with the U.S. marshals in the university's Administration Building, reported by telephone that an angry mob was forming and that the state troopers were nowhere to be seen. We adjourned to the Oval Office, where the President paced the floor.

"What's going on?" the President kept asking his brother. "I thought this had all been agreed to."

Bob was equally disturbed. He had trusted Governor Barnett, but apparently Barnett had double-crossed him and the President.

Kennedy had scheduled a television speech on the Oxford situation for seven-thirty that evening, but he postponed it as matters worsened. The U.S. marshals, led by the late Jim McShane, had formed a protective ring around the Administration Building and, as a result, had become the targets of the bottle-throwing, brick-heaving mob. The marshals were armed only with tear gas. Kennedy went ahead with his speech at 10 P.M. and, immediately after the speech, called and talked with Katzenbach again. He could hear gunfire in the background as Katzenbach told of wounded marshals being carried into the building. "It was like the Alamo," one participant related later.

According to Katzenbach, there seemed to be a real possibility that the building might be overrun and some of the marshals killed. Meredith himself, who had been hidden in a dormitory room, was in imminent danger if he were discovered by the mob.

Kennedy finally ordered U. S. Army troops to the campus. The troops had to come from Memphis, but as the hours passed, they made no progress toward Oxford. Katzenbach warned that the marshals could not hold out much longer if the troops did not arrive.

"Where are the troops?" the President demanded of Cyrus Vance, the Secretary of the Army, but no one seemed to know. The President talked on the phone at one point with the general who was supposedly leading the troops to Oxford and the general indicated he was awaiting orders from the Pentagon.

In his frustration, Kennedy spoke angrily and bitterly to us about the military. "They always give you their pitch about their instant reaction and their split-second timing, but it never works out," he said. "No wonder it's so hard to win a war." I felt he was also reflecting on his experience with the military and the CIA during the Bay of Pigs fiasco.

As dawn approached, an uneasy truce settled over the campus—the marshals had held off the mob. Eventually the troops arrived and Meredith enrolled in the university. We at the White House were stunned with disbelief. It was amazing, for us and for Kennedy, to see how even a President could be misled and disobeyed. Ken and I gave what encouragement and moral support we could, although I don't know why Kennedy had called us there, except to have old friends on hand during one of the worst nights of his career. We had been through a lot together, but never anything quite as frustrating as that.

Three weeks later I was with Kennedy as he campaigned in the Midwest on behalf of our congressional candidates. And I was with Kennedy in his Chicago hotel suite on Saturday, October 20, when he suddenly called in Pierre Salinger and instructed him to tell the press that he had a cold and was canceling his travel schedule to return to the White House.

I was vague as to what was happening. Kennedy didn't give any details and I didn't ask. When our plane landed at Andrews Air Force Base outside Washington, I flew with Kennedy on the helicopter back to the White House. He sat staring silently out the window, chin in hand, obviously in deep thought.

I had no direct involvement in the emergent Cuban missile crisis other than to arrange for and attend the meetings where the President briefed the congressional leaders. While Kennedy and his national security advisers pondered the risks of nuclear war, I tried to focus on the congressional elections. However, I did have one indirect contact with the crisis that, in retrospect, perhaps has a certain grim humor to it.

As nuclear war seemed even a remote possibility, General Chester V. (Ted) Clifton, the President's military adviser, came to my office and told me there was a contingency plan to evacuate the President and his chief advisers to a huge bomb shelter somewhere under the Catoctin Mountains in Maryland, where the government would continue to function. He said that I was among those chosen for survival and that, in fact, I was authorized to take along one secretary. I gave him Phyllis Maddock's name and then inquired about the fate of my wife.

The general explained that Elva was not part of the official party to be whisked away by helicopter to the under-the-mountain sanctuary, but that provision had also been made for her. He gave me a large envelope with instructions for Elva, marked TOP SECRET, and he said it was not to be opened until an alert was sounded. I took it home to Elva, who decided that despite the TOP SECRET instructions, she would like to take an advance look. Once she had read it, she told me she guessed she was doomed, because it involved some rather complicated instructions. She was to put an enclosed sticker on the windshield of her car, then drive down this street to that highway, et cetera—supposedly everyone would clear the way for her—until she reached her designated bomb shelter—all this while

Phyllis and I were safely underground somewhere in Maryland. The whole thing was ridiculous, but deadly serious, too.

One interesting sidelight of the 1962 campaign was Ted Kennedy's race for the Senate in Massachusetts. At the outset, the President had not been enthusiastic about his brother's running. He had to consider how Ted's candidacy would affect his own position. He knew Ted's candidacy would revive the charges of "dynasty" and "nepotism" that had been heard when he appointed Bob as his Attorney General. Thus, the President's basic attitude was that it might be better if Ted ran for state office, perhaps state attorney general, and think about the U. S. Senate later.

The President suggested that I might talk with Ted and point out some of the drawbacks. I didn't follow through on this suggestion, as I felt this was a family matter and an outsider should not interfere. And once Ted decided to run, the President enthusiastically backed him all the way. We never doubted Ted would win. Along with his obvious potential, he had the Kennedy name and the Kennedy organization behind him and, in Massachusetts, that combination was and is unbeatable.

On Election Night, as the first returns came in, I went to the President's office and advised him that Congressman Frank W. Burke of Louisville, Kentucky, a staunch supporter of ours, had been defeated.

"It looks like a damn long night, Larry," he said. I agreed it could be and hurried back to my office to await further returns.

Over the years, the party in power had lost an average of forty-four House seats and five Senate seats in the off-year elections. After all the 1962 results were in, our party lost only five seats in the House and actually gained two seats in the Senate. As far as history was concerned, we had won a victory; but as far as our legislative prospects for 1963–64 were concerned, we faced two more years of the same tough struggle.

The Congress in 1963 closely resembled its predecessor—the final record was similar and talk of a "stalemate" continued. Yet, shortly after Kennedy's death, my office calculated that of our fifty-eight "must" bills for the year, thirty-five had been passed and signed into law.

Among the successes were the approval of the Nuclear Test Ban Treaty, expansion of the Peace Corps, the Clean Air Act, Water Pollution Control, extension of the Juvenile Delinquency Act, the District of Columbia Cultural Center (which became the Kennedy Center for the Performing Arts), a higher education bill, education bills to train teachers of retarded children and to provide aid to medical schools and vocational schools, an equal-pay-for-women bill, the mental-health and mental retardation act, a child-health bill, an increased authorization for housing programs for the elderly, increased benefits for the families of veterans, a $450-million appropriation for accelerated public works, establishment of a Commission on Science and Technology, and a *permanent* increase in the size of the House Rules Committee.

One fact that has seldom been noted is that, at the time of Kennedy's death, we had already made legislative breakthroughs on several major bills that later achieved final passage. For example, on the very morning of Kennedy's assassination, Henry Hall Wilson and Wilbur Mills, after weeks of negotiations and discussions, finally reached agreement on a formula to finance Medicare that was acceptable both to Mills and to the Administration. Thus, with Mills's objections met, the passage of Medicare was inevitable. Henry, bursting with excitement, tried to call me in Texas but was told that the President and his party had just left for Dallas.

The previous month, Kennedy, by his personal intervention, had assured the approval of his civil rights bill by the House Judiciary Committee.

It is a well-known fact that Kennedy, having promised civil rights action in his 1960 campaign, did little with the Congress in this area during his presidency. He took certain executive actions, and his Justice Department was vigorous in promoting voter rights and school desegregation in the South (the locus of most civil rights activity in those simpler days) but he didn't introduce substantial civil rights legislation until the summer of 1963. The reason was simple. The Rules Committee fight had shown us how precarious our congressional majority was. We needed the Southerners to have any majority at all, and we would lose them if we pushed for a civil rights bill; so Kennedy did what he could by executive action, and by his public statements, and waited for the proper time to go to the Congress.

By the summer of 1963, the national mood was beginning to change. The sit-ins and the use of police dogs and fire hoses on demonstrators in the South, and the eloquence of Dr. Martin Luther King and other leaders, had dramatized the issue, and had made it morally imperative that the President take action, and perhaps politically possible that he succeed. Thus, on June 19, he sent to Congress the most far-reaching civil rights bill ever proposed. Congress had in years past defeated many civil rights bills far more tame than this one. It included a ban on discrimination in places of public accommodation, it gave authority for the Attorney General to seek desegregation of public education on his own initiative when students or their parents could not, and it created a Community Relations Service to work with local communities in search of racial progress.

Bipartisan support for this bill was imperative—we were sure to lose many southern Democrats, so the bill could not pass unless we gained Republicans who had not traditionally supported civil rights legislation. At the outset, we thought that the Senate minority leader, Ev Dirksen, might be the key figure in the bill's passage but as it turned out, a truly central figure was Dirksen's counterpart on the House side, minority leader Charlie Halleck, the other half of the celebrated "Ev and Charlie Show," as Dirksen and Halleck's weekly news conference was called by reporters.

Our first obstacle was the House Judiciary Committee, which had as its chairman the venerable Emanuel (Manny) Celler of Brooklyn, and as its ranking Republican William McCulloch of Piqua, Ohio. Both Celler and McCulloch were working hard to see that the Judiciary Committee reported a realistic bill, one that could be passed by the full House and the Senate. However, some liberals on the committee were pushing for a bill that we considered unrealistic, one that simply went too far ever to be passed by Congress. Opponents of civil rights on the committee gladly joined the liberals in supporting the stronger bill, hoping thereby to guarantee that no civil rights bill would pass. Faced with this opposition, our job in the Administration was to persuade the Judiciary Committee to pass a bill with a realistic chance of passing Congress. To that end, Attorney General Bob Kennedy and his deputy, Nick Katzenbach, lobbied tirelessly with the Judiciary Committee, and my staff and I did all we could.

But it was not enough. I finally concluded that we were not going to get our bill out of Judiciary unless the President himself intervened—and intervened successfully. And the person for him to intervene with, I thought, was not committee chairman Celler, or Republican spokesman McCulloch—they had been wonderful, but they simply hadn't been able to swing the votes—but with Charlie Halleck, the minority leader.

It was a measure of our desperation that I urged Kennedy to deal directly with Halleck. The crusty Republican leader fought us daily on the House floor. He was a master of parliamentary procedure and tactical maneuvering, and he was a staunch conservative. Yet he was also a professional, and a man I had always been able to deal with in a cordial manner. Sometimes, before a major House vote, he would invite me to his hideaway office for a martini and a bit of banter, which would usually go something like this:

"Well, I think we're going to beat your pants off tomorrow, O'Toole." He, for some reason always called me O'Toole, much as Ev Dirksen always called me Lawrence.

"No, Charlie, I think you'll find we've got the votes."

"Oh, do you? Well, what's your head count?"

"Well, let's just say I'm confident."

We both had our head counts, down to the last vote, but neither of us was about to reveal this prediction to the other. So we would joke and the next day we'd see who was right.

My relations with Halleck, although cordial, had not been extensive, and Kennedy's had been very limited. But he seemed our last hope of rallying the needed Republican votes in the Judiciary Committee, so Kennedy invited him to his office for a talk. And during that talk, Kennedy discovered something that surprised us, although perhaps it shouldn't have—Halleck was a conservative, he had fought us on countless issues, but he favored civil rights. Indeed, he seemed flattered to be called upon to help.

"Mr. President," he said, "I'd be pleased to talk to some of my fellows and see what I can do. Give me until tomorrow noon, then I'll call you and tell you what I've been able to do."

The next day, I went to Kennedy's office to await the noon call from Halleck that, it seemed, would decide the fate of the civil rights bill. Noon came and went with no call from him. As the minutes ticked by, Kennedy and I gazed at each other in despair. The thought crossed our minds that we had been had, that the crafty Republican leader had only been pulling our legs with his promise of co-operation. Finally, at around 12:45, Kennedy could stand the suspense no longer.

"I'm going to call him," he told me.

It was a measure of his anxiety about the civil rights bill that he was willing to call a Republican leader who failed to make a promised call to the President and who, for all we knew, was sitting in his office with a few cronies having the laugh of his life.

But, once again the President's instinct was good. For when he got Halleck on the line, the minority leader said:

"Mr. President, I'm terribly sorry, I had a hard time catching a couple of my fellows and I just talked to the last one. But I was just about to call you with good news—I've got you the votes to get your bill out of the committee."

Kennedy was overjoyed. With the help of Halleck, and McCulloch as well, he had achieved a major breakthrough. Halleck took some heat from right-wing Republicans, who placed a furled umbrella on his desk to suggest that he had capitulated to the enemy, but he kept his promise and the administration bill was reported out of the Judiciary Committee in late October.

The bipartisan support of the civil rights bill in Judiciary set the stage for bipartisan passage of the bill, by a wide margin,

by the full House. This, in turn, paved the way for bipartisan
passage of the bill in the Senate the next summer. Lyndon
Johnson was President then, of course, and along with him,
Senate minority leader Ev Dirksen rightly received a great
deal of credit for making possible the passage of the civil
rights bill. With all due credit to Dirksen, I think that the
House action had made Senate approval almost inevitable,
and that the unsung hero in this affair has been the other half
of the Ev and Charlie team, Charlie Halleck.

My point is that in both the case of the Medicare bill and of
the civil rights bill, Kennedy had through hard, patient, often
frustrating effort, laid the groundwork for the eventual passage that came under his successor.

I believe that if Kennedy had lived, he would have defeated
Goldwater by a margin similar to Johnson's; he would, therefore, have been backed, in 1965, by the same solid Democratic
congressional majority Johnson had; and he would have
achieved a legislative record in 1965–66 comparable to Johnson's. This, admittedly, is speculation and cannot be proved.
I believe it can be said, however, that Kennedy's legislative
record in 1961–63, with a narrow working majority in the
House, was a most impressive one.

I realize my evaluation conflicts with the assessments of
some journalists who have written about the Kennedy presidency. I firmly believe, however, that these journalists have
tended to overemphasize the few legislative failures in 1961–
63 and have tended to underestimate both the quantity and
the quality of the scores of bills that were passed and became
law. I also realize I am a biased observer of the Kennedy years,
but I urge future historians and scholars *not* to accept without
question the conventional wisdom that Kennedy's record with
Congress was mediocre. Rather, the historians should study
the facts, the record of past Presidents, the make-up of the
Congress, and the actual bills passed.

Sometimes I read about the golden days of Camelot, but I
can't say I remember the Kennedy years that way. Mainly I
remember working like hell. I never played a large role in
Kennedy's social life; Kennedy had his political friends and

his social friends and he usually kept them separate. Camelot may have been burning bright in 1961–63, but if so, I missed it.

Some Friday afternoons I would be working in my White House office and I would hear the roar of a helicopter. I might step to my window and watch as the President, Jackie, the children, and the dogs departed for a weekend at the Cape. Then I would return to whatever head-counting conference I was in or to the thirty or forty phone calls that were usually backed up on my desk. During the 1950s, Elva and I had often rented a cottage at the Cape during the summers, but I don't think I was ever back there during the Kennedy or Johnson years. There just wasn't time. Nor was there time for me to indulge my love of pro basketball—I think I saw one game during the 1960s. Nor was there much opportunity, except on occasional trips to New York, for me to go to the theater. There was just too much work.

This is not to say I had no social life. I may have attended more receptions and dinners and cocktail parties than any other man in Washington during the Kennedy and Johnson years—sometimes Elva would bring my black tie and I'd change in my office and we'd be off for three or four affairs in one evening—but it was all part of my work. At a White House reception for members of Congress and their wives, Elva and I would post ourselves by the door and greet all the guests as they entered and we would be the last to leave when the party was over. It was difficult for me to relax; there was always one more congressman to speak to, one more problem to be heard, one more vote to be sought.

One of the focal points of my "social" life in my White House years was the presidential yacht, the Sequoia. I discovered that the yacht was available to me and, moreover, that most congressmen valued a cruise on the Sequoia almost as highly as a visit to the White House. Frequently, therefore, I would invite groups of fifteen or twenty congressmen and their wives for an evening cruise, complete with drinks, buffet dinner, and some entertainment. In the summers, when the weather was best, we sometimes took the Sequoia out two or three times a week. Cruising down the Potomac under the stars on the President's yacht was about as pleasant a way to spend an evening as I ever experienced and it was also the most effective lobbying device I ever found.

A typical cruise would take us out to Mount Vernon, George Washington's home, several miles upriver in Virginia. At Mount Vernon, by tradition, a record of "The Star-Spangled Banner" would be played. The crew would stand at attention along with the guests and then the captain would turn the *Sequoia* around and head back, at a leisurely rate toward Washington.

Elva, as hostess, kept the parties light and informal. We brought along an accordion player for sing-alongs and we often invited our friend, Congressman Eddie Boland, who loved to sing Irish ballads. Elva would ask Eddie to start off with "When Irish Eyes Are Smiling," and soon we'd have everyone singing, starting with their state songs. The Texans could always be trusted to give us "The Eyes of Texas" and other Lone Star State favorites. At Elva's urging, couples would also dance as we cruised under the stars.

The cruises, however pleasant, were also work. I usually had two or three "targets" for the evening and, in this informal, relaxed setting, I was sometimes able to win co-operation that I might not have achieved in someone's office on Capitol Hill. It was all part of the process.

I suppose we must have taken the *Sequoia* out forty or fifty times in those years. The truth is that, after a while, you wished you were home with a good book. Only once did Elva and I use the yacht for our personal pleasure. One Saturday afternoon we, the O'Donnells, and the members of my congressional relations staff took our families for a cruise.

The O'Brien Sunday morning brunches for members of Congress and other political figures also continued and, on occasion, we would have a congressman to our house during the week. Once in 1963, during discussions on the tax bill, I told Elva that Wilbur Mills was coming for breakfast the next morning. Elva was fond of Wilbur and his wife Polly, and she was up early fixing hot muffins, fresh orange juice, sausage, and eggs and all the trimmings. When Mills arrived he said, to her dismay, he never ate breakfast and would only have a cup of coffee while we talked.

I often had lunch or dinner with members of the Washington press corps, and these events were, of course, a combination of business and pleasure. Some of the journalists were wonderful, delightful people, but there was always the fact that they were seeking information and I wanted to present our legislative program in a good light. Early in 1961 I began having frequent lunches with two of Washington's finest newspapermen, Hugh Sidey of *Time*, whom I'd met during the 1960 campaign, and Peter Lisagor of the Chicago *Daily News*. These were convivial, lighthearted luncheons with much story telling and little politics, and they continue on today.

There were many pleasant dinners with the Joseph Alsops, the Rowland Evanses, and the Joseph Krafts. Dinner with Joe Alsop was more enjoyable than lunch with him. Lunch was business and Joe sometimes appeared to be seeking not so much my views as my confirmation of his views. On the other hand, dinner at the Alsop home always meant the best in food and wine and a fascinating mix of Washington's political, journalistic and social luminaries. We met Alice Roosevelt Longworth, the ageless, sharp-witted grande dame of Washington society, at the Alsop home and we were invited to dinner at Mrs. Longworth's home near DuPont Circle. One evening, as we walked up the stairs to Mrs. Longworth's drawing room, we passed a huge tiger skin that was hanging on the wall, one from an animal I assumed had been shot by her father, Teddy Roosevelt. I noticed that one of the tiger's paws was missing; then, in the drawing room, I saw the paw on top of the piano.

"Mrs. Longworth," I inquired, "how did the paw get separated from the tiger?"

"Oh, Stew shook hands with it one evening," she said, referring to Stewart Alsop, the columnist, "and the paw came off in his hand, so I just put it on the piano."

Some of my most pleasant evenings were spent in New York, when I was able to get away from the pressures of Washington for a few days. Elva and I went to New York in May 1962 for the Democratic fund-raiser at Madison Square Garden, held in conjunction with President Kennedy's birthday. Marilyn Monroe sang an unforgettable "Happy Birthday to You" to Kennedy—a highlight of the evening. Later Arthur Krim gave a party at his townhouse for about a hundred people. Arthur was both the head of United Artists and a major Democratic fund-raiser and he, therefore, moved at the top levels of both the political and the entertainment worlds. Marilyn Monroe was at the party, and I chatted with her, but I don't recall that she said anything memorable. She seemed a quiet, rather shy person. I recall much more vividly that night seeing Jimmy Durante, one of America's great comedians, and Bill Green, one of America's great politicians, singing a duet.

Elva and I would use our infrequent New York trips to catch up on our theatergoing. On a typical evening, we would have dinner at Toots Shor's Restaurant (Toots and his wife "Baby" had become fast friends of ours), go to a play, and then drop by Sardi's Restaurant. Often we would run into Leonard Lyons, the columnist, whom I had met through Toots Shor. Occasionally we would join Leonard as he made his rounds of Manhattan's renowned night clubs. We might catch the show at the Copacabana or one of the other few remaining night clubs. It was ideal to go with Leonard, because we were always taken directly to a ringside table.

Sometimes we would drop by the Plaza Hotel, where Elva and I usually stayed in New York, to catch the show in the Persian Room. Elva might then go on up to bed while Leonard and I continued on our rounds. This was in the heyday of the discotheques and we visited most of them—Arthur's, Trudy Heller's, the Electric Circus, and others whose names are lost to me now—and generally we would close out the evening with a late stop at P. J. Clarke's, the well-known pub on Third Avenue.

Leonard is a small, quick man who had studied to be a lawyer but had soon discovered that he loved being a columnist more. He could stand in the doorway of a club, sweep his eyes over the room, and tell me in seconds whether there was anyone present I should meet. He would usually drop me at a table, then move briskly around the room with his notebook out, sometimes trailed by press agents, as he pursued his chronicle of New York after dark.

I tried to keep as much of Saturday and Sunday as possible open for my family, but I rarely succeeded. It's the old story of life in Washington: there's never enough time for both politics and a family life. We were fortunate, I suppose, that Larry had gone through his formative years during the 1950s, a more relaxed time for me, and was about ready to go out on his own when the hectic Washington years began. He always gave us reason to be proud of him. In June 1963, Elva and I attended Larry's graduation ceremonies at Georgetown Prep. When the various awards were given out, Larry was honored for having the highest grade average in his French class and the second highest over-all grade average in his class.

When the ceremony was over I shook his hand and gave him my congratulations.

"This is wonderful, Larry," I told him. "I never knew you were doing so well."

"You never asked me, Dad," he replied.

In June 1963, when Kennedy was about to leave on his European trip, he arranged for all members of the White House staff of Irish descent to be flown to Ireland for his visit there. We soon discovered a high percentage of "instant" Irish-Americans on the staff and a party of about fifty of us set off for Ireland on one of the presidential back-up planes.

We met the President—fresh from his triumphant stop in West Berlin—at the Dublin Airport and he began a tour of the country of his ancestors. I went with him by helicopter. The visit deeply moved him and rekindled in him a sense of his Irish heritage.

When we reached County Cork, where my parents were born, a motorcade took us to the Cork City Hall, and there, along with the city dignitaries, was my aunt Julia Sweeney, my mother's youngest sister. Kennedy had assigned someone to find out which of his staff members had relatives still living in Ireland. My Aunt Julia lived in Dunmanway, a town near Cork, and Dave Powers had several cousins, who were also at the City Hall ceremony.

My Aunt Julia, an articulate, gray-haired woman with a slight brogue, was making the most of her opportunity. She had brought some neighbors with her and they were thrilled to watch from the VIP section as Kennedy addressed the huge crowd and even more thrilled when, at the end of his remarks, Kennedy said:

"Two of my close associates, Larry O'Brien and Dave Powers, have relatives who are with us today, and I'd like to ask Larry and Dave to introduce them."

So Dave and I presented our Irish relatives while the audience cheered.

At the reception following the speech, my Aunt Julia was introduced to the President.

"I'm pleased to meet you, Mr. Kennedy," my aunt said. "You're very fortunate to have my nephew Lawrence working for you."

The President grinned at her and said, "You may be right."

As the reception ended, I said my good-bys to Aunt Julia, and she looked at me in surprise.

"Lawrence, aren't you going to stay for a few days?"

Fifty thousand people were cheering outside, the motorcade was starting to move, and I told my aunt that I'd better leave Cork immediately or I might never get out. On a later trip to Ireland, I visited Aunt Julia's home in Dunmanway and noted three pictures on her wall—Jesus Christ, John F. Kennedy, and Lawrence O'Brien.

At Shannon Airport, a day or two later, we were all to leave Ireland—Kennedy to continue on to Italy, the rest of us to fly back to Washington. As Kennedy boarded his plane, a choir sang a beautiful version of "Come Back to Erin" and Kennedy was deeply and visibly moved, as were we all. If there was a dry eye at the airport, I missed it.

Once Kennedy was aloft, I fell into conversation with Angier (Angie) Biddle Duke, who was then Chief of Protocol. Angie had a small jet plane that he was about to take to Rome to continue with the presidential party.

"How many will that plane hold, Angie?" I said, half in jest.

"Three," he said. "Come on and go with me."

"I'd love to," I replied, "but I've been traveling with Eddie Boland and Dick Donahue, so there are three of us."

Eddie and Dick appeared on the scene about then and confessed that they, too, would be tempted by a side visit to Rome.

"I'll tell you what," Angie said. "You fellows take my plane and I'll catch a ride on the President's cargo plane. The President's limousine is in it and I'll curl up in the back seat and get some sleep."

"Oh no, we couldn't do that," we protested, but eventually we did. Angie went off to travel in the cargo plane, leaving Boland, Donahue and O'Brien with his plane and pilot.

Then Eddie Boland had second thoughts.

"I think I'll just stay in Ireland and look up some relatives," he said.

It was too late to rescue Angie Duke from the cargo plane, so Dick Donahue and I climbed into Duke's plane and flew to Rome. An embassy official met us at the airport, expecting to find Duke, but finding instead O'Brien and Donahue, who reported that the Chief of Protocol would arrive much later in the cargo plane.

We spent three enjoyable days in Rome and then flew back to Washington on the President's back-up plane. For many days everyone in the White House was aglow from the Ireland trip, including the President. He was given records of the choir that had sung good-by to him at Shannon Airport and of the other groups that had serenaded him along the way. He often played them over the next few months.

Not long after our return Drew Pearson obtained a list of the White House staff people who'd flown to Ireland and published a column about the waste of the taxpayers' money. That was one column that nobody in the White House gave a damn about.

By November 1963 it seemed possible that Senator Barry Goldwater might be the Republican nominee for President the following year. We viewed Goldwater as an ultra-conservative, out of touch with the American political mainstream and thus the easiest man for Kennedy to defeat. President Kennedy's trip to Texas in November was a bit of early-bird campaigning in a key state, and it was also part of his continuing effort to increase his personal influence with powerful members of Congress.

The Texas trip came about at the request of Al Thomas, the Houston congressman who was chairman of the Appropriations Subcommittee on Independent Offices (which approved funds for executive agencies, including NASA). From the day he became President, Kennedy had given special attention to Thomas. He was often invited to the White House and the President would go up to the Hill for the annual Al Thomas Gymnasium Party—for Thomas was the patron saint of the House gym and each year his colleagues would give a party for him there. An easy relationship had developed between Thomas and Kennedy. Kennedy would joke about the extraordinary amount of space-program activity that Thomas had managed to direct back to Houston and would ask if maybe a little of it couldn't go to Massachusetts.

All this attention had paid off, as Thomas' voting record became distinctly more pro-Administration. Thus, one day in the early fall, when Thomas came to my office and asked if the President would be interested in attending a testimonial dinner to be given for him in Houston in late November, I took him directly into the President's office. Thomas repeated how pleased he would be if the President would attend and Kennedy said he would give it serious consideration.

Texas was a long way to go for one testimonial dinner, so once the Houston visit was agreed to we made plans for other stops in San Antonio, Fort Worth, Dallas, and Austin. We'd barely carried Texas in 1960 and we hoped this trip would generate the enthusiasm we needed to give us a more comfortable margin in 1964.

Jackie, who wasn't always enthusiastic about political journeys and who had suffered a miscarriage only three months before, decided to join her husband on the Texas trip. Kennedy was delighted. When we left Washington on the morning of the twenty-first, he was concerned about the weather in Texas, afraid it might not be right for Jackie's wardrobe, and he kept asking General Godfrey McHugh, one of his military aides, to check it.

The weather, the general reported, was variable, perhaps a little warm.

"Damn it, Mac, make up your mind," Kennedy protested. He struck me as being as excited as a little boy to have Jackie accompanying him on this trip.

We flew first to San Antonio, where Vice President Johnson joined us; on to Houston for the Al Thomas dinner and a tour of the Space Center; and then to Fort Worth, arriving around midnight. By the end of that first day, we realized we had a problem on our hands. A bitter feud existed between Vice President Johnson and Texas Senator Ralph Yarborough. Johnson, as Vice President, had continued to involve himself in matters of Texas patronage, and Yarborough, as the state's senior senator and an old foe of Johnson's in Texas politics, bitterly resented what he regarded as a challenge to his prerogatives. Consequently, Yarborough refused to ride in the same car with Johnson. That quickly became the big news story in Texas, so big it threatened to overshadow the visit of the President. On Friday morning, at the Hotel Texas in Fort Worth, Kennedy told me he wanted me to end the Johnson-Yarborough sideshow.

"I don't care if you have to throw Yarborough into the car with Lyndon," he said. "Get him in there."

As we talked in his hotel suite, Kennedy went to a window and looked down at the speaker's platform that had been erected for his appearance. He stared at it for a moment and shook his head.

"Just look at that platform," he said. "With all these buildings around it, the Secret Service couldn't stop someone who really wanted to get you."

I later went downstairs, where the motorcade was waiting, and found Senator Yarborough on the sidewalk. The newspapermen were already on the press bus, but I could see them watching us out the windows.

"Damn it, Ralph," I told the senator. "Look at those reporters watching to see what you do. It's not fair to the President. Why should he suffer because you and Lyndon have a problem? If you really want to help him, you'll get in the car with Lyndon before this thing gets any worse."

Ralph protested he had not intended to hurt the President. He said, "He's having a great trip, the crowds are terrific, everyone's excited. I'm proud to be with him here." He then took another long look at the press bus, turned back to me and quickly agreed to join the Vice President in the car.

I immediately signaled the Secret Service agent standing by the Vice President's car a few feet away and told him Yarborough would be riding with the Vice President and Mrs. Johnson.

"Keep close to the senator and be sure he gets into that car. This is a must." I added.

Then I saw Johnson come out of the hotel.

"Yarborough's going to ride with you," I told him.

"He is?"

"Right."

"Fine," Johnson said, and moments later the two of them drove off together in the open car, all smiles. Unfortunately, this was only a ride to the Fort Worth Airport, to be followed by a short flight to Dallas. Then there would be another motorcade, and I wanted to make sure that Yarborough got back into the car with Johnson for the ride into Dallas.

When we landed at Love Field at about 12:30 P.M., Kennedy moved along the fence shaking hands. Yarborough followed closely behind Kennedy and I followed Yarborough. I was so intent on getting Yarborough into Johnson's car that I missed my own car and the motorcade started to leave without me. I jumped into a convertible with Texas Congressmen George Mahon, Walter Rogers, and Homer Thornberry.

Kennedy's car was four or five cars ahead of us and we could see him waving to the crowds, but the congressmen and I were more intent on studying the people who lined the streets to determine their mood. On the outskirts of Dallas, the crowds were large, but not enthusiastic. My impression was that they'd come out of curiosity and perhaps to glimpse Jackie. Congressman Rogers, somewhat embarrassed, called out "Come on, let's hear it," a few times.

The mood changed, however, as we entered downtown Dallas. Suddenly there were cheering crowds pressing in on the motorcade and throwing confetti. The scene reminded me of New York City's Broadway. The congressmen and I were delighted with the show of enthusiasm. We were rounding a corner—Homer Thornberry was pointing out a building where he'd once had an office—when we heard a shot.

"What was that?" I immediately asked our driver.

"I don't know," he said. "They must be giving him a twenty-one gun salute."

As he spoke we heard additional shots. We had no idea what had happened. The motorcade began to move faster and there was confusion all around us. People were running in every direction. I saw a man with a child in his arms race up a grassy slope. A photographer with cameras slung around his neck jumped on the back of our car and hung on for dear life. He kept pounding the car with his fist and yelling, "Son of a bitch, son of a bitch!"

The photographer hung there while we moved at a high speed, trying to keep up with the cars ahead. We lost them, so we went on to the scheduled destination, the Trade Mart, where Kennedy was to go next. When we got there, other cars from the motorcade were waiting, but not the President's car and I realized something terrible must have happened. Then someone called to us, "He's been shot, he's draped over the back seat!"

We raced to the nearest hospital, where we found the rest of the motorcade, police cars, and great confusion. The police stopped me at the door, but Congressman Al Thomas intervened.

"This is Mr. O'Brien, the assistant to the President," he said, and the policeman stepped aside.

I ran through a maze of corridors until I reached an anteroom where Jackie and Nellie Connally, Governor John Connally's wife, were sitting together. Jackie's pink suit was spattered with blood and she was sitting like stone. As I entered someone said, "John Connally is being moved upstairs to surgery." My immediate thought was he was the one who was seriously wounded. Then Ken whispered to me there was little or no chance the President would live. I turned to Jackie to try to comfort her, but I could not speak.

The next hour was a nightmare. Everything was unreal. I was functioning entirely on reflex action. What is happening? I thought. What will happen next? Events seemed fragmented then and they still seem fragmented in retrospect.

It was chaotic, doctors, nurses running in and out. Medical equipment being wheeled into the room. At one point Jackie and I stepped into the adjoining room where the President's body lay. All I recall is I thought he looked as he always had.

Mac Kilduff, the acting press secretary, kept checking with us. He was distraught. What could he tell the press, he asked? What could he report to the Vice President, who was in another part of the building?

At one point Mac said, "He's dead, isn't he?" near tears. "I've got to tell the press."

"You can't say anything," Ken told him, and the confirmation of the President's death was kept from the world for perhaps half an hour, simply because Ken and I could not bring ourselves to accept it.

Someone sent for a priest and a casket. The casket arrived, and three priests, and a man who said he was the coroner. He ordered that the body could not be removed from the hospital until there had been an autopsy. Jackie had already said, "I won't leave here without Jack." It became an intolerable situation. We argued bitterly with the first official, then with a second official who called himself a judge. Their attitude was that this was no more than another homicide and local rules must be observed.

Finally, we demanded they get out of our way, that we were taking the President out of there. Ken, Dave Powers, General McHugh, and I proceeded to push the casket down the corridor, with Jackie following behind us. The Dallas officials continued to protest, but we pushed past them. Near the exit we encountered one of the priests who blocked our path and insisted that he say more prayers over the body. I shoved him aside. We knew Jackie couldn't stand any more delays and we were fearful the Dallas officials might use additional force to stop us. We finally got the casket into a hearse that was standing by and we piled into a car and sped to the airport behind the hearse.

Several Secret Service agents managed to get the five-hundred-pound casket up the stairs and into Air Force One, but the stairs were too narrow and they scratched the casket and broke one of the handles.

Ken, Dave, and I assisted the agents in placing the casket on the floor of the compartment and securing it. As Jackie and the three of us moved to seats opposite the casket, Vice President and Mrs. Johnson appeared. Lady Bird put her arms around Jackie, whispered her condolences, and the Vice President murmured something to her. The Johnsons then withdrew.

For most of the flight back to Washington, Ken, Dave, and I were alone with Jackie and the casket in the small tail compartment of Air Force One. She spoke at length of what we three had meant to the President. I think that his reaction to his trip to Ireland that summer, his rekindled interest in his Irish heritage, had made her more understanding of the bond that united us.

"You were with him in the beginning and you're with him now," she would say. "That's as it should be." I had never been close to Jackie, but tragedy had made us all part of the same family.

On arrival at Andrews Air Force Base in Virginia, Bob Kennedy immediately boarded the plane. A ramp was placed at the rear door and an honor guard stepped forward to remove the body. We asked them to stand aside and, with Bob, the three of us moved the casket onto the ramp and it was lowered and placed in a hearse. Bob and Jackie rode in the hearse followed in a car by Ken, Dave, and me, to Bethesda Naval Hospital in Maryland where an autopsy was to be performed.

Later that night, while waiting at the hospital, I decided there was another job to be done. At midnight Ken, Dave, and I went to Gawler's Funeral Home on Wisconsin Avenue to select a casket.

"Would you show us the plainest one you have in the middle price range?" I asked the man there.

We all felt that Kennedy should have a plain, inexpensive casket, one any average American might have. The man showed us several and we selected the one with the simplest interior, without ever asking the price. As it turned out, in one final bit of confusion to end that long day, the casket we bought and which Kennedy was buried in, was quite expensive.

We brought the dead President's body to the White House at 4 A.M. and we placed it in the East Room. Jackie asked Ken and me to spend the remainder of the night in the White House. Ken and I went to a bedroom, but we could not sleep, so we talked for hours.

A Mass would be said at 10:00 A.M., to be attended by the family and close friends. Ken and I went downstairs shortly before and we saw Bob Kennedy outside the East Room. He wondered if perhaps the casket should be opened for public viewing and asked Ken and me to decide. However, we felt it would be awkward for us to open the casket with the honor guard present, so we looked for General Ted Clifton, who was handling the funeral arrangements. We couldn't find him, so we did not pursue the matter, and the casket remained closed. We were all thinking in terms of an Irish wake, at which the casket is traditionally open for viewing.

All that weekend, in my White House office, friends came and went, and there were many tears and many reminiscences. Hubert Humphrey, our rival in 1960, came to my office on Saturday morning, just after Mass in the White House, and broke into tears. Early that afternoon, Congressman Bill Green came in and insisted that Ken and I and a few others go to Paul Young's Restaurant for lunch. We took a private room there, but the food was scarcely touched. Bill Green was a tough political pro, one we had gone to hat-in-hand in 1960, but at lunch he was very emotional, often in tears, as we all were. It was like that all weekend.

One thing we didn't do that weekend was any political planning. It was reported that Arthur Schlesinger and others met to discuss whether Bob Kennedy might wrest the 1964 nomination from Johnson. Leaving aside the practicality of such a plan, neither I nor the people I saw that weekend were in any emotional condition for such a discussion.

Monday morning, November 25, Dave and Ken and I were in the upstairs living room of the White House, waiting to join the funeral cortege, which was then on its way from Capitol Hill. We were watching the cortege on television and little John-John Kennedy came into the room and, suddenly, we saw him saluting the televised picture of the cortege.

One of the butlers came in and asked if he could get us anything.

"Let's have a bottle of champagne," Dave said.

The butler brought the champagne and glasses and we toasted Jack Kennedy.

"To the President."

"To the President."

"Good-by, Jack, good-by."

VIII

LBJ

In Dallas, before Air Force One had even taken off, the new President called Ken and me to the stateroom to sit opposite Lady Bird and him.

"The Constitution puts me in the White House," he told us, "but you two are free to make your own choices. I want to urge you to stay and stand shoulder to shoulder with me. I need you more than you need me—and more than Jack Kennedy needed you."

As he spoke, I kept thinking: "*Hell, let's talk about this later.*" In the back of my mind there was the gnawing fear that the Dallas police might arrive and try to take President Kennedy's body off the plane.

I told Johnson about the problem we'd had at the hospital and said I thought we should take off immediately. I knew that the delay was terribly painful to Jackie.

"No, I've talked with the Attorney General," Johnson said. "He thinks I should be sworn in here."

Then it hit me: *This man is President of the United States.* After that, I didn't argue. I just shut my eyes and prayed that the judge would arrive quickly and administer the oath to Johnson.

Johnson had a bowl of soup and changed his shirt. Shortly afterward, Judge Sarah Hughes arrived. She was handed a typed sheet of paper with the wording of the oath. Johnson asked me if I thought Mrs. Kennedy would join him, and I said I would ask her. I noticed the door of the bathroom off the President's bedroom was closed. I asked President

Kennedy's secretary, Evelyn Lincoln, to check with Mrs. Kennedy. Soon Jackie appeared and slowly walked over to join the Johnsons. The group on the plane gathered around. As the judge was about to begin, a steward handed me a brown leather covered book in a white cardboard box, which I assumed was a Bible, and I handed it to her. I later learned the steward had brought it from the President's bedside table. As Johnson placed his hand on it, I glanced at it again and realized it was a Catholic missal. The oath was quickly administered. Jackie, Ken, Dave, and I took our places opposite the casket at the rear of the plane, and we were soon airborne.

After we were aloft, the President again called me and renewed his urgings. "We're being tested," he said. "The world is watching. I need your help." But I just couldn't talk about the future, and the conversation led nowhere.

Johnson made a fleeting reference to a Senate vote on a controversial Russian wheat bill scheduled for the following Monday. Because Kennedy's funeral was Monday, the vote was postponed until later in the week. After the funeral, I returned to the White House, changed from my formal clothes into a business suit, and made an attempt to check the status of the bill. I was trying to keep busy, keep moving.

Wednesday noon, Sorensen, Salinger, and I accompanied the new President to the Hill for his address to a Joint Session of Congress. I found my work continued despite the change of Presidents and by throwing myself into it I could to some degree put aside my grief. I was more fortunate in that respect than O'Donnell, Sorensen, Powers, and others whose jobs had been essentially personal with President Kennedy.

My relationship with Johnson, during his vice presidency, had been friendly but not intimate. There were, as is well known now, some feelings of bitterness by me and other of the Kennedy people during the flight back from Dallas. We didn't like Johnson's taking over Air Force One when his own vice-presidential plane, with identical facilities, was available. We didn't like his delaying the take-off. We resented his calling Jackie "honey." If, in those first days back in Washington, Johnson had been in any way offensive or insensitive toward us, I would have left the government, as some other Kennedy men soon prepared to do. But the opposite was the case. Johnson and his people—Bill Moyers, Jack Valenti, George Reedy, Walter Jenkins—could not have been more considerate.

"I need you, Larry," he told me over and over. "I want you to stay and help me pass Jack Kennedy's program. How can you better honor Jack's memory than to stay and help enact his program?"

I could only agree with him. I decided there was no better tribute I could make to President Kennedy's memory than to stay and continue to work on his legislative program. So I stayed.

I continued to see a good deal of Jackie in the weeks following the assassination. On Thanksgiving morning, she asked Ken, Pierre, and me to accompany her to her husband's grave. After she moved to Averell Harriman's house in Georgetown, Ken and Dave went to see her almost every afternoon, and I often joined them. It was a difficult time. She was lonely, tense, sometimes bitter. The Johnsons were trying mightily to befriend her. One afternoon while I was there, Luci Johnson brought some Christmas gifts for the Kennedy children. Jackie personally went to the door to accept them.

I think that Johnson, in the first days of the Kennedy administration had hoped to play a unique role as Vice President. He thought he could serve as Kennedy's ambassador to Congress, and, also, although no longer Senate majority leader, he could in effect continue as the Democratic leader in the Senate. His hopes suffered two sharp rebuffs. First, his Democratic colleagues in the Senate objected to his plan to continue as chairman of their policy group. Second, Kennedy assigned me as his chief emissary to Congress.

Johnson went out of his way to be friendly to me in those days. In February 1961, he invited Elva and me to dinner at his home. There was snow on the ground, but as soon as we arrived Johnson insisted on taking me outside to see his swimming pool.

"See those Muzak speakers up in the trees?" he said during our tour. "Here, I'll let you hear how it sounds."

He flipped a switch and let me admire the quality of the Muzak system before we went back indoors for a tour of the house. He led Elva and me from room to room, not for just a glance but for detailed commentary on the furniture and mementos that each room contained.

In his bedroom he dug into a drawer, came up with a sportshirt, and pressed it upon me.

"Larry, I want you to have this," he said. "To keep."

Then he seized a bottle of perfume from Mrs. Johnson's dresser drawer.

"Here, Elva, this is for you," he commanded.

Finally the tour ended and we went to dinner. Two other couples were present—the Bobby Bakers and Congressman Jack Brooks and his wife. After an excellent Mexican dinner, Johnson invited the men into his den where he took out his scrapbooks and reminisced at length about his political career. His stories of Texas politics were often hilarious, and there were many affectionate references to Sam Rayburn.

I had put my new shirt on a chair in the hallway and as we said our good nights, I forgot it. But as Elva and I were walking down the sidewalk toward our car, the door burst open.

"Larry, you forgot your shirt," Johnson called and hurried out to give me my gift again. The shirt, which had an LBJ monogram, was too large for me, but I sometimes wore it around the house on weekends.

Elva and I commented later that Johnson's hospitality was of an intensity we had never before encountered.

I appreciated his friendliness, but there was no continuing role for him, as Vice President, to play in our congressional relations program. He was always invited to our strategy sessions in Mike Mansfield's office, but he didn't always attend. He regularly attended the weekly congressional breakfasts at the White House but he rarely volunteered any comment. If he had something to say, he would usually speak to me privately after the breakfast. I recall once when I sought Johnson's support on a Senate matter.

"Larry," he told me rather mournfully, "I'll talk to them, but Claude Desautels has more muscle with those fellows than I do."

He was always highly complimentary of my work. It wasn't his nature to toss praise around lavishly, but he knew Congress and he felt our office was functioning well. Johnson also knew that some members of the Kennedy circle didn't particularly care for him—Kennedy knew it too and that was why he always insisted that Johnson be given every consideration and courtesy. Johnson, for his part, was unfailingly loyal to the President.

As far as I could see, the relationship between Kennedy and Johnson was entirely satisfactory. I saw no indication that Kennedy had considered dropping Johnson in 1964, as some have suggested. There was no reason for him to do so.

As President, Johnson threw himself headlong into his work. He pushed himself day and night to the extent that Mrs. Johnson feared for his health. I saw a great deal of him because my area of operations, Congress, was his number one interest. He took various steps to make sure I'd stay on his staff. He gave Ken and me raises soon after he became President, and just before Christmas, he sent Walter Jenkins to give me my Christmas present, a wristwatch with the initials "LBJ" on its face along with the biblical quotation, "Do unto others as you would have others do unto you." In those first weeks, President Johnson called me almost every day to ask me to go for a swim with him at lunchtime. I wasn't interested in swimming, so I'd make excuses. This went on for a while, until finally, when I'd made one excuse too many, he said, "For Christ's sake, Larry, I'm only asking you to go for a swim. I'm not asking you to change your religion."

Eventually, however, he did get me into the pool. One evening early in 1964 we had a White House reception for congressmen and their wives. It was quite a merry affair and,

as it was breaking up around 8 P.M., Johnson invited some of
us to join him for a swim. There were bathing suits available
for everybody and we went down and continued our party at
the pool. However, there was a heavyweight title fight taking
place simultaneously which interested me more than swimming, so I asked an usher for a radio and a group of us stood in
the shallow end of the pool listening to the fight while the
President dogpaddled around the deep end. When we finished
our "swim" and returned to the dressing room, Johnson and I
got into a rather intense discussion of some legislative matter
—standing in the raw, nose-to-nose, talking for some time while
a number of congressmen looked on open-mouthed.

Johnson expressed his feelings outwardly, whether affection
or anger, to a greater degree than anyone I'd known. When
his wife or daughters entered the room, he always greeted
them with a kiss, then gave them another when they left. He
seemed to reach out in every direction for support, both in
his personal life and in his political life. One aspect of this
was his attending churches of every denomination, including
a Catholic church in southwest Washington. "Larry, I just
went over and visited those little monks of yours," he'd tell
me, "and it was good for me."

President Johnson called me one Sunday early in 1964 with
an invitation.

"Larry, I want you to come play some golf with me at
Burning Tree."

It was a sunny Sunday afternoon and the last thing on my
mind was playing golf.

"Mr. President, I haven't played golf in twenty years. I'd
be terrible."

"You'll be fine. I'll send a car for you."

"Mr. President, really, I don't think . . ."

"Larry, all I'm asking is that you play a few holes of golf
with your President."

"I'll tell you what, Mr. President," I said in desperation.
"My son, Larry, Jr., is home and he plays a little golf. Maybe
he could play with you."

"Okay, okay, but you come too. It's a pretty day and you ought to get out of the house."

I broke the news to Larry that he was about to play a round of golf with the President. He was horrified, since he wasn't much of a golfer either, but there was no way out.

A White House car took us to Burning Tree Country Club, where we met the President and the other members of the foursome, Jack Valenti and Walter Jenkins. Former Illinois Senator Scott Lucas was along as scorekeeper. They went nine holes, a pretty wild nine holes, with the game usually occupying two or three fairways at once, since none of the four was very good. I don't think Johnson had been on a golf course in years either, but he'd decided that a President ought to play golf occasionally. On the drive back to the White House, the President checked over the scorecard that Scott Lucas had kept. It showed that Larry had beaten him by one stroke.

"Larry, would you like for me to autograph this scorecard for you?" the President asked.

"Yes, sir, I'd appreciate it."

"I guess you're going to be active in politics like your father, aren't you?"

"I might, sir," Larry said.

"Well, I'll autograph this scorecard," the President said. "But one lesson you'd better learn if you want to be in politics is that you never go out on a golf course and beat the President."

Johnson was hard on his staff—he'd been notorious for that for years. He gave verbal whippings, but Ken and I, as Kennedy men, were immune from them. Jack Valenti, who was totally devoted to him, was often a target. President Johnson would give him a chewing-out, then five minutes later he might throw his arms around him and tell him how much he needed him. Johnson was intimately involved in the lives of all his top staff people, including the upbringing of their children. I thought there was a basic contradiction in Johnson's nature. He wanted to be loved, but he also wanted to dominate everybody around him. In any event, he was generally more successful in dominating than in being loved. He knew how to put people in awe of him. As far as Congress was concerned, this was reflected in his hard-sell, arm-twisting style of operation which contrasted with Kennedy's more restrained approach.

Politics was Johnson's real interest. No detail of the legislative program was too minute to involve him. Kennedy would give congressional affairs whatever time I requested, but Kennedy had other interests as well. For Johnson, Congress was a twenty-four-hour-a-day obsession. One morning I called him to inform him about a vote we'd lost late the night before.

"Why didn't you call and wake me up and tell me, Larry?" he demanded. "When you bleed, I want to bleed with you."

"Mr. President," I protested, "I don't even know if the switchboard would have put me through at that hour."

"There's a standing order that the switchboard puts you through, at any hour, day or night," he told me, and after that I never hesitated to call him.

Lady Bird Johnson fully shared her husband's interest in legislation. She was a highly intelligent woman, and her years in Washington had given her a keen understanding of the legislative process. It was not at all unusual for her to call me to inquire about the progress of some bill—education or civil rights or Medicare or whatever—and, of course, she took a special interest in "her" beautification bills. Those bills did more than plant flowers and trees. We proposed a tough bill to regulate billboards, one that met fierce resistance from the powerful billboard lobby. This led to prolonged negotiations with congressional leaders—we saw we could not outlaw billboards entirely, so we tried to see just how strong a bill we could pass. Highly technical issues were involved: how far back from the road must billboards be, over what period of years should existing billboards be phased out, and so on. I kept Mrs. Johnson informed of these negotiations on a daily basis, either by phone or by going up to her living quarters to give her a head count. Or, often I would see her in the evening when I was meeting with the President in his office at eight or nine o'clock, and she would come in to urge him to stop working and come have dinner. She and her capable assistant, Liz Carpenter, would actively lobby for her beautification bills, sometimes by phone calls to old friends in Congress, more often by using White House social events as occasions to speak to them. Lady Bird was always astute and effective. She came close to equaling her husband's understanding of Congress, and she perhaps exceeded his understanding of people.

Legislation was intensely personal with Johnson. A vote against one of his bills was a personal rebuff. As President, he'd quickly forgotten the congressional point of view, that self-protection comes before supporting a President. I kept in mind the fact that no one was going to commit political suicide to help us out, but that was exactly what Johnson expected them to do.

President Johnson's passion to have his way once led us into an angry and unfortunate confrontation with Mike Mansfield, the Senate majority leader. There was an effort in progress to close down and consolidate Veterans Administration hospitals for economy, and someone had authorized the closing of a number of hospitals around the country without any consideration of congressional reaction. One of the hospitals was in Montana and, thus, one day without any advance notice, Senator Mansfield got word of the plan by a routine announcemet from the Veterans Administration.

When I dropped by Mansfield's office that morning, he was furious. Fortunately, I convinced him I hadn't known anything about the matter.

"Lawrence," he said, at the end of our brief talk, "I have a message for you to give the President. You tell him I object strenuously to this action and I don't intend to accept it."

That was about as strong a statement as Mike Mansfield normally made, and the President's reply was just as emphatic:

"Those hospitals should be closed and nobody's going to tell me they can't be."

The situation worsened. Mansfield appeared before the House Veterans Affairs Committee to testify against the clos-

ing. Most senators sided with Mansfield. I kept suggesting to
Johnson that perhaps we would do better to leave open one
hospital in Montana than to destroy our relationship with the
majority leader in the Senate. But Johnson was adamant: Mike
Mansfield couldn't push him around.

The end result was predictable. After many weeks of conflict,
the White House gave in; Johnson just couldn't break off with
Mansfield over one hospital.

At that time, when numerous congressmen were unhappy
about the closing of the VA hospitals, we had one of our frequent White House receptions for a group of congressmen and
their wives. These receptions often featured briefings by cabinet
members on current issues. At this particular one, the President
personally responded to questions that had been raised about
the VA hospital closings.

He delivered a long and emotional oration in defense of the
closings. "Our disabled boys deserve the best medical treatment we can give them," he declared. "Why, we're closing
down one VA Hospital in a little Texas town that has become
nothing more than a firetrap. The veterans are all being taken
to a modern new hospital in Memphis, just as they deserve."

His remarks stressed that his own state of Texas was losing a
hospital in the interests of better medical care for the veterans.
He went on to say that the local people in the little Texas town
had been upset about losing jobs because of the closing, but
that was being resolved because the poverty program was making the former hospital into a Women's Job Corps center. The
President concluded proudly that the local people were delighted and thought they'd get more revenue from the Job
Corps than they had from the VA hospital. He was starting to
sit down when a voice boomed out of the back of the room—
the loud, rather husky voice of Congressman Harold Cooley of
North Carolina.

"You gonna burn the women?" Cooley asked.

"What?" the President asked.

"You said it was a firetrap," Cooley said. "You gonna burn
the women?"

Johnson's brilliant presentation was demolished by one question, and he stood speechless for a full minute, searching for a response.

Finally, rather lamely, he said, "I didn't know we had Bob Hope in the audience."

Early in Johnson's presidency, I had wondered about his commitment to the Kennedy program, particularly in the area of civil rights. I knew he would back the legislation, but I wondered if he had a real, deep, gut commitment to civil rights, being a Southerner with strong southern ties. My doubts were tested in 1964.

Liberals in Washington had been fighting for home rule for years with no success. The issue was self-government for the people of Washington, the majority of whom are black. A bill to provide home rule for the District of Columbia was blocked in the House Rules Committee, and the only way to get it to the floor was by a discharge petition, which required the signature of a majority of the House members. Our office, working with District leaders, got about two hundred signatures, but then we reached a standstill. No one else would sign. Finally I went and reported this to the President.

"Why are you giving up?" he roared. "We can win this thing."

He questioned me and discovered that I had a list of twenty-two members who had refused to sign, but whom I thought should sign—they were our last hope. Johnson snatched the list from my hand and grabbed the phone. He stayed on the phone for two hours, calling one representative after another. He persuaded and cajoled and pleaded. He spoke movingly of the inequity of denying democratic government. He told Edna Kelly, a representative from New York, "There's no reason why you can't sign this. I'm begging you. I'm on my knees to you."

He got the signatures, personally and single-handedly. It was a remarkable performance. There was little politically in it for him—home rule was not a national issue. He had done it because he believed in it, and I never doubted his commitment to civil rights after that.

I was in an odd position during Johnson's 1964 campaign for the presidency. On the one hand, he wanted me to organize his campaign, but on the other hand he wanted me to have no role whatsoever in the Democratic Convention at Atlantic City that would nominate him.

President Johnson had always given me the impression that he thought the so-called Irish Mafia had some magic touch in dealing with the big-city leaders like Dick Daley and Bill Green, a touch that he and his people didn't have. His feeling went back to his abortive drive for the 1960 nomination. He couldn't concede that he had then been a regional figure, so far as national politics was concerned, so he decided that the Irish Mafia had somehow outsmarted him. Now, four years later, he wanted us on his side.

But he didn't want us active at the Convention because of his fear that Ken and I might somehow engineer Bob Kennedy's nomination for the vice presidency, even after he had formally removed Kennedy from contention.

There was little possibility of a Kennedy coup at the Convention, but it is true that Bob had wanted the vice-presidential nomination. He wanted it, but Johnson would have absolutely no part of him. Johnson was beside himself for weeks in the early summer trying to find a resolution for the problem.

Eventually, Johnson called Kennedy to his office to settle the matter. Bob came by my White House office beforehand and we speculated on Johnson's probable decision. Bob was realistic. He knew he wasn't likely to be the choice and he knew why—because he and Johnson didn't get along personally, because Johnson wanted to be elected in his own right, because Bob as Vice President might overshadow him, and because Bob as Vice President might challenge him for the nomination in 1968. The polls made clear that Johnson didn't need Bob to win the election, and if he didn't need him, he certainly didn't want him. Bob accepted all this dispassionately, and after we talked awhile he went on downstairs for his appointment with the President. Johnson announced to Bob that he had decided not to select as his running mate any member of his Cabinet—a ploy that rather neatly eliminated Bob, who was of course still the Attorney General. Bob took the decision philosophically—he was not surprised and he was relieved that the uncertainty was over.

Following that meeting, Bob, Ken, and I went to lunch. Bob recounted in some detail his conversation with the President. Upon my return to the office, the President called and asked if I would drop by his office, which I did. I told him I had just had lunch with Bob, and Johnson proceeded to give his version of their talk. When I commented that some points differed from Bob's, he pressed a buzzer and Walter Jenkins came in and read from a long memo that supported Johnson's account. I must have looked skeptical, because Johnson explained that he had dictated the memo to Walter just after Bob left. Later, when I told Bob about that memo, we speculated on whether the meeting had been recorded. Bob noted wryly that Johnson had not been as expansive as usual.

When Johnson rejected him for the vice presidency, Bob had to make a move. To continue in Johnson's Cabinet was unacceptable to Bob. He soon hit upon the idea of running against Senator Ken Keating of New York. We discussed this several times at Hickory Hill in the next few weeks. Bob knew all the problems, including the fact that he would be denounced as a carpetbagger, and not without reason. But the prospects looked reasonably good, and in early September Bob threw himself into the race and won handily.

Once Johnson had eliminated Bob from the vice-presidential sweepstakes, he began his great game of "Who'll it be?" There was hardly a politician in Washington who didn't think that summer that he might be the next Vice President. Johnson loved it and prolonged the suspense with leaks, hints, and rumors.

Hubert Humphrey was the obvious choice, but Johnson didn't want it that cut and dried. He enjoyed keeping people off balance. Humphrey was having fits. He came to see me several times to ask, "What do you hear? What's my status?"

But there was nothing I could tell him. We went through the period when the President frequently pulled polls from his pockets, most of which stated that he'd make a better run without a Vice President. Humphrey, as I recall the polls, was the strongest running mate—he didn't add any support, but he didn't cost any either.

The whole episode was a fantastic exercise. One evening at a reception on the White House lawn, Gene McCarthy, with whom I did not have a close relationship, came up to chat with me several times. He mentioned the high regard he'd always held for Jack Kennedy, which was news to me. At first I didn't understand why McCarthy was going out of his way to make this point so emphatically, but he finally made a passing reference to the fact that he understood Johnson was considering him for the vice presidency.

It finally dawned on me that McCarthy thought I might be advising the President on the selection and he didn't want any memories of the old Kennedy-McCarthy friction to keep me from speaking well of him. I never thought McCarthy was under serious consideration, but, in any event, he was giving me credit where credit wasn't due. The President went through his laundry list of possible running mates with me occasionally, but I knew he was just playing his game—I didn't think for a minute he had any great interest in my opinion. I would make innocuous comments, favorable to all the contenders. Finally one day he pressed me to name my choice.

"Come on, Larry, I want your advice. Who should it be?"

I thought the answer was obvious.

"Mr. President," I said, "I would have to say that Hubert is the best-qualified candidate."

He made no reply, and I had no illusions that my opinion influenced Johnson's final decision.

The Convention in Atlantic City was a strange, cloak-and-dagger affair. Johnson controlled everything, with Walter Jenkins and a newcomer, Marvin Watson, the former Texas Democratic Chairman, as his men on the scene. Marvin proved to be an able co-ordinator. He instituted the tightest procedures any nominating Convention has ever had—a delegate could scarcely go to the bathroom without his okay. All this was intended to prevent any possible move to draft Bob Kennedy for the vice presidency.

Ken and I were stationed in an out-of-the-way motel without any real duties. It wasn't unpleasant, as a vacation trip—we had a nice room, cars at our disposal, invitations to all the receptions, and tickets to the convention floor. But we weren't really involved. Of course, there wasn't much to be involved in. There weren't any candidates in opposition and the platform had already been written in the White House.

From Johnson's point of view, the precautions were sound. I think a draft-Kennedy movement could have developed. The wild ovation when Bob introduced the film memorializing President Kennedy proved that emotions were running high. Johnson shrewdly had the film switched from the first day of the Convention until after the Vice President had been selected. There was absolutely no plan to create a draft-Kennedy movement, yet, Johnson apparently assumed that if there had been such a plan, Ken and I would have been involved.

Once the Convention was past and Bob announced his decision to run for the Senate, Johnson could finally relax—he had always considered Goldwater less of a threat than Kennedy. The President asked me to plan his campaign, and I followed the same procedures I would have for Kennedy—advising on the co-ordination with state and local Democrats, labor, media campaign, and so on. We knew we couldn't lose.

Throughout the fall, I divided my time between the campaign and my legislative duties. We were trying to pass the Medicare bill and we became involved in complicated negotiations with Clinton Anderson, Wilbur Mills, and others in Congress. On several occasions, the President would say he wanted me to get out into the country, to test the political waters for him, to see if Goldwater was making any headway, but he wanted me on Capitol Hill, too. Finally we decided I would make such a tour, but I would keep in touch with the legislative situation by telephone.

I put together a small staff and set up regional meetings with Democratic leaders and labor people. I wanted to listen to their complaints, to evaluate their progress, and to build some co-ordination between the Johnson campaign and their local campaigns. I told the President I would send back reports to him from time to time. Joe Napolitan and Phyllis Maddock were traveling with me, and after our first meeting, we compiled a report and dropped it in the mail to the President. We received word from the White House that this method was too slow and that we should call in the reports.

My reports were quite critical of what I saw. A lack of campaign materials existed in some areas, distribution procedures were lax, local-national co-ordination was poor—nowhere could we find the type of organization that an incumbent President, let alone one who was not short of funds, should have had. It wasn't until I returned from my first trip that I discovered that my reports had caused all hell to break loose in the White House. Walter Jenkins told me that Johnson had been reading them the minute they came in and had been demanding immediate action from his other political aides. Unwittingly, I had made some fellows in Washington pretty unhappy with me. It was Johnson's natural inclination to think that everyone around him was letting him down, and my reports had confirmed his fears.

I made four trips around the country, working especially on a get-out-the-vote effort, and I think we were able to tighten up the campaign structure somewhat. But I don't suggest that my efforts had any significant impact on the outcome of the election. The Republicans lost the 1964 election the day they nominated a man who was too conservative politically and too independent personally to be a winner.

Johnson called me twice on Election Night, elated by his electoral landslide and the huge new Democratic majorities in the House and Senate. "We can wrap up the New Frontier program now, Larry," he told me. "We can pass it all now."

At that point, however, I intended to leave the White House and return to private life, and I so informed Johnson a few days later. He was just as determined to keep me in government as I was to depart. He urged me to spend the Thanksgiving holidays at the LBJ Ranch, but Ken and I had already made plans to take our wives to Palm Beach for a few days.

The situation was complicated by the fact that Ted Kennedy had suggested to me I return to Massachusetts with an eye to running for office, perhaps for the Senate. There had been other suggestions that I seek office, but I never took them very seriously. One reason was that I consider the financial side of politics, as it now exists, demeaning to a candidate. I wouldn't want to ask people for money, and I wouldn't want people who gave me money to feel I was beholden to them. Beyond that, perhaps I lack the necessary ego for office-seeking; I've never felt that my holding public office was essential to the survival of the republic.

Johnson continued to plead his case to me, and he enlisted Democratic leaders in Congress to support him.

"You can't leave now, Larry," he would say. "We've got the votes now to pass it all."

It was, as it had been a year earlier, an unanswerable argument. I had fought the congressional battles for four years, and I had seen some successes, but now, with our new majority in the House, there seemed to be no limit to what we might accomplish. I knew Johnson was giving me his selling job, his four-star treatment, but I knew too that he was right. How do you say no to a President when he says he needs you? I couldn't leave.

I went to Johnson's office one day in January to tell him my decision.

"Mr. President," I said, "I've decided that I will stay on with you on two conditions."

"What are they?" he said, frowning a little.

"First, I would like for you to announce at your next news conference the fact that I submitted my resignation, but that I agreed at your insistence to stay through the 1965 legislative session."

"What's the second condition?"

"That at the end of the session, when I'm ready to resign, you accept my resignation without any further discussion."

I was aware that I might be going too far. He could have

told me to go to blazes with my conditions—he had the votes to pass his program without Larry O'Brien. But I wanted the record clear, and I didn't want to go through another arm-twisting session at the end of the year.

The President stood up and grinned at me.

"I accept your conditions," he said. He walked around the desk and shook my hand. "We'll pass some bills now, we'll show them, Larry," he said.

Not everyone was so pleased. My decision to stay came at about the time that Ken O'Donnell, Dave Powers, and some others of the Kennedy team were leaving the government, and there was some bitterness at my staying. Bob Kennedy strongly recommended that I stay but I heard secondhand what a few of my old associates were saying about me, men I'd been very close to. I knew that some of them hated my guts for staying with Lyndon Johnson. I had to accept that because I believed, and still believe, that my decision was the right one.

IX

THE GREAT SOCIETY

As 1965 began, and I returned to Capitol Hill to work with the Eighty-ninth Congress, it was like entering a new world. Physically the Capitol was the same, but politically it had been turned upside down by the Johnson landslide. The state of Iowa, for example, which for years had returned six Republicans and one Democrat to the House, was now represented by six Democrats and one remaining Republican. The Democratic membership of the House had gone from 258 to 295, and we intended to make the most of the legislative opportunity this presented.

The President spearheaded the effort, giving his program deep and passionate attention. Joseph A. Califano, the President's assistant for domestic affairs, and I were destined to become intimately acquainted. Every day, every hour, it was drive, drive, drive—to use the basketball term, a full-court press. We knew we would inevitably lose some, if not all, of the new Democratic seats in the 1966 elections. We had two years to pass laws—to make history—and we didn't want to waste a minute. The President had the mandate, he had the votes, and they added up to unprecedented power. We intended to maximize that power. Those were heady times for us. In some instances we moved too fast; certainly we made mistakes. But I don't think we were motivated by what Senator Fulbright has called, in another context, the "arrogance of power." The spirit in those days was more the exuberance of power, the joy of having the power given the President by the people, to do the things we all believed needed doing for our country.

Certainly we didn't worry about overburdening our friends in Congress. We were "gung-ho." We had charts prepared showing the exact status of each of our scores of proposed bills, and the President would each week review these charts with the Democratic leaders in Congress and exhort them to do even more to pass them. In cabinet meetings, he would point to Bob Weaver or John Gardner or Bill Wirtz and say, "Why haven't you passed that bill yet? What's wrong with you fellows?"—and the cabinet members, after being put on the spot once or twice, would redouble their legislative efforts.

Johnson expected everyone around him to work just as hard as he did (although that was rarely the case—almost no one worked as hard as he did). It disturbed him when his staff was not on top of every detail of government, particularly of legislation, and he arranged for all of us to have radios in our offices so we could catch the hourly news broadcasts to hear what the wire services were saying about us. Joe Califano had a "hot line" to the President on his desk, and when it rang he could be counted on to burst into action. One day, however, the hot line rang and Califano didn't respond. He missed the call, because he was otherwise occupied in the small bathroom that graced his large White House office. The President later demanded an explanation as to why Joe had not responded to his call, and Califano explained the problem as discreetly as possible.

"We'll have no more of that," Johnson roared, and the next thing Califano knew, the President had arranged for a telephone extension to be placed in his bathroom.

We did everything we could to help the new Democrats who were going out on a limb to help us. Stan Greigg, a freshman representative from Iowa, was typical of the young Democrats who'd been elected in traditionally Republican districts. Stan had operated his family restaurant, been a dean of a college, and served as mayor of Sioux City before he was swept into Congress in the 1964 Democratic landslide. He believed in the Johnson program and supported it all the way, even though he

knew his down-the-line Democratic voting record was hurting
him back home. By 1966, Stan faced opposition from a Republican candidate who denounced him as a "rubber stamp"
for the Administration, a charge made against many who followed their, and the President's, mandate. We did all we could
to help people like Stan. By 1966 I was Postmaster General,
and, somewhat arbitrarily, I arranged a stamp-dedication program in Stan's home town, Sioux City. I went out and rode in
an open car with Stan in a parade that included bands, baton
twirlers, and the rest. Others in the Administration pitched
in to help. Nevertheless, Stan was to be one of the many freshman Democrats defeated in 1966. That was the reality we
faced, two years to do the legislative job that had been bottled
up for a generation.

To assist people like Stan Greigg, we expanded the system
we had established in 1961 whereby our supporters in Congress
could make the first announcement of federal grants and
projects in their districts. There were those in the press and
elsewhere who criticized this as overly political. We thought it
made sense. For example, if one senator from a state supported
a program, and the other opposed it, why not let the one who
supported it get some special credit in the eyes of his constituents?

There were in particular many Defense Department projects
to be announced. Every morning a military officer would appear at Claude Desautels' office with a briefcase full of the
day's announcements.

Naturally our system caused complaints. In one instance,
Senator Margaret Chase Smith of Maine complained bitterly
to Secretary McNamara that Senator Muskie was getting all
the credit for grants to their state. As a ranking member of the
Armed Services Committee, Mrs. Smith was in a position to
make life very difficult for McNamara, so he eventually went
to the President and told him our system of announcing defense projects would have to stop. Johnson was shaken by
McNamara's complaint and called me in to discuss it. I declared that those announcements were our life's blood, our
chief means of supporting those members of Congress who

supported us, and that we absolutely could not give them up. Johnson, somewhat reluctantly, sided with me, and McNamara just had to live with the heat from Senator Smith.

In an effort to ease the situation a bit, we worked out a rather complicated ploy that involved Senator Muskie registering a complaint that *he* was not getting to make enough announcements. That muddied the waters somewhat and calmed Mrs. Smith for a while.

There were other ploys. One occurred in the summer of 1965 when President Johnson journeyed to the Statue of Liberty for an elaborate ceremony at which he signed into law the historic immigration bill. This was, in theory, a nonpartisan event, with leaders of both parties invited. But the word was out for all of us to do all we could for Abe Beame, who was then running for mayor of New York. The President took a helicopter to Liberty Island and the rest of us went over by ferry. When the ferry docked, the politicians scrambled ashore in a great hurry, all wanting to claim a place near the President for the bill-signing ceremony, so they would be in news photographs of the event. I wanted to give Abe Beame a head start, so as he hurried off the boat, I blocked the path of Governor Nelson Rockefeller. I was standing in front of Rockefeller, and it slowly dawned on him that it was no accident that whenever he moved right, I moved right, and when he'd move left, I'd move left. Finally he growled, "Damn it, O'Brien, I'm the governor of New York and I have a right to get off this boat. Get the hell out of my way!"

In later years, when I'd sometimes see Rockefeller at the White House, he would make some joke about, "Hey, Larry, who are you pushing around these days?" I would always pretend not to know what he was talking about.

One of the running jokes in those days was the President's diet. Mrs. Johnson did everything she could to keep him on the diet, and he often went to great lengths to indulge himself in his favorite high-calorie treats. One night I went to his bedroom to discuss a legislative matter with him. He was in his pajamas and sat propped up in bed as we talked. Suddenly he reached under the bed and pulled out a box of pralines—his favorite Texas candy—and quickly swallowed one, as if Lady Bird might burst in the door any moment. He replaced the box, we kept on talking, shortly he grabbed the box again and ate another praline. Then he looked at me somewhat shamefaced.

"I guess I ought to offer you one, shouldn't I?"

"No, thank you, Mr. President," I said, for I, too, was dieting, and pralines weren't one of my weaknesses.

Another time, I accompanied him when he was to throw out the first ball as the Washington Senators opened the baseball season. There was a large party in the President's box—Vice President Humphrey and numerous congressional leaders—and someone ordered hot dogs and began passing them around. After a while I looked around and saw the President sitting doubled over, his head down between his knees, wolfing down a hot dog. Off his diet again, he was afraid that Lady Bird might be watching the game on television and see him eating the hot dog.

Johnson was often called "larger than life" and his sizable ego was often commented on, but there was another, more appealing side of him that these stories suggest—an average American husband and father, trying to diet and failing, turning out lights, and otherwise behaving the way most of us behave. He could be intensely human—I know no better way to put it—and this is a side of that immensely complex man that history should not forget.

There were many legislative victories in those hectic days, but perhaps none was sweeter to us than the passage of Medicare. The Democratic Party had been committed to a program of national health insurance for decades. Franklin Roosevelt, at the time of his death, was planning a health insurance bill to be part of his postwar domestic legislation. His successor, Harry Truman, sent a health insurance bill to Congress in the fall of 1945 but was never able to obtain its passage. Democrats had fought for health insurance in the 1950s, but could not overcome the opposition of President Eisenhower and the American Medical Association. Kennedy, as I have related, was never able to get his Medicare bill out of the House Ways and Means Committee, although on the day of his death, its chairman, Wilbur Mills, had agreed to a compromise that made eventual passage seem certain. On Johnson's second night as President, Saturday night, November 23, 1963, as Henry Hall Wilson and I sat in gloom in the White House, Henry told me of the apparent breakthrough he'd made with Mills the previous day. I thought this so urgent that I had Henry send a draft of the new bill to President Johnson that night.

Johnson was an all-out supporter of Medicare and he hoped to see it pass in 1964. Unlike Kennedy, he entered into direct personal negotiations with Chairman Mills on the details of the legislation. I cannot say that these efforts were particularly effective. The fact we faced throughout 1964, despite signs of co-operation from Mills, was that we lacked majority support for Medicare in either Ways and Means or in the full House. We turned, therefore, to the Senate, where Medicare had failed only narrowly two years earlier. In August, we attached Medicare as a rider to the Social Security amendments, a tactic that enabled us to bypass Senator Harry F. Byrd's Finance Committee, as Senator Byrd was a long-time opponent of Medicare. When a vote was taken, Medicare passed by 49 to 44, with Senator Goldwater, then the Republican nominee for President, among those voting against it. It was the first time, after almost twenty years of effort, that a health insurance bill had passed either house of Congress.

Tagged to the Social Security bill, Medicare then went to a House-Senate Conference Committee where, after a month of heated negotiation, it died, largely because of Wilbur Mills. Mills argued that attaching Medicare to the Social Security bill could jeopardize the bill and that we lacked the votes to pass Medicare in the House. We still wanted a vote even if we lost, to position the Republicans against Medicare just before the 1964 elections. Yet scores of Mills's fellow congressmen desperately wanted not to be put on the spot— to have to choose between the "senior citizens" on the one hand and the AMA on the other—and Mills's action spared them that painful choice.

For all practical purposes, Medicare passed on Election Day. We estimated that we gained close to forty new Medicare votes in the House and at least two in the Senate. Equally important, after years of frustration with the House Ways and Means Committee, we had a seventeen-to-eight majority there.

Early in 1965 Chairman Mills said he'd be pleased to sponsor the Medicare bill in the House if the President wished and the President did wish.

Amazingly, the struggle continued. The AMA, ignoring all political reality, launched a last-ditch half-million-dollar anti-Medicare campaign. Its hope (strategy is too grand a word for it) was to defeat Medicare by gaining support for a program it called the Doctors' Eldercare Program—and which Representative Frank Thompson dubbed Doctorcare. To further complicate things, a Republican introduced a bill similar to Eldercare, which he called Bettercare.

We in the White House were delighted by the AMA's blind opposition to the inevitable. The 1964 elections had weakened the AMA's power in Congress and now its bitter-end battle was offending the friends it had left. We had no problem in the House, but there remained the possibility—the AMA's only hope—that Senator Byrd would bottle up Medicare in his Finance Committee. Because of Byrd's great prestige, the votes in his committee were uncertain.

The President personally solved this problem, with a typically outrageous performance. In mid-March, just after Ways and Means reported out the Medicare bill, President Johnson went on television to describe the program to the nation. With him were nine Democratic leaders of Congress. Each was introduced, and all but Harry Byrd pledged his full support to Medicare. Then, LBJ cornered the straight-backed old Virginian and pressured him into promising quick committee hearings. The exchange went as follows:

THE PRESIDENT: I know that you will take an interest in the orderly scheduling of this matter and giving it a thorough hearing. (Byrd makes no reply.) Would you care to make an observation?

SENATOR BYRD: There is no observation I can make now, because the bill hasn't come before the Senate. Naturally, I'm not familiar with it.

THE PRESIDENT: And you have nothing that you know of that would prevent hearings coming about in reasonable time, not anything ahead of it in the Committee?

SENATOR BYRD: Nothing in the Committee now.

THE PRESIDENT: So when the House acts and it is referred to the Senate Finance Committee you will arrange for prompt hearings and thorough hearings?

SENATOR BYRD (weakly): Yes.

THE PRESIDENT (banging the desk with his fist): Good!

The House voted on Medicare on April 8. Wilbur Mills was given a standing ovation when he introduced the bill, which many were calling the Mills bill. The final challenge in the House was a proposal to replace Medicare with the weak Republican Bettercare bill. This was defeated by a 45-vote margin—almost exactly the number of new Medicare votes we'd gained in the election five months earlier. With that vote it was clear that Medicare would pass, and many representatives who had voted against it previously switched their positions to be on the winning side. The final vote was 313 to 115.

In the Senate, as Senator Byrd had promised, there were prompt hearings. Then Medicare went again to the Senate floor, where it had lost by two votes in 1962 and passed by five votes in 1964. This time it passed by an overwhelming 68 to 21.

On July 30, 1965, President Johnson signed the Medicare bill at the Harry S. Truman Library, Independence, Missouri, in the presence of a distinguished audience which included former President Truman, who had advocated legislation to provide public health insurance some twenty-five years earlier.

The struggle to guarantee medical care to older Americans was, along with the civil rights and education bills, one of the glories of the historic 1965–66 Congress. Yet the passage of Medicare was only part of the larger struggle to provide first-rate medical care to all Americans, regardless of their age. Must an American be sixty-five years old before society cares about his health? Obviously not, and what Medicare was to the 1960s, national health insurance is to the 1970s. Once again, as under Eisenhower, there is strong Republican opposition. Once again, a Kennedy (Senator Ted Kennedy) is leading the fight (in the Senate). And once again the ultimate outcome is as inevitable as tomorrow's sunrise.

For all the high spirits and achievements of 1965–66, we were increasingly aware of an ever-darkening cloud on the horizon, the war in Vietnam.

The problem had begun, of course, under Kennedy. My first memory of the war in Vietnam goes back to a bipartisan breakfast President Kennedy gave for legislative leaders in 1962. Secretary McNamara gave a briefing on the situation in Vietnam. He was decisive and impressive. He explained that there were so many American military advisers in South Vietnam, that they would do such-and-such a job of training our allies, and they would be out by such-and-such a time. I was taken aback. I had no idea we'd made such a military commitment. Charlie Halleck, the House Republican leader, was seated at my right and Ev Dirksen, the Republican Senate leader, was also present. I thought to myself that if I were they, I'd be cross-examining McNamara closely on the statements he'd made. But there wasn't a whisper of doubt, and we passed on to the next item on the agenda.

For the next couple of years there would be periodic reports on Vietnam, usually by Secretaries Rusk or McNamara or by Dick Helms, the CIA Director. They would have charts and maps and would give reports about body counts and kill ratios and bridges bombed. They were extremely confident and, although some of us may have been skeptical, we never felt we were in a position to challenge the wisdom of the experts.

Henry Wilson and I privately commented about these briefings—we'd say the North Vietnamese must be the best engi-

neers in the world, because they'd obviously rebuilt every
bridge in their country at least ten times. We shared a laugh
when I was told that Henry Cabot Lodge, our ambassador to
Vietnam, had asked to have me assigned to Vietnam. Lodge
had decided that what the South Vietnamese needed was
greater political cohesion, and since I was the celebrated
political organizer, obviously I was just the fellow to come
over and tighten things up. President Johnson, to his credit,
vetoed the plan.

Henry and I could joke, but it was all deadly serious to
the President, as it had to be. The war, like everything else,
was immensely personal with him. I'd see him often in his
bedroom the first thing in the morning and I'd say, "How are
you this morning?" and he'd reply, "I didn't sleep well,
Larry. I was up until five waiting for the last of my boys to
come home." He meant the bomber pilots who'd been over
North Vietnam. Some mornings they didn't all come home
and he would be terribly depressed.

Slowly the war became a political issue. Opposition to the
war was beginning to build on campuses and in some liberal
circles, but there was little opposition in Congress. Liberals
in Congress who might otherwise have been expected to oppose the war tended in 1965–66 to give the President the
benefit of the doubt, probably because of his magnificent performance in domestic affairs. The early war critics on the Hill
were Senators Wayne Morse, Ernest Gruening, George McGovern and Frank Church—not the Senate and House leaders with
whom the President met regularly. Still, the opposition was
growing month by month, and I tried, as I would on any political issue, to give the President the best reading I could on how
it was affecting his standing with Congress. My files contain a
number of memos I sent the President in 1965–66, memos that
suggest how the Vietnam issue began slowly to surface as a
political problem for him. These memos also suggest, I think,
that Johnson was by no means unaware of the political backlash caused by his war policy. To the contrary, he knew the
problem. Nonetheless, he went ahead and pursued the war
policy that he believed to be the right one.

The first references to Vietnam in my files are two brief memos to the President dated February 18, 1965. The first noted that a Vietnam debate had been scheduled in the House, that the Leadership would lead the debate supporting the President's policy, and that my office would help them with facts, speech material and so forth.

The second memo noted that a Vietnam debate was scheduled in the Senate and "Dirksen support fine but considerable additional Democratic support available to counteract Church, McGovern, et al." I also noted that a resolution supporting the President's position had been discussed, but was inadvisable since it would be referred to Senator Fulbright's Foreign Relations Committee; instead, I suggested that we circulate an informal statement of support among our Senate allies, and that my office continue to provide them with speeches and statements.

In May 1965, at the President's request, we called congressional offices to learn how the mail was running both on Vietnam and the intervention in the Dominican Republic. In general, we found mail was not heavy and tended to support the President, except in a few eastern states.

In the early months of 1966 I began making trips around the country, with an eye to the fall's congressional campaigns, and I found increasing concern about Vietnam, which I always reported back to the President.

In February, however, my memo on a fund-raising dinner in New Jersey noted that Governor Richard Hughes "made an excellent plea to support you on the Vietnam policy and this was received with obvious strong approval by the audience."

The next month, after a luncheon meeting with the editors of the New York *Times,* I reported, "It was a two-hour Q and A, primarily on Vietnam policy. I reminded them of the attitude of the American people as I see it and confirmed by the polls—your desire for a peaceful resolution and your intention of fulfilling our longtime commitment. I suggested that what was needed today was internal unity and that politics as such did not belong in this area . . . It was apparent to me that there is not unanimity of agreement among them on Vietnam—my impression is some of them, on an individual basis, support you."

In mid-April I spoke at a testimonial dinner for liberal California Congressman Jeffery Cohelan. I noted that Cohelan "chose to speak for twenty minutes stating his extremely dove-like position on Vietnam—I followed him by hitting the Vietnam section of my speech very hard—and audience reaction was cool." In concluding my report I said: "The extent and depth of concern regarding our Vietnam position in northern California surprised me . . . while this past weekend represented nothing more than the quick brush you are able to give an area in a few hours I must say that my impression probably should be checked out further. If accurate this could mean political trouble in the near future."

Johnson was by no means isolated from criticism. His favorite reading material in those days was the Congressional Record. It was, to someone who had spent most of his adult life on Capitol Hill, like his home town paper. Johnson had an aide, Jake Jacobson, a Texas lawyer, who got up before dawn each morning and read through the day's Congressional Record. He would put paper clips at each page where a member of Congress praised or criticized the President, then take the Record to the President's bedroom for him to read as he ate his breakfast. There was much more praise than criticism in those days, but when the latter occurred, Johnson was likely to grab the phone and call me and tell me to find out what was bothering so-and-so.

One instance of this occurred in June 1966, when Johnson read an article in the Scripps-Howard papers in which a number of Democratic congressmen were critical of the war policy. Johnson called and told me to have the staff talk to all of the congressmen that very day and to report to him on what they were saying. Because he believed so fully in the rightness of his policy, Johnson tended to think that if any Democrat criticized him, it was simply a failure of communication, and that if we would just explain our position better the problem would be solved.

We talked to the various congressmen and found most

of them confused and concerned by the war. They wanted
to support the President, but they had elections coming up and
they knew their constituents were disturbed by rising draft
calls and rising battlefield casualties. I wrote a long memo to
the President which concluded with my view that while some
of the congressmen might criticize the war, they were still our
allies and we had to recognize the problems they faced in an
election year:

"When you check the degree of support of these fellows
and realize that while some of this group becomes unnecessarily
and exceedingly anxious and nervous, nevertheless, it is awfully important that we return every one of them we possibly
can next January. The ebb and flow that is bound to take place
with Vietnam, and for that matter possibly the economy, will
of course in turn affect those members in varying degrees. But,
in the final analysis, they have supported you well and I believe
have your best interests at heart within the context of the very
human desire to survive politically. The best procedure is for
us to do what we have been doing—stay close to them."

By then, of course, the 1966 congressional elections were at
hand. We knew we would lose some seats; our hope was to
minimize our losses. I was busy with both Post Office business
and congressional relations and was not deeply involved in the
campaign.

As Election Day neared, the polls looked bad. The President
canceled a planned campaign swing of his own when it
appeared that many of the candidates he would have been
supporting were going to lose. On November 2, I sent the
President my predictions of the elections. I said I thought
we would have a net loss of thirty-two House seats and perhaps
as many as thirty-seven; a net loss of one Senate seat and perhaps two; and a net loss of four governorships. I was too optimistic. We lost forty-seven House seats, four Senate seats, and
eight governorships.

Obviously the public discontent with the war in Vietnam
was a major factor in the Democratic losses in 1966. Equally
damaging, I believe, however, was the growing backlash

against the drive for civil rights that both Kennedy and Johnson had carried out. In the first half of the decade, most civil rights legislation had been directed at southern racial discrimination. But after 1965 the government moved against discrimination in all parts of America and the results were politically explosive.

The reaction in the South, the traditionally Democratic Dixie, was easiest to measure. In 1960, Kennedy, although a Catholic, carried six southern states. In 1964, Johnson, himself a Southerner, carried five southern states. In 1968 the Democratic candidate, Humphrey, carried only one southern state, Texas, and that one only thanks to the three-way split in the vote created by Governor George Wallace of Alabama who, as a segregationist candidate, received 10,000,000 votes and carried five southern states. The Democratic Party was morally right to fulfill its historic commitment to civil rights, and history will so record it, but each legislative victory we won on behalf of minority groups was a setback to our short-term political interests.

With the great Democratic majority of the Eighty-ninth Congress sharply reduced by the 1966 elections, there would be far less major legislation from the Ninetieth Congress in Johnson's last two years as President. The 1965–66 session of Congress was Johnson's finest hour, and all of us who participated in it will always take pride in what was achieved.

It is not my purpose to detail the Johnson legislative record here, but even a summary will suggest its scope. In 1965 we proposed 87 major bills and 84 passed. In 1966 we proposed 113 major bills and 97 of them passed. That totaled 200 measures initiated and 181 approved. Here is a partial list of the legislation passed by the Eighty-ninth Congress:

> The First Session (1965): Medicare; Elementary and Secondary Education; Higher Education; the Farm Bill; the Department of Housing and Urban Development; the Omnibus Housing Act (including rent supplements and low and moderate income housing); Social Security increases: Voting Rights Act; the Immigration Bill; the Older Americans Act; Heart Disease, Cancer, and Stroke

Research and Construction of Facilities; Law Enforcement Assistance Act; National Crime Commission; Drug Controls Act; Mental Health Research and Facilities; Medical Libraries Construction; Vocational Rehabilitation; Arts and Humanities Foundation; Highway Beautification; Appalachia Regional Commission; Air Pollution Control; Water Pollution Control; Child Health Medical Assistance.

The Second Session (1966): The Department of Transportation; Truth in Packaging; Model Cities; Rent Supplements; Teacher Corps; Asian Development Bank; the Clean Rivers Act; the Traffic Safety, Highway Safety and Mine Safety Acts; Narcotics Rehabilitation Act; Health Professional Training; the Child Nutrition Act; the Minimum Wage increase; Urban Mass Transit Act; Bail Reform; the Tire Safety Act; the Public Health Service Reorganization; Medical Care for Military Dependants; and Elementary and Higher Education Funds.

It has sometimes been said that the record of the Eighty-ninth Congress was the greatest since the New Deal legislation of 1933–34. I'm not sure that goes far enough. You can't really compare the two, of course—one an emergency program passed in the midst of economic depression, the other a burst of national self-improvement passed in a time of prosperity. Yet I tend to think, granting my deep personal involvement, that the breakthroughs of the Eighty-ninth Congress—in education, in medical care, in civil rights, in housing—exceeded the New Deal achievements in their impact on American society.

History will, of course, be the final judge of that. I can only say now that a simple listing of bills passed in 1965–66 can in no way convey what they have meant to millions of Americans. The record of the Eighty-ninth Congress is inscribed in the lives of children who received better educations, older people who could face ill health with hope, unemployed men and women who found job opportunities, families that were helped out of slums and into decent housing. Lyndon Johnson made his mistakes and he paid for them, but his record with the Eighty-ninth Congress will live on as a monument to his energy, his vision, and his compassion.

For my part, I was privileged, as an assistant to two Presidents, to play a role in the creation of a new working relationship between the executive and legislative branches of our government. Other men developed the legislation and wrote the messages; my talents did not lie in those areas. But I try to be a perfectionist where organization is concerned, and what I thought I could do was to bring that organizational ability and political judgment to bear on behalf of our legislative program. For too long, Presidents and Congress had eyed each other suspiciously across the great constitutional gulf that separates the two ends of Pennsylvania Avenue.

Our congressional relations office became the instrument by which two Presidents bridged the gap. We proved, I feel, that the two branches can work together productively and with mutual respect. A friend of mine, Joseph Barr, who has been both a member of Congress and Secretary of the Treasury, spoke of our efforts "to build an invisible bridge down Pennsylvania Avenue," in a speech he delivered in the mid-1960s. Barr went on to say:

"This rather simple device of consciously building a bridge across the Constitutional Gulf has helped combine the advantages of a congressional and a parliamentary system. While maintaining the absolute independence of the individual Member of Congress, the O'Brien bridge has in effect opened a parliamentary dialogue in a congressional system. I mean by this that the politicians—the Members and the President— are now engaged in a direct dialogue as they would in a Parliament."

Still, as much pride as we Democrats may take in our legislative record of the 1960s, we must face the fact that we made our share of mistakes. Amid the excitement of 1965–66, we tended too much toward a "batting average" approach to legislation, and I was as guilty of that as anyone. As we pushed scores of new programs, we did not give every one all the attention it deserved. We sometimes promised too much —the "war on poverty" was an example—and we sometimes made the mistake of equating a bill passed with a problem solved.

If we learned nothing else in the 1960s, we learned how deep-rooted are our nation's social and economic problems. They will never be solved in a two-year spurt or, indeed, in an eight-year spurt. I recall the words of President Kennedy as he outlined his goals in his Inaugural Address: "All this will not be finished in the first 100 days. Nor will it be finished in the first 1,000 days, nor in the life of this administration, nor even perhaps in our lifetime on this planet. But let us begin." All that we Democrats can say now, looking back, is that we did the best we could with the facts and the talent available to us to "begin."

While some of the programs we enacted were not perfect, the answer is not to destroy them and put nothing in their place, as the Nixon administration set out to do. The answer, rather, is to improve those efforts. Franklin Roosevelt once made a statement which I think is relevant to our experience in the 1960s:

"Governments can err, Presidents do make mistakes, but the immortal Dante tells us that divine justice weighs the sins of the cold-blooded and the sins of the warm-hearted in different scales. Better the occasional faults of a government that lives in a spirit of charity than the consistent omissions of a government frozen in the ice of its own indifference."

Whatever our failures, they were at least the sins of the warmhearted, and I think they will be weighed by history in different scales than those of the men who followed us to power.

X

POSTMASTER GENERAL

MY APPOINTMENT AS Postmaster General in the late summer of 1965 was one of those strange Johnsonesque exercises that was typical of Johnson in those exuberant days. I was the last to know what was happening, and Johnson thoroughly enjoyed my confusion.

The President knew, of course, that I intended to leave government at the conclusion of the 1965 session of Congress. As I mentioned earlier, I had obtained his specific promise that there would be no further discussion between us when I was ready to resign. But he was not a man who gave up easily.

I see now that Johnson gave me a few clues that summer that something was afoot. At one congressional leadership breakfast meeting, the President unexpectedly said to me:

"I know what's on your mind, and I'm going to win."

"What's that all about?" asked Carl Albert, who was sitting next to me.

"Beats me," I admitted.

A few weeks later, when I was late for a presidential breakfast, Johnson had Jack Valenti call and ask where I was. I arrived at the breakfast soon after, and when it was over, while I was talking with Dean Rusk about the foreign-aid bill, the President approached.

"What are you two talking about?" he demanded.

"The foreign-aid bill," I said, and he nodded and hurried off to a news conference.

I went back to my office and told Phyllis that something

strange was going on, but it was several weeks before I understood what that morning's exchanges had been all about.

I was still in the dark when the President called me into
his office one Friday afternoon in late August, just before he
was to leave for a weekend at the LBJ Ranch. I was then
planning to leave government soon. I had received several
attractive job offers, and some of my friends were again suggesting that I return to Massachusetts politics. I had made up
my mind to decide that weekend what I would do. I had discussed this with associates, and word of my intent had appeared in the Washington newspapers.

When President Johnson summoned me to his office that
afternoon, I assumed it was on routine business. When I
entered, he was standing with his back to me, studying one of
the news tickers he had had installed in his office.

"Well, what is it, Mr. President, good news or bad?" I asked
after a moment, just to break the silence.

He turned and gave me a solemn look.

"Bad news, Larry," he said. "You're going to have to leave
the White House. I'm appointing you Postmaster General!"

I was speechless. As far as I knew, no opening existed—he
had a Postmaster General named John Gronouski. Johnson gave
me no time to collect my thoughts.

"You come on down to the ranch tomorrow and we'll talk
about it there. Okay?" With that, he eased me out of his office.

I returned to my own office, where Mary McGrory of the
Washington *Star* was waiting—we had been in the midst of an
interview when Johnson summoned me. I begged off; my
thoughts were too muddled to give a coherent interview. There
were many reasons why I really wanted to return to private
life. But, as Johnson had expected, I simply found it impossible to turn down a chance to serve in a President's Cabinet.
For an immigrant's son, for a fellow who had worked his way
up the political ladder, it was just too great an honor to refuse.

Secretary Rusk and Postmaster General and Mrs. Gronouski
were on board the air force plane that flew Elva, Larry, and
me down to the LBJ Ranch the next day. I said nothing about
my possible appointment, for I didn't know if Gronouski was

aware that he was about to be replaced. Rusk said nothing either. Lady Bird Johnson, cordial as ever, met our plane, drove us to our cottages at the ranch, and invited us for cocktails and dinner. There was quite a large group for dinner, including Arthur Goldberg, who was then the ambassador to the United Nations, and the evening passed without my having an opportunity to speak to the President about my appointment.

The next morning, Sunday, the Gronouskis, Elva, and I went to early Mass together. When we arrived back at the ranch for breakfast with the Johnsons, the President announced that we'd all go to church together.

"Mr. President," I protested, "I've already been to church."

"It won't hurt you to go to *my* church," Johnson insisted.

Elva and I rode in the car with the President and as we neared the church, Johnson grinned and said, "The press doesn't know you're here—just watch Merriman Smith's face when he sees you."

He loved the secrecy, the pulling rabbits out of his hat, and, sure enough, when we got out of the car outside the church, we heard Merriman Smith, the veteran White House correspondent for United Press International, exclaim to the other reporters, "Hey, there's Larry O'Brien!"

After church, Elva and I drove back to the ranch with Mrs. Johnson and Arthur Goldberg.

"Lyndon has called a press conference when we get back," Lady Bird said. "Does anyone know what it's for?"

"I think he's going to announce the Adlai Stevenson scholarships," said Goldberg, who was Stevenson's successor at the UN.

I had an idea that the press conference might be about me, but I said nothing. I still wanted to talk to the President about my appointment, but he was obviously taking no chances that I'd turn him down.

When we arrived back at the ranch, Bill Moyers directed me to a chair on the porch where I was to sit while Johnson met the press on his front lawn. I was still uncertain about what was happening, when Johnson told the reporters, "You've all heard that Larry O'Brien is leaving the White House, and I want to confirm that report."

He proceeded to announce that Gronouski was the new ambassador to Poland and I was the new Postmaster General.

"Don't be surprised if you see him on the Hill occasionally," Johnson added, grinning widely.

I saw Mrs. Johnson smiling, and I went over and assured her I had been telling her the truth when I said I didn't know what the news conference was all about. She just laughed; I knew she had been through this before.

I went into the house to call my sister in Massachusetts and give her the news. The President grabbed the phone and said, "Well, what do you think of this? Your brother's got two jobs now."

As he suggested, it was no secret that I was to continue in charge of his legislative program, both as Postmaster General-designate and as Postmaster General. In fact, when a reporter had asked who would replace O'Brien on congressional relations, Johnson had laughed and said, "O'Brien."

On our flight back to Washington, Johnson confessed that he'd thoroughly enjoyed the whole process of my appointment, particularly my ignorance of what was happening. Then he explained why a few weeks earlier, he'd called to see why I was late for the legislative breakfast and demanded to know what Dean Rusk and I were talking about. "I was going to announce your appointment that morning without telling you," he said. "The trouble was that Rusk hadn't gotten clearance from the Polish Government for Gronouski to be the new ambassador. When I saw you talking to Rusk, I thought he was tipping you off."

Back in Washington, the Senate unanimously confirmed my appointment as Postmaster General in something under an hour—one reporter called my confirmation hearing a "love-fest." There was one difficult moment during the Senate confirmation hearing when Senator Daniel Brewster of Maryland persistently asked me my position on the mail cover issue. Unfortunately, I hadn't the slightest idea what "mail cover" meant—it referred, I later learned, to the government's power

to monitor people's mail for investigative purposes—so I was
forced to say repeatedly that I would certainly review the
issue thoroughly, as Brewster kept probing for my nonexistent
position on the matter. Despite the "lovefest" on Capitol Hill,
my swearing-in was delayed two months, until November 3.
The fact was that, once Johnson knew I was going to stay, he
wasn't in any hurry for me to get over to the Post Office. He
wanted me to stick with the legislative program until Congress
adjourned. Even after I became Postmaster General, I felt
continual pressure from him to spend less time on postal affairs
and more time on congressional affairs. He insisted that I keep
my White House office and he turned down my repeated suggestion that Henry Hall Wilson—for whom Johnson had high
regard—be named to replace me as special assistant for congressional relations. More than once, Johnson said to me, "Larry,
if you need some more Assistant Postmaster Generals, we'll hire
them, but I want you spending more time on Congress!"

My actual swearing-in came abruptly. After two months of
waiting, I was beginning to doubt it would ever happen. I
went to Texas to make a speech and I called the President,
who was at the ranch recovering from his abdominal surgery,
to wish him good health. "Say, we ought to swear you in," he
declared. "Get Elva and come on down here."

The next thing I knew, Elva and I were at the ranch again
and Johnson had made elaborate plans for my swearing-in
ceremony. I was to be sworn in at a little combination grocery
store and post office at Hye, Texas, near the LBJ Ranch.
Johnson claimed to have mailed his first letter at that post
office a half-century earlier. "Larry is going to find that letter
and deliver it," he quipped.

It was a dreary, overcast November day, but Johnson was
in high spirits as we drove over to Hye. He explained that the
little store was owned by several brothers who had been his
boyhood friends and that he had been responsible for the
present storekeeper's appointment as a postmaster. He reminisced on the boyhood days when he would walk over to
this little store and eat cheese cut from a huge wheel and
crackers out of the cracker barrel.

Perhaps two hundred people and many news photographers were waiting for us outside the store. Johnson took my arm and led me up to his old friend, the storekeeper whom Johnson had named postmaster when he was in Congress.

"I want you to meet your new boss, the Postmaster General," he declared. "Tell him who appointed you as postmaster."

"Jim Farley," the postmaster replied, much to Johnson's chagrin.

"Let's go on inside," Johnson said. "I want to eat some of that good old cheese and crackers from the barrel."

Inside the store, unfortunately, Johnson found that the days of "that good old cheese" were no more. The only cheese in the place was Kraft cheese with each piece wrapped in cellophane, so he unwrapped a piece and ate it for the benefit of the photographers.

As Postmaster General, I inherited the biggest office in Washington (while keeping my White House office as well). The Republicans had begun the construction of the Post Office Building during the Hoover administration, but Roosevelt was President when it was completed and his Postmaster General, Jim Farley, was the first man to occupy the new office, which was about half the size of a basketball court, and had next to it a reception room that *was* the size of a basketball court. It is said that during the early days of the New Deal, that reception room would be filled each morning with job seekers, and that Farley would pass among them, no doubt hiring a few deserving Democrats.

The Postmaster General's office had a fireplace at either end. A portrait of Ben Franklin hung over one fireplace. He was the first Postmaster General and had started one well-honored tradition by putting twenty-odd of his relatives on the payroll. I hung a portrait of Jim Farley over the other fireplace. Farley was, besides being someone I knew and admired, one of the few men who had served both as Postmaster General and as Democratic National Chairman.

Soon after my appointment was announced, I was honored at two parties in Washington—one given by the members of

Congress, the other by a group of Washington reporters. The press party was unique, for while many people give parties for Washington newspapermen, Washington newspapermen rarely give parties for government officials. The party, at the Federal City Club on October 11, featured songs and skits and brief talks including humorous comments by Senator Everett Dirksen, in which he requested I reserve "a few bricks and a little mortar" for post offices in his state. Art Buchwald read an extremely funny speech—so funny, he decided, that he dashed out to phone it in to be his next column.

Over the years I have come to have tremendous respect for the Washington reporter. I'm not speaking just of the big-name columnists, but also of the fellow who's the correspondent for, say, a midwestern daily. These men and women aren't famous, but they're as tough, intelligent, honest, and dedicated a group as I've ever encountered. They worked just as long and hard as we did in government, and for less money. I came to respect the profession so much that when my son worked on his school paper at Georgetown Prep, I encouraged him to consider journalism as a career. (He eventually chose a career in law.)

I was pleased by the generally favorable press comment on my appointment as Postmaster General, but I was bothered by the assumption, widespread among politicians and reporters, that I would be only a figurehead Postmaster General, tending to politics while someone else handled the mails. Yet I had to admit there was cause for the skepticism. And I had to admit, too, that I was starting to have very real doubts about my new job. I feared that the Post Office would be a great letdown after the excitement of the 1965 legislative session. I had some idea what a mess postal service was in, and I wondered if I'd taken on an impossible job when I could have left government on a happy note.

I knew, too, that despite the honor of cabinet status, the Postmaster General was the low man on the cabinet totem pole. At cabinet meetings, I had often wondered why the Postmaster General even bothered to come. His problems seemed not to belong on the cabinet agenda, nor was he likely

Lawrence F. O'Brien with Senator John F. Kennedy, spring 1958.
The Kennedy-O'Brien political partnership began with Kennedy's
first Senate race and ended at the White House.

O'Brien, at the age of seven, with his mother, his sister, Mary, and his father. O'Brien was the son of Irish immigrants who settled in Springfield, Massachusetts.

A political apprenticeship: sixteen-year-old O'Brien behind a typewriter at the western Massachusetts election headquarters of Franklin D. Roosevelt, in 1932. His father, seated to the left of the American flag, was active in local Democratic politics, and young O'Brien was caught up in party work early.

In May 1944, O'Brien married Elva Brassard. The maid of honor was his sister, Mary, and his best man was future Massachusetts governor Foster Furcolo (right). Four years later, O'Brien applied the organizational techniques he'd learned in local elections to help win Furcolo a seat in Congress.

At a 1954 party in Framingham, Massachusetts, the new Mrs. John F. Kennedy is presented to Kennedy workers. O'Brien (at right) first met John Kennedy in 1947, when Kennedy was serving his first term in Congress. Later he became a key adviser and director of the campaign in which Kennedy upset the incumbent Republican Senator Henry Cabot Lodge in 1952.

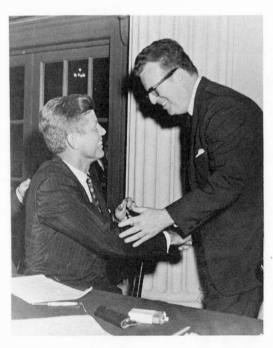

The 1952 victory cemented the Kennedy-O'Brien political partnership. When he ran for re-election in 1958, with O'Brien as director of organization, Kennedy received more votes than any other candidate ever had in Massachusetts, making him a serious contender for the 1960 presidential nomination. Above: Kennedy and aides receive calls from party workers on the eve of the Wisconsin primary. Left: The newly nominated Kennedy congratulates O'Brien, whom he has just named national director of organization for his presidential campaign.

*(Stan Wayman/*Time *magazine)*

November 1960: On election night at Robert Kennedy's house in Hyannis, O'Brien sweats it out with Ted and Bob Kennedy and their sister, Patricia Kennedy Lawford.

Facing a slender Democratic majority on Capitol Hill, Kennedy made O'Brien his special assistant for congressional relations. O'Brien met frequently with the Democratic leadership, as in this 1961 luncheon with House Speaker Sam Rayburn, Vice President Johnson, and Congressman Hale Boggs.

O'Brien quickly became one of Kennedy's principal advisers. Here, in the fall of 1961, he briefs Kennedy before an appearance at a congressional coffee hour. O'Brien was so effective as congressional liaison that *Time* magazine did a cover story on him.

TWENTY-FIVE CENTS

SEPTEMBER 1, 1961

WHITE HOUSE & CONGRESS
Power, Patronage and Persuasion

TIME

THE WEEKLY NEWSMAGAZINE

PRESIDENTIAL AIDE
LARRY O'BRIEN

$7.00 A YEAR

VOL. LXXVIII NO. 9

Dallas, 1963. O'Brien, at the foot of the ramp, follows the blood-spattered Mrs. Kennedy and her secretary, Mary Gallagher, up the steps to Air Force I for the journey back to Washington with John Kennedy's body. *(Cecil Stoughton)*

On board Air Force I: Johnson gazes earnestly at O'Brien (far left) just before Judge Sarah Hughes swears him in as the new President. Johnson was counting on O'Brien to help provide continuity between the two administrations. Behind Johnson is Evelyn Lincoln, Kennedy's secretary. *(Cecil Stoughton)*

Kennedy's body being removed from Air Force I upon arrival in Washington. To Mrs. Kennedy's left are Clint Hill, her secret service man, and O'Brien. *(Wide World Photos)*

O'Brien (right) with Mrs. Kennedy on her Thanksgiving Day 1963 visit to President Kennedy's grave at Arlington Cemetery.

O'Brien agreed to stay on as special assistant to the new President in order to help pass Kennedy's legislation. Above, days after the assassination, he and Johnson discuss the legislative program in the Oval Office.

After the passage of his Great Society legislation (1965–66), President Johnson appointed O'Brien to his Cabinet. In November 1965, O'Brien was sworn in as Postmaster General in front of the Hye, Texas, post office at which Johnson claimed to have mailed his first letter. O'Brien found the postal system near collapse and proposed legislation to create an independent postal corporation. *(Don Stoderl)*

O'Brien, whose Irish immigrant parents could only afford to send him to college at night, beams in June 1967, as his son, Larry III, displays his diploma from Harvard University.

O'Brien resigned his cabinet post to join Robert Kennedy in his bid for the presidency. Here, he and Kennedy workers discuss campaign strategy for the Indiana primary. *(Wide World Photos)*

In 1970, O'Brien became chairman of the Democratic National Committee for the second time. In February 1971, determined to unify the party, O'Brien held an unprecedented meeting of 1972 Democratic presidential hopefuls. From left: O'Brien's assistant Ira Kapenstein, Senator Hubert Humphrey, Committee treasurer Robert Strauss, Senator Fred Harris, Senate Majority Leader Mike Mansfield, Senator Edmund Muskie, O'Brien, Senator Harold Hughes, Senator Henry M. Jackson, Senator George McGovern, House Speaker Carl Albert, and Senator Edward Kennedy.   *(George Tames)*

In the interests of party unity, Chairman O'Brien visited George Wallace in his hospital room shortly after the attempt on his life—the first Democrat to do so.   *(Wide World Photos)*

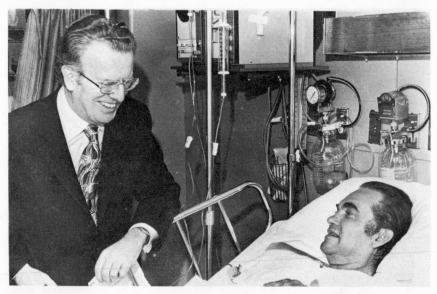

(Cartoon: Jim Dobbins/Boston Herald-American)

O'Brien briefs delegates on rules and procedures at the start of the 1972 convention in Miami Beach. *(Wide World Photos)*

O'Brien and Hubert Humphrey relaxing with a game of pool during the convention, at the time of O'Brien's crucial decision about the "California Challenge." The decision went against Humphrey, an old friend of O'Brien's. *(New York* Times)

Soon after George McGovern and Tom Eagleton became the Convention's choices, McGovern aggravated O'Brien by pleading with him to continue as party chairman, then changing his mind. But here, the three top Democrats clench hands in a show of amity.

(United Press International)

The primary target of Nixon's plumbers, who bugged his office, O'Brien resorted to a public telephone in the lobby of the Water-gate to make his private calls. *(United Press International)*

to have any insight into the domestic and foreign issues that arose for cabinet discussion.

I knew that, on the vital issue of money, the Postmaster General fought a hard, usually a losing, battle on two fronts. First, within the Executive Branch, as the departments and agencies fought for funds, the Post Office always had low priority and often watched its requests cut to the bone by the Bureau of the Budget and the White House. Then it might be cut again by the House Appropriations Committee and cut still again on the House floor and in the Senate. For lack of funds, service grew increasingly worse, but the Post Office's urgent needs for capital investment were never met.

As I dug into my new job in the winter of 1965–66, I found little to encourage me. On December 9 I sent the President a blunt memo, which began:

"I am seriously concerned about the current condition of the Post Office Department. During my first month here, I have attempted to analyze the situation both in Headquarters and in the field. Frankly, postal service has obviously been deteriorating rapidly while mail volume shows an extraordinary yearly increase."

I went on to detail the causes of the problem, which I said included an inadequate budget and serious management deficiencies. Yet my memo, pessimistic as it was, touched only on the Executive Branch aspects of the postal problem. The Post Office's relationship with Congress was an even greater problem. As Postmaster General, I learned my areas of non-control were almost limitless. Congress defined the services of the Post Office and the conditions under which they had to be performed. Congress set the postal rates. Congress fixed the size of the postal work force and established the pay scales, frequently with little regard to revenues. Congress doled out every dime of our funds. Congress wanted better postal service, but it wasn't willing to give the Postmaster General the money or the freedom to do the job.

The workload of the Post Office Department, I found, was truly staggering. When I went to the department, the per capita mail rate was one piece of mail per day for every man, woman and child—that is, 365 pieces of mail a year for every American—and the figure was steadily rising. Mail volume for fiscal 1967 was over 80 billion pieces, more than all the mail handled by all other postal services in the world, and we expected that figure to rise by a third within five years.

Yet the work of handling the mail was being performed with essentially the same facilities that existed prior to World War II, when only one third as much mail was processed. In addition to these problems with physical facilities, the Post Office had serious personnel problems. Pay was poor and chances for advancement were minimal. A disproportionate number of blacks were stalled in the department's lower-level jobs. Morale was low, and the annual turnover rate was a disastrous 21 per cent. Some 92 per cent of these underpaid, dissatisfied postal employees were members of fourteen militant, highly competitive labor unions and the unions bargained with Congress, not with the Postmaster General, for better wages and working conditions.

The result was a postal system that operated on the edge of catastrophe. We were given a glimpse of catastrophe in the massive Chicago tie-up of October 1966, when the world's largest post office was clogged for three weeks with ten million pieces of undelivered mail.

The Post Office was, to say the least, a challenge to my organizational skills, and I set out to find the people and the programs that could provide short-term solutions, while I searched for the long-term reforms I knew were needed.

Not long after my appointment as Postmaster General was announced, I received a call from a young man named Ira Kapenstein, who said he was a special assistant to John Gronouski and that he would like to talk to me. I invited him to my White House office. He then explained that Gronouski had offered him a position at the U. S. Embassy in Poland, but that he would rather continue on at the Post Office, if I felt there would be a place for him on my staff.

I was impressed with the way he presented himself. Ira was then thirty years old, a slender, wiry, rather serious young man, obviously extremely intelligent.

"I'll have to be candid with you," I told him. "I don't feel I can make any long-term commitment. We don't know each other. It might not work out, on either side. But if you like, let's try each other out and see how it goes."

It went extremely well. Ira was a remarkable young man and he soon made himself invaluable to me.

Ira had grown up in New York City, where his mother was employed in the garment district. He worked his way through the University of Iowa's School of Journalism and, upon graduation, got a job as a reporter for the Milwaukee *Journal*. John Gronouski, prior to his appointment as Postmaster General, had been a state official in Wisconsin, and when he had come to Washington late in 1963 he had recruited Ira to come with him. Ira started out as Gronouski's press officer, but soon became involved in all areas of Post Office affairs. Because of the responsibility I could delegate to Ira and some other close associates, I was able to stay atop the Post Office job while still directing the legislative program in the White House.

One day in 1967 Ira came to me with a big smile on his face. "I celebrate a great anniversary today," he told me.

"What's that?" I asked.

"This is the fifth anniversary of my operation for cancer," he explained. "If there's no recurrence in five years, that usually means you've licked it." I was taken aback, because I hadn't known of Ira's previous operation. Certainly there had been no indication, from the tireless way he performed his work, that he had any problem.

Assisted by Ira and a few others, we created the Post Office Department's first Office of Planning. We also upgraded the Office of Research and Engineering to bureau status and hired several dozen new people. We started a $100-million crash mechanization program, including a computer, which eventually will keep track of mail flow and manpower use in the seventy-five largest post offices, and initiated a program to recruit college graduates for management positions.

In an article on the Post Office published in March 1967, a *Fortune* magazine writer said: "To the surprise of just about everyone connected with the postal service—and to the gratification of most of them—O'Brien is turning out to be the strongest, most imaginative boss the Department has ever had . . . Nobody before O'Brien really put together a comprehensive attack on the Department's problems. And nobody before O'Brien brought to the job the forward-looking approach that is routine in any well-run business."

Delighted as I was at *Fortune*'s comments, I found them ironic, for they came only weeks before I unveiled the biggest contribution I would make to the improvement of the Post Office, one that would make the others seem tame by comparison.

I hadn't been at the Post Office long when I decided it should be taken out of the political context entirely and made into a private corporation, perhaps patterned after the Tennessee Valley Authority. I had gone into the job with more political leverage, both with Congress and the President, than any Postmaster General in history, yet I had been able to make only minor improvements in its operations. The assumption that the postal service would somehow always muddle through just wasn't warranted. There had to be radical change or the whole thing was going to collapse.

Early in 1966, I asked four of my most talented assistants to undertake a comprehensive, confidential study of the entire postal service. I asked them to report to me on whether or not the creation of a postal corporation, out of the Cabinet, was a viable answer to the postal mess. If not, what lesser steps might do the job? The young men I asked to answer these questions were Ira Kapenstein; Ronald Lee, whom I hired to run the new Office of Planning; Tim May, our general counsel; and Larry Lewin, my administrative assistant.

Their recommendation, after several months of intensive study, was what I had hoped it would be—that the Post Office be taken out of the Cabinet and made into a nonprofit government corporation. It was an unprecedented proposal, one that was sure to arouse opposition in Congress and among the postal unions.

I said to Ira, "Well, now what do we do with it?"

I first thought that I would take the proposal directly to the President, but it isn't easy to get a President, any President, excited about postal matters. I discussed the plan with Charles Schultze, the Director of the Bureau of the Budget. He was enthusiastic, but the future of the Post Office wasn't really his problem either. I decided I would make the idea public, so we could see what the reaction would be.

I announced the proposal in a speech to the Magazine Publishers Association on April 3, 1967. My plan, as I described it, was that the postal service be taken out of the Cabinet to become a nonprofit government corporation operated by a presidentially appointed board of directors and managed by a professional executive, with a clear mandate on future postal rates.

I stressed the key point of finances. A private corporation would be free of many of the restrictions of appropriated funds. It could issue bonds to obtain capital funds needed for new facilities and modernization. Only such a system, I said, would allow the genius of American managerial skills to be brought to bear on postal service.

The proposal was page one news across the country. In the next few days it inspired several hundred newspaper editorials, the vast majority of them favorable. Some commentators were amused by the idea of O'Brien, the politician, wanting to take the Post Office out of politics and abolishing his own cabinet post in the process, but it was apparent that there was wide support in the press for a plan that promised to relieve the nation's tangled postal situation.

The public approval of the plan impressed the President. It was good government—and good politics, too. I had told Joe Califano, who supported the plan, that I hoped the President would appoint a high-prestige commission to study my proposal. Such a far-reaching proposal was not going to be accepted simply on my say-so; it needed strong, bipartisan backing.

On April 8, just five days after my speech, the President named the President's Commission on Postal Organization,

chaired by Frederick R. Kappel, former chairman of the board
of American Telephone and Telegraph.

After intensive study, the Kappel Commission reported to
the President in June of 1968. It endorsed the proposal fully
and offered detailed ideas on how the changeover might
best be accomplished. At that point, I hoped President Johnson
would quickly translate the Kappel Commission report into a
legislative proposal. I didn't expect it to pass Congress that
year, but I wanted it clearly on the record that this was a
Democratic plan for reform.

Instead, the President took no action. He did not make the
report public for several months and was noncommital regarding it. One problem was that my successor as Postmaster
General, Marvin Watson, urged reforms that stopped short
of removing the postal department from the Cabinet. Ultimately President Johnson did endorse the plan in his final State
of the Union message in January 1969.

After Nixon's election, his choice for Postmaster General,
Winton Blount, an Alabama businessman, came to see me and
said he was excited about the postal corporation plan and that
he'd already discussed it with Nixon. It was no surprise to
see the Nixon administration seize the idea, for it continued
to be good government and good politics too. Blount became
quite a crusader for the plan and in the spring he asked me
to be co-chairman, with former Senator Thruston Morton, of
a Citizens Committee for Postal Reform. That put me in the
position of lobbying for a Nixon bill, but I accepted, because
I considered it at least in part an O'Brien bill.

My support of the bill led to my only two personal meetings
with Nixon. In 1969, when I agreed to co-chair the Citizens
Committee, I was invited to confer with the President at his
San Clemente estate. Nixon greeted me cordially, and we
had coffee and chatted with Blount and Morton. After a while
I realized that Nixon couldn't decide whether to call me
"Larry" or "Mr. O'Brien," so for a time he didn't call me
either, then he came down in favor of Larry. He took me on
a tour of his office, pointing out the various mementos of his
career. My impression was that he was strangely ill at ease.

We went to a pressroom to brief reporters on the postal bill. Nixon walked up to the microphone and said, "Larry, why don't you stand here to my right?"

"Just as long as it's not too far to your right," I quipped. That got a laugh from some in the press, who were clearly amused to see O'Brien as Nixon's guest.

Our second meeting involved fewer pleasantries. It came in August 1970, after Congress passed the Postal Corporation bill. By then I had become Democratic National Chairman and an outspoken critic of the Nixon administration. I can't believe that Nixon was eager to have me to the bill-signing ceremony at the Post Office Department but not to invite me would have been awkward, since I was a former Postmaster General, the co-chairman of the Citizens Committee, and the original author of the proposal.

As the ceremony began, I was curious to see what, if anything, Nixon would say about my role in originally proposing the idea that had been enacted. He was actually quite clever about it. He mentioned the Kappel Commission, and stressed Winton Blount's contribution, but mentioned me only in passing, with a quip about better mail delivery not being a partisan issue. It was a smooth, impressive performance.

But that is just a bit of political byplay. The important point is that in a remarkably short time a controversial plan for restructuring the nation's postal service was accepted by two Presidents, the public, and the Congress.

I have not always been pleased by the manner in which the new Postal Service has been implemented under the Nixon administration. There have been far too many political appointments of unqualified people to top postal positions. There have been serious management mistakes. And there is an inadequate program of congressional relations. Still, the new United States Postal Service has the tools to provide efficient and economic postal service. When those tools are put to use by qualified, dedicated administrators, we can finally achieve first-rate postal service.

XI

JOHNSON WITHDRAWS!

THE DRAMATIC POLITICAL developments of late 1967 and 1968, including the Kennedy and McCarthy campaigns for the Democratic nomination for President, President Johnson's decision not to seek re-election, and Vice President Humphrey's emergence as the candidate, were all deeply interwoven with the ever-worsening U.S. military position in Vietnam and the widening disenchantment with our war policy at home. Before discussing those events, I should note my own attitude toward the war during that period.

In retrospect, I think the evolution of my views on Vietnam was much like that of the average American. I accepted the war at the outset, and was confident the President would resolve it quickly. My thoughts were focused on domestic legislation, and I trusted the military experts who month after month assured us that the end was in sight. It was not until late 1967 that I began to seriously question the war. My concern escalated in 1968 when my son Larry joined the Army with a commitment to serve in Vietnam. And, of course, the fact of the Tet Offensive and the success of Senator Eugene McCarthy's antiwar campaign made it impossible to ignore the potential military and political disaster that the Johnson administration faced. It was only then that I expressed directly to the President my personal doubts about the war.

We had lost ground in the 1966 congressional elections, but we attributed that more to normal off-year attrition than to any widespread anti-Vietnam feeling among the voters. Still, the war had been a factor, the issue was continuing to surface, and the President's hold on the new Congress was not what it had been on the previous one. The mood of Washington was changing. On January 9, 1967, just after the new Congress convened, the President met with Senate Democratic leaders, and there was a full-fledged discussion of the war. Mike Manatos took notes on the discussion, and they suggest the temper of the Senate leadership at that point. Some of the highlights were these:

"Senator J. W. Fulbright—Laid great emphasis on the need to find a way to 'get out' of Vietnam, which he believes was the strongest undercurrent in last year's elections. Expressed concern at what he construed to be certain 'disparities' between the President's position on Vietnam and that of Secretary Rusk when he testifies before the Foreign Relations Committee. The President made clear that if Fulbright would catalogue the area of concern he would speak to Rusk."

"Senator George Smathers—Told of one son just returned from Vietnam, and another about to leave for that area, and the feeling of the first son that 'dissident voices' raised in the Senate on Vietnam was the most serious damper on the morale of our fighting men."

"Senator Richard Russell—Total emphasis on Vietnam. We should 'go in and win, or get out.'"

"Senator Stuart Symington—We are not letting air power reach its enormous capability to shorten war and relieve ground troops."

"Senator Warren Magnuson—We should quit 'nit-picking' on Vietnam, 'with all due respect to my colleague from Arkansas.'"

"Senator Daniel Inouye—Bombing of North Vietnam is most controversial aspect of conflict. Would welcome a candid briefing on bombing results."

"Senator Lister Hill—Endorses Russell view on Vietnam. We should close Hai Phong by sinking ship in harbor."

"Senator Jennings Randolph—Endorses President's handling of Vietnam. Believes we are moving toward victory, hopefully by the end of 1967."

Two points might be made about this meeting. The first is that, clearly, in early 1967, the President was not hearing out-

spoken criticism of the war from the Democratic leaders in the
Senate. Fulbright had some criticism, Daniel Inouye said he'd
like to know more about the results of the bombing, and the
others' main criticism was that the President wasn't pursuing
the war vigorously enough. The second point is that this meeting, however mild its criticisms, was nonetheless the strongest
face-to-face criticism of the war the President had heard. In
previous meetings the war had hardly been discussed at all.

During 1967, while I remained uncertain as to whether the
war was right militarily or diplomatically, I became increasingly aware that it was a disaster politically. The one thing I
felt that I could and should do was to make sure the President
had a complete picture of the damage the war was doing to us
in political terms. I thus sent him many memos in which I reported on talks I'd had with members of Congress about the
war. For example, one in August contained this report on one
particular senator:

"Senator John Pastore—'Our problem is Vietnam—boxes coming back, casualties going up. Back home not a good word
from anyone for us and this attitude is reflected in the Senate.
We are losing good Democrats in droves—a paradox, affluent
society that fears riots but fears Vietnam more. Attitude now is
any Republican can do a better job.'"

It didn't much impress Johnson to learn that, say, Senator
McGovern was talking against the war, because he'd been
against it for a long time. But when someone like Pastore
questioned the war, someone who'd been a staunch supporter
of ours, the President had to be impressed with the seriousness
of the situation.

One means the President used to counter his critics was to
urge his cabinet members to speak out in defense of his Vietnam policy. He made me chairman of a committee on cabinet
"informational activities," which meant that the other cabinet
officers reported to me, and I to the President, on the number
of press conferences and speeches they were making and what
they were saying. The problem was that the cabinet members,
too, were turning away from the war. I recall one cabinet meeting at which only Secretary of Agriculture Orville Freeman,

a Marine hero of the Second World War, spoke out for the President's policy. The others, men like Stew Udall, Willard Wirtz, and Bob Weaver, were depressed, even agonized by the President's policy, but they felt helpless to change it. They knew well what magnificent achievements the President had brought about in domestic areas, and now they saw them all possibly jeopardized by a tragic military adventure.

By late 1967 our thoughts were turning to the presidential election that was only a year away. One congressman commented to me that fall that "if we didn't have Vietnam, we'd repeat 1964 next year." But we did have Vietnam and none of us had any illusions about repeating 1964.

At the President's request, I sent him a long memo early in November in preparation for a meeting to plan our strategy for the 1968 presidential campaign. I recommended that the President not make an early announcement of his candidacy for re-election, that organizing for the campaign nonetheless begin immediately, that he not enter primaries, that he allow supporters in certain key primary states to work on his behalf (the write-in effort in New Hampshire, for example), that he stress his vision of the future, as opposed to the Republican record of obstructionism. This was, essentially, the strategy that was adopted at the meeting and pursued for the next four months.

On November 30, Senator Eugene McCarthy announced he would challenge President Johnson for the Democratic nomination in the New Hampshire and other primaries. The President did not show any immediate concern with this development. He limited himself to stating his personal opinion of McCarthy, which was decidedly negative. McCarthy's candidacy was not taken seriously by anyone around the President. It was regarded as a joke, an annoyance. At that time, it was Bob Kennedy, not Gene McCarthy, who worried Lyndon Johnson. Throughout 1967, whenever Bob criticized the Administration, Johnson regarded it as the start of his presidential candidacy. Bob knew this and got a certain grim pleasure out of the thought that he was annoying Johnson. I am convinced that in 1967 Bob had no thought of running for President the following year, but the fact that he was speaking all over America and receiving favorable public reaction and a good press was enough to irritate and concern the President.

One of the ironies of the situation was that Johnson got along famously with Ted Kennedy.

"I don't know why I can't get along with Bob the way I do with Ted," Johnson would say to me.

I assumed, without saying it, that it was because Ted wasn't likely to run for President the following year.

Throughout January and February of 1968, Bob was under mounting pressure to run for President. McCarthy's candidacy was making his refusal to run look less than courageous to some and McCarthy was rapidly enlisting the support, particularly of the young people, that Bob would need if he did run. Yet Bob knew it was unlikely that he could get the nomination and he was fearful he might tear the party apart if he tried, perhaps ruining his 1972 prospects in the process.

Bob and I had lunch in his Senate office on February 26 and, for the first time, he indicated to me that he might challenge Johnson.

"I don't want to do it, but I may have to," he said. "Johnson's Vietnam policy is a debacle. I'd hoped that if enough of us criticized the war we could turn him around, but, if anything, his policy seems to have hardened. I don't understand Johnson. He scares me. I wonder if he will ever listen to reason."

The New Hampshire primary was only two weeks off and stories were flowing out of that state about the droves of young people flocking to the McCarthy campaign. The fact that Bob did not have a high opinion of McCarthy made his position all the more frustrating. Still, I doubted that Bob would run. He was exasperated and disturbed, but I felt he was too realistic a politician to think he could oust Johnson. As we parted Bob said, "I wish you'd talk to Bob McNamara; I think you'd be interested in his views."

McNamara, who had managed and justified the war in the mid-1960s, had at last turned against it, and as a result departed as Secretary of Defense. He was to be replaced by Clark Clifford, a Washington lawyer and long-time Johnson friend, who was then regarded as a leading hawk on the war. It was an appointment that initially discouraged many of us, but Clifford soon became a major influence on Johnson for a negotiated settlement of the war.

A few days later, McNamara and I had a long talk in my office.

He said the situation in Vietnam was worse than the public knew, that he had tried unsuccessfully to persuade Johnson to alter his policy, and now he feared that Johnson's emotional involvement with the war was such that he could not make objective judgments.

"I think Bob has to run," McNamara told me. "I don't see any other answer."

"A lot of us share your concerns," I told McNamara, "but I'm not sure that Bob's running is the best way to get a new war policy. I still hope it can be changed by pressures from within the Administration." McNamara, however, saw no hope in that approach.

Later that day, Bob Kennedy and I talked. He asked my reaction to what McNamara had said.

"Bob, I'm impressed by his concern about the war and by his admiration for you," I told him. "But I don't think anything McNamara said changes the political realities of the situation."

Bob asked me to have breakfast at Hickory Hill on Saturday, March 2. He spoke of the politicians who were urging him to run. He said Jesse Unruh was having a poll taken in California to determine how well Bob might do in the primary there. I then realized that he was seriously considering running, and I felt that put me in a potentially awkward position.

"Bob," I told him, "you know I share your concern, but I can't ignore the political realities. The only hope I see is that the men around the President can ultimately change his policy, that he has to be impressed by the opposition not only from you, Bob, but from people who have worked with him and have been loyal to him."

Bob frowned and restated his doubts that Johnson would listen to reason.

"Furthermore," I continued, "you know that I will respect the confidentiality of our talks, but you in turn must understand my position. If the President doesn't change his policy, I, too, will face a hard decision down the road, but until then, I will remain loyal to him."

Bob assured me he understood.

I still did not think he would run. He was obviously tortured, but I still felt he recognized the political problems he faced. He and I kept coming back to whether Johnson might somehow be persuaded to change his policy. I strongly recommended that Bob sit down with the President for a direct attempt at persuasion before he made any decision to run. Perhaps Johnson would alter his position rather than have Bob run against him. In any event, I wanted the two of them to meet face to face. I had spent months listening to each of them complaining about the other. If the problem between them could be resolved, it could only be done on a head-to-head basis. Our conversation ended with Bob saying he would consider a meeting with the President and would also advise me of the results of the California poll.

Bob never did follow up on my suggestion for a direct meeting with Johnson, but, after consulting with Bob, Ted Sorensen did meet with the President to propose a national commission to review Vietnam policy, a proposal that Johnson rejected.

Bob called me the next day, Sunday, to say the California poll showed that a slate headed by Jesse Unruh, pledged to Bob, would run strongly in the state. He wasn't excited about the poll, however. We knew it was a "quickie" telephone poll— hardly something to base your future political career on.

Bob also asked me to come to dinner that night. It turned out to be a typical chaotic evening at Hickory Hill, with children and dogs and friends coming and going, everything pretty disjointed, but fun and relaxing. After dinner we all settled down in the big living room—the men in one group smoking cigars and talking politics, the women at the other side of the room. Ted Kennedy, Steve Smith, and John Tunney, Ted's friend and the new California senator, had come by, and there was some desultory talk of the California poll. No one seemed impressed by it and no one urged that Bob become a candidate that night. However, his wife Ethel did say she felt Bob was eventually going to *have* to run, no matter what.

As far as I was concerned, the more pressing political question that night involved Ten Kennedy's plans for the forthcoming Massachusetts presidential primary. Gene McCarthy had entered the primary, the filing deadline was only two days off, and President Johnson had not indicated whether he would himself enter the primary, whether he would encourage Ted Kennedy to enter it, or whether he would ask someone to run as a stand-in candidate for him. Three stand-in candidates who had been discussed were Speaker McCormack, State Senate president Maurice Donahue, and myself.

Ted Kennedy was in an awkward position. It would be highly annoying to him to see McCarthy win the primary and thus control the Massachusetts delegation at the 1968 Democratic Convention. On the other hand, it would be awkward for Ted, as a critic of the war, to run against Gene McCarthy, the anti-war candidate. When I asked Ted his plans that Sunday night at Hickory Hill, he stated flatly that he definitely would not enter the primary.

That left the question to what Johnson would do. Earlier in the year, after seeing a poll conducted among Massachusetts Democrats testing McCarthy's strength against various other candidates, I had written Johnson a long memo. I informed him that all of the candidates had defeated McCarthy in ratios ranging from Ted Kennedy's 80 per cent to 12 per cent (the rest undecided), the President's 72 per cent to 11 per cent, Speaker McCormack's 70 per cent to 20 per cent, to my own 59 per cent to 23 per cent. I pointed out, of course, that this poll was taken well before McCarthy had done any campaigning, that McCarthy had solid organizational potential in the state, and that he'd therefore run stronger in the actual primary.

I said that I was willing to resign from the Post Office and return to Massachusetts to run as Johnson's stand-in, if that was the course of action most helpful to him. However, I noted that his best alternative now might be to enter the primary himself, since he could defeat McCarthy soundly and thus score a clear-cut victory over one of his main anti-war critics.

The weeks went by, with no decision from the President. The Massachusetts leaders were beside themselves, trying to make plans but unable to make them without knowing the President's wishes. March 5, the filing deadline for the April 30 primary, became a day of total confusion. At the White House legislative breakfast that morning, Johnson took me aside and said, "Larry, I want you to know how much I appreciated the offer you made earlier to stand in for me in Massachusetts. You stood solid with me and I'll never forget it."

I knew that meant he did not want me to run as a stand-in for him. I knew, too, that Ted Kennedy would not run. Nor would Speaker McCormack—he had urged me to run. It was still possible that the President would run, however, or that he would allow Maurice Donahue, the State Senate leader, who had expressed a willingness to do so, to run as his stand-in. Throughout that afternoon, frantic phone calls shot back and forth between Boston and Washington, with Donahue standing by, ready to file if he got the word from the White House. In the final hour before the five o'clock filing deadline, Marvin Watson failed to return two calls I made to him. When the chips were down, Johnson was talking only to Marvin Watson and to James Rowe (former assistant to President Roosevelt and a key Democratic political adviser), two of his closest political associates. Perhaps he was just too frustrated to talk to me. In any event, Johnson's silence meant that no one was authorized to run, and I told Donahue he simply could not file under those circumstances.

Letting Gene McCarthy have the Massachusetts delegates was an annoyance to us, but the fact was that he could win the primaries and still not be nominated. I decided Johnson had been wise to stay out of the Massachusetts primary, and I assumed he would do the same with regard to the other primaries.

Two days later, March 7, a story appeared in the New York *Times* quoting a "high official" or "authoritative source" as saying that Johnson definitely would not enter any primaries.

Johnson called me that morning, highly displeased about the story.

"Were you the source of that?" he demanded.

Ira Kapenstein had, in fact, been the source of the story, but I chose not to get into that.

"Mr. President," I responded, "I think the article made sense and I personally agree with it." That further disturbed him.

"I'll make my own damn decisions about the primaries and nobody is authorized to speak for me," he declared. He went on in that vein. His position was understandable—he wanted to keep all his options open—but I didn't appreciate his tone and I broke in to ask:

"Do you have any further comment to make, Mr. President?"

There was silence, and I said good-by and hung up the phone. It was the only unpleasant conversation he and I ever had.

The March 12 New Hampshire primary was at hand and McCarthy was looking stronger. In the finals days, the Johnson people panicked a bit. They ran some rough radio advertisements, implying that a vote for McCarthy was a vote for Hanoi. That was heavyhanded and apparently backfired.

In the end, McCarthy stunned the White House by winning more than 40 per cent of the vote, losing to Johnson by only a narrow margin. I found the results highly significant, a blow to the President's prestige, but I felt a certain detachment from it, for I had been in no way involved in the New Hampshire primary. Johnson kept a clear line between the Massachusetts primary, which he wanted me involved in, and the New Hampshire primary, which he did not want me involved in. I had to assume that he feared the Kennedy forces might stir up a write-in vote for Bob Kennedy and that I might somehow play a role in it. Bernie Boutin, my friend from the 1960 campaign, had directed the Johnson effort in New Hampshire in 1968, and he called me once to apologize for not keeping me posted and to explain that he had been under orders not to communicate with me.

Bob Kennedy had called me on the Saturday before the primary to discuss ever-increasing pressures on him to run, and, when the reports came in from New Hampshire, I realized that his candidacy was inevitable. McCarthy had shown that Johnson was vulnerable. Now Bob would have to prove whether all the conventional political wisdom was mistaken and a sitting President could in fact be denied renomination.

I was not privy to Bob's final deliberations that week; I was in Massachusetts on Post Office business. On Friday, March 15, I spoke at a luncheon ceremony in Boston in connection with the issuance of a John F. Kennedy postage stamp.

Ted Kennedy was also at the luncheon and told me he wanted to talk to me privately following it, but he had to leave early for a flight to Washington and we had no chance to talk. However, he had asked Eddie King's son, Jimmy, a member of his Senate staff, to give me the message that Bob would be announcing his candidacy for President the next day. I watched Bob's televised announcement Saturday morning, then I continued on with my schedule, which included a parade in Holyoke, a wreath-laying at the JFK Memorial in Chicopee, and a speech in Everett on Sunday evening, where I was introduced by Ted Kennedy.

When I returned to Washington late Sunday night, I found a message to call the President's adviser, Jim Rowe. When I reached Rowe the next morning, he read me a telegram that he proposed to send out over our joint signatures to several hundred Democratic leaders. The telegram contained two main points: that each party leader was urged to pledge his support to President Johnson and that Larry O'Brien would direct the President's re-election campaign.

My reaction to the proposed telegram was negative. First of all, I thought it was not only an overreaction to the Kennedy candidacy, but it made no political sense. Secondly, I felt that I was being used and I didn't appreciate it. Until then, Johnson had not involved me in his campaign plans. Now, apparently fearful that I might defect to Kennedy, Johnson was proposing to make me his instant campaign director.

I told Rowe the telegram would boomerang and could not go out over my signature. I also said the matter of my role in the campaign would have to be discussed between the President and me—there could be no emissaries. If the President suddenly wanted to put me out front in his campaign, he should talk to me about it. I then sent a memo to the President which said, in part:

"I have some deep concerns on several counts about the proposal to send telegrams to Party leaders in Congress and across the nation.

"This action—as it was outlined to me this morning following my return from four days on the road—is bound to be construed as a nationwide effort for loyalty oaths, and it would be publicly portrayed in that light. The press and some Party people would read the telegram as a clear sign of panic and over-reaction and would charge that this was an extension of the 'overkill' tactics used in New Hampshire.

"The press will immediately start playing the numbers game with us, and we will have a barrage of inquiries challenging us to specify our batting average in response to the telegrams. Some recipients of the blanket telegram will be afforded the opportunity to get publicity by decrying the action.

"Also, the reference in the draft to 'those who would divide us' is inadvisable. At this early stage, we should not be pointing to those who would divide us. At this point we should let the 'dividers' slug it out among themselves.

"Obviously, it is desirable to have every Democratic official who is willing to do so publicly proclaim his support of you in the coming days and weeks. I believe this can be accomplished through an alternative approach: through concerted personal contacts with the people you would want to reach."

That evening Ted Kennedy came to my home for dinner. We discussed the whole complicated political situation in some detail. Finally, Ted implied that it would be nice if I could head up the Kennedy campaign, but we didn't pursue the subject.

Bob called Tuesday, the next day, and made further reference to Ted's suggestion of the night before. I must say neither Bob nor Ted tried to push me hard. I don't believe they really expected me to leave the Administration to join them, but thought they'd make some effort, just in case.

227

227

The following day, Wednesday the twentieth, I was to address the National Press Club. Bob called me that morning, for he was curious about what I was going to say. I read the part of my speech that said I was in support of President Johnson.

"Larry, I hope I'm not putting you on the spot, announcing my candidacy just before you make a speech to the Press Club. I didn't plan it that way," Bob quipped. Bob's humor was always very, very dry.

"You're not putting me on the spot, Bob," I told him. "You and I both want to see the war ended. You're going about it one way and I'm going about it another."

The President and I had not spoken for several days, but he called me the day after my Press Club speech. He was very warm. He told me he wanted to meet with me soon to discuss the possibility of my heading up his campaign. Then he said a strange thing:

"You are in a position to destroy me."

I told him I disagreed. I thought it was a strange comment for him to make. I perhaps could help him, but I was certainly in no position to destroy him.

That same day, March twenty-first, I sent the President a memo on Vietnam. At the last cabinet meeting he had invited views on Vietnam, and given the Tet Offensive and the worsening political situation at home, I felt the need to add my voice to those calling for a new policy. My memo said in part:

"Through this memorandum, I want to express thoughts that have been developing in my mind. At the outset let me say that while all of us cannot help but have an eye toward the consequences of our policy in terms of next November, my concerns in this area are not in any way politically motivated.

"Viewing our challenge in human terms, it must be apparent to all of us that many Americans are frustrated and deeply concerned that South Vietnam simply is not carrying the burden of the war. I believe we must with all deliberate speed shift this burden to the South Vietnamese where it belongs. I am not suggesting withdrawal, and apparently it is unrealistic to expect meaningful negotiations at this time. Conversely, significant escalation would in all probability be matched by a similar increase on the other side.

"What I am suggesting is a *phasing out* of the tremendous American responsibility for the conduct of the war and a *phasing in* of far greater responsibility by the South Vietnamese themselves. The Government of South Vietnam must increase its troop strength—its fighting capability—as we decrease ours. I feel that the American people would support an Administration which lessened our involvement based on the realistic assessment that the Government and the people of South Vietnam have not fulfilled their obligations."

My growing concerns about the war were shared by others in the Administration, as I learned on the following Monday, the twenty-fifth. Vice President Humphrey came to my office for a late lunch and it was during our conversation that I first learned of Humphrey's doubts about the war. He told me that he had been arranging for some prominent citizens who questioned the war to meet privately with the President. I, in turn, told him about my doubts and the memos I had sent Johnson advising him of the political feedback I was getting. It was amazing—Humphrey and I had been in constant contact for months but weren't aware of each other's views. The problem, as we both knew, was Johnson's tendency to equate criticism with disloyalty.

Later that afternoon, an informal meeting of the Cabinet was held in my office. The traditionally "nonpolitical" members of the Cabinet—the Secretaries of State, Defense, and the Treasury—were not invited, but Johnson had asked me to meet with the others to discuss how they could assist his candidacy in the upcoming Wisconsin primary.

Orville Freeman had already been to Wisconsin and had been heckled by anti-war protestors, but he declared he was going back again and do all he could for the President.

"Either we fight for the Democratic Party," Freeman declared, "or we're going to see this country taken over by the Republicans."

But the other cabinet officers present—Bill Wirtz, Wilbur Cohen, Stew Udall, Ramsey Clark, Bob Weaver—had become despondent about the war and showed no great enthusiasm for campaigning in Wisconsin. Stew Udall stayed behind to talk with me after our meeting broke up. I had not previously talked with Stew about Vietnam, but soon we were discussing whether some type of orchestration or group action by the Cabinet might not have more impact on the President than our individual statement to him. Our thoughts were still vague, but I think some kind of joint statement or action by five or six cabinet officers would almost certainly have come about, had Johnson not taken the dramatic and unexpected action he took less than a week later.

The next day, Tuesday, Ted Kennedy called me.

"Say, Larry," he began, "there's a rumor all over town that you're resigning as Postmaster General to join us."

"You've been misinformed, Ted," I responded, in the same light vein. "As a matter of fact, I'm going out to Wisconsin tomorrow to do some campaigning for the President."

"Well, I just wanted you to know that we've got an office set aside for you in our headquarters with 'Larry O'Brien' on the door. We're ready when you're ready."

"Thanks a lot, Ted," I said. "That's great to know."

The next day, just before leaving for Wisconsin, I sent another memo on Vietnam to the President. This one stressed the political problems the war was causing and it reflected my continuing conversations with many very disheartened Democratic leaders. I had been particularly impressed by my talks with Mayor Daley. We spoke by phone from time to time and he, too, expressed increasing concern about the war. It wasn't that he insisted on withdrawal or had any specific proposals to make; Daley was just another confused fellow questioning whether we were headed in the right direction. "I've got a lot of people out here who are wondering about it," he would say. "How can you explain all those boxes coming back?" I would urge him to repeat his doubts to the President. I don't know if he ever did, but I made a point of advising the President of Daley's concern.

Of course, what Daley said to me was his private opinion.

If a reporter had asked him about Vietnam, he would have said, "I'm behind the President all the way."

My March 27 memo to the President said:

"During the last several days, I have had contacts with a large number of Democratic officials, leaders and workers around the country—both in person and by phone. Without exception, these people are your supporters and also without exception they express serious concerns about our current posture in Vietnam, both in political and in general terms.

"The political aspect came through clearly in the conversations I have had. These people—loyal Administration Democrats—are fearful of the end result in terms of both the Chicago Convention and the November election, if our present Vietnam posture is maintained.

"I know that this is not news to you—that you have been getting the same reports—but it is apparent that these views are becoming more widespread. I have continued to review the problem in my own mind since sending you my memo on March 21, and now I would like to respectfully suggest some possibly dramatic moves that could allay the fears and buoy the spirit of the nation.

"As I suggested in my previous memo, I believe we should vigorously pursue the course of insisting upon greater responsibility by the South Vietnamese people and Government in fighting the War. At the same time, we should publicly express our disappointment and unhappiness with the South Vietnamese failures, both in military terms and in terms of establishing a truly democratic governmental process.

"The Government of South Vietnam could follow this up by making a tangible move toward a greater spirit of democracy: the granting of a general amnesty for political prisoners.

"The next step would be for President Thieu to express his strong desire for peace and his willingness to negotiate with the enemy. President Thieu would specify that on a date certain the South Vietnamese Armed Forces and all allied troops would begin a cease fire. Our Government would support this effort and would announce a bombing pause to begin on the same date.

"As a further effort to dramatize our sincerity, you would announce that you are sending a delegation of prominent Americans to Geneva who will be sitting at the peace table along with representatives of the South Vietnamese Government—ready to negotiate with North Vietnam at the very hour that the cease fire and the bombing pause would be scheduled to start.

"I realize that if we took the above steps or similar steps, the chances for meaningful negotiations and lasting peace would still be questionable. However, I think these moves would accomplish a great deal in making a large segment of the American people understand our sincerity and in convincing them that this Administration will go to the greatest possible lengths to achieve peace.

"We all agree, Mr. President, that our problems in Vietnam transcend political considerations and our search for solutions must not be politically motivated. Nevertheless, the widespread anxieties I have found among our political friends and associates convince me that their fears reflect an ever deepening disenchantment among many segments of the population which have heretofore supported our actions in Vietnam."

I cite this memo as an example of the many, many pressures that were building on the President as he made his agonizing reappraisal of his Vietnam policy. For my own part, it may have seemed presumptuous for me to set out a detailed plan of action for Vietnam. But that had been the job of the experts for far too long.

I flew to Wisconsin, and my day there was climaxed by a pro-Johnson Democratic rally in Milwaukee. We had a good turnout, but as we left the rally we drove by Johnson headquarters and found it dark and empty. A few blocks away we passed the McCarthy headquarters and saw perhaps a hundred young people hard at work inside. That was not a good sign.

I flew from Wisconsin home to Springfield for the opening of a new boys' club. When I returned to my sister Mary's home late that evening, she said Secretary Rusk had called me. Rusk had previously said the President wanted him to talk with me about the proposals in my memos to the President. I decided it was too late to return Rusk's call. The next morning I was in my brother-in-law's car, backing out the driveway to drive to the airport, when Mary called from the door that Rusk was on the phone again. I shouted that I'd miss my plane if I stopped to talked to him, but to say I'd call him from New York. I was going to spend a weekend with my son, Larry, who had just volunteered for the Army, with a commitment to serve in Vietnam.

When I entered the Plaza Hotel that Friday afternoon, the manager rushed up to me.

"Mr. O'Brien," he said, "the President has been calling for you."

"It's all right," I told him. "I've already talked to him." I hadn't, but he seemed so upset I wanted to reassure him. As soon as I got to my room, I called the President.

Johnson began our conversation by noting that he'd been trying to reach me all morning and that Rusk had tried to reach me the previous evening. He went on to say that he'd seen a television report on my Milwaukee speech and it seemed to have been a good rally.

"Mr. President," I said, "it was orchestrated by Post Office people and they put on a good show, but I don't think you should be too enthusiastic because of it."

"Well, what did it look like in Wisconsin?" he asked.

"The most striking thing," I said, "was the closed-down Johnson headquarters and the very busy McCarthy headquarters a few blocks away."

"Well, what do you think will happen?" he asked.

"I don't think it looks good for you."

"Can't you be more definite?"

"Yes," I said, "I think you are going to be badly defeated."

"How bad?" he inquired.

"Sixty–forty," I told him. "Maybe two to one."

His tone changed.

"You were there only one day," he pointed out.

"That's true," I said. "But that's my sense of the situation. Frankly, your supporters are very depressed. They are loyal to you, but they are very depressed. I don't know if they would tell you that, but there it is."

"Well," he said, "Rusk still wants to talk to you."

"Fine, Mr. President, I'll call him."

"No, I'll get him for you."

The next thing I heard was the President clicking the phone and telling the operator to get the Secretary of State for the Postmaster General. I couldn't believe it.

Rusk said the President wanted him to brief me on some significant new developments on the war. He asked if I could come to Washington right away, as he was leaving the city the next day, Saturday. I asked if he couldn't brief me by phone, because I wasn't planning to return to Washington until Sunday, but he said the matters were too confidential for that. He again stressed the President's desire that I be advised, but I was determined to spend the weekend with Larry. We finally agreed that his Under Secretary, Nick Katzenbach, would fill me in when I returned to Washington.

That evening Larry and I had dinner at Toots Shor's. We were joined by Jimmy Breslin, the columnist, and a little later by Jesse Unruh, my old friend from the 1960 Kennedy campaign in California. Jesse, who then was perhaps the leading Democratic figure in California, was bitterly opposed to the war and had been an early booster of Bob Kennedy's candidacy. He spoke at length and with considerable passion about the political situation. "By Christ, we're going to knock Lyndon Johnson out of the box," he declared.

As the evening wore on, Jesse began to get belligerent. At one point he turned to my son and said:

"Why the hell aren't you in the Army? If your father's such a big supporter of the war, why aren't you over there fighting?"

He didn't know that Larry had just joined the Army and might very well be fighting in Vietnam soon. I leaned across the table and told Unruh in no uncertain terms that he had just made the most crass remark I had ever heard. We were nose to nose for a minute—my response was pretty rough—much to the delight of Jimmy Breslin. The next evening we again encountered Jesse. He apologized for his remarks and he joined Larry and me at the Plaza Hotel for a nightcap.

I returned to Washington Sunday afternoon and went directly to my office at the Post Office Building. I never got around to calling Nick Katzenbach for my briefing. The President had scheduled a nationally televised speech that night and I assumed I would learn whatever significant new developments there were from the speech. Later that afternoon, during a meeting at the White House, Marvin Watson asked me where I'd be that evening. I said I'd be at home. I thought the President might be calling me after the speech to get my reaction.

Elva, Phyllis Maddock, Larry, and I sat down to watch the President's speech. Just before it began, the telephone rang. It was Larry Temple, a member of the White House staff, who said he had a message:

"The President wants you to know that at the end of his speech tonight he will announce that he will not be a candidate for re-election."

For a moment I couldn't reply. Then, for some reason, I ended the conversation by saying, "Gotcha!" and hung up. I told the others the news and we were all speechless, disbelieving. The speech began and it went on for half an hour with no mention of a withdrawal from politics. I started to wonder if Temple had been pulling my leg. Then, suddenly, the President announced that he would not seek re-election and the speech was over.

My emotions were mixed. I was pleased by the bombing cutback the President had announced and the new steps toward negotiations. It had been my hope that the New Hampshire setback, followed by a loss in Wisconsin, would force Johnson to a change in his war policy. I had never imagined that he would withdraw and I had not believed that Bob Kennedy could defeat him for the nomination. I had always expected Johnson to be the candidate, probably of a divided party, but, nonetheless, our candidate.

It was impossible not to also feel deep sympathy for Johnson. He was a proud man. He had won a great victory in 1964 and had achieved a remarkable domestic record. Now he faced the prospect of defeat four years later and of carrying hundreds of other Democratic candidates down with him. It must have been with great bitterness that he saw his party and the American people turn against him. After all, those he had looked to for advice had included a number of the Kennedy men. I could not help thinking, although the comparison is perhaps unfair, that if I had given advice on legislative matters that was as demonstrably bad as the advice Johnson received on his Vietnam policy, I would certainly have been fired.

In any event, Johnson had withdrawn, and it was obvious to me that there were two serious contenders for the Democratic nomination, Bob Kennedy and Hubert Humphrey.

"I'll bet you I get two phone calls tonight," I told my companions.

Bob's call came a little before midnight.

"I hope I got to you first," he said.

"You did, Bob," I told him.

"Larry, I'm glad we've kept in touch and I'm glad we've understood each other all the way. Your position has always been a fair one and, now that Johnson has made this decision, I hope you'll join me."

I replied that, under the circumstances, I would of course seriously consider it. Bob did not press me for an immediate yes or no, but he was very excited.

"Here we go again, Larry," he told me. "It's going to be like the old days. You'd better get a good night's sleep tonight because I'm not going to let you sleep from now on. It's a new ball game now."

XII

BOB KENNEDY'S CAMPAIGN FOR
PRESIDENT

WHEN I arrived at my office the next morning, I wrote and sent to the President a letter that said:

"Dear Mr. President:

I am very proud of my President and of my association with you.

I simply want to take this means to express my deep respect and admiration for the position you so courageously took last night. I know from the reactions you expressed to the recent memos I sent you and from our other discussions of your deep concern and your total dedication to a peaceful resolution in Vietnam.

Certainly no American can question your sincerity of purpose. You have the support of all our citizens in your valiant efforts."

At the regular Tuesday legislative breakfast the next day, I asked the President why he had made his momentous political decision.

"I'm doing everything I humanly can do to bring peace," he replied sadly. He looked tired—the burdens of the presidency were aging him. "But there'll always be those who will say all I care about is politics. So now I've done the one thing that proves it's not politics. Larry, I've done everything you fellows urged me to do and more: I've cut back the bombing and I'm trying to negotiate and I won't be a candidate again. I still doubt that it'll work, but I've gone the distance." I felt it could work. He had thrown every chip he had on the table.

Later that day, I received a call from Vice President Humphrey, who had been in Mexico when the President announced his withdrawal. It was a typical Humphrey conversation, filled with humor and enthusiasm, but he was probing my intentions all the way. I said candidly that Bob had contacted me but that my decision had not yet been made. We agreed to talk further.

Ted Kennedy came to lunch with me Thursday and we immediately got down to specifics. We discussed frankly the fact that there were some people in the Kennedy camp, some old associates and some of the newer people, who were not enamored of me because I had stayed with Johnson after Dallas and who would not be overjoyed at my joining the campaign. Ted understood fully. He said I would be in charge and the others would just have to live with it.

He suggested we could have a news conference, to make that point. Bob called later in the day to confirm what Ted had said and to stress that the hour was late, time was short, and he needed me aboard soon.

Hubert called on Friday and began by saying:

"I have three words for you: I need you."

I told him I'd be making my decision very soon. He said he wanted to come to my office the next day for a final talk. I insisted that I would come to *his* office, which I did, and we visited for more than an hour.

"Larry," he insisted, "if you agree to manage my campaign it will make the difference." It was a typical Hubert exaggeration.

"Larry, I know my limitations. I desperately need organization. I have no one who can do that job as it should be done."

We spoke of the good times we and our wives had shared and of some of the legislative battles we had fought together on the Hill. Both of us were moved by the recollections.

It was torture for me to have to choose between Bob and Hubert. Both were my friends. If anything, I was closer to Hubert. We spent more time together socially than Bob and I did, and Elva and Muriel had also become good friends. I remembered the time in 1965 when some friends of mine in Springfield had sponsored a Larry O'Brien Day and Hubert had learned of it and had insisted on flying up for the ceremony. My decision would have been easier if either had been better qualified than the other, but I considered each qualified. Nor was my decision on the basis of going with the probable winner of the nomination. Had it been, Hubert would have been the obvious choice. My decision went deeper than that. It had to do with my roots in Massachusetts, my memories of my years at the side of Jack Kennedy, and my long-time association with and affection for the Kennedy family. It was a personal decision, not a political one. I had to go with Bob.

Hubert understood that and accepted it. Sitting there in his office, we spoke again of the warm feeling that existed between the Humphreys and the O'Briens. And we meant it, both of us. Finally Hubert said to me: "All right, Larry, we will remain friends. Nothing can change that. And I want to make a commitment. I am under no illusions. I have been through one political battle with a Kennedy which didn't work out very well for me. Believe me, I don't look forward to another one—let's stay in touch and I'll get together with you and Bob when it seems appropriate to review our situation and see if we can work something out. I want to avoid a bitter convention battle if I can. Perhaps down the road I won't look as strong as some people think I will. Perhaps Bob won't. In any event, let's agree that Bob, you and I will meet midway in the struggle to see what we might work out." I agreed, and told Hubert that I was sure Bob would too.

My understanding of the conversation was that Humphrey thought if either he or Kennedy was clearly going to get the nomination, the other might withdraw to avoid a bitter convention fight, that either one might instead accept the vice presidency on such a ticket.

Back in my office, I called Bob to tell him of my decision. I told him also of Hubert's suggestion and commitment for future meetings of the three of us at appropriate times. Bob was in complete agreement and mentioned his sincere affection for Hubert. He said, "The worst thing about all this is that we're in a fight with Hubert Humphrey. He's a great guy."

Then Bob asked when I would come aboard. I told him I would be with him as soon as I had submitted my resignation to the President and it was accepted.

I had asked Humphrey to keep my decision confidential, for I felt that the President should get the word directly from me. I requested an appointment with the President but he was away at Camp David, so I did not see him until Wednesday afternoon. He read my letter of resignation carefully and then asked in a low voice, "Are you going with Bob Kennedy?"

"Yes, I am," I replied.

He smiled but chose to make no comment on my decision. Instead, he asked my advice on my successor at the Post Office. I said that since the appointment was presumably only for the remaining nine months of his Administration, he should have in mind rewarding someone who had supported him. We discussed Arthur Krim and all the good work he had done for the party, but the President said he doubted that Arthur would want the job.

"The fellow who has really taken a beating for me and who has been totally loyal and who would be thrilled with this kind of recognition, is Marvin Watson," Johnson said. He asked my opinion and I said, "Marvin certainly has been loyal to you and I think it would be a good appointment." Johnson immediately called Marvin in and told him he was going to be the next Postmaster General. Marvin was as dumfounded as I had been when I received the same news three years before. I shook hands with both of them and made my exit.

I had barely returned to the Post Office when the President called me. He asked if I'd looked at the wire-service ticker. I said I had not and he explained that he'd already gone out and told the press of my resignation. "You read that ticker," he said, "and if I left out any adjectives, it's only because my vocabulary is limited. I want you to know I meant every word of it." I thanked him and when I read the wire-service stories,

I saw that he had indeed been very kind to me in his comments.*

To serve in a President's Cabinet had been the summit of my political career, and I cannot say it was easy for me to walk away from that honor. Other members of the Johnson Cabinet believed in Bob Kennedy's cause, but no other cabinet officer resigned to join his campaign. I wondered if the Kennedys, caught up as they were in their own political drama, understood what my decision had meant to me in human terms. Then a small incident, during the final days between my resignation and my actual departure from government, answered my question.

I happened to meet Ted Kennedy on a flight back to Washington. We walked out of National Airport to the street, where an aide was waiting for him and my limousine and driver were waiting for me. Ted started toward his car, then stopped, looked at my limousine, and walked back over to me.

"Larry, we know you've made a hard decision. You're giving up a lot," Ted said. "I want you to know we understand."

He shook my hand and we parted. I was truly pleased, for Ted in his understated way had shown me that he did understand—not the loss of a limousine, of course, but that I was giving up a great deal that I had worked a lifetime to achieve.

A day or two later, a ceremony was held for me in the departmental auditorium. Many of my friends from Congress and the Executive Branch were there. I made my "farewell address" and at the end of the ceremony the Marine Band played "Auld Lang Syne" and the audience joined in the singing. With their voices ringing in my ears, and with tears brimming in my eyes, I walked off the stage, out of the auditorium, and out of the government I had served as best I could.

The next day, Good Friday, April 12, I was in Indiana, back to the nuts and bolts of politics, back to the chaos of a primary campaign, and back to trying to elect a Kennedy President.

I can't say I was a hard-charging young tiger rushing into action. To some extent, my feeling was, "Well, here we go again." I'd spent a lot of time in Indiana for Jack Kennedy in

* See Appendix.

1960 and there I was, going over the same ground eight years later, for another Kennedy. I can't say I felt the same enthusiasm I had felt the first time. A lot had happened in those eight years. I had held major responsibilities in Washington, yet here I was, back in Indiana, organizing get-out-the-vote drives. I did my job the best I could, but it was a job, not the adventure it once had been.

Indiana went well for us, considering the time we had. Ted Kennedy and Steve Smith had already established the campaign organization and were very active there. I was assisted by Ira Kapenstein whom I had cautioned against leaving the security of the Post Office for the uncertainties of a political campaign. But Ira loved politics and greatly admired Bob Kennedy and insisted on coming with me.

As Ira and I worked to channel volunteers into our traditional Kennedy campaign program, Bob Kennedy was proving that he had the appeal and the ability to be a serious candidate for President. Our great discovery in Indiana was that Bob's support, and potential support, wasn't limited to the young, the black, the liberals, and anti-war people. The workers and their families who lined the streets in Gary and East Chicago to see Bob were very enthusiastic. It wasn't so much a matter of issues as of people making a gut response to a vital, aggressive young candidate.

This discovery led to two key campaign decisions. First, Bob should not limit his personal efforts to his known areas of strength, but should go after the vote of the workers and the ethnic groups. Secondly, in attempting to broaden his base of support, Bob should not present himself as a one-issue candidate, or as a man at the far left of his party, but rather as a national candidate who shared the average American's concern about pocketbook issues and about crime. Thus, in some speeches, Bob began to stress his law-enforcement record as Attorney General. Some purists in our camp saw this as a sellout, but it was only sensible politics by a man who was running a serious campaign for the presidency.

We won Indiana with 42 per cent of the vote. Governor Roger Branigin, running as a favorite son, and in reality as a stand-in for Humphrey, was second with 31 per cent and Gene McCarthy was third with 27 per cent. Jimmy Breslin was with me on Election Night and wrote a column that very well recaptures the flavor of the scene:

> Larry O'Brien sat on the couch with his tie open and a toothpick in his mouth and he waited for the figures with which he has lived his life. Larry O'Brien counted votes for the first time in 1941, when they were all from gin mills and they made him president of the Springfield, Massachusetts, bartenders' union and a politician forever. And last night he sat with his sheets and watched the numbers come in for Robert Kennedy.
>
> "Why don't you try that number again? It's been 13 minutes since we heard from them," O'Brien said to Ira Kapenstein, who works at the mechanics of politics with him.
>
> Kapenstein dialed a number. "Pierre, got any of those precincts yet?" he asked. He nodded and began marking them down on a mimeographed sheet. O'Brien leaned over to watch.
>
> The space said, "Polish ward, South Bend, 9th Precinct, 6th District." Under "Kennedy" Kapenstein wrote 241. Under "Branigin" he put 62. Under "McCarthy" he put 86.
>
> Larry O'Brien sat back on the couch. He took a cigarette out of a pack very slowly. He lit it carefully.
>
> "Well, what do you do now?" he was asked.
>
> "I go to Omaha tomorrow," he said.
>
> Everybody in the room laughed and Larry O'Brien, the professional, got up and went down the hall to see his candidate.

During the Indiana campaign, I made a quick trip to Omaha to check our progress in Nebraska, which held its primary on May 14. While I was there, I ran into Hubert Humphrey in the lobby of our hotel. Although he was officially a non-candidate, there was a Johnson-Humphrey slate entered in the primary and he had come to address a party dinner in an effort to arouse his supporters.

Hubert greeted me warmly and said he hoped I'd join him later that night. He said, "I know you're awfully busy," and I said I certainly was and assumed he was too—we joked about that for a minute. I was wondering later if I should follow up on Hubert's invitation, since I was his chief opponent's campaign director, when I received a call from one of his assistants restating the invitation. I did go to the Vice President's suite and we had a drink and a good talk. Hubert was very relaxed and cordial. I commented on the progress he had been making in terms of delegate support. He agreed that he was doing well but he said he didn't know if it was lasting strength, as he felt much of it was less pro-Humphrey than anti-Kennedy.

"My people in Indiana say you fellows ran a hell of a campaign there," Hubert said. "I'll never make the mistake of underestimating a Kennedy campaign."

I reminded him of his commitment to meet with Bob and me at some midpoint in the campaign, and he said that was still his intention, and that he would await word from me on what I thought was the appropriate time. After an hour's visit, that was how we left it.

We won the Nebraska primary with 51 per cent of the vote to 31 per cent for McCarthy and 14 per cent for the Johnson-Humphrey slate.

The next primary, Oregon, was much different. The groups that had formed a major part of Bob's base elsewhere—Catholics, labor, ethnic groups—were not the prime political forces in Oregon. The new element there, which had not been the significant factor in Indiana or Nebraska, was the academic community—both students and faculty—and they were solidly behind McCarthy. As a result, McCarthy's organization in Oregon was his best of any of the primaries and it was being professionally directed.

You could sense the problem as soon as you entered the state, as there wasn't the movement to Kennedy we'd seen in other states. For the first time, we felt lonely—the crowds weren't large or particularly enthusiastic. In other states, Bob spent a lot of time shaking hands outside factory gates, but there weren't that many factories in Oregon.

The Oregon leaders told us, as they had when Jack Kennedy campaigned there in 1960, that we must avoid a hard-sell campaign in this soft-sell state, so we cut back on hard-sell TV spot presentations, although we did have a massive telephone campaign.

In the final days, the race just wasn't going well. We wondered if there might be some dramatic move we could take to turn it around. The obvious possibility was to accept McCarthy's standing challenge to debate. The weekend before the election, we held a meeting with Pierre Salinger, some of the younger men from the Senate staff such as Peter Edelman and Adam Walinsky, and some of the Oregon people. We discussed the pros and cons of the proposed debate at great length. I tended to favor the idea, although with reservations. Some of the younger men, who didn't think the situation was as bleak as I did, were opposed. We went back and forth for some time without reaching any consensus. Finally, Pierre went down the hall to Bob's suite to report on our conclusions or lack of them. Bob immediately sent back word that he wanted me to come discuss the matter with him so I went to his suite.

"What do you think?" Bob asked. "Is it down the drain?"

I said it could well be. The question then was whether or not the debate might turn the election around. Bob was extremely skeptical about the idea. The problem was not that he might "lose" the debate, but that his accepting it at the last minute would be interpreted as what it in fact was—an act of desperation. A factor in our deliberations was a column by Drew Pearson headlined in the Oregon papers that Bob, when he was Attorney General, had authorized a wiretap on the Reverend Martin Luther King. We discussed the matter in detail. Someone had authorized the wiretap, but whether it had been Bob or the FBI was never clear to me. Whatever the facts, it had become a major issue in the Oregon campaign and we assumed McCarthy would hit it hard on television.

We went over and over the debate issue, continuing our talk as Bob took a bath and dried off. We couldn't reach a clear-cut yes or no so it fell on no by default. Bob was tense and edgy. Just as we were finishing our talk, we heard loud laughter outside his door. Bob threw a towel around his waist and jerked open the door. A couple of his young Senate aides were standing there, along with some girls on the staff. Their laughter, coming when it did, infuriated Bob.

"This is a hell of a thing," he said. "We're about to blow this campaign and you're standing out here laughing. I never told you people to come here from Washington in the first place. I don't know what the hell you're doing here." Bob could be rough when he was angry, and he continued in that vein for a few minutes, slammed the door, and suggested to me that I send some of them back to Washington. I felt we'd do better to get our thoughts back to the primary and whether we could pull it out of the fire.

The last night of the campaign we had a rally in a high school gymnasium in Portland. Perhaps 1,500 people came. When I went back to the hotel, reporters told me that McCarthy had packed 7,000 people into a huge auditorium. That about summed it up—it was McCarthy's state and he could draw five times the crowd.

Bob was campaigning in California on the day of the Oregon voting, May 28, and when he returned that evening the early returns had confirmed our fears of defeat, the first election defeat a Kennedy had ever experienced. Bob was extremely gracious that night. He first went to Edith Green, our Oregon campaign director, and told her he was sorry if he had let her down. That was his approach with all the Oregon leaders who had backed him—that the loss was his, not theirs.

The question then became whether he would send a telegram of congratulations to McCarthy. McCarthy had not extended that courtesy to Bob when we won the two previous primaries, so the real point of Bob's telegram would be to show that he could be gracious in defeat even if McCarthy could not. But there was a lot of bitterness within our group and some argued against sending the telegram. We were in Bob's hotel room and we argued the point for a half hour or so until finally he said angrily: "For Christ's sake, we've lost the primary but we ought at least to be able to resolve this." So we sent the telegram.

California was a different situation. We had a strong organization there, thousands of volunteers, and a great groundswell of pro-Kennedy feeling. We were confident that Bob would win. The goal was to have a big victory that would offset the Oregon loss and be a springboard toward the New York primary and the Convention. One important decision Bob made was to accept McCarthy's challenge to debate. Bob worked hard preparing for the debate and we were all pleased with the outcome.

On Election Night, I went downstairs with Bob when he was going to address the campaign workers in the ballroom of the Ambassador Hotel. It was a typical noisy, enthusiastic victory celebration. I was tired and when Bob began to speak, I said to Ira, "Come on, let's go to my room and watch this on television." I was staying in a bungalow next to the main building and Ira and I were able to see the last few minutes of Bob's victory statement on the TV set. When he finished, I asked Ira to order us some food from room service. Ira dialed the number but the phone just rang and rang. Finally someone picked up the phone and said, "Room service is closed," and slammed down the phone. Ira dialed the operator to complain and the operator said, "It's terrible what's happened."

"What is terrible?" Ira asked.

"Senator Kennedy's been shot."

At just that moment, a big commotion could be seen on the television screen and before Ira gave me the news, I knew what had happened. I slumped in my chair, looked at Ira, and said, "That's it," and the television quickly confirmed our fears.

In Dallas I had not been able to believe that Jack had been shot, in Los Angeles I never doubted that Bob had been. I sat frozen, watching the reports on television. I couldn't move. After a while, Ira suggested that I go to the hospital. "What can I do to help there? I'll just be in the way," I told him. I envisioned another hospital scene like Dallas and I didn't think I could take it. So I spent the night in my room watching television reports and talking to Ira and others who joined us. Early in the morning I called Steve Smith at the hospital. Steve said there was little or no chance Bob would survive. I told him under the circumstances I thought I would return to Washington. He agreed there was nothing I could do to help by staying.

Could Bob Kennedy, if he had lived, have won the Democratic nomination that year? Obviously he was in an uphill fight. At the time of Bob's death, Hubert was very close to having enough committed delegates to be nominated. Indeed, a national poll at that time indicated he had more than a majority. The question that cannot be answered is whether Hubert's support would have held firm. Our strategy was to use the primaries to prove Bob was a winner. Conceivably, the convention delegates, seeking a winner or perhaps in a surge of Kennedy emotion, might have moved from Hubert to Bob in sufficient numbers to give Bob the nomination.

We in the Kennedy camp, in any event, were far from conceding the nomination to Humphrey. We hoped to use the California victory as a springboard to a strong showing in the New York primary on June 18. I flew to New York in mid-May for three days of talks with party leaders. I found that Bob faced a real fight in his own state, for McCarthy was popular and well organized there. And even if Bob had won New York, Humphrey might still have been the nominee.

If Bob had lived, I would, at some point, have pursued the proposed Kennedy-Humphrey meeting after the New York primary. I'm sure it would have taken place because of the respect both men felt for the other. At such a meeting, Hubert would have had two goals: first, to persuade Bob to withdraw before the Convention; second, to persuade him to run as the vice-presidential candidate.

I think it's unlikely that Bob would either have withdrawn before the Convention or accepted the second spot. It wasn't like him to quit any fight and I don't think he wanted the vice presidency. Still, there could have been some points for negotiation between the two men. Assuming Hubert was the nominee, he would have wanted Bob's active support in the campaign, and Bob would have wanted Hubert to pledge an end to the war.

Hubert might have said, "Bob, you know the problem I've

had on Vietnam as a Vice President loyal to his President, but there's not really that much difference between you and me." Hubert could have agreed to support a peace plank acceptable to Bob at the Convention. He would have done so knowing that Johnson might denounce him publicly, but I would have urged him to make the offer. Bob's support in the campaign could have helped Hubert more than Johnson's criticisms could have hurt him. Quite possibly, pressure from Bob might have forced Humphrey to state his position on the war earlier than he did and that, along with active campaigning by Bob Kennedy, might have spelled the difference in what proved to be a very close election. Of course, one could just as easily reverse the roles in this scenario and substitute Bob for Hubert, at least in part. It would be equally intriguing to contemplate the possibility of a Kennedy-Humphrey ticket.

But all this is pure speculation. The reality in June 1968 was that Bob Kennedy was dead. I went to New York for the funeral, and on the day before it was to take place, as I returned from St. Patrick's Cathedral to my room at the Waldorf-Astoria Hotel, a Secret Service man handed me a note. It said the Vice President would appreciate it if I would join him in his suite. I was surprised to learn that Hubert knew I was there. Elva, Phyllis, and Ira were with me, and the four of us went to see Hubert and Muriel. It was a somber visit. Hubert was very depressed, very shaken. He spoke of his affection for Bob and of the terrible uncertainty of life. "Men struggle for worthy goals," he said, "and yet they have no control over their own destinies. It all seems futile and pointless."

The funeral train from New York back to Washington proved to be a long, sad, and emotional journey. People ran out of conversation quickly. At first we watched the crowds along the tracks, but after a while we lost interest, and the news that two onlookers had been struck and killed by the train further depressed us. I was deeply moved by the courage and dignity of Ethel Kennedy as she traveled the length of the train with her son Joe, consoling all of us.

Jackie Kennedy was also on the funeral train. We met in the

aisle of one of the cars and she greeted me with a kiss on the cheek.

"Oh, Larry," she said in a whisper, "isn't it terrible for us to be together again like this? It's unbelievable."

There were a lot of politicians on the train, but I heard no political talk except for Jesse Unruh's comment to me, "Larry, we've got to get moving and get behind a candidate."

But I was in no state of mind to think about politics. After the funeral services, I went home and remained there for several days. It was a mood I had never known before. Following President Kennedy's assassination I had been swept along by Lyndon Johnson and the legislative program, but now I had nothing to do and nothing I wanted to do.

XIII

THE HUMPHREY CAMPAIGN

ABOUT A WEEK after Bob's funeral, Hubert Humphrey came to my home for a visit. He deliberately kept the conversation away from politics. Instead, he extended an invitation to Elva and me.

"Larry, Muriel and I have often mentioned that you've never accepted our invitations to visit us in Waverly."

That was true. The Humphreys had several times invited us to visit their lakeside home at Waverly, Minnesota, but it had never worked out. This time, however, I quickly accepted. Both Elva and I welcomed an opportunity to get out of the house and out of Washington.

I appreciated Hubert's sensitivity in avoiding any references to his campaign, but as he departed I thought I should clear the air.

"Hubert," I told him, "I don't want you to leave with any question in your mind as to my feelings about your candidacy, as opposed to Gene McCarthy's, or any question about my hope to see you the nominee."

He seemed embarrassed and said he had not doubted my position.

The following weekend, Elva and I flew to Waverly, where we saw another side of Hubert Humphrey—the family man, thoroughly enjoying his children, his grandchildren, his neighbors, and his home.

He was meticulous about his house and grounds. He was always raking the grass and sweeping the sidewalks, and every time I put a cigarette into an ashtray, he would leap to his

feet to empty it. He obviously enjoyed his family life as fully
as he did his political life.

On Sunday morning, Hubert insisted on accompanying us
to Mass, and he joined in the services with great enthusiasm.
That afternoon, we all got in his motorboat and went across
the lake to visit some of his friends. We stopped at several
lakeside cottages to say hello or have a cup of coffee. It was
a constant "Hi there, Jim. How are you, Mamie?" with Hubert
enjoying every minute of it. We went out onto his houseboat
that afternoon and for a ride in his antique car. Hubert was
beaming and kept saying, "Isn't this living?" and "What could
be better than this?"

That evening, as we sat in Hubert's kitchen eating crackers
and cheese and drinking beer, Hubert brought up the subject
of his campaign. He reviewed his staff and its weaknesses. He
was somewhat defensive, because he was known as a politician who did not have a solid organization. I stressed how fortunate he was to have Senators Fritz Mondale and Fred Harris
as co-chairmen of his campaign, but he pointed out that their
Senate duties limited their activity. Finally he said he wanted
me to be active in his campaign. I said I was not prepared to
make a decision at that time but I would think about it. As I
considered the matter, I felt there were three obstacles to my
doing so. First, I was contemplating forming a management
consulting and public relations firm, and I questioned whether
I could ask potential clients to wait until after the presidential
campaign. Also, I was anxious that Senators Harris and Mondale agree to my being involved. However, Humphrey later
discussed it with them and they came to my home to urge me
to take charge of the campaign.

Finally, there was my concern about Humphrey's Vietnam
position. In July I had lunch with him at his Capitol office.
The purpose of our meeting was to discuss his position on
Vietnam. I had decided that if his position was acceptable to
me, I would join his campaign through the Convention.

Hubert read me a statement he said he would soon be making public. In it, he favored a bombing halt and a negotiated
end to the war. It satisfied me, and I agreed to join his cam-

paign through the Convention. Hubert told me he was to meet
with the President that evening and he would tell Johnson
about his new position on Vietnam.

"How do you think he'll respond?" I asked.

"I don't know," Humphrey admitted. "I don't think he's going to hug me with joy."

That weekend I watched the papers for word of Humphrey's
statement, but none appeared. I saw him on Monday and
asked how his meeting with Johnson had gone.

"It didn't work out," Humphrey admitted. "Other people
were present and we didn't have a chance to talk. But I'll meet
with him again soon."

About a week later Humphrey visited Johnson at the ranch
and on his return, he told me that the President had advised
him of a major new development on Vietnam. Naturally, he
said, he should not make any statement until after the President had made his announcement. He added that for security
reasons he couldn't reveal the details, but he indicated that the
President was about to take a step that would please the anti-
war people. That was the last I heard of Humphrey's statement, and his position on Vietnam was to haunt us throughout
the Convention and campaign.

As I prepared for the Convention, to be held in Chicago in
late August, I discovered that nobody in the Humphrey organization had the remotest influence on the planning of the Convention. Marvin Watson and a Johnson man at the DNC, John
Criswell, were in total control. We could get no information
about the allocation of hotel rooms, access to the convention
floor, telephones, any of the normal details of convention
planning. The Johnson people had everything tied up. I found
it ironic when the McCarthy camp began complaining that
they were being discriminated against, being frozen out in
favor of Humphrey, because we were receiving exactly the
same treatment.

The division within the Democratic Party over the war can
hardly be overstated. Some prominent Democrats came to me
and urged that Humphrey resign as Vice President to prove his
independence of Johnson. I reported the proposal to Humphrey,

but neither of us took the idea seriously. We knew that the public reaction to his resignation would be very negative, that it would be seen not as an act of courage but one of weakness.

I believed, however, that to be elected Humphrey had to disassociate himself from Johnson's Vietnam policy. Harris and Mondale agreed, but we were by no means a majority in the Humphrey circle of advisers. Jim Rowe, Orville Freeman, and Bill Connell, three of Humphrey's closest associates, all supported the Johnson policy, as did most of the labor leaders and Southerners who strongly supported Humphrey for the nomination.

I wanted to see us recruit many of the former Kennedy supporters into the Humphrey campaign, but I knew we could not unless Humphrey softened his Vietnam position. Yet it soon became apparent to me that Humphrey wasn't going to do or say anything that might be taken as a repudiation of the President, at least until he had the nomination. I, and others, began to hope that we could solve the problem another way. If the Convention could adopt a Vietnam plank that was acceptable to the peace forces, Humphrey could simply run on the Democratic platform. He would not repudiate Johnson, he would simply accept the platform.

Throughout August, a number of people were working to draft a peace plank acceptable to both sides. Ted Sorensen and Ken O'Donnell were two of the leading representatives of the anti-war forces—essentially, the McCarthy delegates and the former Kennedy delegates who were now supporting Senator McGovern's candidacy—and David Ginsburg, a Washington lawyer, along with William Welsh of the Vice President's staff, represented Humphrey in these efforts. Perhaps it was impossible. Perhaps no language could satisfy both sides. For it seemed that any Vietnam plank, no matter how carefully worded, either supported the Johnson policy or repudiated it, and the pro-Johnson forces were not about to see the President repudiated.

Fred Harris and I met twice in Chicago with one of the leading Johnson stalwarts, Governor John Connally of Texas. I'd first known Connally during the Kennedy administration when he was the Secretary of the Navy, and I grew to recognize him as a tough, able political pro. But he was in a hostile mood when Harris and I went to see him, not long after I arrived in Chicago on August 19. The legitimacy of his Texas delegation was under challenge, and he regarded both that and the peace plank as evidence that the eastern liberals were trying to kick around *him*, Lyndon Johnson, Texas, and the South. He bluntly said, "If Humphrey thinks he's got the nomination locked up, he'd better count the delegates again, because all hell will break loose if we're kicked around. He'd better remember we in the South can deny him the nomination if we withdraw our support."

Harris and I met with Connally again the next day and this time he hinted that if Humphrey wasn't careful, Lyndon Johnson's name would be entered in nomination. I took that for the bluff that it was—there had been no show of pro-Johnson feeling at the Convention—but it underscored the uncertainty of Humphrey's position as he struggled for the presidential nomination that had eluded him since 1960.

An important figure in the peace plank effort was Congressman Hale Boggs, chairman of the Platform Committee. David Ginsburg, several others, and I held a secret meeting with Boggs one night to discuss the situation. We did not discuss specific language with him, but we stressed our desire for unity on this emotional issue and our belief that we could win majority support for a compromise plank. Hale's attitude was that he wanted to see unity, and what we were proposing sounded fine to him. It was not until several days later that Hale asked me a casual question that brought me back to reality: "Of course, this has been cleared with the President?"

It hadn't been, and that was to prove our downfall.

By Friday, August 23, the drafters had developed compromise language which seemed to satisfy the peace forces and our representatives. We felt that it could receive the support of a substantial majority of the 110 members of the Platform Committee. But the more important development that day was that Hale Boggs had returned to Washington to confer with the

President on the Russian intervention in Czechoslovakia and had mentioned what was afoot in the Platform Committee.

The upshot was that Charles Murphy, a Washington lawyer and long-time associate of the President, arrived in Chicago as the President's spokesman. Murphy reviewed the draft that Dave Ginsburg and Ted Sorensen and others had agonized over for so long and pronounced it unacceptable. All hope of party unity seemed lost. Ginsburg and I went to Humphrey and told him how serious we felt Murphy's rejection of the compromise plank was. We urged him to call the President and try to persuade him that the agreed-upon language was not critical of him and was essential to the Humphrey candidacy.

Humphrey placed the call, but the President was unavailable. We waited for a while, but it became clear that the President was not going to return the call. Humphrey chose not to comment or complain about the rebuff. Instead, he took the position that the language Murphy was insisting on was not so different from the compromise draft.

"These are just words," he insisted. "I don't see that it's all that important. I don't see that we've upset any applecarts."

I was disturbed by the situation. I had seen the Vice President unable to speak with the President, and I had seen days of sensitive negotiations overturned.

"This could blow the whole campaign," I told Ginsburg. "We might have gotten unity, but this could blow it sky-high."

In the end, Humphrey accepted the Johnson Vietnam plank, and the Convention endorsed it by a two-to-one margin. Johnson got what he wanted—the Democratic Party endorsed his war policy—and Humphrey got what he wanted—the nomination—but the price was very high in terms of bitterness and division within the party.

Humphrey's nomination was never in serious doubt. There was some movement toward drafting Ted Kennedy, but I did not take it seriously. It didn't seem possible to me that Ted, less than three months after Bob's death, could be in any emotional state to run for President. I thought rather, that some of the people who were urging Ted to run were more concerned about *their* political futures than Ted's.

With Humphrey nominated, the remaining question was the selection of a vice-presidential candidate. Ted Kennedy was the one person who would obviously strengthen the ticket, and Humphrey pleaded with him directly, but Ted refused.

The selection finally came down to two senators, Ed Muskie and Fred Harris. Humphrey would have liked to have chosen Harris, who wanted the nomination and had worked hard for him that year. But it was felt that Fred was just a little too young—thirty-seven years old—and from Oklahoma, he did not provide geographical balance for the ticket.

Muskie of Maine, on the other hand, was from the East, experienced, and was fifty-four years old. He was poised and personable, and his "down East" manner would complement Humphrey's mile-a-minute style. There was little doubt, coldly considered, that Muskie would be the more satisfactory candidate, but Humphrey still agonized over the decision because of his personal affection for Fred.

Finally, a choice had to be made. Hubert, Jim Rowe, Bill Connell, and I were in a bedroom in Hubert's suite. Muskie was waiting in the other bedroom and Harris was in the living room. Hubert began tapping me on the chest. "Larry," he said, "if you had fifteen seconds to decide, who would it be?"

"Ed Muskie," I said, and Jim and Bill quickly concurred.

"Okay, let's go," Hubert said. "I'll call them in and Fred can place Ed's name in nomination." He personally advised each of them and that was what happened. As it turned out, the nomination of Muskie was the best decision made in Chicago.

During my two weeks in Chicago, Joe Napolitan worked on an outline of organization, personnel, issues, and media strategy for the Humphrey campaign. I had first known Joe in Springfield in 1956, when he was with a local newspaper. He went on to be a nationally respected political consultant, and we had worked together on a number of campaigns. The outline did not include any involvement by Larry O'Brien in the campaign. I had agreed to help Humphrey only through the

Convention, and I had assured potential clients of my consulting firm that I would be in business the Monday following the Convention.

However, when Humphrey called me in to discuss Napolitan's campaign proposals, he urged me to stay on through the November election. I said that wasn't possible, and that he should be concentrating on people who were available. Late that evening a Secret Service agent came to my suite and said the Vice President wanted to see me. Elva and Joe Napolitan were with me and we knew what Humphrey wanted to discuss. They both urged me not to accept—they knew of my obligations to my future clients. Reluctantly, I went to the Vice President's suite.

As we talked, we could hear the demonstrators chanting "Dump the Hump, Dump the Hump," and worse in the street below his window.

"Larry, do you hear those people down there?" he asked me. "Don't leave me naked. How can I pull all the pieces together in so short a time?"

I was moved by his appeal. Despite my problem with his Vietnam position, Hubert was my friend, one with whom I had shared many a battle on the Hill. Yet I was determined not to change my decision. I had my own future to think of; I couldn't keep going off on "one more campaign" forever.

Then a Secret Service man came in with a note for me. It said: "Elva and I say do it. Joe." Their change of heart, plus Hubert's earnest appeal, caused me to weaken. But I felt that I still had a serious problem with my business clients and I explained the situation to Hubert in detail.

I had, potentially, two major clients for O'Brien Associates, as I planned to call my firm. The first was the three television networks. Two months earlier, James Hagerty, the ABC vice president who had previously been press secretary to President Eisenhower, called me and said the networks were concerned about adverse reaction, both among the public and in Congress, to violence in television programs, and that more generally they wanted to improve their image. I met with the presidents of the three networks and we agreed they would become a client of O'Brien Associates. Our understanding was that I would not fight fires for them, but would rather help them prevent fires—that is, that I would advise them on steps they could take to prevent political and public-relations problems.

My second potential client was Hughes Enterprises, the far-flung empire of billionaire Howard Hughes. In late June I had received a call from Robert Maheu, the executive director of Hughes Enterprises, who said that his boss had asked him to talk with me about possible employment with their company. He asked if my wife and I would consider coming to Las Vegas to talk with him. I was intrigued, and we flew out in early July. I had several talks with Maheu, who explained to me that his employer had a problem I had encountered in other successful men, Jack Kennedy and Lyndon Johnson among them—he didn't think his good works were sufficiently appreciated by the American public. Maheu noted that Howard Hughes had been a pioneer in American aviation, and that Hughes's companies had contributed significantly to the U.S. space program. He noted also that Hughes had created a medical foundation that had supported important research, and that Hughes was an outspoken opponent of underground nuclear testing, a position that many Americans would agree with. But despite this, Maheu noted, Hughes was primarily thought of in terms of his eccentric behavior—his life as a recluse—and he wondered if I might be able to advise him on ways to better present his and his company's story to the public. Subsequently, Maheu wanted my advice on expanding the Hughes television network from an all-sports format into other forms of programming and exploring a settlement of the lengthy Trans World Airlines litigation.

There was, of course, the delicate matter that Hughes wanted to hire me but didn't want to meet me face to face. Maheu raised the issue—he said that was simply Hughes's style of operation, that he, Maheu, had worked for the man for years, and was his chief executive officer, but had never met him.

"We communicate by memo," Maheu explained, "and we have a rule that we're never to show anyone one of Hughes's memos. But I'm going to break that rule now because I don't want you to have any doubts that everything I'm saying comes directly from Hughes himself."

He reached into his desk and took out a memo that was handwritten on a yellow legal pad. In the memo, Hughes told Maheu that he had been watching television and he was highly disturbed by Bob Kennedy's death and the continuing tragedy in the Kennedy family. He said that Kennedy had surrounded himself with some extremely able people and he wondered if any of them might be available to Hughes Enterprises. He said, finally, that he was particularly interested in Larry O'Brien and that he wanted Maheu to find out if O'Brien might possibly join the company.

I did not wish to be an employee of Hughes Enterprises, but we agreed that the firm would become one of the clients of O'Brien Associates.

Both the networks and Hughes, however, had been assured I would be starting in business as soon as the Democratic Convention ended. And, adding to the pressures on me, I had signed a contract to write this book, and there were deadlines to be met.

I outlined these obligations to Humphrey, and the dilemma they put me in. "Hubert," I told him, "I just don't know if these people will wait another two and a half months for me, and it's hard for me to endanger an undertaking that seems to be off to such a good start."

"If I get them to agree to the delay, will that settle it?" he asked.

I said it would, and the next morning Humphrey called Maheu; Frank Stanton, the president of CBS; and Mike Bessie, my book publisher; all of whom agreed to wait until after the election. The only problem came when Bessie refused to believe that Hubert Humphrey was calling and kept insisting that someone was pulling his leg.

In a few days, I moved into the National Committee headquarters in Washington, with Joe Napolitan, Ira Kapenstein, and Phyllis Maddock in offices adjoining mine.

Along with the candidate and members of his staff, Joe, Ira, and I spent the Labor Day weekend in the Humphreys' guest cottage at Waverly trying to put together a campaign. It was terribly frustrating, with only two months left before the election, trying to make decisions that should have been made months earlier. We had no travel plans for the candidate, no media program, no people in key campaign positions, and precious little money. We spent much of the weekend calling people, recruiting staff, often hearing people say that what we wanted done couldn't be done in the time remaining. Yet as the three-day weekend ended, we felt we had at least begun to move, that all hope was not gone.

Money and Vietnam were to be our two most pressing problems for the next two months. The problem of Humphrey's Vietnam position was the one more easily solved. Humphrey could solve this himself. But the money problem could never really be solved. We were caught in a vicious circle: the polls showed that Humphrey would lose, therefore people would not give us money, therefore Humphrey *would* lose. This was at the point when the polls showed Humphrey running more than 15 per cent behind Nixon. We conducted private polls that showed we were stronger than the Harris and Gallup polls indicated. When we publicized them, the press accused us of faking them, but in the end our polls were proven accurate.

I never realized until the 1968 campaign just how unfair the system of private campaign financing is. In the 1960 Kennedy campaign, and the 1964 Johnson campaign, we had been able to hold our own with the Republicans in the fund-raising area, but we never had a chance in 1968. It is a terrible feeling to see your opponent blitzing the nation's television screens and to realize that your candidate, for lack of money, simply can't compete, can't get his message to the voters.

We had hoped to have a six-million-dollar television campaign, but in the end, for lack of money, we only spent half that. Nixon, by contrast, spent $5.2 million, or almost double what we did. He had started his television spots by Labor Day. All we could do was to try to match him in the last two or three weeks of the campaign and hope the viewers by then were tired of his spots and curious about ours.

At one point in the campaign, Humphrey came back from a swing through West Virginia. He was excited. The crowds had been good and there hadn't been the anti-war hecklers who had bedeviled him elsewhere.

"It looked good," he told me, "things are improving."

But one thing bothered him, and he wanted to tell me about it.

"Larry, I don't see any Humphrey signs, any Humphrey literature. I'm out there breaking my butt and I don't see any campaign activity to back me up."

I knew why he hadn't seen any balloons or billboards or brochures. We hadn't wanted to worry him, but now we had to tell him the facts of life.

"We're broke, Hubert," I told him. "We don't have money and we can't get credit. We're not going to have the materials we wanted, and the television campaign has to be cut to the bone. The money just isn't there."

It was a body blow to Humphrey; his enthusiasm left him. He'd been out on the road, campaigning his heart out, doing his job, and he just didn't understand our financial plight.

We discussed the problem at length. It always came back to the polls. There are a good many contributors who, in a close election, give to both parties, insuring that whoever wins, they'll have a foot in the door. But in 1968, with the polls showing Humphrey an apparent loser, these "fat cats," who might have given $10,000 to both candidates, were giving their money to Nixon and nothing to Humphrey.

In the end, the fact that there was any Democratic campaign at all was largely due to organized labor and to a few of Humphrey's close personal friends. Labor contributed more than a half-million dollars, as well as extensive manpower. Many labor leaders were alarmed to see their rank-and-file members about to desert the Democratic Party to vote for George Wallace, and they made an all-out effort to inform their workers of Wallace's poor record on labor-related issues. Several close personal friends of Humphrey's gave till it hurt and they persuaded some other men of wealth to make loans to us, perhaps twenty or thirty loans totaling some $3 million, that enabled us to have at least part of the media campaign we'd hoped for.

Humphrey's position on Vietnam continued to concern me. Some of his other advisers believed that his basic problem was to win back the labor vote from Wallace, and that he should therefore talk tougher on crime and violence and not worry about Vietnam. I certainly shared their concern about the blue-collar vote, but I also believed that Hubert needed to take a Vietnam position that could win back the liberals, the Kennedy and McCarthy people, who seemed likely to stay home on Election Day.

The division within the Humphrey camp over Vietnam came to a head in late September. Ever since the Convention, Humphrey had been reviewing his position on Vietnam, but nothing had been determined. On September 27, I saw an advance copy of a Gallup Poll that showed Nixon with 43 per cent of the vote, Humphrey with 28 per cent and Wallace a strong third at 21 per cent. I thought this poll showed that it was imperative that Humphrey make a dramatic statement on Vietnam, even if it meant running the risk that Johnson would denounce him. We simply had nothing to lose. Fortunately, we had pulled together $100,000 to buy a half hour of national television time and we agreed that the following Monday, Sepember 30, when Humphrey would be in Salt Lake City, was the most convenient time to tape for a nationally televised statement.

In Washington on Saturday morning, two days before the speech, I was shown a copy of what was, I was told, the "final draft" of the Vietnam speech. I read it and hit the ceiling. It was weak; it begged the question—it was a disaster. I sent Humphrey a strong message, via telecopier, which said, among other things, that the speech was a waste of our $100,000.

Humphrey, who was campaigning on the West Coast, called me that afternoon. "Larry, that was quite a telegram," he said. "But there's one problem—that wasn't any final draft you saw. The speech isn't even written yet. Why don't you fly out here and be with me and we'll work on it."

I flew out on Sunday morning and met Humphrey at his hotel suite in Seattle. By then he had read the speech draft I'd seen, and had reacted much as I had. We agreed there had to be a new draft, and we discussed ideas until it was time to fly to Salt Lake City that afternoon.

That night, in Humphrey's hotel suite in Salt Lake City, there was a long, sometimes heated, discussion of the Vietnam speech that lasted until the early hours of Monday morning. Perhaps a dozen people were present. Fred Harris and I did much of the talking for those who wanted a softer line on Vietnam, and Jim Rowe and Bill Connell were the main spokesmen for the Johnson policy.

"You can't expect to be elected President if you turn on the President you served under," Rowe declared. "You can't run on a ticket of disloyalty."

He and Connell predicted that Johnson would denounce any Humphrey call for a bombing halt—a central issue in our debate—and that it might be seen as undercutting the Paris peace talks. Personally, I found it hard to believe that Johnson, however angry, would denounce his own party's candidate for President.

"You have to prove you are your own man," I said to Humphrey as the discussion went on. "You're not going to be elected President unless the people are convinced you stand on your own two feet—and this is the issue you can prove it on!"

Humphrey exploded. "Damn it, I'm on my own two feet," he declared. "I'm sick and tired of hearing about how Lyndon Johnson will react or how Gene McCarthy will react. Let's start thinking about what Hubert Humphrey wants. This is *my* speech and I'll write it myself."

He grabbed a pen and began to work over the speech. The debate continued over the phrasing of one key section, but it was finally clear that Humphrey would call for a bombing halt and thus break with the Johnson position. This drafting went on until three or four in the morning, when I finally decided to leave. I had mixed feelings. The statement was strong, but not as strong as I recommended. When Hubert saw me get up from my chair, he said, "Are you leaving?"

I said I was.

"You're not going to give up that easily, are you?" Hubert said.

"Do you think I'm giving up easily?" I asked.

"No," he said. He smiled at me and I smiled back. What Hubert meant by that, I think, was: "I'm sorry you're leaving not totally pleased."

I wasn't totally pleased, but I was much more so than Rowe and Connell. As I left the room, Jim Rowe said to me, "I think this is wrong, Larry. I think we're making a big mistake."

The actual language of the speech may not, in retrospect, seem to justify all the intense debate. The key passage had more than its share of qualifiers—it was as follows:

"As President, I would be willing to stop the bombing of North Vietnam as an acceptable risk for peace, because I believe that it could lead to success in the negotiations and a shorter war. This would be the best protection for our troops.

"In weighing that risk—and before taking action—I would place key importance on evidence, direct or indirect, by word or deed, of Communist willingness to restore the Demilitarized Zone between North and South Vietnam.

"If the Government of North Vietnam were to show bad faith, I would reserve the right to resume the bombing."

The first paragraph was the one I wanted to see. The ones after that were the qualifications that Rowe and Connell urged be added.

The speech had an immediate dramatic impact on both the candidate and the campaign. Soon after he delivered the speech, Humphrey received a telegram of congratulations from Ted Kennedy and he was beaming as he showed it to us. He was a new man from then on; it was as if a burden had been lifted from his shoulders. And the impact on the campaign itself was just as great. The crowds began to swell, the hecklers died out, a little money began to come in, and many of the anti-war liberals began to support us—we began, in short, to move toward a more normal Democratic campaign for the presidency.

Yet we never won back all the liberals. Too many of them argued that it didn't make any difference—Humphrey was no better than Nixon—and so they didn't work, or even vote, for the Democratic candidate. These defections were symbolized by Gene McCarthy's performance that fall. When he finally got around to endorsing Humphrey, his statement was so tepid as to be worthless. I have never had much use for fair-weather Democrats and the 1968 campaign reinforced my sentiments. There was ample evidence to persuade any Democrat that Humphrey would make a far better President than Nixon. For those who refused to accept that in 1968, subsequent events emphasized the point even more. As President Kennedy said in 1960: "There may be thousands of Americans more qualified to be President than me, but the choice is between two, Nixon and myself."

In contrast to McCarthy's attitude, both George McGovern and Ted Kennedy worked hard for Humphrey; McGovern pledged his full support to the ticket immediately after Humphrey's nomination, despite their differences over the war. Ted Kennedy made his first political appearance after Bob's death at a Humphrey rally in Boston, one in which both of them were silenced by angry anti-war hecklers. Ted also made some television tapes with Humphrey, and near the end of the campaign Ted called and asked me if there was anything else he could do. I spoke with Humphrey and we decided that another television segment, something out of the ordinary, was what we needed.

At Ted's suggestion, we settled on a film of the two of us walking on the beach at the Cape, in an unrehearsed conversation. Ted and I reminisced on the 1960 campaign and how hard Humphrey had worked for John Kennedy that year, and we stressed the respect and affection that had existed between Bob Kennedy and Humphrey. We used this film on Humphrey's final election eve television program.

Nixon ran a campaign of avoidance—he avoided the issues, he avoided Humphrey, and he avoided the people. We were never able to get a handle on him. It was a clever campaign. If we'd been ahead, we'd probably have avoided him, too. If he had lost the election, however, as he nearly did, it would have been because of his remaining above the battle in the final days of the campaign when the gap was obviously closing.

We tried hard to make an issue of his refusal to debate Humphrey. Nixon obviously was not going to debate, but we hoped his refusal could be used to put him on the defensive. We were sure Nixon was afraid of the debate issue, for he still blamed his debates with John F. Kennedy for his loss in 1960.

To keep the issue alive, we urged our allies on Capitol Hill to push through a bill to waive the equal-time law, so fringe candidates could not prevent a Nixon-Humphrey debate from taking place. We got the equal time suspension through the House, after a dramatic session in which Speaker McCormack invoked his authority to lock the members in the House chamber until he had a vote. However, in the Senate, majority leader Mansfield and Senator John Pastore, who was chairman of the subcommittee that would handle the bill, argued that since Nixon obviously was not going to debate, an effort to pass the equal-time bill would be labeled "just politics." That, I confess, was probably true. We would have liked to keep the issue alive through Senate debate but this didn't happen and it fizzled out.

We tried to make an issue of Nixon's running mate, Spiro Agnew. We felt that he compared rather poorly with Ed Muskie and we did everything we could to force the comparison. Near the end of the campaign, despite our financial bind, we ran a half-hour biography of Muskie. And on the final night telethons, Muskie was virtually a co-performer with Hubert, whereas Agnew was nowhere to be seen on the Nixon program. We had one television spot of about thirty seconds of hysterical laughter followed by the question, "Agnew for President?" We canceled it after getting protests from our own people that it was too tough and might backfire. We did use another one that featured the sound of a heartbeat followed by a voice saying "Imagine Spiro T. Agnew a heartbeat away from the presidency." I wouldn't argue, however, that Agnew hurt the Nixon ticket. He was chosen as a sop to the South and border states and his blunders, or the attacks on him, didn't lower his appeal in those areas.

We seriously considered using films of two of Nixon's most famous public appearances—the "Checkers Speech" of 1952 and the "last press conference" after his defeat by Pat Brown for governor of California in 1962—as part of our campaign. I sat through screenings of both of them to determine if they would be effective. I decided against using the "last press conference" because I feared that some viewers, rather than being disturbed at how petty, self-pitying and erratic Nixon was, might be impressed by his attacks on the press, for anti-press feeling was running high in the 1968 campaign.

I thought more seriously about using the "Checkers Speech." It was such vintage Nixon. Pat Nixon sat primly while Dick spoke piously of his little dog Checkers and his wife's plain Republican cloth coat. I thought people would react negatively to the speech's obvious corn and insincerity. But we didn't use the Checkers Speech, partly because of our money problem, and partly because we feared a backlash.

On October 31, five days before the election, President Johnson announced a halt of the bombing in Vietnam. We had hoped that Johnson would make some peace gesture that would aid the Humphrey campaign, but this action came too late for major impact. There was no time for it to sink into the public mind, no time for Humphrey to follow up on it. Instead, South Vietnamese President Thieu, who obviously wanted to see Nixon elected, got the last word by charging President Johnson with the "betrayal of an ally."

Humphrey peaked that final weekend. He was given a tremendous reception at the Astrodome in Houston and on Monday he drove through the streets of Los Angeles like a conquering hero, surrounded by the kind of crowds that had greeted Bob Kennedy that spring. I found my hopes rising. By Election Day, as we flew from California to Minnesota, we knew we were in a contest. Winning was a possibility.

The early returns were not encouraging that night. They

showed us losing New Jersey. I called Governor Dick Hughes in the hope the report might be wrong. It didn't seem realistic that we'd lose New Jersey while winning Pennsylvania, New York, Connecticut, and Massachusetts. Dick Hughes called back to say the report was accurate, and the loss of New Jersey was a serious blow to our hopes.

We had been concentrating in the final weeks on big states like New Jersey and Michigan. We saw no hope of carrying the southern states and only faint hope of carrying two or three border states. Thus we had to do better in the big states than Kennedy did in 1960. We had to carry two states we lost in 1960, Ohio and California, and retain Illinois, which we had won narrowly. We also had to carry Texas and New Jersey, both of which we felt fairly confident about.

But it was more than we could pull off. We carried Texas, thanks to the three-way split with Wallace, but we lost Ohio, California, and Illinois, as well as New Jersey, all by close margins, and they cost us the election. In all, Humphrey carried 13 states and the District of Columbia, for 191 electoral votes, to Nixon's 32 states and 301 electoral votes and Wallace's 5 states and 46 electoral votes.

I stayed with Hubert, Muriel, and their family in their Minneapolis hotel suite until he conceded in the early hours of Wednesday morning. Both Hubert and Muriel accepted the defeat with dignity, although of course emotions ran high in all of us that night. The Democratic presidential era that had begun with such high hopes eight years before was coming to an end. The man we had defeated eight years before, and about whom we all had such grave doubts, was to be our President. It was not a happy time for any of us, but there was nothing to do but accept the judgment of the people.

I might add a personal note about the Humphrey campaign. It had many problems, and it ended in a bitter defeat, but I would have to say that I enjoyed it immensely because it was the campaign in which I was given full control in all areas. In the 1960 Kennedy campaign I was director of the campaign organization, and Bob Kennedy was the over-all chairman. In 1964 I was chiefly the political adviser in a campaign that was obviously going to be won. In 1972 . . . well, we'll get to 1972 in due course. But in 1968, Humphrey understood his needs, and he wanted me to have full authority over all aspects of the campaign—the media program, organization, issues, the whole thing. I savored the challenge, the day by day uphill struggle that took us so close to victory. I don't believe in "moral victories," but I wouldn't be honest if I didn't say that I was proud of how far we moved in those two hectic months, or if I didn't say I enjoyed every minute of it.

On the day after the election, I flew back to Washington. Elva and I took a brief vacation in Europe, and then I was busy through the holidays with my business affairs. In January, however, as the Nixon Inauguration neared, I made an appointment with the outgoing President, Lyndon Johnson.

We were both leaving politics and I wanted to make sure he left office with a full understanding of my admiration for all that he had accomplished as President and my deep appreciation for all that he had done for me.

I went to his office at 5 P.M. one January afternoon and we talked for almost two hours. His able assistant, Jim Jones, later a congressman from Oklahoma, came in several times to remind Johnson of his other appointments, but the President waved him away. He asked who would be succeeding me as chairman of the Democratic National Committee. I said I understood it would be Fred Harris, and Johnson was noncommittal. We reminisced about the legislative battles we'd been in together, but his closing comments to me were about his concern for his two sons-in-law who were serving in Vietnam. "I'm not a President where those two boys are concerned," he said. "I'm just a worried father." I told him I understood his feeling because my own son was about to leave for Vietnam and I would be praying for his safe return.

"I wish every success to the new President," he said. "I've done everything I could. I can't think of anything I could have done that I didn't do."

Hubert Humphrey called on the afternoon before the Inauguration. He said he and Muriel would like to drop by that evening and I urged him to do so. I knew this was a difficult time for him. The next day, as the outgoing Vice President, he would have to stand and watch the man who had defeated him, Richard Nixon, sworn in as President. However, he was in a lighthearted and relaxed mood. We did reminisce about the campaign, how close it had been, and its very closeness had made the defeat all the more difficult to accept. There were so many "ifs" to the Humphrey campaign—if we'd had a little more money, if the bombing halt had come sooner . . . But that was behind us now. Hubert said he didn't want this Democratic era to end without again saying how much he appreciated my efforts in his behalf. He and I were both out of politics now; he back to Minnesota to teach and write, I to New York for a new business venture; and we parted on that last night of the Johnson administration with the four of us reflecting on our friendship and our determination that it would continue, whatever the future might hold.

XIV

NATIONAL CHAIRMAN

IN LATE November of 1968, after Elva and I had returned from our trip to Europe, I was busy re-establishing O'Brien Associates. Hughes Enterprises, the television networks, and other clients had agreed to wait for me until after the election, and now I was anxious to get started. In early December, however, my business plans changed abruptly when I received an unexpected, highly attractive offer from Wall Street.

I was contacted by an old friend of mine, George Bissell, who was related through marriage to Murray McDonnell, the chairman of the board of McDonnell & Co., a major and long-established Wall Street brokerage firm. I had never met Murray McDonnell, but I knew the McDonnell family by reputation as a prominent Irish-Catholic family. Murray McDonnell's younger brother Sean, an officer of the firm, had recently died of a heart attack while still in his thirties. George Bissell said Murray McDonnell was anxious to see me, and we held a series of discussions which led to Murray's asking me to become president of McDonnell & Co.

I agonized over the decision. I felt an obligation to the clients of O'Brien Associates, and I wanted to be my own boss. At the same time, I was attracted by the security offered by McDonnell & Co., as opposed to the uncertainties of starting my own business. By early December I had decided I simply could not refuse the McDonnell offer, and I notified the clients of O'Brien Associates of my decision. Both Phyllis Maddock and Ira Kapenstein agreed to join me at McDonnell, although, I must say, they did not enter the venture with the high degree of enthusiasm that I felt.

It soon became evident that my enthusiasm was misplaced. My arrival on Wall Street coincided with a general worsening of the national economy. Several brokerage houses failed; others merged. Shortly, I realized that McDonnell had serious financial and operational problems. The stock-market situation continued to deteriorate, and Murray McDonnell was unable to secure new capital. In August, after seven months with the company, I resigned, and some seven months later the company went out of business. I left McDonnell with no ill will, but it was obvious that I had chosen the wrong time to begin a career on Wall Street and that my decision to join McDonnell & Co. had been a serious mistake.

I have often been asked if politics is not a tough, dirty business and been met with skepticism when I replied that, with few exceptions, the politicians I have known have been honorable men. I might say that Wall Street in 1969 struck me as a far more ruthless world than anything I have known in politics —at least until 1972 and the Nixon Watergate era. It was a time of panic, of course, with fortunes being lost and careers ruined. I saw men who had been with a company for decades fired by telegram, just like that, without warning or sympathy. You don't often see people treated that way in politics.

When I resigned as president of McDonnell & Co., and my stock in the company was worthless, I found myself sitting across a desk from a stony-faced banker. A few months earlier he had warmly welcomed me to Wall Street and advised me to sign a note approaching six figures to cover the purchase of that stock. Now he was demanding immediate payment of the note. I had just sold my home in Washington and he urged that I turn over the proceeds as partial payment.

Fortunately, with the help of a friend, I had the pleasure of handing that banker a check for the full amount of the note and telling him I would wait while he brought me the balance of my modest checking account, down to the penny, because I didn't intend ever to do business with him or his bank again. During that same week, Elva and I thought we would be literally evicted from our New York apartment, which was owned by McDonnell & Co. Elva was close to tears—but again our friend saved us. Now, he has been fully repaid but our experience was a reminder of just how tough the world of high finance can be. I'll take the world of politics anytime.

In the fall of 1969, I once again began to organize O'Brien Associates, which had never actually begun operations the previous year. I sought out clients, I opened offices on Park Avenue, and I held a news conference to discuss my clients and activities.

During this period, my son was serving as an intelligence officer in Vietnam. He arrived there in March 1969 and stayed for thirteen months. Larry's year in Vietnam was a time of great anxiety for Elva and me. We waited for the mail every morning, worried if no letter came, and we watched the news every night, to see where the bombing had been that day and what the casualty figures were. Even in the most chaotic months at McDonnell & Co., I could find time most days to write handwritten letters to Larry. Once I ran into John Kenneth Galbraith on a plane and he spoke of our shared experience of having sons of military age. Ken noted that it had given an "extra dimension" to his opposition to the war. Certainly that was my experience. It's one thing to realize that the war is a military fiasco or a national disaster; it's quite another thing to realize that your son might be killed there.

During 1969, I made two business trips to the Philippines, and each time I arranged to fly on to Vietnam to visit Larry. During one of my visits, military officials arranged a briefing for me. I was there, of course, as a private citizen, but the briefing was arranged as a courtesy and out of regard for my former status as a cabinet officer. Larry was called in to attend the briefing and he took a seat in the back of the room. The briefing struck me as overly optimistic, but I chose not to question it—I had been hearing overly optimistic briefings on Vietnam for eight years. However, Larry began closely questioning the colonel who was conducting the briefing. I almost fell out of my chair when I heard him. But a general in attendance began answering this young lieutenant's rather pointed questions.

As soon as possible, I announced that I was late for my next appointment. When we were safely outside, I asked Larry why he'd chosen to speak out.

"I couldn't sit there and listen to all that bull," he said, or words to that effect.

As 1970 began, I was busy with O'Brien Associates and with work on this book. Then, early in February, Senator Fred Harris resigned as chairman of the Democratic National Committee and I found myself under intense pressures to replace him.

The unsalaried post of national chairman was not, to be sure, much of a plum at that point. Our party was divided and deeply in debt. I had been surprised when Fred Harris sought the post a year earlier. He apparently hoped the chairmanship would work to his political advantage by giving him national visibility, but instead his increasing association with the liberal wing of the Democratic Party was giving him political problems back in Oklahoma.

A number of reporters called me on the day Harris announced his resignation and I told them all that I was not the least interested in the job. Hubert Humphrey called me a few days later and said that as the party's titular leader he felt a responsibility to recommend a new chairman to the National Committee, whose members were to meet within thirty days to elect a replacement for Harris. Humphrey asked me to refrain from flatly ruling out the possibility until we had time to talk in person.

I agreed to do so, but I made it clear to him that I was not a candidate. However, in the days ahead, pressures continued to build. Humphrey called to report that Bob Strauss, a Dallas lawyer and Texas national committeeman, had agreed to become the party's treasurer if I became chairman. I commented that any man who would become the treasurer of a party that was over nine million dollars in debt was obviously a good Democrat.

Humphrey and I met in Washington and he told me he had been in touch with party leaders around the country and there was a consensus that I was the man for the job. I replied that

I doubted if any real consensus existed, since, for example, I'd heard that George Meany, head of the AFL-CIO, was cool toward my return.

"Let's just see about that," Hubert responded and immediately called Meany, who told him he could be comfortable with me as chairman.

I discussed the situation at length with Elva, Phyllis, Joe Napolitan, and Ira Kapenstein. Their view was that I had done my share for the party over the years and that I had my private life and my own financial situation to consider. I found myself agreeing with them.

I was tempted, of course. I've been in politics too long ever to be immune to its call. The prospect of trying to help unite our badly divided party was a challenge. There was the added incentive of joining the fight against the Nixon administration, both in that fall's congressional elections and in the preparations for the 1972 campaign.

But I decided I could not do it and, after advising Humphrey, I made a public statement that I was not a candidate.

I assumed the matter was closed. However, after the executive committee of the National Committee began its deliberations, I received a call from the chairman, Colonel Jake Arvey, a close friend of mine and the long-time Democratic leader in Chicago, who announced that the executive committee had unanimously drafted me. "We don't want any response from you now," he said. "Just think about it." While I thought about it, there was a call from Humphrey and I filled him in on what was taking place. He was highly amused and pleased. "We've got you on the spot now," he said.

I began to be swayed by the mounting pressures. Finally, I said I would accept the draft of the executive committee if it was backed up by similar approval of the full National Committee. Eventually Arvey and other party leaders persuaded the active announced contenders not to enter the race so that my selection would be unanimous. Given that on-the-record support from the National Committee, I accepted the chairmanship.

Some reporters wrote that I had engineered a brilliant political coup to obtain this unanimous draft. That wasn't true. I did not seek the job and I accepted only when old friends in the party persuaded me.

In early March of 1970, soon after my return to Washington, I had a breakfast reunion with some friends in the press corps. Their blunt attitude was: "O'Brien, you're crazy! What are you doing here?"

They knew, as did I, that the party was a shambles. Not only did our debt total some $9.3 million; despite Fred Harris' efforts, it had increased rather than decreased in 1969.

Even more serious than our financial plight was the deep division within our party, the worst I had ever seen. The problem encompassed far more than our loss of the 1968 election. We had lost in 1952 and 1956 and remained reasonably united. But in 1970 the bitter divisions of 1968 still existed—hawk versus dove, liberal versus conservative, reformer versus regular —and no reconciliation was in sight.

The National Committee was, I thought, the proper forum, indeed the only forum, through which the party might be united. It had been in existence for more than a century; it represented all the states and territories; and it had, through its executive committee, its elected membership, its chairman, and its full-time staff in the Washington headquarters, the potential for visible and effective leadership.

I intended to be an aggressive chairman. My first priority, I felt, was to undertake vigorous internal reorganization of the DNC and its staff. New staff members were hired, including John Stewart, formerly a legislative assistant to Vice President Humphrey, as our director of communications; Joe Mohbat, a prize-winning young reporter for the Associated Press, as press secretary; Stan Greigg, whom I'd known when he was a congressman from Iowa, as director of political organization. They joined Geri Joseph, our vice chairman; Dorothy Bush, the party's long-time secretary, and Bill Welsh, a former Humphrey aide, who was the committee's executive director.

Ira Kapenstein, who had worked with me at the Post Office, on the Humphrey campaign, and at McDonnell & Co., became my deputy chairman. Bob Strauss, the Dallas lawyer, came aboard as treasurer, and later, after Geri Joseph resigned, I brought in Mary Lou Berg as the committee's first salaried, full-time female vice chairman. Also, Joe Califano, who had been LBJ's special assistant for domestic affairs, agreed to serve as our unpaid general counsel.

With this revitalized staff, we were able to develop better communications within the party. We created offices representing the governors and the state chairmen. We held meetings and receptions with the Congress to improve the DNC's traditionally poor relations there. We increased the research facilities we could make available to Democratic candidates for Congress, and once again we updated and revised the O'Brien Campaign Manual. In September, we had the first political strategy meeting ever held on national closed-circuit television, with some eight thousand Democrats in eighteen cities participating.

These nuts and bolts jobs needed doing, but it was not my intention to be just a nuts-and-bolts chairman. I meant to be a major spokesman for our party. There was no precedent for the kind of chairmanship I envisioned, but neither was there precedent for the condition of the party at that point. I saw myself in a free-wheeling role, one limited only by my own time and imagination. For the first time in my political career I didn't have any responsibility to an employer—a President or would-be President—and I intended to do my own thing.

In the spring of 1970, Nixon too often held the national stage without challenge. His most outrageous statements would go without rebuttal. Our party's titular head, Hubert Humphrey, was concentrating on winning election to the Senate, and Senators Muskie and Kennedy were also absorbed with their home-state Senate races.

I thought the situation demanded that I speak out forcefully for the party, despite the risk of offending some members of Congress. In the months ahead I was often tougher than our presidential contenders felt they could be. I denounced "Nixonomics" and the Nixon-Agnew "politics of fear." Agnew became a special target of mine at a time when many Democratic leaders chose not to take him on.

I did not expect to make my attacks with impunity. The White House could never persuade my counterpart at the Republican National Committee, the pleasant, low-key Rogers Morton, to attack me with sufficient vigor, so they unleashed Senator Robert Dole, Morton's eventual successor as Republican chairman, who began denouncing me almost daily. Also, a right-wing writer began circulating, at White House urging, scurrilous stories about my business and political activities, but these rarely saw print. The only attack that received much publicity was Agnew's sarcastic remark at a Republican fund-raising dinner that thanks to my "adroit management" McDonnell & Co. had gone broke. I issued a statement demanding an apology, but privately I wasn't bothered. McDonnell's financial problems were a matter of record. If that was the worst charge the Republicans could make about me, I was in good shape.

In fact, I welcomed Agnew's attacks. By directing his fire at me, he reinforced my status as the Democratic Party's spokesman. As far as I was concerned, Agnew was playing into my hands.

In addition to speaking out myself, I wanted to make it possible for other Democrats to express themselves by fighting for greater equity in the manner in which television time was allocated between the "in" and the "out" parties. In mid-March I said, on "Meet the Press":

"Recently my predecessor asked to purchase time from the television networks to present our case to the American people and solicit funds. One major network flatly refused to allow that purchase of time, and let me sum up by saying that I am not going to stand idly by and allow that to happen. They will be hearing further from me."

I kept that promise. In 1970, we began a battle for basic reform of the rules governing political broadcasting. Our efforts were spurred on by our belief that nothing less than the survival of the two-party system hung in the balance. We faced the fact that in 1968 the Republicans had outspent us by two-to-one on television time, and they were prepared to do the same in the 1970 and 1972 elections. Moreover, the President can request free, prime-time television virtually at will, and Nixon was taking full advantage of that power. In his first eighteen months as President, Mr. Nixon appeared on prime evening television more than Presidents Eisenhower, Kennedy, and Johnson combined in the same period of time. Besides his aggressive use of free television time, he had appointed an able but partisan figure, Dean Burch, the former Goldwater aide and Republican chairman, as chairman of the Federal Communications Commission. Also, Nixon had assigned his Vice President the task of trying to intimidate television newsmen and executives by denouncing their objectivity and by making thinly veiled threats of FCC action against those who displeased the Administration.

Soon after I returned as chairman, Bob Strauss and I wanted to buy radio and television time for fund-raising appeals and also for brief comments on political issues. We knew this might be impossible. CBS had already refused to sell us a half hour of prime time, saying it only sold time "for political purposes . . . during elections." ABC had a policy against selling time for the solicitation of funds, and many local radio stations would not sell time for the discussion of "controversial" issues.

I understood the networks' attitude. Why risk the wrath of the President or of some viewers by selling time for "controversial" political messages when you are doing very well selling your time for non-controversial dog-food and deodorant commercials? Why indeed—except that our two-party system can't survive if one party is denied access to the dominant communications medium.

The Democratic Party had to raise money if it was to survive, and our fund-raising effort was doomed in the face of the existing network policies. In May we, therefore, asked the FCC for a ruling that broadcasters cannot refuse to sell time for fund raising and for discussion of public issues. But a ruling was not issued until August.

Another significant struggle in the area of access to television time was launched in May, also. We made our first request for equal time to respond to the President after his televised

speech of April 30 announcing the United States invasion of
Cambodia. We made the request of all three networks and
James Hagerty, vice president of ABC, called and advised me
his network would grant us one-half hour of prime time. It was
our first breakthrough. I was speaking on Saturday, May 9, to a
Democratic dinner in Milwaukee and I delivered a hard-hitting attack on Nixon's Indochina policy, which was carried by
the ABC network.

In June I received a call from Dr. Frank Stanton, the president of CBS, who said CBS would voluntarily sell us sixty-second segments for the purpose of fund raising, "without confin-
ing these announcements to campaign periods." Also, Stanton
said, CBS was offering us twenty-five minutes of free time at
10 P.M. on July 7 "for presentation of the Committee's views"
followed by five minutes of CBS commentary. Stanton said this
free time was for the first of a four-part series of "Loyal Opposition" programs by the Democratic Party.

We intended to make maximum use of this free time, and
we therefore devised an unprecedented and, as it turned out,
controversial, format, one that evolved from our belief that
Nixon was his own worst enemy. A large part of the program
was given over to film clips of Nixon himself—making his
pledges and predictions on the economy, the war, and other issues—followed by my factual rebuttals telling what he had
actually done.

The first "Loyal Opposition" show was hardly off the air before the Republican protests commenced. Rogers Morton accused me of making an "inaccurate personal attack" on the
President, but he never explained how it was either inaccurate
or personal. Much of the Republican fire was directed at Stanton and CBS. He was denounced by Republican leaders as a
tool of the Democrats and, when he appeared before a Senate
subcommittee, he was raked over the coals by irate Republicans. Unfortunately, the Democrats on the committee did not
defend Stanton. Senator John Pastore later said to me, "You
know, Larry, you *were* highly political on that show." I agreed.
Of course, I was political; I was *supposed* to be political.

The television issue flared up again in August. First, the FCC ruled on the petition we had filed in May. The commission decreed that broadcasters *could* refuse to sell time to political parties for discussion of public issues. It also concluded that the broadcasters could sell us time for brief fund-raising appeals, but that this was not made mandatory. FCC Chairman Dean Burch also declared: "We have expressly rejected any principle embodying right of reply or rebuttal to the President . . . We find that there is no obligation to provide time for countering addresses to those of the President."

It was obvious by then, if there had ever been any doubt, that we could expect no equity from the Republican-dominated FCC, so Joe Califano decided to go ahead with plans for an appeal to the United States Court of Appeals.

A few days later I was in New York and received an unexpected invitation to have lunch with Dr. Stanton at CBS. This was about a month after the first "Loyal Opposition" show, and we had been waiting for word from CBS regarding the scheduling of the next three "Loyal Opposition" shows. I assumed one would be in August, with the third program in September and the fourth in October. That was the logical format to coincide with the congressional elections in November.

When I arrived in Stanton's office, one of his lawyers was with him, and Stanton seemed upset. Just after the first "Loyal Opposition" show, he had told me how pleased he was with its imaginative format and the press response it had received. But that was before he had taken a beating both from Republican leaders and from many of his affiliates, which were owned by Republicans who did not want to present Democratic rebuttals to the President.

It was not until 1973, when the Watergate investigations brought to light many internal White House memoranda, that we realized just how disturbed Nixon had been by the "Loyal Opposition" program or that we learned he had assigned his Special Counsel, Charles Colson, to bring all possible pressure to bear toward the cancellations of the series.

Stanton reviewed with me the problems that he had faced as a result of the show and the fact that he had received little or no support from Democratic spokesmen other than myself.

Then he dropped his bombshell—the date for the second "Loyal Opposition" show, he said, would be November 17, two weeks *after* the congressional elections. That might get the Republican Party off his back, but it obviously made the program meaningless politically. He also said that for the second show, unlike the first, he wanted to approve the format in advance.

I was stunned, but I managed to come back with a surprise of my own. I informed him that our counsel, Joe Califano, was prepared to file a suit with the United States Court of Appeals, challenging the recent FCC ruling. This came as a surprise to Stanton and his lawyer, who had hoped the FCC ruling would end the whole controversy. I told them that, in light of their changed position on the "Loyal Opposition" series and of the other two networks' reluctance to grant equity toward our party, I had no alternative but to pursue every opportunity open to me, be it the FCC, the courts, the Congress, or the forum of public opinion.

Stanton then asked if, because of the problem he'd had with his affiliates, I might write CBS to express the Democratic Party's appreciation for carrying the first "Loyal Opposition" program. I said I'd be glad to and I was sorry I neglected to do so before. I felt a good deal of sympathy for Stanton. He had taken a courageous stand and for his trouble he'd been denounced by the Republicans, criticized by his affiliates, and received precious little support from our party.

The final blow to the "Loyal Opposition" concept came about a week later. The Republican National Committee had petitioned the FCC for equal time to respond to the first "Loyal Opposition" program—ignoring, of course, that the program had itself been a response to the President. The FCC granted this illogical request and CBS, faced with the prospect of endless responses to responses, killed the series.

The struggle over the "Loyal Opposition" series suggests the basic problem in the issue of access to television for the party out of power. There are no rules or guidelines governing the issue. Television thus becomes a no man's land of political power plays. We pushed the networks until CBS gave us a little time; the White House pushed back until the series was canceled. That is definitely not the way to decide how the public should be informed on national issues. There is a desperate need for Congress to pass laws that grant reasonable access to radio and television to the party out of power, whichever party it may be.

Related reforms are also needed. We must end the unfair system that permits a well-financed candidate to purchase two or three—or ten—times more television time than his opponent. A reasonable amount of *free* television time should be made available to all candidates, on a public-service basis, and additional *paid* time should be sold at the station's lowest commercial rates. The purpose of political campaigns is not to enrich the nation's radio and television stations.

In the fall of 1970, Congress passed a bill to limit campaign spending on television. It was a good bill, but President Nixon cynically vetoed it. His veto was a political victory for his well-financed party, but a defeat for the democratic process.

We began the fight for fair play in the allocation of free television time in 1970. We continued it throughout my three years as chairman. We lost more battles than we won, but I think we will prevail in the long run. I do not expect this Republican administration to permit the needed reforms, but I am hopeful that the next Democratic administration will put aside partisan concerns and surrender some of the power of incumbency in the interest of preserving the two-party system of government.

For me, the 1970 congressional campaign began the day I returned as national chairman. Political columnists were focusing on the disarray of the Democrats and were speculating that the Republicans might sweep the elections and gain control of Congress. Our disarray was undeniable, but I thought Nixon was vulnerable and that our party could do well in the off-year elections.

The gap between Nixon's promises and his performance was beginning to show. He had not ended the war, the economy was a mess, and he had been hurt politically by the Senate's rejection of two of his Supreme Court appointments—Clement F. Haynesworth and G. Harrold Carswell. I began hitting hard at the "crisis of confidence" in Nixon's leadership. Nixon, however, read his status reports differently, for he chose to make himself and his record the central issue in the campaign. He chose the candidates, raised their money, and stumped tirelessly for them. It would have been a great personal victory if he had won. As a politician, I admired his audacity—a President *should* lead his party—but as a Democrat, I was glad to see him gamble and lose.

Three issues stood out in 1970: the war, the economy, and a third, more complicated issue, sometimes called "law and order." On the latter, the Nixon-Agnew strategy was to lump together street crime, political dissent of all degrees, and alleged "softness" or "permissiveness" and to denounce their political opponents as "soft on crime," "radical liberals," "effete snobs."

Agnew acted as Nixon's hatchet man in 1969, with his attacks on newsmen and anti-war militants, but he soon shifted to his real targets—those politicians of either party who opposed the Administration. By mid-1970, his attacks on "radical liberals," a term that stretched from the Black Panthers to liberal Republicans, were receiving tremendous publicity; and he stood tall in the public opinion polls. When Agnew came charging into their states, many Democratic leaders would arrange to be elsewhere.

I was glad to take on Agnew. I felt that his tactic of lumping sincere and legal dissenters with criminals and Communists extended far beyond the accepted boundaries of political debate. Like Senator Joe McCarthy, he questioned not only his opponents' judgment but their motives and patriotism. Moreover, as the campaign progressed, I sensed that Agnew's smears were becoming counterproductive. Nixon had given Agnew an impossible assignment. A voter might disagree with, say, Adlai Stevenson III's liberal views, but few voters are going to be convinced that someone like Stevenson is a dangerous radical. Nixon and Agnew were underestimating the intelligence of the voters, and, in time, they only created sympathy for the men they smeared.

I kept waiting for Agnew to switch from the low road to

the high, to climb out of the gutter and to strike some note of statesmanship. But he never did, and when Nixon began his own intensive campaigning in the final weeks, his tone was no more elevated than was Agnew's. I was amazed when I realized that Nixon intended to base his entire campaign on demagoguery. It was a blunder, as Nixon realized when the returns were in.

Hubert Humphrey helped turn around the "soft on crime" issue with a speech in August when he called on liberals to speak out just as strongly against crime and violence as the Republicans. Democrats across the nation began following his advice. Adlai Stevenson III, for example, began wearing an American flag pin in his lapel and stressing his anticrime record in the state legislature. Democrats generally followed suit and the phony "law and order" issue began to peter out.

I was personally offended by the Nixon-Agnew charge that we Democrats condoned violence, especially since I had been close to two national leaders who had died violent deaths in the 1960s. During a campaign speech I made in Albuquerque, New Mexico, in early October I made pointed reference to that fact. "We know violence," I said. "We've lived with it." I went on to recall my association with John and Robert Kennedy, and what I said had a sobering effect on my audience. I returned to this theme in a speech to the National Press Club in Washington in late October. There was absolute silence as I spoke of the deaths of the two Kennedys and of my outrage at the Republican statements about our being soft on violence, and Ed Muskie used this same theme in his election eve telecast when he asked, "How dare they?" (insinuate that Democrats condone violence).

By Election Day the violence issue had been neutralized or perhaps turned slightly in our favor.

The war in Vietnam was another issue that was neutralized by Election Day.

In the spring I had been critical of Nixon's invasion of Cambodia. When ABC gave our party a half hour to respond to Nixon's explanation of the invasion, I declared that the President "has finally proven the ineffectiveness of his leadership" and had made "a tragic decision based on a series of extreme misjudgments." Turning to the domestic consequences of the invasion, which by then included the shootings at Kent State, I said:

"I can only speculate in sorrow whether those young people would have been killed were it not for the Nixon-Agnew-Mitchell inflammatory rhetoric—the rhetoric that appeals to the fears and prejudices and darker impulses that lurk within mankind."

It was a tough speech—possibly too tough, for some of my critics within the party reacted adversely—but I thought the occasion called for plain talk.

However, as the election neared, memories of the Cambodian invasion dimmed, and the main issue became the pace of American withdrawal from Vietnam. On October 8, in a televised address, Nixon announced a proposal for a ceasefire. In a statement the next day, I said I "very much welcomed" the proposal. I added: "The issue of ending the Indochina War is not in the political arena. We take the President and his spokesmen at their word that these proposals were not made to influence the November elections."

Actually, I viewed both Nixon's proposal and my response as highly political. I was taking a "me too" position on his peace plan because I thought that was the best we Democrats could do on the war issue. We were in a weak position to criticize Nixon. We might think the pace of his troop withdrawals was too slow, but he was withdrawing them, whereas we Democrats had sent them over there. If Vietnam was to be debated in the campaign, it would hurt us more than the Republicans. If Nixon wanted to take the issue out of politics, that was fine. In effect, that is what happened and I don't think the war had significant impact on the election results.

The economy was the one issue that Nixon could not neutralize or take out of politics. He kept promising that prosperity was just around the corner, but the price of hamburger kept rising and so did the unemployment rate. The Nixon administration's handling of the economy had been inept at best and heartless at worst, and I hit "Nixonomics" as hard as I could. In my October speech to the National Press Club I said:

"Unemployment is a key issue, to be sure. But it isn't that so many millions are out of work . . . It's that so many who are out of work and the people who depend on them have no feeling that anyone in power sees their plight or understands their humiliation . . . or gives a damn. They are not statistics . . . They are fathers and mothers and young people with names and families and pride and human needs . . . They did not come into this world to help President Nixon balance his books or compensate for fiscal ineptness."

In the end, it was the economic issue, the price of hamburger, that the Nixon-Agnew bombast could not overcome.

Jim Hagerty of ABC called me the weekend before the election and said the Republicans had asked to purchase a half hour of prime time on election eve. Hagerty said that if the Democrats wanted to buy fifteen minutes that evening, his network would limit the Republicans to the same amount of time. Hagerty may have suspected that we Democrats couldn't raise the necessary money, but this offer suggested that our months of battling the networks had at least created a little more sensitivity to our position on the equal-time issue.

My reply to Hagerty was that the networks should donate prime time to both parties. (The irony of my position was that I wouldn't have known what to do with the time if they'd given it to us. The DNC couldn't have arbitrarily given it to Muskie or Humphrey or any presidential contender, and there might have been objections if I had made myself the spokesman. Probably, I would have called on Mike Mansfield or Carl Albert.)

I learned at about the same time that a group headed by former Ambassador Averell Harriman was working, independent of the National Committee, to raise money to put Senator Muskie on television. Their fund-raising effort succeeded—while my effort to get free time did not—and the result was that Muskie's dignified appeal for reason and unity contrasted beautifully with the film of an angry arm-waving "law and order" speech by Nixon that the Republicans chose to broadcast. Nixon later denied any involvement in selecting that film, but the choice perfectly reflected the type of campaign he had chosen to lead. He had promised to unite the country, but his 1970 political strategy was to further divide it, and his strategy was repudiated by the voters.

Far from achieving the Republican sweep of Congress he had sought, Nixon's party lost twelve seats in the House and picked up only two in the Senate—far short of the number needed for control. Our party scored an impressive net gain of eleven governorships. On a district-by-district basis, the Democratic candidates ran an average of 3 per cent better nationally than we had in 1968.

All in all, 1970 had been a good year for the Democrats. At its start, the pundits were proclaiming our party politically dead. At its end, the same pundits were saying that Richard Nixon might be a one-term President. That was not to be, but we would later learn that his 1970 setback, and his fear of defeat in 1972, inspired the thirst for political espionage that eventually led to Watergate.

With the congressional elections behind us, it was time to think ahead to the coming presidential election. One of our concerns was to try to keep our party's numerous presidential contenders from tearing the party further apart in the 1972 primary elections. To that end, on the evening of February 9, 1971, in my apartment at the Sheraton Park Hotel, I convened what I believe to be an unprecedented meeting of our party's presidential contenders. Those present, in addition to myself, Bob Strauss and Ira Kapenstein from the Democratic National Committee, were House Speaker Albert, Senate Majority Leader Mansfield, and seven senators who were potential candidates for the Democratic nomination in 1972—Hubert Humphrey, Ed Muskie, Henry Jackson, George McGovern, Ted Kennedy, Harold Hughes, and Fred Harris. Senator Birch Bayh was also invited but was out of the country.

It was a tricky—some critics said a presumptuous—thing for me to select more than a year in advance, the party's potential presidential candidates. The only announced candidate was

McGovern, whom few people took seriously. Obviously my list
was an inclusive one, although not inclusive enough to please
everyone. Gene McCarthy's friends complained because he
wasn't invited and Sam Yorty, the mayor of Los Angeles, called
for my resignation after he learned of the meeting. I invited
Ted Kennedy because, despite his disclaimers, he was widely
viewed as a logical candidate; and I invited Wilbur Mills to
our second meeting when he had begun to be discussed as a
dark-horse contender.

I maintained top secrecy, lest the press learn of the meeting.
Most of my staff knew nothing of it, and even the guests did
not know the purpose until they arrived. I had feared that if
I told them I was calling a meeting of potential candidates for
President, they would assert their non-candidacy and decline
the invitation. Nor did they have any way of knowing who else
was invited, and there was a lot of head-turning and joking
each time the door opened and another "contender" arrived.

When everyone was present, I told my guests what I had in
mind. As national chairman, I was responsible for planning
the 1972 National Convention, and I wanted all potential candidates to be involved in the planning. I wanted their support
for the party's proposed delegate selection reforms. And I
wanted to minimize intraparty bloodletting in next year's primaries.

My guests greeted my proposals with enthusiasm. Hubert
Humphrey declared that it would be a shame if we didn't have
a picture of this unprecedented gathering, and we got on the
phone and located a photographer. We proceeded on to dinner
and a long, productive discussion.

We agreed that evening, and I was authorized to inform the
press, that the Democratic contenders for the presidential nomination in 1972 would concentrate their fire on the Nixon administration, not on each other; that they would support the
party reforms; that they would assist Democratic National
Committee fund-raising efforts; and that they would work with
the Democratic National Committee in its fight for increased
"Loyal Opposition" access to television.

At a later meeting, we reached our most important agreement: a ceiling on each candidate's media spending—five cents per registered voter in the primary states and three cents per voter in the non-primary states. This agreement helped everyone, and it meant that money saved in the spring could be used against Nixon in the fall. It was closely adhered to, with the only charges of violation being exchanged by Humphrey and McGovern in the last days of the California primary.

In late December 1971, several friends of Wilbur Mills came to see me at my New York apartment and asked me to resign as national chairman to head a Mills for President campaign. When I recovered from my initial surprise, I told them that what they requested was impossible because I intended to continue as national chairman through the Convention and I would be a neutral chairman throughout.

Later Mills and I met and I reiterated my position of neutrality. He accepted this. We then discussed the primaries and the fact that a candidate can sometimes win a "moral victory" in a primary without actually winning the most votes. I cited Humphrey's "moral victory" over Kennedy in Wisconsin in 1960 and Gene McCarthy's similar "victory" over President Johnson in New Hampshire in 1968. Mills eventually entered the New Hampshire primary, the year's first, but without success.

I mentioned that Ira Kapenstein was present at my initial meeting with the Democratic contenders on February 9, 1971. That was to be expected, for Ira had been deeply involved in all my activities since 1965—at the Post Office, in the Kennedy and Humphrey campaigns, at McDonnell & Co., and finally as deputy chairman of the National Committee. His energy, his enthusiasm, and his dedication to his work never failed; but, tragically, the cancer that he thought had been arrested reappeared. In 1969, while we were at McDonnell & Co., he came to me and said he thought he'd detected a warning sign. In short order, he had entered the hospital for an operation, returned to work, and re-entered the hospital for yet another operation.

His condition seemed to have stabilized, and he eagerly accompanied me to the National Committee. He continued to return to New York each week for treatment, but never spoke of his health. On Friday, February 26, 1971, Ira and Phyllis and I had lunch together in the Watergate Restaurant. I noticed that Ira wasn't eating and that he was impatient with the service—he said he had a lot of work to do and wanted to get back to the office. He worked late that night, but on Saturday he began to feel terribly ill and on Sunday morning he told his wife, Betty, that he'd better enter the hospital. He died in the hospital on Sunday evening, just seventeen days past his thirty-fifth birthday.

His loss was a terrible blow to me and to everyone who had known him. He had been both a valued friend and trusted adviser. After Ira's death, we helped establish a trust fund to assist in the education of his three children, one to which many journalists and political figures contributed generously.

It was far easier to achieve a semblance of unity among the party's six or eight presidential contenders than to achieve unity in the party itself—that is, among the millions of people in America who consider themselves Democrats but sometimes disagree on the issues. The main instrument for achieving party unity was, and continues to be, the party reforms that were begun in the aftermath of our disruptive 1968 Convention, reforms that went to the basic question of how our party selects its candidate for President.

Many states, of course, hold presidential primary elections to choose their delegates to the National Convention. But in a larger number of states, party leaders had traditonally appointed the delegations. Thus, it was possible for a candidate to win the primaries but not the nomination, if enough party leaders opposed him.

The issue came to a head in 1968. The two anti-war candidates, McCarthy and Kennedy, swept the primaries, but Humphrey won the nomination. The result was division and disillusion among many Democrats. In effect, they decided that the Democratic Party was not democratic.

Yet anti-war forces won one important victory at the 1968 Convention—the creation of two commissions on party reform:

the Commission on Rules and the Commission on Party Structure and Delegate Selection.

The members of both commissions had been selected by Fred Harris when he was national chairman, and, I believe, the make-up of the two commissions was clearly weighted toward the liberal wing of the party, rather than being representative of the party as a whole.

The Commission on Rules was the less controversial of the two. Led by its competent chairman, Representative James G. O'Hara of Michigan, the commission adopted new procedures to streamline our party's National Conventions. Its deliberations led to the elimination of the traditional "spontaneous" floor demonstrations for candidates, a reduction in the number of seconding speeches for presidential nominees, a reduction of media access to the floor of the Convention, and other steps to make the National Convention less of a circus and more of an efficient business meeting.

The Commission on Party Structure and Delegate Selection was the one that caused widespread disagreement within the party, for it dealt with the more complicated and controversial issues. The first chairman of the commission was Senator McGovern, with Senator Harold Hughes as vice chairman. When McGovern later resigned to become an announced candidate for President, Representative Donald M. Fraser was named to replace him.

The basic and most controversial reform endorsed by the McGovern commission was a requirement that *all* of the delegates to the National Convention must be elected. This was not difficult in the twenty-two states that already had primary elections scheduled in 1972, but it meant major changes in the rest of the states. In some "non-primary" states, party leaders had traditionally appointed their delegations; in others, party caucuses were held, but they were often poorly publicized, poorly attended, and held far too early to be significant. The McGovern commission guidelines required that such party caucuses be in the year of the election, be well publicized, and be open to *all* Democrats.

The commission then went one crucial step further. It required "state parties to overcome past discrimination by" taking "affirmative steps":

—to encourage minority group participation, including representation of minority groups on the national convention delegation in reasonable relationship to the group's presence in the population of the State.
—to encourage representation on the national convention delegation of young people—defined as people of not more than 30 nor less than eighteen years of age—and women in reasonable relationship to their presence in the population of the State.

These requirements obviously needed interpretation. What were the "affirmative steps"? What was a "reasonable relationship"? Each requirement was followed, in the commission report, by a reference to Footnote 2, which further confused the issue. The footnote read: "It is the understanding of the Commission that this is not to be accomplished by the mandatory imposition of quotas."

The footnote symbolized the built-in ambiguity of the guidelines—an ambiguity that I think was encouraged by some members of the McGovern commission and its staff. We wanted minority groups, young people, and women on the delegations, but we didn't want a quota system. What was to be done if an open caucus produced an all-white, all-male delegation or an all-black, all-female delegation? How can an open election comply with a "reasonable relationship" requirement?

By the time I returned as national chairman early in 1970, the McGovern commission had already held hearings across the country and had adopted its proposed new delegate selection guidelines. Its activities had, however, created a good deal of confusion and suspicion among party leaders and labor leaders. My concern, therefore, was with the definition and implementation of the guidelines. I had to "sell" the new rules to the national party as a whole and particularly to the state party leaders who would have to live with them, to work with them, and to enforce them. At the same time I was aware that many of the reform advocates on the McGovern commission and its staff viewed me as an establishment figure who would somehow try to "sell out" the party reforms. I accepted their suspicions as inevitable and felt that my actions would be the best proof of my commitment to an open party. Reform was imperative and I and virtually every member of the National Committee wanted reform. What I also wanted, and what we did not achieve in 1972, was reform that led to party unity, not reform that came at the price of continuing division within the party.

The reforms succeeded in achieving an unprecedented mixture of young and old, black and white, males and females at our Convention, but these advances resulted in great ill will in other segments of the party. Many party leaders, informed they must run for election to their delegation after years of taking their appointments for granted, stayed home. Other leaders ran, often pledged to Muskie; were defeated by young McGovern supporters; and responded with indignation. Organized labor viewed the new rules as an attempt by liberals to lessen its influence in the selection of the Democratic candidate. Many traditional Democrats—working people, members of ethnic groups, older people—watched this struggle on the evening news and thought: "It's O.K. that you're bringing in the kids and the blacks, but what about us?" In short, in bringing in some groups, we made others feel ignored.

I have sometimes asked myself whether I, as a national chairman committed to party unity, might not somehow have foreseen the problems that arose out of the McGovern commission reforms. The guidelines had been adopted by the commission. They were supported by me and unanimously approved by the Democratic National Committee after careful review. That review was supposed to resolve any ambiguities, including any ambiguity there might be in Footnote 2. We understood it to mean that there was to be no quota system. Yet that didn't prove to be the case. Most party leaders, fearful of challenges at the Convention, chose to play it safe by assuring that their delegations included the appropriate percentages of women, blacks, and young people. And McGovern as a candidate, carefully balanced his slates, which put pressure on the other candidates to do the same. But that was a total denial of the purpose of the reforms, which stated that there was to be an open process, a democratic process.

I don't think anyone could have foreseen in 1970—not I, not George McGovern, not George Meany—the results of the guidelines two years later. We were feeling our way, taking steps no major political party had ever taken. We knew that the old rules had brought deep divisions in 1968 and we were groping toward something better.

But in 1972, of course, we realized that the new rules, in their application, favored the candidate with determined, tenacious followers. McGovern had those followers. If another candidate had organized his supporters for a fight in each of the non-primary states, the outcome might have been different. Muskie, in particular, ran for President in 1972 as if the 1968 rules still applied, relying on party leaders without emphasizing grass-roots activity.

The party was as deeply divided in 1972 as it had been in 1968, and no rules, however written, could have satisfied both sides any more than a "compromise plank" on Vietnam could have reconciled both sides in 1968. In 1968 the establishment elements of the party got their man nominated and in 1972 the anti-establishment or anti-war elements got their man nominated, but neither side could win the election without the other. Thus, we lost in 1972 just as we lost in 1968—by defeating ourselves. The divisions were just too deep to be overcome.

The continuing struggle over the new party rules brought me into conflict, in October 1971, with the man who was then the front-runner for the nomination, Ed Muskie. It was not a confrontation I sought, but I gave it my all, for it seemed that Muskie was trying to intrude upon my authority as national chairman.

At issue was the acting chairmanship of the Credentials Committee for the National Convention. Since it was likely there would be many contested delegations to the Convention, the Credentials post became a highly important one. I had the responsibility to recommend someone to the full National Committee and my selection was Patricia Roberts Harris, a Washington lawyer who had previously been U.S. ambassador to Luxembourg and dean of the Howard University Law School, Washington, D.C. I had known Mrs. Harris only slightly, but a number of people urged me to make use of her talents in some capacity at the Convention. After Bob Strauss and I had a luncheon conversation with her, we felt she would be an excellent choice for the Credentials post.

Senator Harold Hughes, who had been vice chairman of the McGovern commission and was considered a leader in the re- form movement, informed me that he hoped to be the acting chairman of the Credentials Committee. He began actively soliciting support among members of the National Committee.

I decided, however, that Mrs. Harris would be better for the position. As I saw it, she was at least as well qualified as Hughes (she was a lawyer, which he was not, and this was a judicial post), she was just as committed to reform, she was less controversial, and she would not bring to the post any per- sonal political ambitions. Also, Congressman Jim O'Hara, the chairman of the Rules Commission, had told me that both he and Congressman Don Fraser, the chairman of the Commis- sion on Delegate Selection, thought it would be a mistake to have a Credentials chairman who had been a member of the McGovern commission. This, he said, was nothing against Hughes, but they thought there was a basic conflict of interest involved. In effect, the McGovern commission had performed a legislative function—writing the new rules—and the Creden- tials Committee would perform a judicial function—interpreting the new rules.

The irony of the ensuing Hughes-Harris contest for the Credentials chairmanship was that, since Hughes was a leader in the reform movement, Mrs. Harris was viewed by some as an "anti-reform" candidate—a rather ridiculous view, since she was black, a woman, and a liberal.

The Hughes-Harris contest ultimately involved some of the candidates for President, along with other Democrats in the Congress. Suddenly, everyone seemed to be telling me and the National Committee members what course of action to follow. Finally, Senator Muskie became involved when he called me two nights before the election and informed me that he was instructing his people to lobby for Hughes and was issuing a press release stating his support for Hughes over Mrs. Harris. I understood Muskie's motives. He very much wanted an endorsement from Senator Hughes, who had a following in the anti-war movement. Nonetheless, I hit the ceiling; this was too much. Under the rules, it was my responsibility to nominate a candidate for this post and I did not think Senator Muskie should become involved in the matter.

"Ed," I told him, "I'm supporting Pat Harris, with no holds barred. I'll put my reputation on the line for her. I don't see what you're doing in this, since this is my area of responsibility."

"Wait a minute, Larry," Muskie said, but I didn't want to wait a minute and the conversation was soon terminated. Muskie apparently saw me in the old role of national chairman—as simply a front man for the party powers. I thought he knew me better than that. That night I told my staff I wanted a detailed head count of the National Committee members in the Hughes-Harris race.

The lobbying was thick and heavy by Wednesday morning when the National Committee met. Muskie's aides were lobbying for Hughes, although in some instances not enthusiastically; my aides were lobbying for Mrs. Harris; and George Meany's representatives were also lobbying for her. It was later reported in the *New Republic* that I had brought labor's people into the battle as part of a stop-McGovern effort. That was ridiculous. In October 1971, no one was worrying about McGovern. Labor's goal was to block Hughes, whom Meany regarded as a "far-out" left-wing reformer.

The vote was to follow a "unity luncheon" that turned out not to be as unifying as we'd hoped. I introduced all the presidential contenders, and McGovern, Fred Harris and Muskie all got up and endorsed Hughes. Humphrey deftly complimented both candidates. Scoop Jackson received the most applause when he declared that his role as a senator did not encompass getting involved in DNC matters. To me, that was the real issue.

The vote itself was anticlimactic. Mrs. Harris defeated Senator Hughes by a two-to-one margin. Later that day Hughes issued a press release in which he declared: "This is the first real combat on the big moral issues within our Party since 1968 . . . We have just begun to fight." I thought that somewhat overblown. He hadn't exactly been defeated by Senator Eastland.

There was an interesting aftermath to the episode. Muskie and McGovern had both been wooing Hughes for his endorsement, and backing him for Credentials chairman was part of their strategy. The McGovern people were confident that Hughes, as an outspoken anti-war leader, would support their man, and they were astounded when Hughes endorsed Muskie. In the middle of the Hughes-Harris contest, Frank Mankiewicz, a McGovern top adviser, had said to one of my aides, "How can you sleep nights working for O'Brien?" Later, after Hughes endorsed Muskie, he retracted that statement.

As the party primaries began in the spring, I was as surprised as most people to see Senator McGovern emerge as the front-runner for the nomination. Before the primaries, I had shared the conventional wisdom that Muskie was the likely nominee, that Humphrey might move up if Muskie slipped, and that Kennedy could never be ruled out, despite his avowals of non-candidacy. I had viewed McGovern as a determined candidate, but one whose support was too narrow to win him the nomination.

Obviously, I underestimated McGovern and, also, the impact of the new party rules on the nominating process. McGovern's primary campaign was smart and well organized. His followers, motivated by their hatred of the war in Vietnam, were at that moment the most vital force in the Democratic Party. Only George Wallace's followers shared their passion, but the Wallace people were not well organized. Muskie had many governors and senators supporting him, but not the foot soldiers. In state after state, party leaders pledged to Muskie would be defeated in party caucuses by students and housewives pledged to McGovern. Clearly, something historic was happening within our party.

As the neutral party chairman, I viewed the primaries with a measure of detachment, but many party regulars, along with AFL-CIO President George Meany, were doing all they could to stop McGovern.

I had been in communication with Meany about the new party rules and other matters since I returned as national chairman in 1970. Our relationship was cordial, but Meany viewed the Democratic Party as disorganized and ineffectual in comparison to COPE, the AFL-CIO's political arm. Obviously, I could not accept that view.

I spoke with Meany about the new rules in 1971, and he denounced them as part of a liberal attempt to take over the party.

"The rules have been adopted," I told him. "It's too late to debate whether they're good or bad. You have your people well organized all over the country. You should study the new rules and use them to your advantage, just like everyone else."

For too long, however, labor ignored the new rules. For a time, in the early party caucuses, word went out to labor people to run as uncommitted delegates. This strategy failed. It was almost impossible to elect uncommitted delegates, because you can't beat somebody with nobody. You can't get people excited about supporting Mr. X. I had lunch one day with a labor organizer who'd just come back from caucuses in Georgia. "We had buses," he said. "We had box lunches. We got our people there. But the meetings would drag on until our people began to drift away. The McGovern people would stay till midnight and they won."

Labor eventually changed strategy and told its people to run as delegates for whoever was strongest in their area—Humphrey, Muskie, Jackson—anyone but McGovern. Ultimately, labor was to claim there were more labor delegates at the 1972 Convention (approximately 500) than at any previous Democratic Convention.

A few weeks before the National Convention was to open in

Miami, I received an unexpected visit from one of George Meany's chief political advisers. The man indicated, in a rather roundabout way, that he hoped some action could be taken to stop a McGovern nomination. I made it clear that I was neutral with regard to the nomination and would continue to be. I assumed a stop-McGovern effort would develop at the Convention, but I was not going to be part of it. Perhaps my visitor hoped that I, by some ruling at the Convention, could help stop McGovern. Certainly there have been times in the past when a convention chairman, with one bang of his gavel, destroyed someone's candidacy, but that wasn't what I had been working toward for a year and a half. The people who wanted to stop McGovern could have stopped him in the primaries, if they had planned their strategies more intelligently. I certainly had no intention of pulling their chestnuts out of the fire.

On the morning of Saturday, June 17, I was in Miami Beach where I had spent several days working on arrangements for the Democratic Convention that was to open there three weeks later. About 8 A.M., I received a call from Stan Greigg, the DNC's deputy chairman, who informed me that early that morning, five burglars had been arrested at gunpoint in our National Committee headquarters in the Watergate office building. Stan's story was fragmented at that point. The police had taken him to the jail for a look at the five men, but he did not recognize any of them. The police also took him to a room in the nearby Watergate Hotel where the burglars had sophisticated electronic equipment and burglary tools. The police had also told Stan that the burglars had in their possession a large number of one-hundred-dollar bills.

At that point, neither Stan nor I knew what to make of the break-in. We were troubled and suspicious but we had no hard evidence to suggest that the burglars were politically motivated. I flew back to New York that morning to review the film we were to use at the Convention. On the flight up, I discussed the break-in report with Nick Kostopulos, one of my assistants and frequent traveling companion, and we agreed it made no sense. The next day, Sunday, I was flying to New Orleans to speak to the U. S. Conference of Mayors. At La Guardia Airport, just as I was boarding the plane, I was called to the telephone. It was Stan Greigg again.

"Larry, this is unbelievable, but James McCord, one of those burglars, works for the Committee for the Re-election of the President" (CRP).

I was stunned. It all seemed unreal. There was no time for discussion—my plane was leaving—so Stan and I agreed we'd talk later. I flew to New Orleans with no idea what this strange event was leading to. It was possible that McCord was acting on his own. At the New Orleans airport I had a call waiting from Joe Mohbat, my press secretary, who informed me that former Attorney General John Mitchell, the director of CRP, had just issued a statement denying that CRP had anything to do with the break-in.*

Joe and I agreed that I should make some public comment. Obviously I had to be extremely careful about what I said. The situation was changing hour by hour. I authorized Joe to issue a statement in which I declared that the break-in "has raised the ugliest questions about the integrity of the political process that I have encountered in a quarter-century of political activity."

I delivered my speech the next morning, then flew back to Washington, where I met with Joe Califano, Stan Greigg, Joe Mohbat, and John Stewart to discuss the unfolding story of the break-in and our response to it.

There was one thing certain. We wanted to get to the bottom of this—we wanted the whole story, no matter where it led. There was reason to suspect that the break-in and wire-tapping had been authorized by the officials of CRP; and there was the possibility that the trial might lead even higher. We wanted the facts, and we knew they would not be easily attained. One decision we made, acting on Joe Califano's legal advice, was to file a lawsuit against CRP. In this way, the judicial process would help us get to the truth.

* See Appendix.

As we discussed the elements of the lawsuit, I reflected on the 1960s and the Republican leaders in the Congress. Senator Ev Dirksen, Congressmen Charlie Halleck and Jerry Ford and their colleagues had consistently fought our program but without rancor. They had been hard-nosed but never mean or personal. Similarly I recalled previous national campaigns when Democrats and Republicans had fought hard, but there had been nothing remotely comparable to this. I concluded in my mind that when the facts finally surfaced, they would not involve the Republican Party as a whole. This prompted me to appeal directly to President Nixon, urging him to name a Special Prosecutor to investigate the facts surrounding Watergate and to prosecute those responsible. Unfortunately, the President was not to act on this request until a year later.*

I announced our one-million-dollar damage suit against CRP, the burglars, and other defendants, still unknown, at a news conference the next morning. At that time I made a longer statement on the break-in, one that said in part:

"We know that as of the moment of his arrest at gunpoint just 10 feet from where I now stand, Mr. McCord was in the pay of the Committee for the Re-election of the President, where he has an office. If John Mitchell's reflex attempt to conceal that fact is any signal of what is to come from the Republican Party and Administration, I fear we shall be a long time getting at the truth.

"I am obviously concerned over this case because it is my Party that was the victim of this police-state tactic. But those of you who have followed my public position over the past two years will understand when I say that the crisis here goes far beyond the physical privacy of a political committee's offices.

"At a time when the Democratic Party—through great struggle—has turned itself inside out to make politics a free and open process responsive to the people, we now see politics, as practiced this weekend, brought down to the gutter level.

"At a time when national polls demonstrate beyond a doubt a national cynicism toward politics and the political process,

* See Appendix.

Americans now read and hear of cheap cloak-and-dagger intrigue at the national political level. We learned of this bugging attempt only because it was bungled. How many other attempts have there been? And just *who* was involved?"

It would be a long time before we and the American people got an answer to my question.

XV

MIAMI BEACH

IN RETROSPECT, I think of the 1972 Democratic National Convention as the greatest challenge I ever faced. The party rules provided that I, as national chairman, had the responsibility "to plan, arrange, manage, and conduct" the Convention. Under the rules, I was the temporary chairman of the Convention and, because no other major party figure wanted the job—they all remembered the chaos of the 1968 Convention—I became its permanent chairman as well and delivered the Convention's first address. Finally, I was to be called upon to decide a bitterly disputed parliamentary point that seemed likely to determine the party's nominee for President.

It was a hectic two weeks, filled with high drama and low comedy, but when it was over I was satisfied. We had experienced none of the violent discord of the 1968 Convention. A subsequent national poll showed that most people agreed that our Convention was fair and open—while many had doubts about our candidate, they accepted that he was fairly chosen. That had been my goal in the more than a year of planning that led us to Miami Beach.

In that planning, I was pleased to have the assistance of Richard J. Murphy, whom I'd been associated with in the 1960 campaign and when he was Assistant Postmaster General for Personnel. Dick took the thankless job of convention manager and stuck with it through months of frustration out of loyalty to the party and to me.

When you set out to plan a Convention, you must first decide where and when to have it. The "where" was not a difficult decision for us. We discovered only one city, Miami Beach, that both wanted us and had the facilities to accommodate us. As for the "when," I wanted as early a Convention as possible, so the candidate chosen would have maximum time to campaign. I considered breaking all precedent and having a Convention in June, but practical considerations, including the fact that California's primary was not until June 6, forced us to wait until mid-July.

The "where" of the Republican convention was not initially a problem for the Republicans either. They selected San Diego. This surprised us because we had not received any serious offer from that city. Later, a connection between the Republican decision and the International Telephone and Telegraph Corporation (ITT) was to surface. Reports indicated that the Sheraton Corporation of America—a subsidiary of ITT—had pledged up to $400,000 to help underwrite San Diego's bid to host the Republican Convention. We further learned that eight days after the selection of San Diego, the Justice Department had approved an out-of-court settlement of three pending ITT merger cases.

On December 13, 1971, I wrote to Attorney General John Mitchell calling on him to make public the full record of the ITT merger.* I received a reply to my letter from Deputy Attorney General Richard Kleindienst,* which did not adequately respond to my inquiry. The matter did not end there. Congress, the Watergate Committee, and the Special Prosecutor's Office have delved into the affair, but at this writing, the full story is yet to emerge.

One continuing problem we had prior to the Democratic Convention was finding qualified people to play major convention roles. I had a long talk with Carl Albert about his serving as permanent chairman of the Convention, as he had in 1968, but he told me to forget it, there was no possibility that he would repeat that nightmare. No major Democrat wanted to be the chairman of the Convention—despite the priceless television exposure involved—and it fell by default to me. I also had trouble finding a chairman of the Platform

* See Appendix.

Committee. Senators Fritz Mondale and Gaylord Nelson, among others, turned me down. Finally I turned to the academic community and recruited Professor Richard Neustadt of Harvard, who agreed with reluctance and served with distinction.

Arranging the Convention was a difficult task. The logistics of the entire effort were staggering—we had to insure the housing of five thousand delegates and alternates, several thousand reporters (which comprised the biggest press corps in convention history we were told) and several thousand party and international VIPs. And the problems were endless. There were never enough tickets, even with 15,000 seats in the hall—as we estimated as many as 50,000 people were in Miami Beach for the Convention. The press never thought it had enough space or floor passes. Political leaders and media figures had countless sons and daughters they wanted to serve as pages for the Convention, and many of them had some undiscovered Maria Callases in their family who they felt should sing "The Star-Spangled Banner" each night of the Convention. There was also a southern congressman who was insistent that we make use of some live and kicking donkeys from his state, perhaps in a "Democratic Donkey" parade through the streets of Miami Beach.

Amid the inanities, very serious questions existed about security at our Convention. We wanted to avoid the violent outbreaks that had caused us such damage in Chicago in 1968. But, in addition, we felt threatened—a first in all my years of politics—by political espionage and political sabotage—a very real concern since agents of the Republican Party had been caught breaking into and wiretapping our National Committee offices only weeks before. Subsequent Watergate testimony indicated that the "Liddy plan" did indeed call for bugging my hotel suite, sabotaging the air-conditioning system in the convention hall, using call girls to lure unwary Democratic politicians onto yachts where any misdeed would be photographed and later used for blackmail.

To try to avert demonstrations outside the hall, Dick Murphy held a long series of meetings with leaders of Students for

a Democratic Society, the Vietnam Veterans Against the War,
and other protest groups, and these discussions contributed to
the lack of violent demonstrations during our Convention. To
handle security inside the hall, we employed a private security
force, the Andy Frain Service. A week or so before the sessions
were to begin, I was presented with a detailed report on what
was to be done in the event of bomb threats, demonstrations,
sit-ins, and the like. My favorite portion of their report—which
was read to me aloud and with a straight face—was the following:

"V. MARIJUANA SMOKE-IN:
  A. Small Numbers of Persons
    1. The Chair will be instructed to ignore it.
    2. Andy Frain Ushers and DNC people will talk to
    these people and try to discourage them (peer group
    pressure is encouraged).
  B. Mass Smoke-In
    1. The Chair will refuse to admit it is marijuana.

"VI. NUDE-IN:
  A. Have sufficient quantity of blankets available.
  B. Cover them and have Andy Frain personnel escort
  them off the floor in a non-abrasive manner."

Fortunately, we were spared either a smoke-in or a nude-in
—although later testimony indicated that G. Gordon Liddy
had at least contemplated staging a nude-in for us.

It's a terrible feeling to suspect you are being spied on, to
have to have your phones checked for bugs every morning, to
find yourself suddenly suspicious of strangers. We even were
worried that our security reports to the Secret Service were being forwarded to the White House and to whomever had
bugged our Watergate offices. The Service had an office in the
convention hall. One of the follow-up stories on the Watergate
burglary stated that Alfred C. Wong, deputy assistant director
of the Secret Service, had recommended James McCord, one
of the burglars, for his job with the Committee to Re-elect the
President. That fact upset Dick Murphy, who told the head of
the Secret Service detail in Miami Beach he was concerned

about the tie-in with McCord. Later that day I received a call from James J. Rowley, the Director of the Secret Service, whom I had known in my White House days. He said he was disturbed that Murphy didn't trust his people. I told Jim that I would like to know more about the link, if any, between Wong and McCord, for I could not apologize for Murphy's actions until I did. No such assurance was forthcoming, however. And when a couple of politically appointed lawyers from the Justice Department appeared at a later date and asked for office space at the convention hall, supposedly for official business, Dick Murphy refused the request, saying he'd be "damned" if he'd "give space to Nixon's spies." Already, the fallout from Watergate had begun to poison the air.

In the end, the Republicans abandoned their espionage plans, the youthful demonstrators were nonviolent, and our most serious security problem was caused by members of the National Welfare Rights Organization, who "crashed" our final meeting of the Arrangements Committee at the Fontainebleau Hotel. We had a few Andy Frain guards at the door, but a hefty welfare mother pushed past them—in fact, knocked one of them down—led by Ralph Abernathy and George Wiley. There were cries of "Let's get em!" as they surrounded the committee members and as several invaders headed toward the podium where I was standing. The next thing I knew was that my security guards—provided for me by Florida Governor Reubin Askew—were hustling me out the door, through the kitchen, and up the elevator to my suite. But after catching my breath I insisted on going back downstairs, over the strenuous objections of the security men. I found Ralph Abernathy making a speech and I went up and greeted him and the others with him.

The demonstrators were demanding six hundred floor passes. I told their leaders that we should appoint a joint committee to determine what might be worked out. Their requests for floor passes were way out of line, but the committees were appointed and met to negotiate. We eventually gave the group a few gallery seats, and some NWRO people did get onto the

convention floor when members of the New York delegation
gave them their own credentials.

In the weeks leading up to the Convention, I had continued
my efforts to build good will with the AFL-CIO but without
great success. I gave George Meany's representatives virtually
everything they asked for. A direct telephone line was installed
between George Meany and me. Meany used it once, when he
called immediately after McGovern's nomination to leave a
message for me: "Tell O'Brien George Meany was opposed to
George McGovern yesterday, he is opposed to George McGovern today, and he will be opposed to George McGovern tomorrow and forever." I got the message.

The AFL-CIO had sixty-four box seats each night of the
Convention, more than anyone else, including the presidential
candidates. They had twenty-five floor passes each night, again
the largest number given anyone. I arranged for them to have
a trailer just outside the hall, but about the time the Convention opened they decided they didn't want a trailer. Apparently they had determined that the outcome of the Convention
would not be to their liking, and they would therefore maintain a "lower profile."

I called the Convention to order on the evening of Monday, July 10. I had selected Governor Reubin Askew of Florida to deliver the Convention's traditional keynote address,
because I wanted to recognize both the South and the Democratic governors. However, I broke tradition by scheduling the
keynote speech on the Convention's second night, and delivering my own opening address on the first night. I did this because I felt a deep personal responsibility for the success of
the Convention and I hoped that my speech might set the
proper tone. In it, I returned to a theme I had used in a hundred other speeches for more than two years—that the Democratic Party must regain the trust of the American people by
talking straight with them. Perhaps the heart of the speech
was:

"I think it comes down to this: do we have the guts to level
with the American people?

"How do we level? We begin, I believe, with a few simple steps. We cool the excessive political rhetoric. We lighten the purple prose. We do not promise what we know cannot be delivered by man, God or the Democratic Party.

"There is not a politician or a churchman or a businessman or a magician in this country who can fulfill all those dazzling promises. But we have lacked the courage to say this. Instead, we have promised something to everybody, and then hoped that nobody would keep score.

"It didn't work. The people can count. They can keep score. And they aren't easily fooled.

"We have short-changed them in terms of specific accomplishments—jobs, houses, schools, safe streets—and have lost much of their trust along the way. Now, we must stop kidding the American people. We must tell them the truth. I recognize, of course, that this idea runs counter to the whole history of American political talk.

"But just imagine what it would be like to elect a President who made only modest, straightforward campaign promises, and then seriously went about fulfilling them.

"That has *never* happened. But it could."*

It was a tough speech—and was intended to be—not tough on Nixon, whom I had lambasted in scores of other speeches, but tough, rather, on my own party and on myself, insofar as I had been one of those Democrats who had promised more than our party could deliver. I viewed the speech as a statement of fact. We *had* promised too much, we *had* lost the faith of the people, and it was time for us to go hat in hand to try to win back their trust.

Once I had delivered my opening address, much of the pressure was off, as far as I was concerned. I still had to preside over the Convention but our vice chairman, the lovely and able Yvonne Braithwaite Burke, now a congresswoman from California, alternated with me, and I would sometimes take walks on the convention floor. Up on the podium you felt a long way removed from the delegates and it was a pleasure to

* See Appendix

wander among them and shake hands and talk. They were a
wonderful group. My pleasure was tempered, however, by the
failure of the McGovern forces to compromise on the seating of
Mayor Richard Daley's Illinois delegation. His delegation had
been duly elected in a statewide primary, unlike the challeng-
ers, but *both* delegations had been willing to compromise. The
ouster of the Daley delegation was the most damaging thing
that happened to McGovern at the Convention.

One of the Convention's dramatic moments came on Tuesday night when Governor George Wallace addressed the delegates. He spoke from a wheelchair, having been crippled by a
would-be assassin's bullets only two months earlier. To me,
Wallace's appearance before the Convention highlighted a long
effort to bring him back into the Democratic Party. Early that
year, when it appeared that Wallace might enter several Democratic primaries, some of my associates urged me to take action
to keep him out of the primaries on the grounds that he was not
a Democrat but a spoiler who would use our primaries for publicity, then run a third-party campaign for the presidency, as
he had in 1968, or support Nixon.

Insofar as I could influence events, I wanted to avoid another
three-man contest for the presidency in 1972. I wanted a two-
man, head-to-head Democrat versus Republican race. I felt
that the voters should choose between the two major parties,
not cast a vote for George Wallace as an easy out.

As far as the primaries were concerned, I didn't think Wallace should be able to have it both ways. If he wanted to run
in the Democratic primaries, he should abide by the rules of
the Democratic Party, which meant that his delegates must
not support any candidate other than the eventual Democratic
nominee for President. Ideally, I wanted Wallace and his followers inside the Democratic Party, not outside it. I wanted to
pin Wallace down and he, of course, wanted to keep his options open.

Late in January, Wallace agreed that his delegates to the
Convention would abide by all party rules. That was all the
party could legally require, and I immediately directed that
Wallace be treated as a full-fledged candidate for the Demo-

cratic nomination and be given the same treatment as all contenders by the National Committee.

Certainly I was not alone in hoping he would return to our party. By the spring even George McGovern was saying that he would consider finding a place for Governor Wallace in a McGovern administration. However, the injuries Wallace suffered on May 15 removed him from that year's presidential race, and it is impossible to say what might have happened if he had remained healthy. I visited Wallace in his hospital room eight days after the assassination attempt and he thanked me for the courtesies being extended to him and to his delegates. At the Convention, and at a subsequent meeting at President Johnson's funeral, Wallace again stressed to me how much he had appreciated the courteous treatment he had received.

The most important action I took at the Convention came in the last hectic days before the Convention actually convened. The party regulars who still hoped to prevent George McGovern's nomination had seized upon the possibility of stripping McGovern of 151 delegate votes he had won in California's winner-take-all primary. While the new party rules had encouraged the apportionment of a state's delegates on the basis of the percentage of the vote each candidate received in the primary, Don Fraser, chairman of the Commission on Delegate Selection, had conducted personal negotiations with California party leaders and had agreed that California could keep its traditional "winner-take-all" primary in 1972.

McGovern had defeated Humphrey in California and, under the rules governing the primary, won all 271 of the state's delegate votes. However, the Humphrey forces belatedly argued that they should be given votes in proportion to the popular vote Humphrey and the other contenders received—151 delegate votes, which might have prevented McGovern's nomination.

The Humphrey position prevailed in the June 29 meeting of the Credentials Committee, but it was, in turn, challenged by the original California delegation in a legal action. The suit progressed through the courts and when the Supreme Court refused on July 7 to become involved in the matter, the issue became one for the full Convention to decide.

Since McGovern apparently had the 1,509 votes needed for a first-ballot nomination it seemed likely that he also had the support to carry the California issue. However, the stop-McGovern people raised a serious parliamentary issue. It was obvious that the contested delegates could not vote on their own challenge; consequently, instead of the full 3,016 eligible votes there would be 2,865 eligible votes. What then constituted a majority? The stop-McGovern people argued that the proper majority was still 1,509. The McGovern people argued that a majority was simply a majority of those eligible to vote; in this case 1,433. Everyone knew that McGovern clearly had 1,433 votes, but without the contested California delegates there was a possibility he might not have 1,509 votes. Thus, if he lost the "majority" issue he might lose the California challenge and perhaps the nomination.

The responsibility to rule on the question of what constituted the proper majority fell to me.

In retrospect, the issue may not seem difficult. A majority is a majority of those present and eligible to vote. To make an analogy, if all nine members of the Supreme Court vote on a case, it takes five to make a majority, but if only seven vote, the majority becomes four—it doesn't remain at five. Yet the issue by no means seemed easy at the time. There were no clear precedents; there was some ambiguous language to deal with and some of the nation's best lawyers were arguing both sides of the issue. Moreover, legalities aside, it was an issue with tremendous political consequences. It might decide whether or not McGovern was the party's nominee and thus affect the direction of the party for years to come. From a personal point of view, I knew that whichever way I ruled, I would make enemies, in some instances of men who had been my close associates. But the decision had to be made, and it was mine to make.

For legal guidance, I consulted Joe Califano, the Democratic National Committee's general counsel; Congressman Jim O'Hara, the parliamentarian for the Convention; and Lee

White, former assistant special counsel to Presidents Kennedy and Johnson. They, in turn, conferred with Lewis Deschler, parliamentarian of the House of Representatives and sought opinions from legal experts on the Harvard and Yale Law School faculties.

While the legal consultations were in progress, there were political consultations as well. McGovern's two top aides, Frank Mankiewicz and Gary Hart, came to my suite on Saturday, July 8, to state their case. Mankiewicz indicated that if the ruling went against McGovern, his delegates would blow the lid off the Convention. I told him my decision would not be swayed by that possibility. McGovern visited me a little later and took a milder approach, saying he was sure I'd do the right thing. Humphrey also came by that day.

"I'm not here to lobby you, Larry," he assured me. "Just to pay a courtesy call. I hope you'll see things my way, but I'll abide by whatever decision you make."

It happened that I had a pool table in my suite and, rather than talk politics, Hubert and I relaxed with a game of pool, much to the enjoyment of my staff and Hubert's Secret Service entourage.

Hubert and I didn't have to discuss the situation, we both understood it. He was a man who had sought the presidency for a dozen years, who I felt would have made a good President, and who was making what would probably be his last pursuit of that elusive prize. His friend for a dozen years, his campaign manager four years before, was called upon to make a decision that conceivably could give him the nomination. Hubert must have known his legal case was weak, and he also knew I would not let personal feelings influence my judgment.

Humphrey and McGovern were diplomatic in their talks with me, but when Joe Califano and Jim O'Hara met to discuss the legal issues with representatives of Muskie, Humphrey, Jackson, and Wallace, tempers flared, and there were threats of an oust-O'Brien effort if the ruling went in favor of McGovern.

On Sunday morning, I met for two hours with Califano, O'Hara (who was, incidentally, a Humphrey supporter), and

Lee White. They concluded that a simple majority of those *eligible* to vote would constitute a majority on the California issue, and I concurred.

When Joe Califano informed representatives of the other candidates of my position, Humphrey's representative, Washington lawyer Max Kampelman, angrily declared that O'Brien should be ousted. He rushed from the room and returned with a statement which he read, supposedly on behalf of Humphrey, saying that this ruling was an act of personal hostility toward Senator Humphrey. Later, Kampelman and Governor Wallace's spokesman called for a vote of no-confidence in me by the Convention. Sherwin Markman, Muskie's spokesman, said he disagreed with the ruling but disassociated himself from any attack on the integrity of O'Brien, O'Hara, or Califano.

That evening I shared an elevator with Sterling Munro, administrative assistant to Scoop Jackson. He gave me a cool look and when he got off the elevator he said, "Larry, Scoop is triple-pissed!" That pretty well summed up the feelings of the stop-McGovern forces. Passions ran high. Following my ruling, I learned that meetings were taking place, including representatives of Scoop Jackson, George Wallace, and organized labor, to discuss a "takeover" of the Democratic Party. McGovern had not actually been nominated yet and elements of the Party and labor, in anticipation of McGovern's defeat in November, were already making plans for their eventual control of the Party.

Some people may never forgive me for my ruling, but I've never met any impartial lawyer who questioned the ruling, and I continue to think it was absurd of the stop-McGovern people, having failed in the primaries, to hope I could bail them out at the last moment with an illogical parliamentary ruling. For my part, I divorced the parliamentary issue from the question of what candidate it might help or hurt. All I sought was to make the decision with a clear conscience.

Finally, it was over. George McGovern was our party's nominee and he stood on the platform with Kennedy, Humphrey, Muskie, Jackson, and other party leaders in the traditional Democratic show of unity. The band played, the delegates cheered, and for a fleeting moment I let myself dream that somehow this show of unity might be lasting and might carry us on to victory in November.

At the conclusion of each National Convention, the National Committee traditionally meets and elects a new chairman, normally one nominated by the party's new presidential candidate.

In the months leading up to the 1972 Convention, reporters often asked me if I would be willing to continue as chairman after the Convention, and I repeatedly stated that I would not. My feeling was that there was no more appropriate time for me to take a bow and say my good-bys than on the night I banged the final gavel on the 1972 Convention. Then the party's new nominee would be free to select his own chairman.

During the spring of 1972, Senator McGovern several times told reporters and told me that if nominated he would ask me to stay as chairman. I took these statements with a grain of salt, for as long as I was chairman and he was a candidate, it was in his interest to seek my favor. But on Friday, July 14, the day of the National Committee meeting, when he was to name his choice for the chairmanship, he continued to urge me to remain in the post, and an unfortunate series of events occurred.

There were two party breakfasts that morning, but I slept through them both, and took a call from McGovern in mid-morning, not long before the start of the National Committee meeting.

"Larry, I expected to see you at breakfast this morning," he began.

"You're the candidate, George," I told him. "You have to go to those things, but I don't."

"I've got to talk to you about the chairmanship," he said.

"There's no time to discuss it," I said. "The meeting starts in twenty minutes."

"I saw the report that your decision is irrevocable. Is that correct?"

"Yes, it is," I said, "and, as you know, your responsibility is to recommend a new chairman at the meeting."

Then I went downstairs to open the National Committee meeting.

As the roll was being called, I was handed a message to call McGovern at his suite in the Doral Hotel. I turned the gavel over to Mary Lou Berg, our vice chairman, and called McGovern from a pay phone in the hotel corridor.

"Surely we can talk for a minute," he said. "I'm only two minutes away."

"George, I'm certainly not avoiding you," I replied. "Let me see what I can do."

I reported to the committee that Senator McGovern had a conflict in his schedule, which in fact he did, and couldn't arrive until afternoon. I therefore suggested that we adjourn for a leisurely lunch and reconvene at 2 P.M.

Stan Greigg, Joe Napolitan, and Joe Mohbat went with me to McGovern's suite at the Doral. Several of McGovern's advisers were present, including Frank Mankiewicz, Jean Westwood, and Pierre Salinger, along with Mrs. McGovern, and he suggested that he and I go into another room for a private talk. He ordered some lunch for us and said how much he appreciated my fairness as convention chairman. We agreed that the Convention had gone well. Then, the pleasantries completed, he got down to business, saying he wanted me to reconsider my decision. Over my protests, he insisted that my staying as chairman was vital to his campaign, and he stressed that I could have the job on my own terms, with full autonomy.

McGovern can be a persuasive man, and finally I told him I would consider the matter, but that I wanted to discuss it with my three associates, who were waiting in the next room.

"Fine, I'll bring them in," he said. He left the room, and Greigg, Napolitan, and Mohbat joined me. When I told them the situation, they were not enthusiastic about my staying, but they felt that I should stay through the election out of loyalty to the party. I agreed, with a similar lack of enthusiasm, and the four of us sat there for a while, until we began to wonder where McGovern was. Then he reappeared and said he needed to speak with me privately again.

My associates left the room. McGovern seemed upset. He said, "Larry, you know how busy I've been, picking a Vice President and working on my acceptance speech. I just didn't realize what's been going on. I've just been told that the woman's caucus is mad as hell at me and they're demanding a woman as chairman. How would you feel about being co-chairman with Jean Westwood?" (the national committee-woman from Utah)

I told him there was no provision in the committee rules for co-chairmen. I added that, if I stayed, it would only be through the election and that it would be fine with me if he wanted to name Westwood after that.

"I'm not sure I could sell that," he said. "These women are adamant. Some of my people think there has to be a change."

I was more stunned than angry. "You're the nominee of the Democratic Party," I said. "You say you haven't caught up with what's going on. I've never dealt with a candidate who doesn't make his own decisions."

McGovern looked unhappy but made no reply. "I have a suggestion," I said finally. "The National Committee is waiting for us. Let's turn back the clock to before we had this discussion. It's unfortunate that you insisted on my coming here at all."

"I guess we have no alternative," he said.

"Okay, the clock is turned back."

"What do you want to do?" he asked.

"I've got to get back to the meeting."

"Why don't we ride over together?" he suggested.

I said that would be fine, and Jean Westwood and Pierre Salinger, who was McGovern's choice for vice chairman of the DNC, joined us for the ride back to the National Committee meeting.

Later accounts, from people who were present, indicated that quite a scene had taken place when McGovern informed his inner circle that he was persuading me to stay on as chairman. Apparently, Gary Hart (who had joined the group after

316 No Final Victories

my arrival) and Mankiewicz strongly rejected the idea, perhaps because they viewed me as a threat to their own roles in the campaign. Jean Westwood, who wanted to be the new chairman, was reportedly in tears. Also reportedly upset, but for a quite different reason, was McGovern's wife Eleanor, who insisted that it would be a serious blunder to lose me as chairman. Apparently McGovern felt he had to side with the prevailing view of his advisers, who had done so much to help him win the nomination.

Quite a charade ensued at the National Committee meeting. McGovern stood up and eulogized me, explaining how he'd used all his persuasive power to change my decision to step down as chairman. "Three times in the past three weeks I have called Larry O'Brien and asked him to remain as chairman of the party," he said. That was true enough, although he left out the events of the previous hour. But, that was our agreement—to turn back the clock.

I said my good-bys to the National Committee and went up to my suite as McGovern's choice, Jean Westwood, an early McGovern supporter, was being elected the new national chairman. I was annoyed by McGovern's behavior—it was all so unnecessary—but I was not unhappy with the outcome. I had achieved my goal. The Convention had been a success, and I was at last returning to private life.

XVI

THE MCGOVERN CAMPAIGN

I FLEW BACK to Washington and on Sunday afternoon went by my office at the National Committee to pick up a few personal belongings.

Elva called me there from home to report that I had an "urgent" message to call Senator McGovern. I was in no mood to return McGovern's calls, urgent or otherwise. However, he must have guessed my whereabouts, because there was a call from him minutes later.

He said he wanted to talk to me and asked me to name the time and place. I told him I was having my staff to my apartment that night for a snack, and suggested he come by after that. Our little party broke up about ten-thirty—it wasn't that gala an affair, for we were all still exhausted from Miami Beach—and McGovern arrived a few minutes later. He gave Eleanor's regards to Elva. I offered him a drink, but he took instead a dish of ice cream left over from our party. He sat across from me, eating the ice cream, looking tired and unhappy, as he told me how very disturbed he was about what had happened between us at Miami Beach.

"Eleanor says it's the worst mistake I've ever made in politics," he said. "And she may be right. I'm furious about the way my staff behaved. They overstepped their authority and I'm not going to put up with any more of that."

Finally he began to urge me to join his campaign. "It's not easy for me to come here," he said. "You have every reason to refuse. But I would like to create the position of national campaign chairman for you. You can have whatever staff you

want, be my campaign spokesman, and work with labor and
party leaders. I'd planned to ask Ted Kennedy to take that
position, but under the circumstances I think it would be better
if you did."

It was a strong, very personal appeal and he pressed me for
an immediate decision. "I'm flying out to the Black Hills tomorrow. Could you meet me at the airport in the morning for
an announcement to the press?"

"George, there's no way I'm going to make this decision tonight," I told him. "I'm in no mood for it. You know I'll support the ticket, but you'll have to give me time to think it over."

I should say that I am aware that I have described a good
many scenes wherein political figures urged me to join their
campaigns, and that this may seem the height of immodesty.
In my defense, I can only say that the scenes are true, and
that they accurately reflect the conflict I often felt between my
political life and my personal life.

I might say, too, that I often felt that the various candidates
who sought my help overstated its importance. No one man
holds the key to a successful political campaign; if such a
man existed, he would achieve immediate fame and fortune.
The interest Humphrey and McGovern and others had in involving me in their campaigns reflects the fact that there are
very few people who have political experience at the national
level. In my own case, my role in the 1960 and 1964 campaigns, plus my work on Capitol Hill, brought me into contact with hundreds of leading Democratic political figures. A
candidate who has to organize a national political campaign
in a very short time—a Humphrey in 1968, a McGovern in 1972
—needs someone on his team who can pick up the phone and
deal on a first-name basis with party leaders all over the
country. In McGovern's case, I was strongest where he was
weakest, with party regulars and some elements of organized
labor, so it came as no surprise to me that he wanted me. I
wasn't sure, however, that I wanted to work for a man who'd
given me such a difficult time at Miami Beach.

For the next two days, I talked at length with some of the
people who had worked with me at the Democratic National

Committee and who, if I joined the McGovern camp, would feel obligated to join it with me. Their views were sharply divided. Some said it was absurd, that I could forgive McGovern his behavior at Miami Beach, but that didn't mean I should join his campaign for three months. Others said that I didn't owe McGovern anything, but I still owed the party something. That, in the end, was my own feeling—that if you're a Democrat, a committed, activist Democrat, you can't pick and choose your years, or be upset by personal considerations. It was apparent that McGovern was not likely to win the election, but it was important that he and other Democratic candidates make the strongest possible showing and I felt there was a duty to work toward that end.

I notified McGovern of my decision, and on Wednesday, July 20, when he flew back to Washington to vote on the minimum wage bill, he held a news conference to announce me national campaign chairman. McGovern declared that I would be his "liaison with the Democrats in Congress, the Democratic governors, Democratic mayors, . . . etc.," that I would be "a foremost consultant on the over-all policy and strategy of my campaign," and that I would "direct a separate entity whose overriding goal will be to unite the support of key Democrats across the country."

With that impressive send-off, I embarked on the three worst months of my life. It was a nightmare. There were frustrations arising from the disorganization of the McGovern campaign and from McGovern's uncertainty about what he really wanted my role to be. There were the huge problems for which, despite our best efforts, we could find no effective answers, such as the fallout from the Eagleton affair and the opposition of George Meany and numerous party regulars. All this was coupled with the growing realization that Nixon was running a smart, incredibly well-financed campaign. He wasn't making the mistakes of 1970 again. He didn't go out and wave his arms and yell about law and order. In fact, it was similar to 1968; we couldn't flush him out. He stayed in the White House, aloof from the press, above the battle. He had already done his most effective campaigning months before in Peking and Moscow. He neutralized the war issue with his last-minute "peace is at hand" promise. He had vetoed the campaign spending bill that would have put the Democrats on an equal footing with the Republicans. He played every card in the deck.

Nonetheless, I don't think Nixon won in 1972 so much as we Democrats lost, and in what I say about the McGovern campaign I don't mean to point the finger at anyone. The fact is that McGovern, with all his problems, ran only about 4 per cent behind Humphrey's 1968 showing—about 40 per cent of the vote compared with about 44 per cent. Once again our party was divided, and, given these divisions, in my judgment no Democrat could have won in 1972.

On July 27 my staff and I moved into our offices on the eighth floor of McGovern's headquarters at 1910 K Street on the edge of downtown Washington. Stan Greigg and I took a tour of the building and received a warm greeting from McGovern's young people.

The Eagleton affair had just erupted and McGovern had not yet made his decision. However, when I talked that day to Henry Kimelman, McGovern's chief fund-raiser, he declared that Eagleton would have to go, simply because of what the situation was doing to his money-raising efforts.

McGovern did not consult me on the Eagleton matter. If he had, I would have advised a different course from the one he followed. Tom Eagleton can, of course, be faulted for not advising McGovern of his history of mental health problems before he accepted the vice-presidential nomination. But McGovern was naïve if he thought the issue would just go away in a few days. McGovern was called upon to make a hard, dispassionate political judgment. If he had resolved the matter amicably with Eagleton at the outset, instead of leaving it up in the air for a week, he could at least have minimized the damage. He should have had the same press conference the first day that he eventually had a week later, picturing the withdrawal as Eagleton's own. Instead, McGovern agonized for a week, stated his 1,000 per cent support of Eagleton, and the story remained front page news. In the end, the outcome was the same, except that by then the episode had become a public test of McGovern as a decision maker, and his performance raised doubts in the minds of millions.

Once Eagleton had withdrawn, the question was whom McGovern would choose to replace him on the ticket. And on Tuesday, August 1, the day after Eagleton's withdrawal, McGovern told me that I was among those being considered. I was pleased but not totally surprised—as he had told me of his previous consideration of me at Miami Beach. But my pleasure was tempered by apprehension at the prospect of suddenly becoming a candidate for national office.

On that Tuesday, McGovern invited Elva and me to join Eleanor and him for dinner at Washington's Jockey Club. We had a pleasant, three-hour dinner at that excellent French restaurant, with the vice presidency as the main topic of discussion.

"Let's discuss the candidates, present company excluded," McGovern said jokingly.

"Well, it's pretty hard for me to be objective," I replied, in the same vein.

"You know I considered you at Miami Beach and that's still the case," he said seriously. "I know your pluses and minuses."

I gave him my evaluations of the various contenders. I didn't push for any one man—I had no special preference. I stressed that one element of his decision must be what was best for his candidacy, and he emphasized that this time he alone would make the decision. It was obvious that he continued to hope that Ted Kennedy could be persuaded to be his running mate, which proved to be as unrealistic then as it had been at Miami Beach.

As is well known, McGovern ultimately offered the vice presidency to Humphrey and to Muskie and both turned it down. Muskie said on Friday, August 4, he was going up to Maine to think it over, and the joke around Washington was that he might think it over until Election Day. While Muskie was pondering, McGovern gave me a call early Friday afternoon. He said, "Larry, if Ed turns me down, I'm going to be back to you immediately. And I expect him to turn me down."

I concluded he meant he would be back to me not for more advice, but as his choice for Vice President.

On Saturday morning, Muskie announced he would not run, and I began getting calls from people who wanted me to push for the nomination. Instead, I told my staff that no effort was to be made on my behalf.

Later that morning I received an indirect report that Sarge Shriver was McGovern's choice. I was not surprised, as I knew that Henry Kimelman, his campaign treasurer, Frank Mankiewicz and Pierre Salinger had been campaigning hard for Shriver. I knew Sarge would do a good job—as, indeed, he did, for Sarge is an articulate, intelligent and energetic man.

Early that afternoon, McGovern called.

"Larry," he began, "I've got something to say that will be disappointing to you. I've made my decision and it's Sarge Shriver."

I was prepared to applaud his choice, but instead I found myself resenting his suggestion that I would be disappointed. I'd said nothing to him to indicate that I wanted to be on the ticket or that I'd be disappointed if I wasn't.

"However," he went on, "you'll be pleased to know that in our polls you did well. But you're identified as a politician, and we feel we should stay away from a political image."

By then I was pretty irritated. The gist of what he had said was, "Larry, you're a good fellow, but you're a politician and therefore unfit for high office." What, I wondered, were Eagleton, Humphrey, Muskie, and Shriver—what was McGovern himself—if not politicians?

I was annoyed by McGovern's remarks, and some of my friends were outraged and thought I should leave the campaign. The ones who'd originally said I shouldn't join the campaign were quick with their "I-told-you-so's."

But I *had* joined the campaign and it was time for me to settle into my new job and determine just what the national campaign chairman could do.

As I looked around the McGovern headquarters, I saw that the campaign had its pluses along with its problems—as a politician I once knew in Massachusetts used to say, it had its longcomings as well as its shortcomings. The campaign had many bright, dedicated people, the kind we had in the Kennedy campaigns, who'd work until they dropped. It also had the finest grass-roots financial support of any political campaign in my lifetime. There was a large room in the headquarters where you could go day or night and see dozens of volunteers busy opening a seemingly endless stream of envelopes containing a dollar or ten dollars or twenty dollars. I'd never seen anything like it before. Sometimes as I'd watch those contributions pouring in, I'd think of the Humphrey campaign in 1968 and reflect that Hubert would have been President if he'd inspired that kind of grass-roots support.

One of the campaign's major problems was a lack of internal communication. At the top level, Gary Hart, Frank Mankiewicz, and I each took responsibility in given areas. Essentially, I was in charge of liaison with Democratic officeholders, party regulars, and labor; Hart was in charge of liaison with McGovern's own state-by-state organization; and Mankiewicz traveled with the candidate as his chief adviser. The problem was that there was lack of co-ordination among the three of us.

Gary Hart was a Colorado lawyer in his early thirties who had worked in Bob Kennedy's campaign in 1968. He was soft-spoken, dedicated, and capable. He had put together McGovern's effective grass-roots organization during the primaries and he continued to direct the organization during the national campaign. He was performing the job I performed in 1960, and he once told me that he had studied our procedures and learned from them.

Gary was McGovern's emissary to the "new politics" people, and I was his emissary to the Democratic Party. Out in the field, of course, our two constituencies were often in sharp conflict.

Frank Mankiewicz, formerly Bob Kennedy's press secretary, and I were not well acquainted, even though we had both worked in Bob's 1968 campaign. We did not see much of one another in the McGovern campaign since he was generally on the road with the candidate. That was regrettable, because there was a great need for co-ordination on the issues and as far as I could see, Mankiewicz had good judgment. Nixon had dozens of "surrogate" spokesmen popping up all over the country, and when these stand-ins made a statement, we needed to be ready with a prompt reply, but that was rarely the case, which was frustrating to our issues co-ordinator, Ted Van Dyk. In Humphrey's campaign, we had various policy groups working on position papers with specific direction as to when and how they'd be used. In McGovern's campaign, papers and speeches were circulating, but the process always seemed disorganized.

It would be difficult to fault McGovern's primary campaign, but I think that he and his people suffered from an inability to shift gears from a primary campaign to a presidential campaign. The two are entirely different. You can be nominated as the leader of a faction, but you cannot be elected unless you present yourself as the party's national leader. Once nominated, your first step should be to win the support of those who opposed you for the nomination. Kennedy did so in 1960 by putting Johnson on the ticket, and Johnson did so in 1964 by endorsing Kennedy's liberal programs. But McGovern was never able to shift from being the liberal, anti-war candidate to being the Democratic Party's candidate.

One of the first things we noted when we moved into the campaign headquarters was that the sign over the door said simply "McGovern Headquarters"—the word "Democratic" was nowhere to be seen. Similarly, his slogan on TV and on his literature had been "McGovern . . . For the People." We were able in the early weeks of the campaign, to get the word "Democrat" over the door and into the literature, but we were never able to make Democratic Party loyalty basic to the McGovern campaign. In 1960 Kennedy had proclaimed proudly, and effectively, that he was the candidate of the party of Wilson, Roosevelt, and Truman, while his opponent was the candidate of the party of Harding, Coolidge, and Hoover.

McGovern never took up that cry, for I think that in 1972 his thoughts about the party were far more complex. I had known McGovern in the 1960s as a party loyalist, a man who almost singlehandedly had built the Democratic Party in South Dakota, a staunch supporter of the Kennedy and Johnson legislative programs. But McGovern had passionately opposed President Johnson's war policy, and I think that by the time he ran for President, he had distinctly mixed feelings about his own party, or at least significant elements of it.

If McGovern had mixed feelings about the Democratic Party, some of his followers' feelings were not mixed. They seemed to view the Democratic Party as an enemy, or at best as a slightly repugnant means to an end. Gary Hart and I once had a long talk about the difference between the 1960 and 1972 campaigns. The gist of what Gary said was this:

"In 1960 you Kennedy people came on the scene at about the same age as we are, you worked hard, you made sacrifices, you built an organization, you won the primaries and you won the nomination. So did we. But your people had a commitment not only to John Kennedy, but to the Democratic Party. Most of our people not only have not been active in the Democratic Party, they have no interest or commitment to it. They look upon the party purely as a vehicle for George McGovern's candidacy, because the system requires that.

"The point is that you, as Director of Organization in 1960, could elicit from local Democratic leaders some sense of accountability to you. You could issue orders. You had discipline. But discipline emanates from involvement with the Party and the system. For example, I had a local McGovern co-ordinator make a wild-eyed speech the other day that caused us a lot of problems. He's our co-ordinator because he was our leading supporter in his area in the early stages of the campaign. I can't call him and tell him to shut up because he *won't* shut up. I have no discipline over him. That's the difference between 1960 and 1972."

I thought Gary's comments were perceptive. Many of McGovern's supporters were very young people, people to whom Franklin Roosevelt was a figure out of history and John Kennedy a dim memory from their grade-school days. To them, the Democratic Party meant only one thing: Vietnam. McGovern won their allegiance by opposing the war, but we, as a political party, were starting from scratch with their generation. I now find considerable evidence that many of the young veterans of the McGovern campaign are currently involved in our party's affairs and I am confident their numbers will grow. The continuing challenge we face is to bring them to our cause, not by pointing out the sins of one Republican administration, but by convincing them that our party, with all its faults, is the one that shares their ideals and their determination to build a better tomorrow.

August was the worst month of the campaign. In the middle of the month four of my aides, Stan Greigg, Dick Murphy, Joe Mohbat, and John Stewart sent me a long critique of the campaign at that point. They said, among other things:

"The political unit is not transmitting vital information to other sections. The issues unit has little input into scheduling or political decisions. There is no reliable internal information system to disseminate positions, statements, etc., among all persons who should know. The DNC functions more or less independently of everyone else. The candidate makes statements on the road without adequate consultation and advice of issues experts. And so it goes.

"The result has been two weeks where McGovern has continued to decline in the polls and where each day's performance is marred by at least one unfortunate event that wipes out the positive efforts. McGovern continues to look bad and the campaign gives little indication of really beginning to move."

They recommended that I take over the campaign in order to give it unity and central direction. They added:

"No doubt some persons will be unhappy and uncomfortable if you actively move to implement your role as Campaign Chairman. But we believe that a far greater number of the McGovern staff would be overjoyed at such a development, particularly if it resulted in their being able to do a more effective job. We would appear to be in a situation where each section of the campaign *wants* to relate more effectively to the other sections but doesn't know how."

I agreed with their analysis but not with their solution. I was not interested in a *coup d'état*. McGovern knew the problems his campaign was having. Occasionally he would suggest that my role be altered—that I travel with him more, or that I make more speeches, or that I exercise more control—but there was no followup.

Our organizational problems were the focus of a meeting at McGovern's home in Northwest Washington on the evening of August 30. Gary Hart, Mankiewicz, and Jean Westwood, my successor at the Democratic National Committee, were present. On this particular evening, Westwood came in carrying a bulging briefcase and launched into a detailed explanation of a voter-registration drive in one of the boroughs of New York City. McGovern sat taking notes on a yellow legal pad. As Jean Westwood went on, I became increasingly impatient, until finally I broke in.

"I've never seen a candidate for President concern himself with the details of a voter-registration drive," I told McGovern. "You can't do that and function as the candidate too."

McGovern agreed that perhaps we could move on to other matters, and, having gotten started, I decided to get something else off my chest:

"You're the candidate of the Democratic Party," I said, "a party that has millions of adherents, but the only time we ever hear the word Democrats is in John Connally's 'Democrats for Nixon.' You're being cast as the candidate of some fringe group. You've got to run as a Democrat. Maybe we should start saying that there still is a Democratic Party and that, hopefully, you'll be moving it through the 1970s."

"You couldn't be more right," McGovern agreed enthusiastically, and the remainder of the meeting was devoted to discussing how best he could stress traditional party loyalties for the duration of the campaign.

But, while McGovern was committed to this, we continued

to experience great difficulty in securing party loyalty from many traditional Democrats.

Harry Truman once said that a President spent most of his time trying to persuade people to do things they ought to do without any persuasion. A lot of my time was spent that way during the McGovern campaign, trying to persuade Democratic Party regulars to support the Democratic candidate for President. The problem was that these regulars—Democratic mayors, governors, state chairmen, congressmen—were convinced McGovern could not win, so they didn't want to waste time, money, and political prestige on his candidacy.

I spent many hours talking to hundreds of these people, trying to appeal to their party loyalty or to their dislike of Nixon, but too many of them had already made up their minds to write off McGovern and concentrate on state and local races. I could arrange a unity meeting here or an endorsement there, but I failed to generate much enthusiasm for McGovern among party regulars. They had made their judgments, on the basis of ideology or self-interest, or other factors, and what I had to say rarely swayed them.

I was also charged with working with labor. We sought labor support through a committee that included such AFL-CIO leaders as Joseph Beirne of the Communications Workers, Joseph Keenan of the Electrical Workers, Floyd (Red) Smith of the Machinists, and Jerry Wurf of the Federal, State, County and Municipal Employees. Despite George Meany's opposition to McGovern, that committee lined up the support of the officers of forty-two international unions who represented a majority of the union members in America. In August Red Smith and Leonard Woodcock of the United Auto Workers arranged a joint session of their unions' top people—the first such meeting ever to occur between the two unions—and invited me to speak. I did, and it was heartwarming to talk to those strong and dedicated people who had been through many struggles in the past and who were meeting this challenge, no matter what the polls or George Meany said.

The hard fact, however, was that despite the best efforts of the officers of the forty-two unions, they couldn't convince their rank and file. Too many union members who had won good wages and working conditions in large part through the efforts of the Democratic Party were hell-bent on voting for Richard Nixon.

We were also working to strengthen congressional support for McGovern. On the evening of September 13 about forty leading Democrats in Congress, including the Democratic leadership, came to my apartment to discuss campaign strategy. The session turned out to be candid, even brutal, but highly productive. These men were frustrated and they welcomed a chance to get it out of their systems. The persons most critical of McGovern's campaign were usually those closest to him; time after time, a senator would begin, "You all know that George and I are close friends, but . . ."

Abe Ribicoff complained of the lack of co-ordination with him and with other senators. When McGovern had spoken on welfare, Ribicoff declared, he had said all the wrong things —and Ribicoff, an expert on the subject, could have helped out if anyone had asked him.

Adlai Stevenson complained about McGovern's amnesty position, declaring that he just couldn't defend it in Illinois.

Warren Magnuson, when there was talk of more research on the issues, declared, "We don't need more research; we need a campaign."

Congressmen Tip O'Neill, John McFall, Hale Boggs, and others chimed in with similar comments. It was rather like a session of Congress; every few minutes someone would make a little speech and the others would nod their agreement. But the speeches and comments were helpful. They cleared the air. Gary Hart, and other McGovern staffers whom I'd invited to meet the congressional leaders, sat through the discussion and later responded to the criticisms.

We then proceeded to do what we could to improve the situation. Each member appointed a staff co-ordinator to work with John Stewart on a series of speeches to be delivered daily on the House and Senate floors. Plans were begun for appearances around the country by congressional leaders, and for closer ties between McGovern's speechwriters and congressional staff sources. All in all, our "bitch session" was one of the more productive meetings of the campaign.

One day in mid-campaign, Dick Hatcher, the black mayor of Gary, Indiana, called me and said there was a man I should talk to, who had an idea that might turn the campaign around.

I asked who the man was. Dick said he couldn't tell me, that the whole thing was extremely confidential, but that this fellow might have the key to victory for McGovern, and that he would be back in touch with me about a meeting.

Hatcher called again when I was in New York for a weekend. He said the man, whom he still refused to identify, would be in a certain hotel on Sunday afternoon and that I should meet him there. I was not sure I wanted to make such a mysterious visit, even to meet a person who might turn the campaign around, so I suggested instead that the man come to my apartment at the United Nations Plaza on Sunday afternoon. Hatcher said this would be acceptable.

At the appointed time on Sunday, my doorbell rang and I opened the door. A lean black man was standing there holding a briefcase. He greeted me in a cordial manner, came in, sat down, and started talking.

He was Dick Gregory, the comedian who had become a spokesman for civil rights and for the anti-war movement. He had, I remembered from newspaper stories, several times fasted for long periods to dramatize his objection to the war in Vietnam.

Now Gregory was telling me, with great conviction and eloquence, that George McGovern should begin a fast to dramatize his opposition to social injustice in America, that such an action would impress the American people with his sincerity and would help persuade them to elect him President.

I was impressed by Gregory's dedication, his sincerity, and, not least of all, by his obvious good health—he was himself a fine testimonial for the good effects of fasting. Unfortunately, I could not share his judgment that a McGovern fast would turn the campaign around.

As the campaign progressed, many of us were increasingly unhappy with McGovern's TV spots. McGovern was still using the same spots that he had used in the primaries in the spring, low-keyed films of him talking informally with small groups of people. These had been fine for the spring, but in the fall, with McGovern twenty points behind in the polls, it was time to try something different. I was among those who favored spots that attacked Nixon's record and hammered at the above-the-battle "presidential" aura with which he had surrounded himself.

In late September I called Tony Schwartz, a gifted New York filmmaker who had done several spots for us in the 1968 Humphrey campaign, perhaps most notably the "heartbeat" spot which questioned whether the voter really wanted Spiro Agnew a heartbeat away from the presidency.

Tony said he'd be glad to produce some spots for us, even that late in the campaign, and I sent John Stewart up to work with him. By late October, Tony had produced five hard-hitting TV spots—one on Vietnam, showing a mother and her dead child in a bombed-out village, one on inflation and the shrinking dollar, one on Watergate, one that urged the undecided voter to return to the Democratic Party, and one giving people's views on Nixon.

After viewing the films, the top staff agreed that the Vietnam spot should not be used because Nixon had neutralized the war issue with Kissinger's "peace is at hand" promise, but that we should go ahead with the "Watergate" and "undecided voter" spots. By then, however, it was the first of November, with only days left in the campaign, too late for them to have much impact. Thus, the television offensive was another might-have-been of the McGovern campaign. It had probably been the best-financed media campaign in the history of the Democratic Party and there were none of the last-minute cutbacks we were forced to make in 1968. But McGovern, faced with conflicting advice, had failed to shift from the soft-sell of spring to the hard-sell television effort which would have been effective in the fall. As in other areas of the campaign, the gears had not been shifted.

Throughout the campaign, we often called for a debate between the two candidates. Obviously Nixon was not going to debate, but from time to time we would remind the voters that he had once gone on record in favor of debates between presidential contenders.

My thoughts kept returning to my own 1970 television show, when I used film clips of Nixon's campaign promises and contrasted them with his actual performance. Finally I made a proposal to McGovern: we could stage a Nixon-McGovern "debate" using film clips of Nixon to present his side.

McGovern at first rejected the idea as unfair, but I stressed that we would do everything possible to be fair to Nixon, and in late September McGovern gave me the go-ahead. I assigned John Stewart to follow through, and he contacted Emile de Antonio, a well-known maker of documentary films to produce the "debate." De Antonio began collecting and putting together Nixon film clips, and Charles Guggenheim, McGovern's own filmmaker, filmed McGovern's half of the debate one hectic day in Detroit when the candidate was tired and not at his best. De Antonio put the film together, and one evening in late October, McGovern sat down with some staff people to watch a screening of this unprecedented "debate."

When the screening was over, McGovern ordered that the "debate" must never be shown. Everyone agreed we had been too fair. Nixon had won.

One of my jobs as national campaign chairman was to be a principal spokesman for the campaign. In retrospect, I think it might have been better if I'd concentrated on that role exclusively, perhaps undertaking a national speaking tour, rather than spinning my wheels trying to bring party regulars into line. As it was, I issued almost daily blasts at Nixon, I participated by telephone in a series of regional news conferences, and I talked privately with a steady stream of reporters and columnists who made their way to my eighth-floor office.

One of my major topics was the unfolding Watergate scandal. For a time, I let myself hope that Watergate might be the miracle that could turn the election around. McGovern and I hit hard at the issue, hoping to arouse in the nation the outrage we felt at the break-in and the bugging and the probability of White House involvement in it.

On August 24, I declared: "The plain truth is this: we are now witnessing one of the most outrageous and blatant political cover-ups of this generation. Richard Nixon and John Mitchell recognize that the facts in this case, if spread before the American people, would place their entire re-election campaign in gravest peril."

My charges were denounced as "political" by the White House and largely ignored by the press, which was then, with a few exceptions, treating Watergate as a "caper." Everything that McGovern and I said about Watergate was eventually proved to be true—and more. Yet our efforts to make Watergate a campaign issue failed. The American people had tuned out Watergate. The truth was too awful to accept, so people chose not to think about it, or to regard it as a "caper" or as "politics as usual."

What did succeed in gaining widespread attention, however, was demagogic distortion such as a statement by Senator Hugh Scott: "The McGovern campaign is the campaign of the three A's: acid, abortion, and amnesty."

As the election approached, I had no illusions about the outcome. Publicly, I avoided being pessimistic—one day, when I insisted to columnist Rowland Evans that the gap was closing, he proposed a little bet on the matter, giving me heavy odds, and my official optimism cost me five hundred dollars. Privately, I thought McGovern might at best carry five states. A day or two before the election, when an angry McGovern told a heckler, "Kiss my ass," some of our people facetiously said that might be the miracle that would turn the campaign around. Others suggested it was probably the best single comment he made in the campaign. It humanized him.

On Election Night, as the bad news came in, I called McGovern in South Dakota to offer my condolences and to compliment him on the fight he had personally waged. He had, after all, been a dedicated candidate and had campaigned tirelessly. He thanked me for my efforts and commented that until the final few days he felt he would pull off an upset. He also brought up the episode of his Doral Hotel suite in Miami Beach concerning the Democratic chairmanship, and said how much he regretted what had happened. I thought it was remarkable that a man going through what McGovern was enduring that night would recall that incident.

A meeting of the National Committee was to be held a month after the presidential election, and Jean Westwood, my successor as national chairman, faced strong opposition. Organized labor, the South, and various anti-McGovern elements of the party who viewed Westwood as a symbol of the McGovern takeover were determined to oust her. This was, of course, a significant part of the plan that originated at the Miami Beach Convention. Bob Strauss, who had been the National Committee's treasurer during my 1970–72 chairmanship, emerged as the candidate of the oust-Westwood coalition.

I decided to take a close look at the situation, and I would have to say that I was interested. I had spent three years working for an open party and I found I could not be indifferent to the fact that many of the people supporting Bob Strauss were determined, as they put it, to "reform the reforms."

On the other hand, I did not want to become involved in a bitter, bloody fight for the chairmanship of a deeply divided party. Three years earlier I had been unanimously drafted to lead the party, but no such unanimity existed by December 1972. Labor resented what they saw as my "pro-McGovern" ruling at the Convention. Many of McGovern's supporters, while preferring me to Strauss, wanted someone they considered more liberal.

If there had been evidence of strong support for me, I might have become a candidate. But my judgment was that while my candidacy would prevent Strauss's election, I could not be elected unless other candidates dropped out. The prospect of possibly prevailing on a second or third ballot had no appeal to me, and I would not be a party to a stop-Strauss movement; Bob had earned the right to seek the chairmanship by his good record as the party treasurer.

So, I sent word to the National Committee meeting that my name was not to be placed in nomination. As it turned out, Bob Strauss won a three-way race on the first ballot by a slender margin and, from my observations, he has gone on to acquit himself well as chairman.

XVII

WATERGATE—AND BEYOND

IN MAY 1973 I experienced one of the happiest days of my life, when my son Larry was married to Helen Powell, a lovely young schoolteacher he had met in New York. After completing his military service, Larry had returned to Columbia Law School. Upon his graduation he joined an outstanding New York firm—Breed, Abbott & Morgan. I've taken immense pride in the course of Larry's life in recent years, particularly because I've so often seen how adversely political life can affect the lives of children of public men. But Larry has always shown himself to be an intelligent and independent-minded young man, and Elva and I could not have been more pleased with his career and his marriage.

Larry's wedding was a bright spot in an otherwise grim season. A few weeks after his wedding I watched as another young man, Jeb Stuart Magruder, confessed on national television that he had participated, along with John Mitchell, John Dean, and G. Gordon Liddy, in the original planning for the breaking-in and bugging of my office. When asked the motivation for this plot, Magruder replied:

"Well, I think at that time we were particularly concerned about the ITT situation. Mr. O'Brien has been a very effective spokesman against our position on the ITT case and I think there was a general concern that if he was allowed to continue as Democratic National Chairman, because he was certainly their most professional, at least from our standpoint, their most professional political operator, that he could be very difficult in the coming campaign. So we had hoped that information might discredit him."

Those words still stun me and horrify me. What kind of people are these who think it is their right to decide who shall be "allowed" to lead the opposition party? What kind of mentality is this that assumes the way to counter a political critic is to burglarize his office in search of something with which to blackmail or discredit him?

A man came up to me on a plane not long ago, studied my face intently, obviously trying to place me, and finally exclaimed, "Oh, I know you—you're the victim of Watergate!"

In truth, we are *all* victims of Watergate. The criminal actions of the Nixon administration have not only diminished the liberties of its selected victims but have tragically eroded every citizen's confidence in our form of government. The great challenge facing America today is not simply to punish the wrongdoers but to restore the nation's confidence in its democratic system.

Yet, the man on the plane was partly correct. As Magruder's statement and an abundance of other evidence makes "perfectly clear," I was a prime target of the Watergate espionage operation and of many other forms of harassment as well; and I wouldn't be honest if I didn't say the experience has affected me. From the first confused day in June 1972 when I learned of the break-in, right up to the present moment, my life has seemed to be cut off from reality. I have been caught up in lawsuits. I have gradually learned of the full extent of the White House program "to get O'Brien." I have seen innocent people suffer personally, politically, and financially simply because they were friends of mine and thus considered "enemies" of their government. I have watched the White House and its political allies attempt to persuade the public that somehow I could have avoided Watergate and, therefore, I must share the blame. Yes, for me Watergate has been a continuing aggravation, one that seems to have no ending.

As I have related, three days after the break-in I filed a one-million-dollar damage suit against the Committee for the Re-election of the President, and I called upon the President to name a Special Prosecutor to conduct a thorough and impartial investigation*—a suggestion he chose to ignore. On June 23, six days after the break-in, I contacted Senator Sam Ervin to explore the possibility of his Subcommittee on Constitutional Rights investigating the circumstances of Watergate. Senator Ervin said it was his judgment this was not appropriate, for it appeared that the FBI was then conducting an intensive investigation. I concurred in his judgment, for the number of FBI agents who were examining our offices and interviewing our staff did indicate a major investigation was under way.

This conclusion was supported the following day when I received a telephone call from L. Patrick Gray, the Acting Director of the FBI—a man I had never met. Gray told me he was disturbed by reports suggesting the FBI was not conducting a thorough investigation. "That is simply not true," Gray told me. "I assure you this matter will be pursued wherever it leads, regardless of my position in the Administration. Let the chips fall where they may." I told Gray I appreciated his call, and he concluded our talk with an unexpected comment: "Mr. O'Brien, we Irish Catholics must stick together."

On July 7, following Gray's call, I was visited by two Secret Service agents in my suite at the Fontainebleau Hotel in Miami Beach, where I was preparing for our Convention. One of the agents was Paul Rundell, Associate Director of the Secret Service and over-all co-ordinator of convention security. The other agent was Clint Hill whom I had known during my White House years and who was with us in Dallas at the time of President Kennedy's assassination. They told me they had been instructed to report to me that the FBI's exhaustive examination of the National Committee offices had uncovered no telephone bugs or other electronic devices—that "the place was found to be clean." I accepted their report without question. I knew the FBI had torn the place apart—removing ceiling panels, dismantling radiators, and the like—and if they said there were no bugs, then I assumed there were no bugs. Later evidence, of course, revealed that bugs had been placed

* See Appendix.

on my phone and that of Spencer Oliver, Executive Director of the Association of State Democratic Chairmen. To this day I cannot explain the discrepancy between those facts and the report I was given.

Through the early stages of the Watergate affair, little interest was shown in it by the Congress. The House Banking and Currency Committee's Chairman Wright Patman did attempt to hold hearings on "laundered money" reportedly used in financing the break-in, but his effort was thwarted by intensive White House lobbying.

This congressional disinterest was matched by the press. They, along with the White House, treated the break-in merely as a "caper," a "third-rate" burglary. The major exceptions to this were the Washington *Post's* Bob Woodward and Carl Bernstein, who maintained close contact with our deputy chairman, Stan Greigg, during this period, and columnist Jack Anderson. However, press interest did rise sharply by September.

Watergate was kept alive in the early months because of the determination of Judge John Sirica to get to the truth and because of the civil suit we had filed against the Committee for the Re-election of the President. In September, however, Judge Charles R. Richey of the U. S. District Court, who was handling our civil suit, began to question whether trying the suit might prejudice criminal action against the Watergate burglars. So, on September 21, just as our lawyers were about to depose John Mitchell, Judge Richey halted further depositions and ordered that those already taken be placed under seal. This meant there would be no trial of our suit before the election and no disclosure of the information contained in the depositions.

The civil suit was eventually resumed after the election. But in March 1973, another problem arose for me. Joe Califano, my counsel, advised me that Judge Richey had questioned whether his firm, Williams, Connolly and Califano, might have a possible conflict of interest, as the firm also represented the Washington *Post*. The *Post* then faced certain legal actions by

CRP, which were designed to discover the sources of its reporters' Watergate stories.

Califano told me that the members of his firm had met and reluctantly decided they should cease to represent me. He said he would help me to locate new counsel and we contacted a number of Washington attorneys, some of them old friends from the Kennedy and Johnson administrations. I found, among these old friends, a reluctance to handle my case. While appalled by Watergate, it was clear that they felt involvement with me would antagonize the Nixon administration and might jeopardize their law practices. Consequently, I was without counsel on the eve of my departure for a long-planned trip to Ireland.

That evening, without solicitation by me, Edward P. Morgan of the Washington law firm of Welch and Morgan, hearing of my situation, contacted me and volunteered to represent me. I will always be grateful to Ed Morgan and his associates, particularly Charles A. McNelis, who have stayed with me through this difficult period. This experience with old friends was disturbing because, as Democratic Party chairman, I had decided from the outset that any judgment I received for damages would go to the party. I had determined I would not personally profit in any way from what I considered to be a national tragedy.

There were two important Watergate developments in the early months of 1973. In February the Senate authorized the creation of a special Watergate Committee to be chaired by Senator Sam Ervin. In May, at long last, the Administration reluctantly agreed to name a Special Prosecutor and Archibald Cox was appointed to the post. I applauded both developments.

The Senate Watergate Committee was given a twofold mandate: to investigate Watergate and to make specific recommendations for political reform to the Congress. The committee did a credible job of investigating Watergate. The long parade of witnesses, highlighted by John Dean's lengthy confession and John Ehrlichman's determined "stonewalling" did much to inform the public on the facts of Watergate. Also, the committee's discovery of the presidential tapes was to be of historic importance.

The committee did less well, however, in fulfilling its legislative mandate. It conducted hearings from the spring of 1973 through the spring of 1974 but made no legislative proposals to the Congress. I had hoped the committee would make its proposals while it had overwhelming public attention and support. I fear that, with the passage of time and the focus of Watergate directed elsewhere, the opportunity for maximum impact of the committee's recommendations may have passed.

While I generally approve of the record of the Watergate Committee, I do wonder about the activities of some of the committee's staff. On the several occasions when I was interrogated at length by both Republican and Democratic staff members, I was prepared to tell what I knew about the break-in, the damage we had suffered, and my proposals to prevent future Watergates. However, only two items were of any particular interest to them.

On the Republican side, a theory was advanced that ultimately became known as Senator Howard Baker's "double agent" theory. It was suggested I had advance notice of the Watergate break-in, that I took no precautions to avoid it, that it was an entrapment, that indeed I might have tipped off the Washington police to have them at the ready so the capture of the burglars could be a political coup for the Democrats. Beyond that, so the theory went, former CIA agent James McCord, an employee of CRP, might have been a "double agent" and former FBI agent Alfred C. Baldwin, who had been hired by McCord to monitor the taps on our phones for CRP, could also have been a "double agent." Indeed, O'Brien might have been involved with the CIA in the whole plan.

I recall one occasion when I was subjected to a prolonged grilling by Republican counsel in pursuit of the Baker theory. It was based on a letter I had found in my files and voluntarily turned over to the committee. The letter was from a concerned Democrat saying he had heard rumors in New York that the Democratic Party might be subject to electronic surveillance in the 1972 campaign. I instructed John Stewart of our staff to follow it up, which he did. After contact with the author of the letter and others, Stewart was unable to discover any specifics that would support the writer's concern. Nevertheless, the Republican lawyers intensely pursued the theory that I had advance notice of the break-in. "Why didn't the DNC take precautions to prevent a break-in," I was asked. "Why didn't you have closed-circuit television, as CRP did? Why didn't you have your own security police as CRP did?" I told them we not only lacked the money for a CRP-style security network but that, more to the point, the Democratic Party is an open party and wants people to come and go freely. We do not do business in an armed camp, like our well-financed and apparently insecure counterparts at CRP. I informed them that we had experienced at least two previous break-ins and reported them to the Washington police. They promptly investigated and concluded the break-ins were routine burglaries. Nevertheless, we had had our office locks changed as a result.

All of this made no impression on the Republicans. They continued to peddle their preposterous theory that I had advance notice. It received considerable press coverage and contributed to my feeling that I was living in a world turned topsy-turvy.

The air of unreality was not confined to my dealings with the Republican members of the committee staff, however. I soon had cause to question the views of Sam Dash, the committee's chief counsel, and some of his colleagues on the Democratic side as they became obsessed with discovering "the real motive" for Watergate.

I had, over the months, been presented with a dozen theories on the reason for the break-in. One theory was that the break-in occurred because I was in contact with the Castro regime in Cuba. According to that theory, the Democratic Party was considering a plank in its platform calling for the recognition of Cuba and for that reason, Castro sympathizers were secretly contributing money to the Democratic Party. The fact that four of the Watergate burglars were anti-Castro Cuban-Americans seemed to give some superficial credence to this ridiculous idea.

A second theory that surfaced was that, as I had been publicly attacking the ITT-Republican Convention arrangements,* I might have had ITT documents of concern to the Republicans in my files. My information on the ITT case had come from Jack Anderson's column and other sources on the public record and I had no knowledge of purloined documents.

Finally, Sam Dash and some of his colleagues came up with their own theory—the break-in occurred because of the consulting relationship my firm, O'Brien Associates, once had had with Hughes Enterprises. The theory was that I might have had some knowledge of the $100,000 that Hughes had given Nixon through Nixon's friend Bebe Rebozo and I might have some documentation of that gift in my files. The truth was that my knowledge of the $100,000 came long after the break-in and, as in the ITT case, was based on what I read in the newspapers. Furthermore, if I'd had any documentation about that gift, no one would have been more anxious than I to see such information made public.

So much for theories. I do not deal in theories. I prefer to deal in political realities and facts.

The political realities surrounding Watergate were: Democratic National Chairman O'Brien had crisscrossed the country in the 1970 off-year election vigorously attacking the record of the Nixon administration and the White House, in turn, attacked O'Brien, primarily through Spiro Agnew, but the Republicans suffered a defeat in that election. O'Brien was repeatedly demanding equal time on television for the Democratic Party through the courts and the Federal Communications Commission, which was strenuously opposed by the White House. O'Brien had publicly decried the White House's violation of citizen's right of privacy in demanding and securing personal tax returns from the Internal Revenue Service, and his charges had resulted in congressional inquiry. O'Brien had demanded full disclosure of the facts concerning the Administration's approval of the controversial ITT merger; O'Brien was persistently and vigorously attacking the Administration's record of domestic failure. And furthermore, O'Brien was, of

* See Appendix.

course, known in the White House as a Kennedy man. Those were the political realities at the time of the planning of Watergate.

Now let's look at the *facts* of Watergate, on the public record. A meeting took place in Attorney General John Mitchell's office in early 1971. In addition to Mitchell, those present were John Dean, Jeb Magruder, and G. Gordon Liddy. A program was presented by Liddy with a budget of $1,000,000 for political espionage on the Democratic Party with O'Brien as a prime target. Apparently, no objections were raised to the project, but Liddy was told that his budget was excessive and he should revise it.

Later, the same group reconvened in the Attorney General's office. Again, presumably no objections were raised to the project, but Liddy was told his revised budget of $500,000 was still too high.

Liddy and his associate, E. Howard Hunt, Jr., were not deterred. They contacted Charles Colson, a presidential assistant, to seek his help. He, in turn, urged Jeb Magruder "to get off the dime," indicating it was vital to get moving on O'Brien. Haldeman's office was also urging more and better political intelligence, particularly on O'Brien.

Under these pressures, Magruder again met with John Mitchell. Magruder reported the project was finally approved, but at a reduced budget of $250,000. Magruder notified the White House of this approval and gave the go-ahead signal to Liddy.

According to testimony, the elements of the project included the following: the bugging of O'Brien's office in the DNC, the bugging of McGovern's campaign headquarters, the bugging of O'Brien's suite and the DNC National Convention headquarters at the Fontainebleau Hotel in Miami Beach, the disruption of the Democratic Convention by disconnecting the air-conditioning system in the heat of a Miami summer, and a myriad of other activities.

So, Bernard Barker and his Cuban-American friends were again recruited. They were not given any specific instructions other than they were to be involved in a national security project. The first target was the DNC—one break-in was aborted; the next was successful, but the information secured by photographing my documents was non-productive and the bug on my phone malfunctioned. CRP and the White House were dissatisfied.

So back again—to photograph more of my documents, correct the malfunctioning phone bug, and install electronic devices which would pick up conversations in my office.

What was the purpose of these illegal acts—what was the "real reason" for the Watergate break-in? The political realities and the facts show conclusively that the objective of Watergate was to secure all possible information that would help destroy the Democratic Party and its chairman. It is as simple as that.

However, the facts also are that long before Watergate and well beyond it, an extensive program of surveillance and harassment against me, perhaps the most extensive ever directed for political purposes by our government against a private citizen was being carried out. Its goal was both to discredit me politically and to cripple me financially, and it was directed not only at me but at my friends and business associates. This get-O'Brien operation culminated with the burglary and bugging of my National Committee office, but it had been in progress for more than two years, ever since I returned as Democratic chairman. I may never know just how extensive this operation was, but its main elements, as I now know them, were the following:

INTERNAL REVENUE SERVICE HARASSMENT. Soon after my return to the DNC, I accused the White House of illegally obtaining individual tax returns from the IRS and using them for political purposes. This was, of course, denied. But later that year I was subjected to a full field audit of my 1969 tax return followed by an audit of my 1970 return and then in 1973 an unbelievable reaudit of my 1969 return. My accountant told me these were the most intensive audits he'd ever seen. The result was a complete failure for the White House and ultimately a reluctant clean bill of health for me.

It was only after the Watergate revelations, when I had

learned of some high-level Nixon administration memos on the subject, that I could be sure of what I had suspected—that the audits were entirely political in nature. They represent a particularly insidious form of political harassment, because it is so terribly expensive to pay the lawyers and accountants you must employ to prove your innocence.

INVESTIGATION. Soon after I returned as national chairman in 1970, the White House private investigator, John Caulfield, was assigned to investigate my business and financial affairs. His efforts led to highly inaccurate memos that White House officials gave to reporters, urging the reporters to question me about various allegations. The reporters always recognized the allegations and insinuations as the trash they were and some would call me to inform me that a smear campaign was in progress.

The charges made against me included a suggestion that President Johnson and I were somehow involved in clandestine dealings with regard to the awarding of government contracts. White House memos show that an extensive investigation was made in this matter and failed to turn up one iota of evidence to support the charges. Also, the White House claimed I was soliciting or accepting kickbacks from firms that wanted to have exhibits at the 1972 Democratic Convention. In truth, exhibitors made legitimate proposals to both parties regarding the 1972 conventions and were turned down by both parties.

Throughout my three years as national chairman there were a series of break-ins and suspicious activities that I now realize were part of the White House surveillance. My apartment at the Sheraton Park Hotel in Washington was entered at least twice and documents were stolen from it. There were also at least two attempts to break into an apartment I used on East Sixty-eighth Street in New York, where I kept my government files and records. It happened that the apartment was just around the corner from the FBI's New York headquarters, and when unidentified persons occasionally asked the doormen about my activities, I attributed the inquiries to the natural curiosity of the FBI. Similarly, waiters in Washington and New York restaurants would sometimes tell me that other customers had asked who my lunch or dinner companions were, but I ascribed that, also, to normal curiosity. Now I am forced to suspect that much of this was part of the White House surveillance program.

DUKOR MODULAR HOMES. A vicious campaign of harassment was carried out against my friend George Bissell and his Dukor Modular Homes, a California-based sudsidiary of his Dukor Industries, Inc. I've known George Bissell since we were young men growing up together in Springfield. In 1969 his company became a client of O'Brien Associates and I served on the board of directors of Dukor Modular Homes. Because of my close association with Dukor, the White House directed a program of government discrimination against Dukor Modular Homes.

Sources within the Federal Housing Administration have confided that the Regional Director of the FHA ordered that no applications from Dukor were to be acted upon without his personal review—a highly unusual practice. On at least three occasions, legitimate applications for FHA loans were turned down, in at least one instance after initial approval. At the time George thought he was simply encountering bad luck or bureaucratic ineptitude. We now know that White House operatives were trying to drive him out of business. In fact, his modular home program was virtually ruined, at a substantial financial loss to him.

THE DYSON AFFAIR. Just as insidious is the case of Charles Dyson of the Dyson-Kissner Co., a New York-based company. I met Charlie Dyson a few years ago as a result of our sons having served together in Vietnam. Ours was a social relationship—I didn't even inquire what his politics were. When I was seeking office space for O'Brien Associates, he arranged for me to occupy space in his suite of offices on Park Avenue. We saw each other only occasionally, but our friendship was not unnoticed by the White House sleuths. When the White House "enemies list" was made public in the spring of 1972, Charlie Dyson's name was in the "top twenty," with the notation "friend of Larry O'Brien."

So there you have it: a prominent businessman becomes an

"enemy" of the White House because he is friendly with a Democratic politician whose son served with his son in Vietnam. Had Charlie Dyson's phone been tapped? Had his companies been discriminated against in their dealings with the government? Who can say?

PUBLIC AFFAIRS ANALYSTS. Public Affairs Analysts, Inc., was formed in 1969 to provide political education programs for corporate employees. I was scheduled to be a major stockholder along with Cliff White, who is of course a leading Republican political figure, Joe Napolitan, and Martin Haley, and I was given an equal stock option with them. Shortly thereafter I returned to the National Committee, so I did not exercise my stock option, nor was I active in PAA until my return to private life early in 1973. White House memos show that the offices of PAA were invaded at White House direction, that my involvement with PAA was fully investigated, and that there were detailed discussions of how best to "embarrass" me or, as one memo puts it, "to keep O'Brien on the defensive."

LEGAL ACTION. In response to my suit against the Committee for the Re-election of the President, Maurice Stans filed a five-million-dollar suit against me, alleging malicious abuse of the judicial process and libel. A memo from CRP lawyer Kenneth W. Parkinson to the White House dated September 11, 1972, had stated that the facts in the case "do not support a claim of actual malice" and he therefore had not recommended a suit by Stans against O'Brien. A memo sent the next day from John Dean to H. R. Haldeman also had stated: "The facts known to us do not support a claim of actual malice." But it went on to say, "However, the filing of the action would have obvious media advantages." And so Stans sued me.

My attitude toward all this activity can perhaps best be described in a comment that Republican Senator Lowell Weicker of Connecticut made to former presidential assistant Charles Colson:

"I deal in hardnose politics, you deal in crap."

It must be said, however, that this program of harassment had its impact on me. It hurt, and in a lot of ways. The most obvious one is financial. I paid thousands of dollars in fees to accountants and lawyers as a result of the IRS harassment. But the financial pressures are only the beginning. The IRS investigation and the Stans lawsuit were a constant drain on my time and energies. The phone calls from lawyers, the depositions, the press inquiries, were a never-ending distraction.

One obvious goal of a program of harassment is to hurt the victim's reputation. No one likes to admit he's being investigated by the IRS. Nor is it any fun to know that someone is circulating scurrilous stories about your business and political life to the newspapers. The harassment hurts in other, very personal ways. George Bissell is an old and valued friend, and I can never forget now that, simply for being my friend, he lost thousands and thousands of dollars—it's a high price to put on friendship.

Make no mistake about it—the government can grind you down. The Nixon administration harassment never silenced me, but I would be dishonest if I didn't admit that it hurt me financially, sapped my energies, and often left me deeply depressed.

But my personal problems are not the real issue. The actions of the Nixon administration amount to a profound corruption of our form of government. Can our two-party system survive in the face of police-state tactics by which the party in power tries to discredit and indeed destroy the opposition party? And, leaving criminal activity aside, can the two-party system survive when the incumbent party has unlimited access to the communications medium and all but unlimited campaign funds?

I will not pretend to be optimistic. This nation faced a crisis of confidence even before Watergate. I said early in 1972, in an address to a joint session of the New Mexico state legislature, that the political system itself was on trial—it was, and it still is. Millions of people ask whether our system will ever again produce strong, compassionate, trustworthy leaders. Even before Watergate, apathy and cynicism were widespread. People just don't trust politicians or feel that they, the people, really have a voice in government. Now we are, in a sense,

asked to evaluate the American experience, two hundred years
of it, and to judge whether our unique political experiment
has any relevancy to the demands and challenges of modern
America. More and more people ask: has our system outlived
its usefulness? Should it be discarded? Indeed, *has* it been
discarded?

There is much cause for pessimism, but there is also cause
for hope. For all our problems, for all the cynicism, most
Americans still believe in the democratic system and still look
to the ballot box as their means of achieving good government
—if people do not trust politicians, they still trust the political
system. There is little support for any fundamental change in
the existing constitutional system or for the overthrow of existing democratic institutions. The critical issue in American
politics in the mid-1970s is *how* the government can once again
be made to function with competence, with equity, and above
all with integrity.

In Watergate's aftermath, many reforms of our political process have been suggested. Some are urgently needed; others
deserve the most careful scrutiny—for it would compound the
tragedy if Watergate led us to hasty, ill-advised changes in
our method of governing.

There are three political reforms that I support wholeheart-
edly:

First, we must have equal access to radio and television for
both major political parties. So long as the President can have,
at will, free time on national television to state his case on
controversial issues without equal time for rebuttal, the people
will have to make decisions without knowing the facts. The
networks have slowly moved in this direction in recent years,
at least in part because of the pressures and lawsuits we of the
Democratic National Committee brought to bear in 1970–72,
but informal agreements aren't enough. Equal time should be
the law. There should also be provision for televised debates
between the opposing presidential candidates, along the lines
of the 1960 Kennedy-Nixon debates. The incumbent President should not be allowed to hide behind the "duties of the
office" shield to escape debating. He is a politician seeking re-

election, and if he is fearful of defending his record in open debate, he doesn't deserve to be re-elected.

Some restrictions should be placed on the format of paid political advertisements. Slick, sometimes subliminal, selling techniques have too often been used to confuse, mislead, and scare the voter, rather than to inform him. Complex issues are often deliberately reduced to absurdity in thirty- or sixty-second spot commercials. I am thinking, for example, of the 1972 Nixon spot that "explained" the issue of defense spending in terms of a hand (presumably McGovern's) knocking toy ships and airplanes off a table. Or, for that matter, of the 1964 "Daisy Girl" spot used by the Democrats, which linked Barry Goldwater to the nuclear incineration of little girls. This kind of misleading political advertising, by both parties, should be ended. Political candidates should be required to appear personally in their television films rather than the present practice whereby inept candidates are hidden away while the ad-men create a new image for them. Actually, I think the stress should be less on paid political advertising and more on television and radio being required to provide public-service time for debates between candidates and question-and-answer sessions between candidates and reporters. The purpose of political campaigns is not to profit the owners of television stations, although that is one result of the present system.

Second, we must have reform in campaign financing. A national election is little more than a joke if one candidate is able to pour twice as much money as his opponent into paid television time. Our goal must be public financing of all federal elections. First, we should achieve public financing of presidential elections. When it proves successful, as I believe it would, we would move on to public financing of House and Senate elections. My personal preference is the dollar checkoff, which I have strongly supported for years, whereby each taxpayer voluntarily allocates one of his tax dollars to go into a public campaign fund and, thus, has direct participation in financing the electoral process. The dollar checkoff, along with the elimination or drastic reduction of private contributions, could revolutionize American politics.

We often say, "one man, one vote," but that is not enough. It should be "one man, one vote, one dollar." It is a mockery to say that the average man's vote equals the millionaire's vote, so long as the millionaire's vote can be supplemented with a $100,000 contribution to buy television time that will influence thousands of other votes. We must stop the "fat-cat" system of political financing and until we do, we will never restore public confidence in the political process.

Along with the *cost* of campaigns, I think we should give serious consideration to the *length* of campaigns, the amount of time they are allowed to go on. An incumbent President, be he Nixon in 1972 or Johnson in 1964, holds an all but overwhelming advantage when he can start planning and organizing his campaign a year or more in advance, while his challenger cannot really finalize planning until he is nominated, perhaps three or four months before the election. Obviously a President, in one sense, is always campaigning, but it would be possible to restrict the kind of political activity that the Committee for the Re-election of the President started on Nixon's behalf early in 1971.

Third, we must work for fuller and more complete voter registration and voter participation in elections. A democracy by definition does not work if half of the people do not take part in the process. It isn't simply a matter of people being too lazy or uninterested to vote. In many areas of the country, the political establishment makes it hard for people to register. There are residency laws that in effect disenfranchise thousands of people in our highly mobile society. In rural areas, the registration office is often in a distant courthouse that is only open during the hours that most people work. In years past, blacks found it almost impossible to vote in some areas, and in recent years college students have often been the victims of discriminatory registration procedures.

Clearly, we should take every step to make registering and voting easier. Registrars should go to the people, as they have in some states, by setting up booths at schools and churches and libraries and shopping centers. Beyond this, a citizen should be able to register to vote by the simple mailing of a postcard registration form.

We have another responsibility beyond seeking reform of the registration laws. We must seek out the people who have not voted, particularly the young and the poor, and try to have them understand why it is crucial that they do. A person who is struggling for economic survival rarely sees how casting a vote will matter to the day-to-day reality of his or her life. We must explain to people the political facts of life—that a vote-less American is a powerless American.

Other political reforms have been proposed in the aftermath of Watergate, some of them dealing with such vital questions as the way we select our President and Vice President and the possibility of new restraints on presidential power.

One oft-discussed reform is the idea of a national primary to select the parties' nominees for President. The basic idea is that on a given day in each presidential election year, probably in the spring, both political parties would hold national primary elections and the winners of the Republican primary and the Democratic primary would then be the two candidates who would run against one another in the November election.

The national primary has one big selling-point: it seems to place the nominating process directly into the hands of the voters. Yet I think that when the idea is examined closely, it presents many difficulties. For example, who would be eligible to run in the national primary? How is eligibility decided? And, once you have decided who can run, you must decide who can vote. Obviously, registered Democrats vote in the Democratic primary and registered Republicans in the Republican primary, but can they cross over and vote in each other's primary? What about the millions of voters who belong to neither party? Can they pick their primary?

And what would be required to win a national primary? A majority vote? Forty per cent of the vote? Or, in a field of candidates, can someone be nominated for President with 20 or 25 per cent of the vote? Obviously not, so the answer would be to have a runoff between the top two vote-getters. And that costly process might well lead to voter fatigue before the year was over—a national primary, a national primary runoff, then, finally, the general election.

Not the least of my objections to the national primary is the very reason that makes some people favor it—it would weaken the party system. If the presidential candidates are chosen in a national primary, the two parties become less and less significant. Would you still have a party convention, if the presidential nominee was already chosen, just to select a Vice President and draft a platform? My own belief is that we need a stronger two-party system, not a weaker one, because the parties provide leadership and focus to our continuing national political dialogue.

Our current system of selecting Democratic candidates for President is, admittedly, a hodgepodge, but it is an evolving system, one that can be improved and one that I think we should not lightly discard—no system that produced the nominations of Franklin Roosevelt, Adlai Stevenson, and John Kennedy can be entirely without merit.

In 1972 some twenty-three states held presidential primaries, and the other states held party caucuses and conventions to choose their delegates to the National Conventions. In the Democratic Party, we did everything we could to make our delegate selection procedure truly open and democratic. The system will be further reformed and perfected by 1976. This, I think, is the direction we should move in—make the process open and make the results *binding* on its delegates. Granting that the present procedure is cumbersome, time-consuming, and expensive, it nonetheless presents a true test, a kind of political obstacle course, of the candidates' capacities and voter appeal. A national primary, however, would tend to lead to the nomination of whoever happened to be the best-known person in each party on a given day in the spring. No, my instinct is to stay with our existing nomination procedure, but to continue to improve it and open it to all citizens. And I think that as we continue to open up the Democratic Party's decision-making process, the Republican Party will inevitably be forced to move in the same direction.

What of the Vice President? How should he be selected? My

own opinion—and it is not original with me—is that the best thing we could do about the Office of Vice President would be to abolish it. But, since that action does not seem likely to happen, I think we should at least schedule our convention programs so that the new presidential candidate has *two* full days to make his recommendation for Vice President known to the delegates, thus preventing the kind of chaotic, you've-got-five-minutes-to-decide activity that we saw in 1960, 1968, and, with such unhappy results, in 1972.

There have been suggestions that the convention delegates should nominate the Vice President, fully independent of the presidential candidate, perhaps at a separate convention, but I strongly disagree with such proposals. If we are to have a Vice President, it is imperative that he be compatible with the President.

Numerous suggestions have been made, as a result of Richard Nixon's excesses as President, for new checks or restraints on presidential power. Perhaps the most sweeping of these is the proposal for a one-term limit on Presidents. I oppose the one-term limit today, just as I oppose the two-term limit that was enacted in reaction to Franklin Roosevelt's having been elected four times. Let the people decide. If the people want a particular man as President two or three or four times, why should their wishes be frustrated? If you believe in democracy, you have to place your ultimate trust in the good judgment of the American people, and you have to assume that our system will produce more Roosevelts and Kennedys than Nixons and Hardings.

One of the worst aspects of the Nixon presidency—one of his worst offenses against our political traditions—was the secrecy, the isolation he brought to the office. We need an open presidency, one in which the President deals candidly and regularly with the people and the press. This is not something we can legislate, but something that an aroused public should demand. Certainly, one of the few encouraging aspects of the Nixon scandals has been signs of revitalization among the

American press, particularly, the outstanding investigative reporting that those scandals have inspired.

The presidency must be open to meet the challenges of a free society, but it must also remain strong. We must not let the illegalities of the Nixon administration panic us into abandoning our traditional concept of the separation of powers and the traditional system of checks and balances that exists between the three branches of government. My experience in government has made me a firm believer in the concept of executive privilege in matters relating to the President's discharge of his constitutional responsibilities. Obviously there is no right of executive privilege where illegal activities are charged or where political activities beyond the scope of the President's duties are involved, but neither should the Watergate experience set any precedents that will allow congressional "fishing trips" into White House files or White House affairs.

There should continue to be confidentiality on all legitimate business carried on within the White House itself. I have served as a White House assistant to two Presidents, and I don't think I could have done my job properly if I had thought that my every word or my every document would some day be publicized. I made many extremely candid reports to Presidents Kennedy and Johnson on why I thought this or that member of Congress was taking a particular position, and it would have been hard for me to give the President my blunt, sometimes scathing judgments if I thought my memos would some day be printed in the newspapers—or, heaven forbid, that my verbal remarks were being taped and might some day be played on Capitol Hill. Again, I stress the distinction between legal and illegal situations. If a President or a presidential aide is accused of a crime, let all relevant memos be brought forth. But we must not allow a reaction to the illegal acts of one Administration to set precedents that might cripple the legal activities of future Administrations.

I think there is a clear distinction between cabinet officials, who must be available to testify before the Congress, and presidential assistants, who traditionally have not been subject to Senate confirmation or available to testify. I myself have served in both roles, and it was altogether proper that when I was Postmaster General I was always on call to appear before the appropriate congressional committees. But a presidential assistant has a different role, a more intimate advisory role; less governmental and more personal. Give Congress the power to reject or to interrogate the President's closest aides and you give it the potential power to cripple the presidency, and that we must never do.

Congress has many means to check presidential excess. It has the power to accept or reject virtually all presidential appointments. It has the power to call cabinet members and other appointees to testify. It has the power to cut off Executive Branch funds or to reject Executive Branch legislative proposals. It has the power to investigate, to criticize and to publicize, and it has the power to remove the President from office through the constitutional process of impeachment. I think the answer to our present crisis of confidence is not to give the Congress more checks on the presidency; the need, rather, is for the Congress to be more vigilant in using the checks it has.

Whatever the difficulties of our political system, I think the answer lies not in changing systems but in changing our approach to politics. And I think the kind of reforms I support— particularly access to television, campaign spending, and citizen participation—would go a long way toward accomplishing this.

Ideally, reforms of this nature would be bipartisan, and I hope that both Democrats and Republicans will support them in the crucial days ahead. But my view of what America needs in this time of crisis is not exclusively bipartisan. My partisanship is well known and it has not been diminished in recent years. This nation needs a revitalized, united Democratic Party, one that can again give the dynamic and progressive leadership it provided under Wilson, Roosevelt, Truman, Kennedy, and Johnson.

I am not one of those who think that Watergate means an automatic Democratic victory in 1976—far from it—for Watergate has discredited both parties and the political process for many Americans. Today we Democrats are a divided party and we will continue to lose the presidential elections so long as we remain divided. The great Democratic coalition of 1932–64 was torn apart by two historic issues—the war and the drive for racial equality. Yet our division need not be permanent. The war is behind us now. The racial issue will always be with us as long as there is prejudice, but I am confident that most Americans are coming to realize that we can't turn back the clock, that the equal rights laws are on the books and they must be accepted, and that basic decency calls for compassion and understanding. There are remaining racial issues in the courts, however, and they must be resolved there.

Our divisions over these issues did cost us the presidency in 1968 and 1972. We must be united or we will lose again in 1976. We have carried out our historic party reforms and we are continuing to perfect them. We have brought a new generation of political activists into our party and they have brought new vigor to the party, but we must now bring those same activists into a working coalition with the traditional Democrats—the working men and women, the ethnic groups—those Democrats who felt that the party had no place for them in 1968 and in 1972.

If we are to be united—"workingman" and "intellectual," black and white, questioning youth and concerned senior citizen—it can only be on the basis of shared goals, on a recognition by all groups that they need the others in order to achieve their political ends. What are these goals? I realize that words like equality and opportunity and justice may have grown stale with overuse, but they still have meaning and they can still unite men and women of good will. We still need tax laws that are fair and equitable. We need protection for the consumer. We need national health insurance. We need a first-rate education for every American, regardless of his financial condition. We need to end festering poverty in the midst of general prosperity. We need to preserve our environment and we need safe streets and the sanctity of our homes. We have, in short, an unfinished agenda from the 1960s that we must face up to in what remains of the 1970s. There were no final victories in the sixties and there may be none now, but there is much to be done. We have lost eight precious years, and it is time to get moving again.

Who are our party's future leaders? Not long ago four students came to my table in a New York restaurant and said they'd like to talk about politics. It was a good talk, but when I asked them who they looked to as national leaders, they could not come up with a single name. That is a sad commentary on our party's present situation, but new leaders will emerge.

Those young people also asked me a question that many others have: "Do you miss politics?" And I gave them an honest answer: "You bet I do." I've had the opportunity to participate in both the campaign process—the electing of Presidents—and in the more difficult governmental process—the struggle to enact a President's program. Now that I'm out of political life, I follow its day-to-day drama in the newspapers, on television, and in talks with my old friends in Washington. There are countless times when I second-guess the participants, when I think of what I would do if I were still in the arena. But, as I told those young people, the profession of politics is not like other professions. You are left with memories and scrapbooks, but little provision for your later life. After a lifetime of uncertainties, there comes a point when you must think of yourself, your family, and your future. Do I miss it? Of course I do. Do I have plans to return to it? No, I don't.

My private prediction of the Democratic presidential candidate in 1972 proved to be wrong, so I won't try to predict the 1976 nominee, but a few general observations may be in order.

There is a group of older, well-known Democratic leaders, men like Senators Jackson, Humphrey, and Muskie, who have sought the presidency before and may well continue that quest in 1976. They are men of ability and experience, yet it remains to be seen, as they grow older and the electorate grows younger, if the party will turn to them again.

Then there is a group of younger, lesser-known men, senators, governors, congressmen, who are surfacing in the national consciousness and may seek the presidency in 1976 or thereafter. Senators Mondale of Minnesota and Bentsen of Texas, and Governor Gilligan of Ohio are examples—and there are many more. Such rising political figures will continue to be tested in the political arena. Some will be up for election in 1974 and the strength of their showings may point the way to 1976, as Jack Kennedy's overwhelming Senate victory in 1958 helped project him into the 1960 presidential race.

Finally, in a classification by himself, in a truly unique position, there is Ted Kennedy. He has inherited the Kennedy name and much of the ardent following that his two brothers developed over so many years. Despite the Chappaquiddick tragedy, he remains the most visible Democratic leader in America today, the one whom millions of Democrats look to as the party's only rallying point, and he has demonstrated in the Senate that he is an able leader and legislator.

Yet, to my mind, there is a continuing cloud over Ted's otherwise strong prospects for the presidency. He, like his brothers before him, arouses the strongest passions in people, both pro and con. When I contemplate the emotions that would be aroused by another Kennedy campaign and when I remember that his two brothers were shot down by fanatics, I find myself deeply concerned that history might repeat itself. In considering the possibility of Ted's candidacy for the presidency, I would have to weigh the national need against my affection for him and his family and I am saddened to say I would be inclined to conclude that I do not think he should run. To say that is to make a terrible indictment of our society and the darker passions within it today, but I was in Dallas and in Los Angeles and I can't forget.

So our leadership is uncertain now. We are passing through a time of transition. But when I look back to the late 1950s, when the critics said Jack Kennedy was too young and too inexperienced and too Catholic to lead the nation and were proved so wrong, I cannot but think that in the next few years another dynamic leader will emerge. I don't mean another Jack Kennedy—we shouldn't expect that, for it does no good to turn our eyes to the past. Perhaps in the early 1960s the nation had a vision of Camelot, but there was no Camelot. What there was, rather, was an extraordinary, dynamic young politician who was able to inspire this nation, to bring out the best in us, and to appeal to our nation's limitless wellsprings of hope and compassion and decency.

"It's a long way from Mattoon Street, O'Brien," Eddie Boland used to say to me sometimes when we'd meet at the White House; he as a member of Congress, I as the Postmaster General. And he was right. It had been a long way from the rooming house on Mattoon Street where I grew up in Springfield. When I look back over my life, with all its ups and downs, I am struck more than anything by how immensely fortunate I have been, by the opportunities this country gave me. My parents came to this country with no money and little education, but by their hard work they made a good life for themselves and their children. My sister Mary and I grew up in the Depression, with no luxuries, but I was able to work my way through night law school and both of us went on to better lives. The third generation, my son Larry and Mary's daughter Katherine, a Radcliffe student, can look forward to a future of limitless opportunity. What an amazing progression, in three generations, from penniless immigrants to young people with wonderful educations and the whole world opened up before them. It could only have happened in America, in this magnificent democracy of ours, and we should all be ever thankful for the priceless gifts of freedom and opportunity, but we must be ever vigilant that they are preserved for our children and our children's children.

APPENDICES

1. Letter from President Lyndon B. Johnson to Lawrence F. O'Brien following O'Brien's resignation from the Johnson Cabinet upon his decision to campaign for Bob Kennedy—1968.
2. Chairman O'Brien's letter to Attorney General John Mitchell, December 13, 1971, re ITT and financing of the 1972 Republican National Convention.
3. Deputy Attorney General Richard G. Kleindienst's reply to O'Brien letter to Mitchell of December 13.
4. Statement of John Mitchell, Sunday, June 18, 1972, the day after the break-in of the DNC headquarters.
5. Chairman O'Brien's statement on Sunday, June 18, 1972, following the Mitchell statement.
6. Telegram from Chairman O'Brien to Attorney General Kleindienst on June 18, 1972.
7. Reply to O'Brien telegram by Henry Petersen, Assistant Attorney General, June 19, 1972.
8. Letter to President Nixon from Chairman O'Brien requesting a Special Prosecutor, June 24, 1972.
9. Telegram sent by O'Brien to Nixon from Miami Beach, July 2, 1972.
10. Kleindienst reply to June 24 letter to Nixon, July 3, 1972.
11. Ronald Ziegler responds for the President, July 3, 1972.
12. O'Brien again writes to President Nixon, requesting a Special Prosecutor, September 1, 1972.
13. Opening Address by Chairman O'Brien to the Democratic National Convention in Miami Beach, July 10, 1972.

THE WHITE HOUSE

WASHINGTON

April 10, 1968

Dear Larry:

I accept your resignation with regret.

I have been proud and grateful to have you serve
your country during these times. Few men have
known your privilege of serving two Presidents
for eight momentous years.

Your contributions have left an enduring mark in
an unprecedented record of legislative achievement,
a uniquely vigorous and visionary management of
our postal system.

Your Cabinet colleagues are equally indebted to
you for your unselfishness. We are reluctant to
see you leave.

Mrs. Johnson and I appreciate your friendship. We
hope that you and Elva will find nothing but happiness
and success ahead.

Sincerely,

Honorable Lawrence F. O'Brien
Postmaster General
Post Office Department
Washington, D. C. 20260

Ltr hand delivered: 12/13/71

DEMOCRATIC
NATIONAL COMMITTEE   2600 Virginia Avenue, N.W.   Washington, D.C. 20037   (202) 333-8750

LAWRENCE F. O'BRIEN
Chairman

December 13, 1971

Dear General:

Continuing public reports about the methods of financing the
1972 Republican National Convention raise a serious cloud over the
recent out-of-court settlement by the Department of Justice of three
antitrust cases involving International Telephone & Telegraph Corp. (ITT).

The reports indicate that the Sheraton Corporation of America
-- a subsidiary of ITT -- has pledged a $400,000 underwriting of the
City of San Diego's bid to host your party's presidential nominating
convention next August. According to press accounts unrefuted by
administration spokesmen, San Diego was the personal choice of the
President.

Eight days after the selection of San Diego was announced by
the Republican National Committee, the Department of Justice and ITT
announced agreement on an out-of-court settlement of three pending ITT
merger cases (involving Hartford Fire Insurance Co., The Grinnell Corp.,
and Canteen Corp.).

As national chairman of the Democratic Party, I call on you
today in your dual roles of chief law enforcement officer of the United
States and chief political adviser to the President to make public the
full record of your decision to settle with ITT as well as ITT's involvement
in financing your party's convention next year.

Specifically:

--Before the selection of San Diego as host city, did Chairman
Bob Wilson of the House Republican Campaign Committee meet privately
in New York with ITT officials and if so, to what purpose?

- 2 -

—After the selection of San Diego, did Congressman Wilson (whose district includes San Diego) meet with Deputy Attorney General Kleindienst to discuss resolution of the government's antitrust case against ITT, or any other aspect of that case? If so, why?

—Are you able, through a candid exposition of all the facts, to allay any suspicion that there is a connection between ITT's sudden largesse to the Republican Party and the nearly simultaneous out-of-court settlement of one of the biggest merger cases in corporate history -- to ITT's benefit?

—At a period in our political history when the American people are seriously questioning the fairness and responsiveness of the political process to all the people, I earnestly hope that you, General, will see the urgency of making the record in the San Diego-ITT case absolutely clear.

Sincerely,

Lawrence F. O'Brien
Chairman

The Honorable John N. Mitchell
The Attorney General
U. S. Department of Justice
Washington, D. C.   20530

December 13, 1971

Honorable Lawrence F. O'Brien
Chairman
Democratic National Committee
2600 Virginia Avenue, N.W.
Washington, D.C. 20037

Dear Mr. Chairman:

The Attorney General has asked me to respond to your letter of December 13, 1971, for the reason that, since he became the Attorney General, he has removed himself from any matter coming before the Department of Justice which could or has involved the International Telephone and Telegraph Corp. (ITT). As you may know, his former law firm has performed legal services for some of the subsidiary corporations of ITT prior to the time that Mr. Mitchell assumed his responsibilities as the Attorney General. Therefore, I have discharged the responsibility of the Attorney General from time to time as and when necessitated by any matter which would involve action of decision by the Attorney General. I have of course done so as the Deputy Attorney General and as required by law.

I have no knowledge, direct or indirect, that the Sheraton Corporation of America, a subsidiary of ITT, has pledged $400,000 or any other sum underwriting the city of San Diego's bid to host the Republican National Convention next August. I do not know whether San Diego was the personal choice of President Nixon. Similarly, I was not consulted about or involved in any way directly or indirectly, in connection with the selection of San Diego by the Republican National Committee.

The settlement between the Department of Justice and ITT was handled and negotiated exclusively by Assistant Attorney General Richard W. McLaren, who is in Europe at the present time and is not expected to return until the evening of December 20th, 1971. Upon his return I will request that he communicate with you immediately with respect to the matters raised by your letter. While I am positive that Mr. McLaren had absolutely no knowledge of any pledge by the Sheraton Corporation of America to underwrite the city of San Diego's bid to host the Republican National Convention next August, I will let him respond directly to you in that regard. Mr. McLaren kept me generally advised as to the course of negotiations with ITT and with his reasons for endeavoring to work out a settlement with it. Prior to the final conclusion of these settlement negotiations and the effectuation of a settlement agreement between the Department of Justice and ITT, Mr. McLaren made his final recommendation in the matter to me, with which I concurred. Again, I will leave it to Mr. McLaren to more specifically discuss the details of and reasons for that settlement agreement on behalf of the Department of Justice.

With respect to Congressman Bob Wilson, I have no knowledge whether he met privately in New York with ITT officials at any time and with respect to any purpose. I can say, however, that I have never discussed with Congressman Wilson any matter of any kind for any reason within the past year. Indeed, I have no personal recollection of ever discussing any matter pertaining to the operation of the Department of Justice with Congressman Wilson at any time within the past three years, except possibly recommendations that he might have had with respect to the appointment of persons to the Federal Judiciary or to other positions within the Department of Justice. Immediately prior to my preparation of this letter to you I called Congressman Wilson and I related to him the foregoing recollection of mine with respect to talking to him, and he completely confirmed it.

I firmly believe the American people are entitled to know at all times how their public servants arrive at the decision-making process. Assistant Attorney General McLaren will be able to provide that information upon his return. The American people, however, may well begin to question the fairness and responsiveness of the political process when they read of alleged statements of fact, alluded to by you in your letter to the Attorney General which were made without any factual basis or substance whatsoever. I am sure that you will assist Assistant Attorney General McLaren in setting the record straight in this matter as soon as he returns.

Sincerely,

(signed Richard G. Kleindienst)

Richard G. Kleindienst
Deputy Attorney General

STATEMENT OF JOHN N. MITCHELL, SUNDAY, JUNE 18, 1972, regarding the break-in to Democratic National Committee Headquarters and the role of James McCord, one of the men apprehended, as reported in the New York *Times*, Monday, July 19, 1972:

. . . Mr. McCord "is the proprietor of a private security agency who was employed by our committee months ago to assist with the installation of our security system.

"He has, as we understand it, a number of business clients and interests, and we have no knowledge of those relationships.

"We want to emphasize that this man and the other people involved were not operating either on our behalf or with our consent. I am surprised and dismayed at these reports.

"There is no place in our campaign or in the electoral process for this type of activity, and we will not permit or condone it."

STATEMENT BY CHAIRMAN LAWRENCE F. O'BRIEN
SUNDAY, JUNE 18, 1972
FOLLOWING JOHN MITCHELL'S STATEMENT

Continuing disclosures in the wake of Saturday's bugging incident at the DNC raised the ugliest question about the integrity of the political process that I have encountered in a quarter-century of political activity.

No mere statement of innocence by Mr. Nixon's campaign manager, John Mitchell, former Attorney General, will dispel these questions—especially as the individual allegedly involved remains on the payroll of the Nixon Campaign organization as filed with the Congress.

Only the most searching professional investigation can determine to what extent, if any, the Committee for the Re-election of the President is involved in this attempt to spy on Democratic Headquarters.

I call upon Attorney General Kleindienst to order an immediate and thorough investigation by the FBI. This investigation must remain open until we know beyond a doubt what organization or individuals were behind this incredible act of political espionage.

We shall anxiously await the Attorney General's response.

TELEGRAM FROM CHAIRMAN LAWRENCE F. O'BRIEN TO ATTORNEY GENERAL KLEINDIENST, SUNDAY, JUNE 18, 1972.

Coinciding with my press statement of this same day, I sent a telegram to Attorney General Kleindienst urging him "to order an immediate and thorough investigation by the FBI. Only the most searching professional investigation can determine to what extent, if any, the Committee for the Re-election of the President is involved in this attempt to spy on Democratic Headquarters."

"No mere statement of innocence by Mr. Nixon's campaign manager, John Mitchell, former Attorney General, will dispel these questions."

"The investigation should continue until we know beyond a doubt what organization or individuals were behind this incredible act of political espionage."

Department of Justice   JUN 21 1972
Washington 20530

June 19, 1972

Mr. Lawrence F. O'Brien
Chairman
Democratic National Party
2600 Virginia Avenue, N.W.
Washington, D. C.

Dear Mr. O'Brien:

Your telegram of June 18, 1972, to Attorney General
Kleindienst concerning the arrests made on June 17, 1972, of the
persons who had entered rooms occupied by the headquarters of your
party has been referred to this office for consideration and reply.

As indicated in published reports concerning this incident,
the Federal Bureau of Investigation immediately initiated a full
scale investigation thereof. I trust this will serve to assure you
that all aspects of this matter will receive the fullest consideration
and that based upon the completed investigation, we will move
vigorously to secure appropriate disposition of such Federal violations
as the full investigation may disclose.

Sincerely,

HENRY E. PETERSEN
Assistant Attorney General

June 24, 1972

Dear Mr. President:

Last week a group of men was apprehended after breaking into the national headquarters of the Democratic Party. I am sure you will agree that their action constituted an infringement of the First Amendment right of political association of millions of American citizens. The prompt and fair investigation of this matter is of the gravest concern to all Americans, regardless of political affiliation.

During the past week there have been numerous reports in the press which are profoundly disturbing. Of particular concern are those reports which indicate a relationship of the action of these men last week to official organs of the Republican Party, members of the White House staff and security agencies of the United States Government.

Mr. James W. McCord, Jr., one of the men who was arrested at gunpoint by the police, was closely associated with The Committee for the Re-election of the President and with the Republican National Committee. Mr. McCord was the Security Coordinator for The Committee for the Re-election of the President and the Republican National Committee. Mr. McCord and the men apprehended with him at the time of the arrest had walkie-talkie radios which were authorized to operate on channels granted by the Federal Communications Commission exclusively for the use of the Republican National Committee.

The events that have been revealed to date, particularly in the context of a presidential campaign, make this case one of vital importance. I am sure you share my concern that the investigation of this matter and its eventual prosecution be conducted in a manner that will credit the integrity of the American judicial process. Of equal importance is the need to assure that all Americans can be confident that this investigation is conducted promptly and with complete objectivity and fairness to all concerned. At stake here are America's most cherished constitutional rights—rights of free speech and free association.

Accordingly, I respectfully request that you direct the Attorney General to appoint a Special Prosecutor of unimpeach-able integrity and national reputation, and provide him with whatever resources he requests to investigate the facts surrounding this violation of First Amendment rights and to prosecute those responsible to the full extent of the law.

Sincerely,

Lawrence F. O'Brien
Chairman

The President
The White House

TELEGRAM SENT BY DEMOCRATIC NATIONAL
CHAIRMAN LAWRENCE F. O'BRIEN
TO PRESIDENT RICHARD M. NIXON
SUNDAY, JULY 2, 1972, FROM MIAMI BEACH, FLORIDA

Dear Mr. President:

A week ago, I wrote to request that you direct the Attorney General to appoint a Special Prosecutor to investigate the case against the five men arrested in the headquarters of the Democratic National Committee in the early morning hours of June 17.

To date, you have chosen not to reply to my request. Indeed, I am informed that you have referred the matter to the Committee for the Re-election of the President as a "political matter."

You are by now familiar with the facts of the case as developed so far—including recent information that potentially incriminating materials seemingly related to the intrusion upon our property have been found in the office of a consultant to your special assistant, Mr. Colson, in the Executive Office Building of the White House complex.

You know, of course, that the men arrested in our offices had in their possession walkie-talkie radios operating on frequencies granted exclusively to the Republican National Committee and that each new development in this case points to a relationship between the men arrested and the Central Intelligence Agency, the White House, and perhaps other key agencies of the United States Government.

I am aware, Mr. President, that in a recent news conference you deplored this break-in, which was a blatant attempt at political espionage on a major political party, and I appreciate those views.

But I am sure you recognize, as I do, the grave implications —going to the First Amendment rights of all Americans—in the growing number of questions that remain unanswered to date. I know that you share my concern and desire that a thorough and impartial investigation be conducted so that the American people may be assured that justice is done.

Mr. President, I would now suggest that it is your decision whether this unparalleled case lands in the political arena or is treated in a cold, impartial manner that will ensure that the constitutional rights of all Americans are protected.

I repeat, therefore, my request that you direct the appointment of a Special Prosecutor of unimpeachable integrity and national reputation and provide him with whatever resources he requests to investigate the facts surrounding this apparent violation of constitutional rights.

Lawrence F. O'Brien, Chairman
Democratic National Committee

Office of the Attorney General
Washington, D.C.

July 3, 1972

Mr. Lawrence F. O'Brien
Chairman
Democratic National Committee
2600 Virginia Avenue, N.W.
Washington, D.C. 20037.

Dear Mr. O'Brien,

This will acknowledge receipt and thank you for
your letter of June 24, 1972 to the President,
which has been forwarded to me for response.

You may be assured that the recent incident
involving the breaking and entry of the
headquarters office of the Democratic National
Committee is being fully and thoroughly investigated
by the Federal Bureau of Investigation, and that
this Department will prosecute violators of the
Federal law to the fullest extent.

Sincerely,

Richard G. Kleindienst

RGK:tl

ZIEGLER RESPONDS FOR THE PRESIDENT, JULY 3, 1972.

The New York *Times* reported on July 4, 1972, that "In San Clemente, California, where Mr. Nixon is taking a working vacation, Ronald Ziegler, the President's press secretary, said that the President had rejected Mr. O'Brien's suggestion. He said that Mr. Nixon was confident that the FBI and other law enforcement agencies would conduct a thorough investigation."

It had been further reported that Ziegler stated there would be no reaction from the President to "anything Larry O'Brien sends around."

September 1, 1972

Dear Mr. President:

I am most disturbed by Attorney General Kleindienst's recent statements concerning the bugging of Democratic headquarters as reported in Wednesday's Washington *Post*, particularly as they are set against your subsequent remarks to the press at San Clemente.

If the account of the Attorney General's interview is accurate, and if you meant what you said, it only deepens my concern that your refusal to appoint an independent special prosecutor in this case will deny to the American people the full, expeditious and forthright investigation that is clearly their right in the present circumstances.

The Attorney General is quoted in the *Post* story as promising "the most extensive, thorough and comprehensive investigation since the assassination of President Kennedy." This analogy with the work of the Warren Commission goes directly to the point I have made in requesting that a special prosecutor be appointed to conduct the government's investigation of the Democratic headquarters bugging case.

It was precisely to achieve a totally open and forthright investigation that President Johnson asked the Chief Justice of the United States, along with a panel of public officials of unimpeachable integrity, to conduct the official inquiry into the assassination of President Kennedy. It is precisely your refusal to appoint a special prosecutor to establish the facts of the present case that flies in the face of Mr. Kleindienst's promise to conduct an ". . . extensive, thorough and comprehensive investigation."

You, or your spokesmen, have repeatedly dismissed the request for the appointment of a special prosecutor. At San Clemente you suggested that the numerous investigations currently underway precluded the need for a special prosecutor. To the contrary, since three of the six investigations you cited (Clark MacGregor, Maurice Stans and John Dean) are being conducted by persons representing Republican groups directly implicated in the crime itself, it is patently obvious that a totally disinterested special prosecutor is called for.

The doubts concerning the Justice Department's handling of this case are seriously compounded by the Attorney General's statement that "It's not a matter of looking into the conduct of government officials, but alleged criminal acts on the part of private individuals." Does this mean that the government's chief law enforcement agency has, out of hand, decided to ignore the possibility that government officials may have been involved in the bugging of Democratic headquarters, even though numerous leads point directly to official involvement? This statement, in itself, is sufficient to disqualify the Justice Department from any further responsibility for the criminal investigation of the Watergate bugging affair.

How does this statement by Attorney General Kleindienst square with your pronouncement at San Clemente that ". . . no one in the White House staff, no one in this administration, *presently employed*, was involved in this very bizarre incident"? Does this mean that the past employees of the White House and your administration *were* involved in the affair? If so, is the Attorney General suggesting that these persons will be immune from prosecution from the Justice Department? I believe this matter must be clarified without further delay.

The Attorney General's suggestion that the Democratic Party "would like to set aside the whole system of criminal justice" shows a woeful lack of understanding of what is at stake in this investigation. Indeed, our suggestion that a special prosecutor take charge of the case is motivated solely by the desire to ensure that the integrity of our system of criminal justice is preserved in this case. How can this be done when as Mr. Kleindienst acknowledges, "the President's Justice Department (is) investigating people working with the President"? And how does that statement gibe with his declaration that "It's not a matter of looking into the conduct of government officials . . ."?

The Attorney General is quoted as saying "I think so" when asked whether he knew who was behind the bugging incident. How can the public be assured that whatever information he may have is being shared with the federal grand jury? Are we equally assured that the grand jury is proceeding as expeditiously as possible in this case, with no effort on his part to delay possible indictments with an eye to the political calendar?

The entire tone, as well as the content, of the Attorney General's published remarks, when coupled with your statements at San Clemente, display an appalling lack of sensitivity to the issues at stake in the investigation of the Watergate case. A most serious crime has been committed. A growing body of evidence points to the direct involvement by persons in your administration or in your campaign organization. In light of these facts, it is more imperative than ever for you to appoint an independent and politically disinterested special prosecutor to discover the facts, without regard for the political considerations that obviously dominate this entire matter.

The integrity not only of our system of criminal justice, but of the two-party system in America, demands no less.

Sincerely,

Lawrence F. O'Brien

The Honorable Richard M. Nixon
The White House
Washington, D.C.

OPENING ADDRESS BY DEMOCRATIC NATIONAL
CHAIRMAN LAWRENCE F. O'BRIEN
TEMPORARY CHAIRMAN OF THE 1972 DEMOCRATIC
NATIONAL CONVENTION
MIAMI BEACH CONVENTION CENTER, JULY 10, 1972

Fellow Democrats. Fellow Americans. I welcome you to Miami Beach and the Democratic National Convention of 1972.

We have come here to a great playground, but, as proceedings later in the evening will undoubtedly confirm, we have not come here to play. We have come to work—to work in harmony and in honest, open disagreement. And we have come to find out whether the Democratic Party has anything to say to the people of the United States.

We must begin with a candid appraisal.

Whoever we are—city dweller, farmer, housewife, worker, student, businessman—we seem powerless to stop a war, to make our streets safe for our families, to enforce fair policies of taxation, justice, or economic opportunity. Messages have been sent, but institutions, both public and private, do not seem to hear. "Time! Give us time!" say the politicians, educators, and administrators . . . when they hear us at all. But governments have collapsed, violent revolutions have swept across whole nations, and societies have vanished altogether—because the only answer to the people's desperate message was: "Give us time!"

More than time is required.

If any institution is to remain alive in a self-governing society, it must respond truthfully to the voices of those being squeezed by the problems—to the voices of those who see their lives destroyed, their sons dead, their hopes blighted, their freedoms restricted, while their institutions sit in fat and splendid isolation—and their cries of distress become minor statistics in bureaucratic reports. Those cries come from every sector of American life.

Yet, if we listen carefully, we can also hear quiet affirmations of hope.

This is America today . . . a country we devoutly love, but a country torn with anguish—so that our love is often clouded by bitterness and despair. Listen, then, to the people.

"It comes from the people up." These simple, direct words sum up what many people have been saying. And in spite of a growing cynicism that is affecting the two-party democratic process, we have discovered in these last months that some people have *not* despaired. Their record turnouts in primaries and state conventions are clear evidence that a faith in political leaders and institutions still does exist.

As the National Democratic Chairman, it is tempting for me to capitalize on these feelings with the standard old political remedy: "Send a Democrat to the White House. Throw out Mr. Nixon and his Republican friends, and your problems will be over." Such a message would have two weaknesses: it wouldn't be true. And nobody would believe it.

Now make no mistake: I am proud to be a Democrat, and I am proud of our Party's record. In good men—good women —good ideas—and good works, the Party of the People is unmatched.

But an excessive pride in the past, coupled with future promises that few people believe, have brought our Party— along with other institutions—to the present crisis of truth. *Both* political parties and their leaders are on trial this year.

For the Democratic Party, the trial takes place this week . . . in Miami Beach . . . right here in this hall . . . right now.

What can we say for ourselves as this trial begins? We must not proclaim to America that the Democratic Party has all of the answers to all the problems. But we must find at least *some* of the answers to take to the people for their judgment on Election Day.

We must write a platform that uses the *good* things of the American past as an intelligent springboard into the American future—a platform that inspires people with its imagination and good sense.

But we must do *more* than that.

Our nominee must be even better than the Platform. Because the Platform does not become the President—the person does.

We need a constructive candidate who will not promise everything, but who will be certain after becoming President to *deliver* what has been promised.

To put it simply, our first concern in these next few crucial days must be to act in such a way that Americans will be able to say about us: "I trust these men and women. I trust this Party."

For three years, we have been laying the foundation for their trust. We have *rebuilt* the Democratic Party.

We have anchored our reforms in a voice for everyone, a place for everyone, a fair shake for everyone.

Some of you will say that the number of reforms has been too many. Some of you will say that the number of reforms has been too few. Some of you—perhaps a dozen—will say that the number of reforms is just right.

But I think we would all agree that the reforms we have seen this year will be more than casually significant in the history of the Democratic Party. But now we must take our reforms to the people—all of them.

The first challenge we face this week is to decide whether party reform will in fact make the Democratic Party better able to deal with our real problems, *or* whether party reform turns out to be an exercise in self-destruction.

To succeed, we need everyone.

To succeed, we need those who this year have said for the first time that they will fight beside us.

To succeed, we *also* need those who, through thick and thin, for better or worse, in agreement and disagreement, have labored with us for a lifetime in the great tangled vineyard of American politics.

We need *everyone,* and all of us here must figure out how we *get* everyone. But we begin with you—the delegates and alternates to this convention. And it is a good beginning, for *who* you are and *how* you got here is one of the most exciting and hopeful stories of this presidential year.

1972 will be remembered as the year that the American grass roots came back to life.

As I look at the packed agenda here on the podium, I can tell you that getting here was only half the job. *Now* we must go to work. The hours will be long. The job will be tough. But we must prove to the American people that the Democratic Party should again be entrusted with America's future.

I think it comes down to this: do we have the guts to level with the American people? Only *you* can answer this question —nobody else.

How do we level? We begin, I believe, with a few simple

steps: we cool the excessive political rhetoric. We lighten the purple prose. We do not promise what we know cannot be delivered by man, God or the Democratic Party.

There is not a politician or a churchman or a businessman or a magician in this country who can fulfill all those dazzling promises. But we have lacked the courage to say this. Instead, we have promised something to everybody, and then hoped that nobody would keep score.

It didn't work. The people can count. They *can* keep score. And they aren't easily fooled.

We have short-changed them in terms of specific accomplishments—jobs, houses, schools, safe streets—and have lost much of their trust along the way. Now, we must stop kidding the American people. We must tell them the truth. I recognize, of course, that this idea runs counter to the whole history of American political talk.

But just imagine what it would be like to elect a President who made only modest, straightforward campaign promises, and then seriously went about fulfilling them.

That has *never* happened. But it could.

We cannot abolish poverty with a stroke of the pen. But we can feed hungry children.

We cannot end unemployment with a stroke of the pen. But we can stop pursuing those policies in which an administration deliberately encourages the loss of jobs in a misguided effort to slow down inflation.

We cannot eliminate racial tension with the stroke of a pen. But we can make the government fair to everyone—even when the people have not yet been touched by fairness in their hearts.

Thomas Paine put it this way: He said that not a place on earth might be so happy as America. But it is true today as it was during the American Revolution that the road to that happiness has discomfort and sacrifice and sadness along the way. If anybody tells you differently, don't believe him. Not even if he's a Democrat.

There is no easy escape from the burdens that must be assumed by every citizen if we are to have a decent society.

Some will say that Americans are tired of making sacrifices. I say the American people are better than that. I say that they will make the sacrifice if they can see the *sense* of the sacrifice. And when we level with them, that is *exactly* what we show them.

By far the great majority of you are sitting for the first

time as delegates to a national convention. Your neighbors have sent you here—and now some splendid opportunities are going to be thrust upon you.

By taking a large enough viewpoint, you have a chance to make the party reforms work.

By being honest, direct, and realistic, you have a chance to consciously break the vicious cycle of overpromising and underproducing that has corrupted us all.

By keeping your vision of America intact and clear, you have a chance to pass that vision on, not just to the voters in November, but eventually to the people who will follow all of us—to the people who will be the Americans as we begin our third century as a nation.

My friends, these are great chances! They are here tonight. They may not come again.

I urge you to reach out and *take* these chances. And if you reach out in that good spirit, you will touch the heart of every American in this land.

INDEX